24 FAVORITE ONE-ACT PLAYS

EDITED BY BENNETT CERF
and
VAN H. CARTMELL

Dolphin Books
Doubleday & Company, Inc.
Garden City, New York

24 Favorite One-Act Plays was originally published by
Doubleday & Company, Inc. in 1958.

Dolphin Books edition: 1963

PS
634
.C43
1963b

FOREWORD

In the fifteen years that have somehow slipped by since the editors of this volume made their first selection of *Thirty Famous One-Act Plays* (a collection, incidentally, that has sold nearly a hundred thousand copies and that still flourishes in a Modern Library Giant edition), the one-act play has come of age on Broadway.

It always *was* popular and appreciated in arty theaters tucked away in Greenwich Village cellars and converted stables, and in amateur circles throughout the country. Unsung, underpaid, and truly dedicated off-Broadway producers understood the appeal and validity of a full evening's worth of three or four varied expertly wrought one-acters. Only big-shot managers on the "Main Stem" did not.

To them, a one-act play was something you dug up as a curtain raiser when the main bill of the evening could not be made to suffice by itself. We still recall the bitter plaint made some years ago by one veteran producer. "Nobody ever sold a single extra ticket because of a one-act play added to the program," he stated, with all the authority of a man whose last four Broadway attractions had been dismal failures, "but what can you do when an author you've been counting on is so busy skiing in Switzerland and skin diving in Acapulco that he can't deliver three full acts in three full years? Take the last thing I just opened in New Haven. We held the curtain till 8:45 and stretched both intermissions out to twenty-two minutes—and still they were playing the exit march at 10:37. It's a lucky thing for me those Yale boys weren't carrying switchblade knives. I gotta get a curtain raiser before we open on Broadway for sheer self-protection. Know something adequate in one simple set that's in the public domain?"

Even on Broadway today, however, the one-act play,

enthusiastically fostered by popular playwrights like Noel Coward, Thornton Wilder, Arthur Miller, Tennessee Williams, and William Inge, has come into its own. You will recognize in this volume some of the plays that brought about the change. Their taut construction and economy of dialogue will hold a special appeal for readers who have been plowing through some of the padded, endless, thousand-page novels publishers have been foisting on an arm-weary public. These one-acters may raise another thought in your minds, too: how many full-length plays of the past four or five years would have been infinitely more rewarding—and successful—if they too had been compressed into a single act?

In selecting the contents for this volume, the editors tried in general to pick representative plays that could be staged advantageously by groups with limited funds and facilities. We omitted, naturally, any plays that had been included in our first collection. And we thought it unwise to include more than one play by any author, though the temptation was strong to double up on some of the more popular practitioners. The result, we hope, will be as varied and provocative a collection as is possible today.

The late Eugene O'Neill always insisted that it was a lot easier for a conscientious playwright to expand a compact one-act playlet into a full-length drama than to reverse the process. Cutting his own plays was not Mr. O'Neill's forte. Like many a lesser dramatist he usually countered a request for a cut with "Confound it, that's the best scene in the play!"

At the tryout of *Ah, Wilderness*, the curtain fell so late that the stagehands demanded overtime. George M. Cohan, the star, furthermore, introduced new business and mannerisms with every succeeding performance. Everybody connected with the Theatre Guild beseeched O'Neill in vain to wield his blue pencil. Finally, Russel Crouse, publicity representative at the time, volunteered to try.

O'Neill liked Crouse—as did everybody else—and let him make his pleas without interruption. "I'll think over what you've said," he promised. The next morning he phoned Crouse and said, "You'll be happy to learn I've cut out fifteen minutes."

Crouse scarcely could believe his ears. "When? How?" he sputtered. "I'll be right up to get the changes."

"There aren't any changes in the TEXT," O'Neill assured him, "but, you know, we've been playing this thing in four acts. *I've decided to cut out the third intermission.*"

At the back of this volume there are short biographical notes of all the playwrights represented. Only one or two of the plays are in the public domain. For acting or reproduction rights, the editors refer you to the holders of the copyrights, all clearly indicated in the acknowledgments preceding each play. This book, however, will have achieved its chief purpose if it serves to make the one-act play more popular with an armchair audience. Many a reader who has a tendency to skip all but the dialogue in a novel insists that he can't read a play. We suggest that this book offers him an excellent opportunity to see if he cannot remedy this infirmity.

How we can justify the inclusion under the head of "favorite" plays one that has never before been published and another which is an adaptation of a short story may be questioned. We can only answer that any arbitrary selection of anthology material is necessarily subject to the prejudice of the compilers and plead guilty to liking Mr. Inge's play and Miss Parker's story very much indeed.

We might also in this connection note that we have included two plays, one of them a bit too saccharine for our taste and the other undeniably "corny" simply because of their extraordinary popularity with little theatre groups for decades past.

Happy reading!

Van H. Cartmell

Bennett Cerf

CONTENTS

A MEMORY OF
TWO MONDAYS

by Arthur Miller

CHARACTERS

BERT
RAYMOND
AGNES
PATRICIA
GUS
JIM
KENNETH
LARRY
FRANK
JERRY
WILLIAM
TOM
MECHANIC
MISTER EAGLE

A MEMORY OF TWO MONDAYS

The shipping room of a large auto-parts warehouse. This is but the back of a large loft in an industrial section of New York. The front of the loft, where we cannot see, is filled with office machinery, records, the telephone switchboard, and the counter where customers may come who do not order by letter or phone.

The two basic structures are the long packing table which curves upstage at the left, and the factory-type windows which reach from floor to ceiling and are encrusted with the hard dirt of years. These windows are the background and seem to surround the entire stage.

At the back, near the center, is a door to the toilet; on it are hooks for clothing. The back wall is bare but for a large spindle on which orders are impaled every morning and taken off and filled by the workers all day long. At center there is an ancient desk and chair. Downstage right is a small bench, boxes, a roll of packing paper on the table, and general untidiness. This place is rarely swept.

The right and left walls are composed of corridor openings, a louverlike effect, leading out into the alleys which are lined with bins reaching to the ceiling. Downstage center there is a large cast-iron floor scale with weights and balance exposed.

The nature of the work is simple. The men take orders off the hook, go out into the bin-lined alleys, fill the orders, bring the merchandise back to the table, where KENNETH *packs and addresses everything. The desk is used by* GUS *and/or* TOM KELLY *to figure postage or express rates on, to eat on, to lean on, or to hide things in. It is just home base, generally.*

A warning: The place must seem dirty and unmanageably chaotic, but since it is seen in this play with two separate visons it is also romantic. It is a little world, a home to which, unbelievably perhaps, these people like to come every Monday morning, despite what they say.

It is a hot Monday morning in summer, just before nine.

The stage is empty for a moment; then BERT *enters. He is eighteen. His trousers are worn at the knees but not un-respectable; he has rolled-up sleeves and is tieless. He carries a thick book, a large lunch in a brown paper bag, and a* New York Times. *He stores the lunch behind the packing table, clears a place on the table, sits and opens the paper, reads.*

Enter RAYMOND RYAN, *the manager. He wears a tie, white shirt, pressed pants, carries a clean towel, a tabloid, and in the other hand a sheaf of orders.*

RAYMOND *is forty, weighed down by responsibilities, afraid to be kind, quite able to be tough. He walks with the suggestion of a stoop.*

He goes directly to a large hook set in the back wall and impales the orders. BERT *sees him but, getting no greeting, returns to his paper. Preoccupied,* RAYMOND *walks past* BERT *toward the toilet, then halts in thought, turns back to* BERT.

RAYMOND. Tommy Kelly get in yet?

BERT. I haven't seen him, but I just got here myself. (RAYMOND *nods slightly, worried*). He'll probably make it all right.

RAYMOND. What are you doing in so early?

BERT. I wanted to get a seat on the subway for once. Boy, it's nice to walk around in the streets before the crowds get out . . .

RAYMOND (*he has never paid much attention to* BERT, *is now curious, has time for it*). How do you get time to read that paper?

BERT. Well, I've got an hour and ten minutes on the subway. I don't read it all, though. Just reading about Hitler.

RAYMOND. Who's that?

BERT. He took over the German government last week.

RAYMOND (*nodding, uninterested*). Listen, I want you to sweep up that excelsior laying around the freight elevator.

BERT. Okay. I had a lot of orders on Saturday, so I didn't get to it.

RAYMOND (*self-consciously; thus almost in mockery*). I hear you're going to go to college. Is that true?

BERT (*embarrassed*). Oh, I don't know, Mr. Ryan. They may not even let me in, I got such bad marks in high school.

RAYMOND. *You* did?

BERT. Oh, yeah. I just played ball and fooled around, that's all. I think I wasn't listening, y'know?

RAYMOND. How much it going to cost you?

BERT. I guess about four, five hundred for the first year. So I'll be here a long time—if I ever do go. You ever go to college?

RAYMOND (*shaking his head negatively*). My kid brother went to pharmacy, though. What are you going to take up?

BERT. I really don't know. You look through that catalogue —boy, you feel like taking it all, you know?

RAYMOND. This the same book you been reading?

BERT. Well, it's pretty long, and I fall asleep right after supper.

RAYMOND (*turning the book up*). "War and Peace"?

BERT. Yeah, he's supposed to be a great writer.

RAYMOND. How long it take you to read a book like this?

BERT. Oh, probably about three, four months, I guess. It's hard on the subway, with all those Russian names.

RAYMOND (*putting the book down*). What do you get out of a book like that?

BERT. Well, it's—it's literature.

RAYMOND (*nodding, mystified*). Be sure to open those three crates of axles that came in Saturday, will you? (*He starts to go toward the toilet.*)

BERT. I'll get to it this morning.

RAYMOND. And let me know when you decide to leave. I'll have to get somebody—

BERT. Oh, that'll be another year. Don't worry about it. I've got to save it all up first. I'm probably just dreaming anyway.

RAYMOND. How much do you save?

BERT. About eleven or twelve a week.

RAYMOND. Out of fifteen?

BERT. Well, I don't buy much. And my mother gives me my lunch.

RAYMOND. Well, sweep up around the elevator, will you? (RAYMOND *starts for the toilet as* AGNES *enters. She is a spinster in her late forties, always on the verge of laughter.*)

AGNES. Morning, Ray!

RAYMOND. Morning, Agnes. (*He exits into the toilet.*)

AGNES (*to* BERT). Bet you wish you could go swimming, heh?

BERT. Boy, I wouldn't mind. It's starting to boil already.

AGNES. You ought to meet my nephew sometime, Bert. He's a wonderful swimmer. Really, you'd like him. He's very serious.

BERT. How old is he now?

AGNES. He's only thirteen, but he reads the *New York Times* too.

BERT. Yeah?

AGNES (*noticing the book*). You still reading that book?

BERT (*embarrassed*). Well, I only get time on the subway, Agnes—

AGNES. Don't let any of them kid you, Bert. You go ahead.

You read the *New York Times* and all that. What happened today?

BERT. Hitler took over the German government.

AGNES. Oh, yes; my nephew knows about him. He loves civics. Last week one night he made a regular speech to all of us in the living room, and I realized that everything Roosevelt has done is absolutely illegal. Did you know that? Even my brother-in-law had to admit it, and he's a Democrat. (*Enter* PATRICIA *on her way to the toilet. She is twenty-three, blankly pretty, dressed just a little too tightly. She is not quite sure who she is yet.*)

PATRICIA. Morning!

AGNES. Morning, Patricia! Where did you get that pin?

PATRICIA. It was given. (*She glances at* BERT *who blushes.*)

AGNES. Oh, Patricia! Which one is he?

PATRICIA. Oh, somebody. (*She starts past for the toilet;* BERT *utters a warning "Ugh," and she remains.*)

AGNES (*she tends to laugh constantly, softly*). Did you go to the dance Saturday night?

PATRICIA (*fixing her clothing*). Well, they're always ending up with six guys in the hospital at that dance, and like that, so we went bowling.

AGNES. Did he give you that pin?

PATRICIA. No, I had a date after him.

AGNES (*laughing, titillated*). Pat!

PATRICIA. Well, I forgot all about him. So when I got home he was still sitting in front of the house in his car. I thought he was going to murder me. But isn't it an unusual pin? (*To* BERT, *who has moved off*). What are you always running away for?

BERT (*embarrassed*). I was just getting ready to work, that's all. (*Enter* GUS. *He is sixty-eight, a barrel-bellied man, totally bald, with a long, fierce, gray mustache that droops on the right side. He wears a bowler, and his pants are a little too short. He has a ready-made clip-on tie. He wears winter underwear all summer long, changes once a week. There is something neat and dusty about him—a rolling gait, bandy legs, a belly hard as a rock and full of beer. He speaks with a gruff Slavic accent.)*

PATRICIA. Oh, God, here's King Kong. (*She goes out up one of the corridors.*)

GUS (*calling after her halfheartedly—he is not completely sober, not bright yet*). You let me get my hands on you I give you King Kong!

AGNES (*laughing*). Oh, Gus, don't say those things!

GUS (*going for her*). Aggie, you make me crazy for you!

AGNES (*laughing and running from him toward the toilet door*). Gus!

GUS. Agnes, let's go Atlantic City! (AGNES *starts to open the toilet door.* RAYMOND *emerges from it.*)

AGNES (*surprised by* RAYMOND). Oh!

RAYMOND (*with plaintive anger*). Gus! Why don't you cut it out, heh?

GUS. Oh, I'm sick and tired, Raymond. (AGNES *goes into the toilet.*)

RAYMOND. How about getting all the orders shipped out by tonight, heh, Gus—for once?

GUS. What I did? I did something?

RAYMOND. Where's Jim?

GUS. How do I know where's Jim? Jim is my brother? (JIM *enters, stiff. He is in his mid-seventies, wears bent eyeglasses; has a full head of hair; pads about with careful tread.*)

JIM (*dimly*). Morning, Raymond. (*He walks as though he will fall forward. All watch as* JIM *aims his jacket for a hook, then, with a sudden motion, makes it. But he never really sways.*)

GUS. Attaboy, Jim! (*To* RAYMOND). What you criticize Jim? Look at that!

JIM (*turning to* RAYMOND *with an apologetic smile*).

Morning, Raymond. Hot day today. (*He goes to the spike and takes orders off it.*)

RAYMOND. Now look, Gus, Mr. Eagle is probably going to come today, so let's have everything going good, huh?

GUS. You can take Mr. Eagle and you shove him! (*AGNES enters from the toilet.*)

RAYMOND. What's the matter with you? I don't want that language around here any more. I'm not kidding, either. It's getting worse and worse, and we've got orders left over every night. Let's get straightened out here, will you? It's the same circus every Monday morning. (*He goes out.*)

AGNES. How's Lilly? Feeling better?

GUS. She's all the time sick, Agnes. I think she gonna die.

AGNES. Oh, don't say that. Pray to God, Gus.

GUS (*routinely*). Aggie, come with me Atlantic City. (*He starts taking off his shirt.*)

AGNES (*going from him*). Oh, how you smell!

GUS (*loudly*). I stink, Aggie!

AGNES (*closing her ears, laughing*). Oh, Gus, you're so terrible! (*She rushes out.*)

GUS (*laughs loudly, tauntingly, and turns to BERT*). What are you doin'? It's nine o'clock.

BERT. Oh. (*He gets off the bench*). I've got five to. Is your wife really sick? (*He gets an order from the hook.*)

GUS. You don't see Jim wait till nine o'clock! (*He goes to JIM, who is looking through the orders, and puts an arm around him*). Goddam Raymond. You hear what he says to me?

JIM. Ssh, Gus, it's all right. Maybe better call Lilly.

GUS (*grasping JIM's arm*). Wanna beer?

JIM (*trying to disengage himself*). No, Gus, let's behave ourselves. Come on.

GUS (*looking around*). Oh, boy. Oh, goddam boy. Monday morning. Ach.

JIM (*to* BERT, *as he starts out*). Did you unpack those axles yet?

GUS (*taking the order out of* JIM's *hand*). What are you doing with axles? Man your age! (*He gives* BERT JIM's *order*). Bert! Here! You let him pick up heavy stuff I show you something! Go!

BERT. I always take Jim's heavy orders, Gus. (*He goes out with the orders.*)

GUS. Nice girls, heh, Jim?

JIM. Oh, darn nice. Darn nice girls, Gus.

GUS. I keep my promise, hah, Jim?

JIM. You did, Gus. I enjoyed myself. But maybe you ought to call up your wife. She might be wonderin' about you. You been missin' since Saturday, Gus.

GUS (*asking for a reminder*). Where we was yesterday?

JIM. That's when we went to Staten Island, I think. On the ferry? Remember? With the girls? I think we was on a ferry. So it must've been to Staten Island. You better call her.

GUS. Ach—She don't hear nothing, Jim.

JIM. But if the phone rings, Gus, she'll know you're all right.

GUS. All right, I ring the phone. (*He goes and dials.* JIM *leaves with his orders.* PATRICIA *enters.*)

PATRICIA. Morning, Kong!

GUS. Shatap. (*She goes into the toilet as* GUS *listens on the phone. Then he roars*). Hallo! *Hallo!* Lilly! Gus! *Gus!* How you feel? *Gus!* Working! Ya! Ya! *Gus!* Oh, shatap! (*He hangs up the phone angrily, confused.* JIM *enters with a few small boxes, which he sets in a pile on the table.*)

JIM. You call her?

GUS. Oh, Jim, she don't hear nothing. (*He goes idly to the toilet, opens the door.* PATRICIA *screams within, and* GUS *stands there in the open doorway, screaming with her in parody, then lets the door shut.* JIM *starts out, examining his order, a pencil in his hand, as* KENNETH *enters, lunch in hand.* KENNETH *is twenty-six, a strapping, fair-skinned man, with thinning hair, delicately shy, very strong. He has only recently come to this country.*)

JIM. Morning, Kenneth.

KENNETH. And how are you this fine exemplary morning, James?

JIM. Oh, comin' along. Goin' to be hot today. (*He goes out.* KENNETH *hangs up his jacket and stores his lunch.* GUS *is standing in thought, picking his ear with a pencil.*)

KENNETH. Havin' yourself a thought this morning, Gus? (GUS *just looks at him, then goes back to his thought and his excavation*). Gus, don't you think something could be done about the dust constantly fallin' through the air of this place? Don't you imagine a thing or two could be done about that?

GUS. Because it's dusty, that's why. (*He goes to the desk, sits.*)

KENNETH. That's what I was sayin'—it's dusty. Tommy Kelly get in?

GUS. No.

KENNETH. Oh, poor Tommy Kelly. (BERT *enters*). Good morning to you, Bert. Have you finished your book yet?

BERT (*setting two heavy axles on the bench*). Not yet, Kenneth.

KENNETH (*his jacket in his hand*). Well, don't lose heart. (*He orates*):

> "Courage, brother! do not stumble
>   Though thy path be dark as night;
>   There's a star to guide the humble;
>   Trust in God, and do the Right."

By Norman Macleod.

BERT (*with wonder, respect*). How'd you learn all that poetry?

KENNETH (*hanging up his jacket*). Why, in Ireland, Bert; there's all kinds of useless occupations in Ireland. "When lilacs last in the dooryard bloomed . . ."

GUS (*from the desk*). What the hell you doin'? (BERT *goes to order hook.*)

KENNETH. Why, it's the poetry hour, Gus, don't you know that? This is the hour all men rise to thank God for the blue of the sky, the roundness of the everlasting globe, and the cheerful cleanliness of the subway system. And here we have some axles. Oh, Bert, I never thought I would end me life wrappin' brown paper around strange axles. (*He wraps*). And what's the latest in the *New York Times* this morning?

BERT (*looking through orders on the hook*). Hitler took over the German government.

KENNETH. Oh, did he! Strange, isn't it, about the Germans? A great people they are for mustaches. You take Bismarck, now, or you take Frederick the Great, or even take Gus over here—

GUS. I'm no Heinie.

KENNETH. Why, I always thought you were, Gus. What are you, then?

GUS. American.

KENNETH. I know that, but what *are* you?

GUS. I fought in submarine.

KENNETH. Did you, now? An American submarine?

GUS. What the hell kind of submarine I fight in, Hungarian? (*He turns back to his desk.*)

KENNETH. Well, don't take offense, Gus. There's all kinds of submarines, y'know. (BERT *starts out, examining his order*). How's this to be wrapped, Bert? Express?

BERT. I think that goes parcel post. It's for Skaneateles.

GUS (*erupting at his desk*). Axles parcel post? You crazy? You know how much gonna cost axles parcel post?

BERT. That's right. I guess it goes express.

GUS. And you gonna go college? Barber college you gonna go!

BERT. Well, I forgot it was axles, Gus.

GUS (*muttering over his desk*). Stupid.

KENNETH. I've never been to Skaneateles. Where would that be?

BERT. It's a little town upstate. It's supposed to be pretty there.

KENNETH. That a sweet thought? Sendin' these two grimy axles out into the green countryside? I spent yesterday in the park. What did you do, Bert? Go swimmin' again, I suppose?

GUS (*turning*). You gonna talk all day?

BERT. We're working. (*He goes out.* KENNETH *wraps.*)

KENNETH. You're rubbin' that poor kid pretty hard, Gus; he's got other things on his mind than parcel post and—

GUS. What the hell I care what he got on his mind? Axles he gonna send parcel post! (*He returns to his work on the desk.*)

KENNETH (*wraps, then*). Can you feel the heat rising in this building! If only some of it could be saved for the winter. (*Pause. He is wrapping*). The fiery furnace. Nebuchadnezzar was the architect. (*Pause*). What do you suppose would happen, Gus, if a man took it into his head to wash these windows? They'd snatch him off to the nuthouse, heh? (*Pause*). I wonder if he's only kiddin'—Bert. About goin' to college someday.

GUS (*not turning from his desk*). Barber College he gonna go.

KENNETH (*he works, thinking*). He must have a wealthy family. Still and all, he don't spend much. I suppose he's just got some strong idea in his mind. That's the thing, y'know. I often conceive them myself, but I'm all the time losin' them, though. It's the holdin' on—that's what does it. You can almost see it in him, y'know? He's holdin' on to somethin'. (*He shakes his head in wonder, then sings*):

> Oh, the heat of the summer,
> The cool of the fall.
> The lady went swimming
> With nothing at all.

Ah, that's a filthy song, isn't it! (*Pause. He wraps*). Gus, you suppose Mr. Roosevelt'll be makin' it any better than it is? (*He sings*):

> The minstrel boy to the war has gone,
> In the ranks of death . . .

(PATRICIA *enters from the toilet.*)

PATRICIA. Was that an Irish song?

KENNETH (*shyly*). All Irish here and none of yiz knows an Irish song.

PATRICIA. You have a terrific voice, Kenneth.

GUS (*to* PATRICIA). Why don't you make date with him?

KENNETH (*stamping his foot*). Oh, that's a nasty thing to say in front of a girl, Gus! (GUS *rises.*)

PATRICIA (*backing away from* GUS). Now don't start with me, kid, because— (GUS *lunges for her. She turns to run, and he squeezes her buttocks mercilessly as she runs out and almost collides with* LARRY, *who is entering.* LARRY *is thirty-nine, a troubled but phlegmatic man, good-looking. He is carrying a container of coffee and a lighted cigarette. On the collision he spills a little coffee.*)

LARRY (*with a slight humor*). Hey! Take it easy.

PATRICIA (*quite suddenly all concerned for* LARRY, *to* GUS).

Look what you did, you big horse! (LARRY *sets the coffee on the table.*)

LARRY. Jesus, Gus.

GUS. Tell her stop makin' all the men crazy! (*He returns to his desk.*)

PATRICIA. I'm sorry, Larry. (*She is alone, in effect, with* LARRY. *Both of them wipe the spot on his shirt*). Did you buy it?

LARRY (*embarrassed but courageous, as though inwardly flaunting his own fears*). Yeah, I got it yesterday.

PATRICIA. Gee, I'd love to see it. You ever going to bring it to work?

LARRY (*now he meets her eyes*). I might. On a Saturday, maybe.

PATRICIA. 'Cause I love those Auburns, y'know?

LARRY. Yeah, they got nice valves. Maybe I'll drive you home some night. For the ride.

PATRICIA (*the news stuns her*). Oh, boy! Well—I'll see ya. (*She goes.*)

GUS. You crazy? Buy Auburn?

LARRY (*with depth—a profound conclusion*). I like the valves, Gus.

GUS. Yeah, but when you gonna go sell it who gonna buy an Auburn?

LARRY. Didn't you ever get to where you don't care about that? I *always* liked those valves, and I decided, that's all.

GUS. Yeah, but when you gonna go sell it—

LARRY. I don't care.

GUS. You don't care!

LARRY. I'm sick of dreaming about things. They've got the most beautifully laid-out valves in the country on that car, and I want it, that's all. (KENNETH *is weighing a package on the scales.*)

GUS. Yeah, but when you gonna go sell it—

LARRY. I just don't care, Gus. Can't you understand that? (*He stares away, inhaling his cigarette.*)

KENNETH (*stooped over, sliding the scale weights*). There's a remarkable circumstance, Larry. Raymond's got twins, and now you with the triplets. And both in the same corporation. We ought to send that to the *Daily News* or something. I think they give you a dollar for an item like that. (BERT *enters, puts goods on the table.*)

BERT. Gee, I'm getting hungry. Want a sandwich, Kenneth? (*He reaches behind the packing table for his lunch bag.*)

KENNETH. Thank you, Bert. I might take one later.

GUS (*turning from the desk to* BERT). Lunch you gonna eat nine o'clock?

BERT. I got up too early this morning. You want some?

KENNETH. He's only a growing boy, Gus—and by the way, if you care to bend down, Gus—(*indicating under the scale platform*) there's more mice than ever under here.

GUS (*without turning*). Leave them mice alone.

KENNETH. Well, you're always complainin' the number of crayons I'm using, and I'm only tellin' you they're the ones is eatin' them up. (*He turns to* LARRY). It's a feast of crayons goin' on here every night, Larry. (*Enter* JIM *with goods, padding along.*)

JIM. Goin' to be hot today, Gus.

GUS. Take easy, what you running for? (JIM *stops to light his cigar butt.*)

KENNETH (*reading off the scale weights*). Eighty-one pounds, Gus. For Skaneateles, in the green countryside of upper New York State.

GUS. What? What you want?

KENNETH. I want the express order—eighty-one pounds to Skaneateles, New York.

GUS. Then why don't you say that, goddam Irishman? You

talk so much. When you gonna stop talkin'? (*He proceeds to make out the slip.*)

KENNETH. Oh, when I'm rich, Gus, I'll have very little more to say. (GUS *is busy making out the slip;* KENNETH *turns to* LARRY). No sign yet of Tommy Kelly in the place, Larry.

LARRY. What'd you, cut a hole in your shoe?

KENNETH. A breath of air for me little toe. I only paid a quarter for them, y'know; feller was sellin' them in Bryant Park. Slightly used, but they're a fine pair of shoes, you can see that.

LARRY. They look small for you.

KENNETH. They are at that. But you can't complain for a quarter, I guess.

GUS. Here. (GUS *hands* KENNETH *an express slip, which* KENNETH *now proceeds to attach to the package on the table. Meanwhile* JIM *has been leafing through the orders on the hook and is now leaving with two in his hand.*)

KENNETH. How do you keep up your strength, Jim? I'm always exhausted. You never stop movin', do ya? (JIM *just shakes his head with a "Heh, heh"*). I bet it's because you never got married, eh?

JIM. No, I guess I done everything there is but that.

LARRY. How come you never did get married, Jim?

JIM. Well, I was out West so long, you know, Larry. Out West. (*He starts to go again.*)

KENNETH. Oh, don't they get married much out there?

JIM. Well, the cavalry was amongst the Indians most of the time.

BERT. How old are you now, Jim? No kidding.

KENNETH. I'll bet he's a hundred.

JIM. Me? No. I ain't no hunderd. I ain't near a hunderd. You don't have to be a hunderd to've fought the Indians. They was more Indians was fought than they tells in the schoolbooks, y'know. They was a hell of a lot of fightin' up to McKinley and all in there. I ain't no hunderd. (*He starts out.*)

KENNETH. Well, how old would you say you are, Jim?

JIM. Oh, I'm seventy-four, seventy-five, seventy-six—around in there. But I ain't no hunderd. (*He exits, and* KEN-NETH *sneezes.*)

BERT (*he has put his lunch bag away and is about to leave*). Boy, I was hungry!

KENNETH (*irritated*). Larry, don't you suppose a word might be passed to Mr. Eagle about the dust? It's rainin' dust from the ceiling! (BERT *goes out.*)

GUS. What the hell Mr. Eagle gonna do about the dust?

KENNETH. Why, he's supposed to be a brilliant man, isn't he? Dartmouth College graduate and all? I've been five and a half months in this country, and I never sneezed so much in my entire life before. My nose is all— (*Enter* FRANK, *the truckdriver, an impassive, burly man in his thirties.*)

FRANK. Anything for the West Bronx?

KENNETH. Nothin' yet, Frank. I've only started, though. (JIM *enters with little boxes, which he adds to the pile on the bench.*)

FRANK. You got anything for West Bronx, Jim? I've got the truck on the elevator.

GUS. What's the hurry?

FRANK. I got the truck on the elevator.

GUS. Well, take it off the elevator! You got one little box of bearings for the West Bronx. You can't go West Bronx with one little box.

FRANK. Well, I gotta go.

GUS. You got a little pussy in the West Bronx.

FRANK. Yeah, I gotta make it before lunch.

JIM (*riffling through his orders*). I think I got something for the East Bronx.

FRANK. No, West Bronx.

JIM (*removing one order from his batch*). How about Brooklyn?

FRANK. What part? (*He takes* JIM's *order, reads the address, looks up, thinking.*)

JIM. Didn't you have a girl around Williamsburg?

FRANK. I'll have to make a call. I'll be right back.

GUS. You gonna deliver only where you got a woman?

FRANK. No, Gus, I go any place you tell me. But as long as I'm goin' someplace I might as well—you know. (*He starts out.*)

GUS. You some truckdriver.

FRANK. You said it, Gus. (*He goes out.*)

GUS. Why don't you go with him sometime, Kenneth? Get yourself nice piece ding-a-ling—

KENNETH. Oh, don't be nasty now, Gus. You're only tryin' to be nasty to taunt me. (RAYMOND *enters.*)

RAYMOND. Didn't Tommy Kelly get here?

GUS. Don't worry for Tommy. Tommy going to be all right.

LARRY. Can I see you a minute, Ray? (*He moves with* RAYMOND *over to the left.*)

RAYMOND. Eagle's coming today, and if he sees him drunk again I don't know what I'm going to do.

LARRY. Ray, I'd like you to ask Eagle something for me.

RAYMOND. What?

LARRY. I've got to have more money.

RAYMOND. You and me both, boy.

LARRY. No, I can't make it any more, Ray. I mean it. The car put me a hundred and thirty bucks in the hole. If one of the kids gets sick I'll be strapped.

RAYMOND. Well, what'd you buy the car for?

LARRY. I'm almost forty, Ray. What am I going to be careful for?

RAYMOND. See, the problem is, Larry, if you go up, I'm

only making thirty-eight myself, and I'm the manager, so it's two raises—

LARRY. Ray, I hate to make it tough for you, but my wife is driving me nuts. Now— (*Enter* JERRY MAXWELL *and* WILLY HOGAN, *both twenty-three.* JERRY *has a black eye; both are slick dressers.*)

JERRY AND WILLY. Morning. Morning, Gus.

RAYMOND. Aren't you late, fellas?

JERRY (*glancing at his gold wrist watch*). I've got one minute to nine, Mr. Ryan.

WILLY. That's Hudson Tubes time, Mr. Ryan.

GUS. The stopwatch twins.

RAYMOND (*to* JERRY). You got a black eye?

JERRY. Yeah, we went to a dance in Jersey City last night.

WILLY. Ran into a wise guy in Jersey City, Mr. Ryan.

JERRY (*with his taunting grin; he is very happy with himself*). Tried to take his girl away from us.

RAYMOND. Well, get on the ball. Mr. Eagle's— (*Enter* TOM KELLY. GUS *rises from the desk.* BERT *enters, stands still.* RAYMOND *and* LARRY *stand watching.* KENNETH *stops wrapping.* TOM *is stiff; he moves in a dream to the chair* GUS *has left and sits rigidly. He is a slight, graying clerk in his late forties.*)

GUS (*to* RAYMOND). Go 'way, go 'head. (RAYMOND *comes up and around the desk to face* TOM, *who sits there, staring ahead, immobile, his hands in his lap.*)

RAYMOND. Tommy. (JERRY *and* WILLY *titter.*)

GUS (*to them*). Shatap, goddam bums!

JERRY. Hey, don't call me—

GUS. Shatap, goddamit I break you goddam head! (*He has an axle in his hand, and* RAYMOND *and* LARRY *are pulling his arm down.* JIM *enters and goes directly to him. All are crying, "Gus! Cut it out! Put it down!"*)

JERRY. What'd we do? What'd I say?

GUS. Watch out! Just watch out you make fun of this man!

I break you head, both of you! (*Silence. He goes to* TOM, *who has not moved since arriving*). Tommy. Tommy, you hear Gus? Tommy? (TOM *is transfixed.*)

RAYMOND. Mr. Eagle is coming today, Tommy.

GUS (*to all*). Go 'head, go to work, go to work! (*They all move;* JERRY *and* WILLY *go out.*)

RAYMOND. Can you hear me, Tom? Mr. Eagle is coming to look things over today, Tom.

JIM. Little shot of whisky might bring him to.

GUS. Bert! (*He reaches into his pocket*). Here, go downstairs bring a shot. Tell him for Tommy. (*He sees what is in his hand*). I only got ten cents.

RAYMOND. Here. (*He reaches into his pocket as* JIM, KENNETH, *and* LARRY *all reach into their own pockets.*)

BERT (*taking a coin from* RAYMOND). Okay, I'll be right up. (*He hurries out.*)

RAYMOND. Well, this is it, Gus. I gave him his final warning.

GUS (*he is worried*). All right, go 'way, go 'way. (AGNES *enters.*)

AGNES. Is he—?

RAYMOND. You heard me, Agnes. I told him on Saturday, didn't I? (*He starts past her.*)

AGNES. But Ray, look how nice and clean he came in today. His hair is all combed, and he's much neater.

RAYMOND. I did my best, Agnes. (*He goes out.*)

GUS (*staring into* TOMMY's *dead eyes*). Ach. He don't see nothin', Agnes.

AGNES (*looking into* TOMMY's *face*). And he's supposed to be saving for his daughter's confirmation dress! Oh, Tommy. I'd better cool his face. (*She goes into the toilet.*)

KENNETH (*to* LARRY). Ah, you can't blame the poor feller; sixteen years of his life in this place.

LARRY. You said it.

KENNETH. There's a good deal of monotony connected with the life, isn't it?

LARRY. You ain't kiddin'.

KENNETH. Oh, there must be a terrible lot of Monday mornings in sixteen years. And no philosophical idea at all, y'know, to pass the time?

GUS (*to* KENNETH). When you gonna shut up? (AGNES *comes from the toilet with a wet cloth. They watch as she washes* TOM's *face.*)

KENNETH. Larry, you suppose we could get these windows washed sometime? I've often thought if we could see a bit of the sky now and again it would help matters now and again.

LARRY. They've never been washed since I've been here.

KENNETH. I'd do it myself if I thought they wouldn't all be laughin' at me for a greenhorn. (*He looks out through the open window, which only opens out a few inches*). With all this glass we might observe the clouds and the various signs of approaching storms. And there might even be a bird now and again.

AGNES. Look at that—he doesn't even move. And he's been trying so hard! Nobody gives him credit, but he does try hard. (*To* LARRY). See how nice and clean he comes in now? (JIM *enters, carrying parts.*)

JIM. Did you try blowing in his ear?

GUS. Blow in his ear?

JIM. Yeah, the Indians used to do that. Here, wait a minute. (*He comes over, takes a deep breath, and blows into* TOM's *ear. A faint smile begins to appear on* TOM's *face, but, as* JIM *runs out of breath, it fades.*)

KENNETH. Well, I guess he's not an Indian.

JIM. That's the truth, y'know. Out West, whenever there'd be a drunken Indian, they used to blow in his ear. (*Enter* BERT, *carefully carrying a shotglass of whisky.*)

GUS. Here, gimme that. (*He takes it.*)

BERT (*licking his fingers*). Boy, that stuff is strong.

GUS. Tommy? (*He holds the glass in front of* TOM's *nose*). Whisky. (TOM *doesn't move*). Mr. Eagle is coming today, Tommy.

JIM. Leave it on the desk. He might wake up to it.

BERT. How's he manage to make it here, I wonder.

AGNES. Oh, he's awake. Somewhere inside, y'know. He just can't show it, somehow. It's not really like being drunk, even.

KENNETH. Well, it's pretty close, though, Agnes. (AGNES *resumes wetting* TOM's *brow*.)

LARRY. Is that a fact, Jim, about blowing in a guy's ear?

JIM. Oh, sure. Indians always done that. (*He goes to the order hook, leafs through.*)

KENNETH. What did yiz all have against the Indians?

JIM. The Indians? Oh, we didn't have nothin' against the Indians. Just law and order, that's all. Talk about heat, though. It was so hot out there we— (JIM *exits with an order as* FRANK *enters.*)

FRANK. All right, I'll go to Brooklyn.

GUS. Where you running? I got nothing packed yet. (*Enter* JERRY, *who puts goods on the table.*)

FRANK. Well, you beefed that I want to go Bronx, so I'm tellin' you now I'll go to Brooklyn.

GUS. You all fixed up in Brooklyn?

FRANK. Yeah, I just made a call.

AGNES (*laughing*). Oh, you're all so terrible! (*She goes out.*)

JERRY. How you doin', Kenny? You gittin' any?

KENNETH. Is that all two fine young fellas like you is got on your minds?

JERRY. Yeah, that's all. What's on your mind? (FRANK *is loading himself with packages.*)

GUS (*of* TOMMY). What am I gonna do with him, Larry? The old man's comin'.

LARRY. Tell you the truth, Gus, I'm sick and tired of worrying about him, y'know? Let him take care of himself. (GUS *goes to* LARRY, *concerned, and they speak quietly.*)

GUS. What's the matter with you these days?

LARRY. Two years I'm asking for a lousy five-dollar raise. Meantime my brother's into me for fifty bucks for his wife's special shoes; my sister's got me for sixty-five to have her kid's teeth fixed. So I buy a car, and they're all on my back—how'd I dare buy a car! Whose money is it? Y'know, Gus? I mean—

GUS. Yeah, but an Auburn, Larry—

LARRY (*getting hot*). I happen to like the valves! What's so unusual about that? (*Enter* WILLY *and* JERRY *with goods.*)

WILLY (*to* JERRY). Here! Ask Frank. (*To* FRANK). Who played shortstop for Pittsburgh in nineteen-twenty-four?

FRANK. Pittsburgh? Honus Wagner, wasn't it?

WILLY (*to* JERRY). What I tell ya?

JERRY. How could it be Honus Wagner? Honus Wagner— (RAYMOND *enters with a mechanic, and* WILLY *and* JERRY *exit, arguing.* FRANK *goes out with his packages.* GUS *returns to his desk.*)

RAYMOND. Larry, you want to help this man? He's got a part here. (LARRY *simply turns, silent, with a hurt and angry look. The mechanic goes to him, holds out the part; but* LARRY *does not take it, merely inspects it, for it is greasy, as is the man.*)

RAYMOND (*going to the desk, where* GUS *is now seated at work beside* TOM KELLY). Did he move at all, Gus?

GUS. He's feeling much better, I can see. Go, go 'way, Raymond. (RAYMOND *worriedly stands there.*)

LARRY (*to mechanic*). Where you from?

MECHANIC. I'm mechanic over General Truck.

LARRY. What's that off?

MECHANIC (*as* BERT *stops to watch, and* KENNETH *stops packing to observe*). That's the thing—I don't know. It's a very old coal truck, see, and I thought it was a Mack, because it says Mack on the radiator, see? But I went over to Mack, and they says there's no part like that on any Mack in their whole history, see?

LARRY. Is there any name on the engine?

MECHANIC. I'm tellin' you; on the engine it says American-LaFrance—must be a replacement engine.

LARRY. That's not off a LaFrance.

MECHANIC. I know! I went over to American-LaFrance, but they says they never seen nothin' like that in their whole life since the year one. (RAYMOND *joins them.*)

LARRY. What is it, off the manifold?

MECHANIC. Well, it ain't exactly off the manifold. It like sticks out, see, except it don't stick out, it's like stuck in there—I mean it's like in a little hole there on top of the head, except it ain't exactly a hole, it's a thing that comes up in like a bump, see, and then it goes down. Two days I'm walkin' the streets with this, my boss is goin' crazy.

LARRY. Well, go and find out what it is, and if we got it we'll sell it to you.

RAYMOND. Don't you have any idea, Larry?

LARRY. I might, Ray, but I'm not getting paid for being an encyclopedia. There's ten thousand obsolete parts upstairs—it was never my job to keep all that in my head. If the old man wants that service, let him pay somebody to do it.

RAYMOND. Ah, Larry, the guy's here with the part.

LARRY. The guy is always here with the part, Ray. Let him hire somebody to take an inventory up there and see what it costs him.

RAYMOND (*taking the part off the table*). Well, I'll see what I can find up there.

LARRY. You won't find it, Ray. Put it down. (RAYMOND *does, and* LARRY, *blinking with hurt, turns to the mechanic*). What is that truck, about nineteen-twenty-two?

MECHANIC. That truck? (*He shifts onto his right foot in thought.*)

LARRY. Nineteen-twenty?

MECHANIC (*in a higher voice, shifting to the left foot*). That truck?

LARRY. Well, it's at least nineteen-twenty, isn't it?

MECHANIC. Oh, it's at least. I brung over a couple a friend of mines, and one of them is an old man and he says when he was a boy already that truck was an old truck, and he's an old, old man, that guy. (LARRY *takes the part now and sets it on the packing bench. Now even* GUS *gets up to watch as he stares at the part. There is a hush.* RAYMOND *goes out.* LARRY *turns the part a little and stares at it again. Now he sips his coffee*). I understand this company's got a lot of old parts from the olden days, heh?

LARRY. We may have one left, if it's what I think it is, but you'll have to pay for it.

MECHANIC. Oh, I know; that's why my boss says try all the other places first, because he says youse guys charge. But looks to me like we're stuck.

LARRY. Bert. (*He stares in thought*). Get the key to the third floor from Miss Molloy. Go up there, and when you open the door you'll see those Model-T mufflers stacked up.

BERT. Okay.

LARRY. You ever been up there?

BERT. No, but I always wanted to go.

LARRY. Well, go past the mufflers and you'll see a lot of bins going up to the ceiling. They're full of Marmon valves and ignition stuff.

BERT. Yeah?

LARRY. Go past them, and you'll come to a little corridor, see?

BERT. Yeah?

LARRY. At the end of the corridor is a pile of crates—I think there's some Maxwell differentials in there.

BERT. Yeah?

LARRY. Climb over the crates, but don't keep goin', see. Stand on top of the crates and turn right. Then bend down, and there's a bin— No, I tell you, get off the crates, and you can reach behind them, but to the right, and reach into that bin. There's a lot of Locomobile head-nuts in there, but way back—you gotta stick your hand way in, see, and you'll find one of these.

BERT. Geez, Larry, how do you remember all that? (AGNES *rushes in.*)

AGNES. Eagle's here! Eagle's here!

LARRY (*to the mechanic*). Go out front and wait at the counter, will ya? (*The mechanic nods and leaves.* LARRY *indicates the glass on the desk*). Better put that whisky away, Gus.

GUS (*alarmed now*). What should we do with him? (LARRY *goes to* TOM, *peeved, and speaks in his ear.*)

LARRY. Tommy. Tommy!

AGNES. Larry, why don't you put him up on the third floor? He got a dozen warnings already. Eagle's disgusted—

GUS. Maybe he's sick. I never seen him like this. (JIM *enters with goods.*)

JIM. Eagle's here.

LARRY. Let's try to walk him around. Come on. (GUS *looks for a place to hide the whisky, then drinks it.*)

GUS. All right, Tommy, come on, get up. (*They hoist him up to his feet, then let him go. He starts to sag; they catch him*). I don't think he feel so good.

LARRY. Come on, walk him. (*To* AGNES). Watch out for

Eagle. (*She stands looking off and praying silently*). Let's go, Tom. (*They try to walk* TOM, *but he doesn't lift his feet.*)

AGNES (*trembling, watching* TOMMY). He's so kindhearted, y'see? That's his whole trouble—he's too kindhearted.

LARRY (*angering, but restrained, shaking* TOM). For God's sake, Tom, come on! Eagle's here! (*He shakes* TOM *more violently*). Come on! What the hell is the matter with you, you want to lose your job? Goddamit, you a baby or something?

AGNES. Sssh! (*They all turn to the left. In the distance is heard the clacking of heel taps on a concrete floor.*)

GUS. Put him down. Larry! (*They seat* TOM *before the desk.* AGNES *swipes back his mussed hair.* GUS *sets his right hand on top of an invoice on the desk*). Here, put him like he's writing. Where's my pencil? Who's got pencil? (LARRY, KENNETH, AGNES *search themselves for a pencil.*)

KENNETH. Here's a crayon.

GUS. Goddam, who take my pencil! Bert! Where's that Bert! He always take my pencil! (BERT *enters, carrying a heavy axle.*)

BERT. Hey, Eagle's here!

GUS. Goddam you, why you take my pencil?

BERT. I haven't got your pencil. This is mine. (GUS *grabs the pencil out of* BERT'S *shirt pocket and sticks it upright into* TOM's *hand. They have set him up to look as if he is writing. They step away.* TOM *starts sagging toward one side.*)

AGNES (*in a loud whisper*). Here he comes! (*She goes to the order spike and pretends she is examining it.* LARRY *meanwhile rushes to* TOM, *sets him upright, then walks away, pretending to busy himself. But* TOM *starts falling off the chair again, and* BERT *rushes and props him up. The sound of the heel taps is on us now, and* BERT *starts talking to* TOM, *meantime supporting him with one hand on his shoulder.*)

BERT (*overloudly*). Tommy, the reason I ask, see, is because on Friday I filled an order for the same amount of coils for Scranton, see, and it just seems they wouldn't be ordering the same exact amount again. (*During his speech* EAGLE *has entered—a good-looking man in his late forties, wearing Palm Beach trousers, a shirt and tie, sleeves neatly folded up, a new towel over one arm. He walks across the shipping room, not exactly looking at anyone, but clearly observing everything. He goes toward the toilet, past* AGNES, *who turns.*)

AGNES. Good morning, Mr. Eagle.

EAGLE (*nodding*). Morning. (*He goes into the toilet.*)

KENNETH (*indicating the toilet*). Keep it up, keep it up now!

BERT (*loudly*). Ah—another thing that's bothering me, Tommy, is those rear-end gears for Riverhead. I can't find invoice for Riverhead. I can't find any invoice for gears to Riverhead. (*He is getting desperate, looks to the others, but they only urge him on*). So what happened to the invoice? That's the thing we're all wondering about, Tommy. What happened to that invoice? You see, Tom? That invoice—it was blue, I remember, blue with a little red around the edges—

KENNETH (*loudly*). That's right there, Bert, it was a blue invoice—and it had numbers on it—(*Suddenly* TOM *stands, swaying a little, blinking. There is a moment's silence.*)

TOM. No, no, Glen Wright was shortstop for Pittsburgh, not Honus Wagner. (EAGLE *emerges from the toilet.* BERT *goes to the order spike.*)

LARRY. Morning, sir. (*He goes out.*)

TOM (*half bewildered, shifting from foot to foot*). Who was talking about Pittsburgh? (*He turns about and almost collides with* EAGLE). Morning, Mr. Eagle.

EAGLE (*as he passes* TOM *he lets his look linger on his face*). Morning, Kelly. (EAGLE *crosses the shipping room and goes out.* AGNES, KENNETH, *and* GUS *wait an instant.* JIM *enters, sees* TOM *is up.*)

JIM. Attaboy, Tommy, knew you'd make it.

TOM. Glen Wright was shortstop. Who asked about that?

GUS (*nodding sternly his approbation to* BERT). Very good, Bert, you done good.

BERT (*wiping his forehead*). Boy!

TOM. Who was talking about Pittsburgh? (AGNES *is heard weeping. They turn*). Agnes? (*He goes to her*). What's the matter, Ag?

AGNES. Oh, Tommy, why do you do that?

PATRICIA (*calling from offstage left*). Aggie? Your switchboard's ringing.

AGNES. Oh, Tommy! (*Weeping, she hurries out.*)

TOM (*to the others*). What happened? What is she cryin' for?

GUS (*indicating the desk*). Why don't you go to work, Tommy? You got lotta parcel post this morning. (TOM *always has a defensive smile. He shifts from foot to foot as he talks, as though he were always standing on a hot stove. He turns to the desk, sees* KENNETH. *He wants to normalize everything.*)

TOM. Kenny! I didn't even see ya!

KENNETH. Morning, Tommy. Good to see you up and about.

TOM (*with a put-on brogue*). Jasus, me bye, y'r hair is fallin' like the dew of the evenin'.

KENNETH (*self-consciously wiping his hair*). Oh, Tommy, now—

TOM. Kenny, bye, y'r gittin' an awful long face to wash!

KENNETH (*gently cuffing him*). Oh, now, stop that talk!

TOM (*backing toward his desk*). Why, ya donkey, ya. I bet they had to back you off the boat!

KENNETH (*with mock anger*). Oh, don't you be callin' me a donkey now! (*Enter* RAYMOND.)

RAYMOND. Tom? (*He is very earnest, even deadly.*)

TOM (*instantly perceiving his own guilt*). Oh, mornin', Ray, how's the twins? (*He gasps little chuckles as he sits at his desk, feeling about for a pencil.* RAYMOND *goes up close to the desk and leans over, as the others watch— pretending not to.*)

RAYMOND (*quietly*). Eagle wants to see you.

TOM (*with foreboding, looking up into* RAYMOND's *face*). Eagle? I got a lot of parcel post this morning, Ray. (*He automatically presses down his hair.*)

RAYMOND. He's in his office waiting for you now, Tom.

TOM. Oh, sure. It's just that there's a lot of parcel post on Monday. . . . (*He feels for his tie as he rises, and walks out.* RAYMOND *starts out after him, but* GUS *intercedes.*)

GUS (*going up to* RAYMOND). What Eagle wants?

RAYMOND. I warned him, Gus, I warned him a dozen times.

GUS. He's no gonna fire him.

RAYMOND. Look, it's all over, Gus, so there's nothing—

GUS. He gonna fire Tommy?

RAYMOND. Now don't raise your voice.

GUS. Sixteen year Tommy work here! He got daughter gonna be in church confirmation!

RAYMOND. Now listen, I been nursing him along for—

GUS. Then you fire me! You fire Tommy, you fire me!

RAYMOND. Gus! (*With a stride* GUS *goes to the hook, takes his shirt down, thrusts himself into it.*)

GUS. Goddam son-of-a-bitch.

RAYMOND. Now don't be crazy, Gus.

GUS. I show who crazy! Tommy Kelly he gonna fire! (*He grabs his bowler off the hook. Enter* AGNES, *agitated.*)

AGNES. Gus! Go to the phone!

GUS (*not noticing her, and with bowler on, to* RAYMOND).

Come on, he gonna fire me now, son-of-a-bitch! (*He starts out, shirttails flying, and* AGNES *stops him.*)

AGNES (*indicating the phone*). Gus, your neighbor's—

GUS (*trying to disengage himself*). No, he gonna fire me now. He fire Tommy Kelly, he fire me!

AGNES. Lilly, Gus! Your neighbor wants to talk to you. Go, go to the phone. (GUS *halts, looks at* AGNES.)

GUS. What, Lilly?

AGNES. Something's happened. Go, go to the phone.

GUS. Lilly? (*Perplexed, he goes to the phone*). Hallo. Yeah, Gus. Ha? (*He listens, stunned. His hand, of itself, goes to his hatbrim as though to doff the hat, but it stays there.* JIM *enters, comes to a halt, sensing the attention, and watches* GUS). When? When it happen? (*He listens, and then mumbles*). Ya. Thank you. I come home right away. (*He hangs up.* JIM *comes forward to him questioningly. To* JIM, *perplexed*). My Lilly. Die.

JIM. Oh? Hm! (LARRY *enters.* GUS *dumbly turns to him.*)

GUS (*to* LARRY). Die. My Lilly.

LARRY. Oh, that's tough, Gus.

RAYMOND. You better go home. (*Pause*). Go ahead, Gus. Go home. (GUS *stands blinking.* RAYMOND *takes his jacket from the hook and helps him on with it.* AGNES *starts to push his shirttails into his pants.*)

GUS. We shouldn't've go to Staten Island, Jim. Maybe she don't feel good yesterday. Ts, I was in Staten Island, maybe she was sick. (TOMMY KELLY *enters, goes directly to his desk, sits, his back to the others. Pause. To* TOM). He fire you, Tommy?

TOM (*holding tears back*). No, Gus, I'm all right.

GUS (*going up next to him*). Give you another chance?

TOM (*he is speaking with his head lowered*). Yeah. It's all right, Gus, I'm goin' to be all right from now on.

GUS. Sure. Be a man, Tommy. Don't be no drunken bum.

Be a man. You hear? Don't let nobody walk on top you. Be man.

TOM. I'm gonna be all right, Gus.

GUS (*nodding*). One more time you come in drunk I gonna show you something. (AGNES *sobs. He turns to her*). What for you cry all the time? (*He goes past her and out.* AGNES *then goes. A silence.*)

RAYMOND (*breaking the silence*). What do you say, fellas, let's get going, heh? (*He claps his hands and walks out as all move about their work. Soon all are gone but* TOMMY KELLY, *slumped at his desk;* KENNETH, *wrapping; and* BERT, *picking an order from the hook. Now* KENNETH *faces* BERT *suddenly.*)

KENNETH (*he has taken his feeling from the departing* GUS, *and turns now to* BERT). Bert? How would you feel about washing these windows—you and I—once and for all? Let a little of God's light in the place?

BERT (*excitedly, happily*). Would you?

KENNETH. Well, I would if you would.

BERT. Okay, come on! Let's do a little every day; couple of months it'll all be clean! Gee! Look at the sun!

KENNETH. Hey, look down there! See the old man sitting in a chair?
And roses all over the fence!
Oh, that's a lovely back yard!
(*A rag in hand,* BERT *mounts the table; they make one slow swipe of the window before them and instantly all the windows around the stage burst into the yellow light of summer that floods into the room.*)

BERT. Boy, they've got a tree!
And all those cats!

KENNETH. It'll be nice to watch the seasons pass.
'That pretty up there now, a real summer sky
And a little white cloud goin' over?
I can just see autumn comin' in
And the leaves falling on the gray days.

You've got to have a sky to look at!
(*Gradually, as they speak, all light hardens to that of winter, finally.*)

BERT (*turning to* KENNETH). Kenny, were you ever fired from a job?

KENNETH. Oh, sure; two-three times.

BERT. Did you feel bad?

KENNETH. The first time, maybe. But you have to get used to that, Bert. I'll bet you never went hungry in your life, did you?

BERT. No, I never did. Did you?

KENNETH. Oh, many and many a time. You get used to that too, though.

BERT (*turning and looking out*). That tree is turning red.

KENNETH. It must be spectacular out in the country now.

BERT. How does the cold get through these walls?
Feel it, it's almost a wind!

KENNETH. Don't cats walk dainty in the snow!

BERT. Gee, you'd never know it was the same place—
How clean it is when it's white!
Gus doesn't say much any more, y'know?

KENNETH. Well, he's showin' his age. Gus is old.
When do you buy your ticket for the train?

BERT. I did. I've got it.

KENNETH. Oh, then you're off soon!
You'll confound all the professors, I'll bet!
(*He sings softly.*)
"The minstrel boy to the war has gone . . ."
(BERT *moves a few feet away; thus he is alone.* KENNETH *remains at the window, looking out, polishing, and singing softly.*)

BERT. There's something so terrible here!
There always was, and I don't know what.
Gus, and Agnes, and Tommy and Larry, Jim and Patricia—

Why does it make me so sad to see them every morning?
It's like the subway;
Every day I see the same people getting on
And the same people getting off,
And all that happens is that they get older. God!
Sometimes it scares me; like all of us in the world
Were riding back and forth across a great big room,
From wall to wall and back again,
And no end ever! Just no end!
(*He turns to* KENNETH, *but not quite looking at him, and with a deeper anxiety.*)
Didn't you ever want to be anything, Kenneth?

KENNETH. I've never been able to keep my mind on it, Bert. . . .
I shouldn't've cut a hole in me shoe.
Now the snow's slushin' in, and me feet's all wet.

BERT. If you studied, Kenneth, if you put your mind to something great, I know you'd be able to learn anything, because you're clever, you're much smarter than I am!

KENNETH. You've got something steady in your mind, Bert; Something far away and steady.
I never could hold my mind on a far-away thing . . .
(*His tone changes as though he were addressing a group of men; his manner is rougher, angrier, less careful of proprieties.*)
She's not giving me the heat I'm entitled to.
Eleven dollars a week room and board,
And all she puts in the bag is a lousy pork sandwich,
The same every day and no surprises.
Is that right? Is that right now?
How's a man to live,
Freezing all day in this palace of dust
And night comes with one window and a bed
And the streets full of strangers
And not one of them's read a book through,
Or seen a poem from beginning to end
Or knows a song worth singing.

Oh, this is an ice-cold city, Mother,
And Roosevelt's not makin' it warmer, somehow.
(*He sits on the table, holding his head.*)
And here's another grand Monday!
(*They are gradually appearing in natural light now, but
it is a cold wintry light which has gradually supplanted
the hot light of summer.* BERT *goes to the hook for a
sweater.*) Jesus, me head'll murder me. I never had the
headache till this year.

BERT (*delicately*). You're not taking up drinking, are you?

KENNETH (*he doesn't reply. Suddenly, as though to retrieve
something slipping by, he gets to his feet, and roars out*):
"The Ship of State," by Walt Whitman!

"O Captain! my Captain! our fearful trip is done!
The ship has weathered every wrack,
The prize we sought is won . . ."

Now what in the world comes after that?

BERT. I don't know that poem.

KENNETH. Dammit all! I don't remember the bloody poems
any more the way I did! It's the drinkin' does it, I think.
I've got to stop the drinkin'!

BERT. Well, why do you drink, Kenny, if it makes you
feel—

KENNETH. Good God, Bert, you can't always be doin' what
you're better off to do! There's all kinds of unexpected
turns, y'know, and things not workin' out the way they
ought! What in hell *is* the next stanza of that poem?
"The prize we sought is won . . ." God, I'd never believe
I could forget that poem! I'm thinkin', Bert, y'know—
maybe I ought to go onto the Civil Service. The only
trouble is there's no jobs open except for the guard in
the insane asylum. And that'd be a nervous place to
work, I think.

BERT. It might be interesting, though.

KENNETH. I suppose it might. They tell me it's only the
more intelligent people goes mad, y'know. But it's six-

teen hundred a year, Bert, and I've a feelin' I'd never dare leave it, y'know? And I'm not ready for me last job yet, I think. I don't want nothin' to be the last, yet. Still and all . . . (RAYMOND *enters, going to toilet. He wears a blue button-up sweater.*)

RAYMOND. Morning, boys. (*He impales a batch of orders on the hook.*)

KENNETH (*in a routine way*). Morning, Mr. Ryan. Have a nice New Year's, did you?

RAYMOND. Good enough. (*To* BERT, *seeing the book on the table*). Still reading that book?

BERT. Oh, I'm almost finished now. (RAYMOND *nods, continues on.* BERT *jumps off the table*). Mr. Ryan? Can I see you a minute? (*He goes to* RAYMOND). I wondered if you hired anybody yet, to take my place.

RAYMOND (*pleasantly surprised*). Why? Don't you have enough money to go?

BERT. No, I'm going. I just thought maybe I could help you break in the new boy. I won't be leaving till after lunch tomorrow.

RAYMOND (*with resentment, even an edge of sarcasm*). We'll break him in all right. Why don't you just get on to your own work? There's a lot of excelsior laying around the freight elevator. (RAYMOND *turns and goes into the toilet. For an instant* BERT *is left staring after him. Then he turns to* KENNETH, *perplexed.*)

BERT. Is he sore at me?

KENNETH (*deprecatingly*). Ah, why would he be sore at you? (*He starts busying himself at the table, avoiding* BERT'S *eyes.* BERT *moves toward him, halts.*)

BERT. I hope you're not, are you?

KENNETH (*with an evasive air*). Me? Ha! Why, Bert, you've the heartfelt good wishes of everybody in the place for your goin'-away! (*But he turns away to busy himself at the table—and on his line* LARRY *has entered with a container of coffee and a cigarette.*)

BERT. Morning, Larry. (*He goes to the hook, takes an order.*)

LARRY (*leaning against the table*). Jesus, it'd be just about perfect in here for penguins. (BERT *passes him*). You actually leaving tomorrow?

BERT (*eagerly*). I guess so, yeah.

LARRY (*with a certain embarrassed envy*). Got all the dough, heh?

BERT. Well, for the first year anyway. (*He grins in embarrassment*). You mind if I thank you?

LARRY. What for?

BERT. I don't know—just for teaching me everything. I'd have been fired the first month without you, Larry.

LARRY (*with some wonder, respect*). Got all your dough, hch?

BERT. Well, that's all I've been doing is saving. (*Enter* TOM KELLY. *He is bright, clean, sober.*)

TOM. Morning!

KENNETH (*with an empty kind of heartiness*). Why, here comes Tommy Kelly!

TOM (*passing to hang up his coat and hat*). Ah, y're gettin' an awful long face to wash, Kenny, me bye.

KENNETH. Oh, cut it out with me face, Tommy. I'm as sick of it as you are.

TOM. Go on, ya donkey ya, they backed you off the boat.

KENNETH. Why, I'll tear you limb from limb, Tom Kelly! (*He mocks a fury, and* TOM *laughs as he is swung about. And then, with a quick hug and a laugh*). Oh, Tommy, you're the first man I ever heard of done it. How'd you do it, Tom?

TOM. Will power, Kenny. (*He walks to his desk, sits*). Just made up my mind, that's all.

KENNETH. Y'know the whole world is talking about you, Tom—the way you mixed all the drinks at the Christmas party and never weakened? Y'know, when I heard it was you going to mix the drinks I was prepared to light a candle for you.

TOM. I just wanted to see if I could do it, that's all. When I done that—mixin' the drinks for three hours, and givin' them away—I realized I made it. You don't look so hot to me, you know that?

KENNETH (*with a sigh*). Oh, I'm all right. It's the sight of Monday, that's all, is got me down.

TOM. You better get yourself a little will power, Kenny. I think you're gettin' a fine taste for the hard stuff.

KENNETH. Ah, no, I'll never be a drunk, Tommy.

TOM. You're a drunk now.

KENNETH. Oh, don't say that, please!

TOM. I'm tellin' you, I can see it comin' on you.

KENNETH (*deeply disturbed*). You can't either. Don't say that, Tommy! (AGNES *enters.*)

AGNES. Morning! (*She wears sheets of brown paper for leggins.*)

KENNETH. Winter's surely here when Agnes is wearin' her leggins.

AGNES (*with her laughter*). Don't they look awful? But that draft under the switchboard is enough to kill ya.

LARRY. This place is just right for penguins.

AGNES. Haven't you got a heavier sweater, Bert? I'm surprised at your mother.

BERT. Oh, it's warm; she knitted it.

KENNETH. Bert's got the idea. Get yourself an education.

TOM. College guys are sellin' ties all over Macy's. Accountancy, Bert, that's my advice to you. You don't even have to go to college for it either.

BERT. Yeah, but I don't want to be an accountant.

TOM (*with a superior grin*). You don't want to be an accountant?

LARRY. What's so hot about an accountant?

TOM. Well, try runnin' a business without one. That's what you should've done, Larry. If you'd a took accountancy, you'd a—

LARRY. You know, Tommy, I'm beginning to like you better drunk? (TOMMY *laughs, beyond criticism*). I mean it. Before, we only had to pick you up all the time; now you got opinions about everything.

TOM. Well, if I happen to know something, why shouldn't I say—(*Enter* RAYMOND *from the toilet.*)

RAYMOND. What do you say we get on the ball early today, fellas? Eagle's coming today. Bert, how about gettin' those carburetor crates open, will ya?

BERT. I was just going to do that. (BERT *and* RAYMOND *are starting out, and* AGNES *is moving to go, when* GUS *and* JIM *enter. Both of them are on the verge of staggering.* GUS *has a bright new suit and checkered overcoat, a new bowler, and new shoes. He is carrying upright a pair of Ford fenders, still in their brown paper wrappings—they stand about seven feet in height.* JIM *aids him in carefully resting the fenders against the wall.* KENNETH, AGNES, *and* LARRY *watch in silence.* PATRICIA *enters and watches. She is wearing leggins.* WILLY *and* JERRY *enter in overcoats, all jazzed up.*)

WILLY. Morning!

JERRY. Morn—(*Both break off and slowly remove their coats as they note the scene and the mood.* GUS, *now that the fenders are safely stacked, turns.*)

GUS (*dimly*). Who's got a hanger?

KENNETH. Hanger? You mean a coat-hanger, Gus?

GUS. Coat-hanger.

JERRY. Here! Here's mine! (*He gives a wire hanger to* GUS. GUS *is aided by* JIM *in removing his overcoat, and they both hang it on the hanger, then on a hook. Both give it a brush or two, and* GUS *goes to his chair, sits. He raises his eyes to them all.*)

GUS. So what everybody is looking at? (BERT, WILLY,

JERRY *go to work, gradually going out with orders.* JIM *also takes orders off the hook, and the pattern of going-and-coming emerges.* PATRICIA *goes to the toilet.* TOM KELLY *works at the desk.*)

LARRY (*half-kidding, but in a careful tone*). What are you all dressed up about? (GUS *simply glowers in his fumes and thoughts.* RAYMOND *goes over to* JIM.)

RAYMOND. What's he all dressed up for?

JIM. Oh, don't talk to me about him, Ray, I'm sick and tired of him. Spent all Saturday buyin' new clothes to go to the cemetery; then all the way the hell over to Long Island City to get these damned fenders for that old wreck of a Ford he's got. Never got to the cemetery, never got the fenders on—and we been walkin' around all weekend carryin' them damn things.

RAYMOND. Eagle'll be here this morning. See if you can get him upstairs. I don't want him to see him crocked again.

JIM. I'd just let him sit there, Ray, if I was you. I ain't goin' to touch him. You know what he went and done? Took all his insurance money outa the bank Saturday. Walkin' around with all that cash in his pocket—I tell ya, I ain't been to sleep since Friday night. 'Cause you can't let him loose with all that money and so low in his mind, y'know . . .

GUS. Irishman! (*All turn to him. He takes a wad out of his pocket, peels one bill off*). Here. Buy new pair shoes.

KENNETH. Ah, thank you, no, Gus, I couldn't take that.

RAYMOND. Gus, Eagle's coming this morning; why don't you—

GUS (*stuffing a bill into* KENNETH's *pocket*). Go buy pair shoes.

RAYMOND. Gus, he's going to be here right away; why don't you—

GUS. I don't give one goddam for Eagle! Why don't he make one more toilet?

RAYMOND. What? (BERT *enters with goods.*)

GUS. Toilet! That's right? Have one toilet for so many people? That's very bad, Raymond. That's no nice. (*Offering* BERT *a bill*). Here, boy, go—buy book, buy candy. (LARRY *goes to* GUS *before he gives the bill, puts an arm around him, and walks away from the group.*)

LARRY. Come on, Gussy, let me take you upstairs.

GUS. I don't care Eagle sees me, I got my money now, goddam. Oh, Larry, Larry, twenty-two year I workin' here.

LARRY. Why don't you give me the money, Gus? I'll put in the bank for you.

GUS. What for I put in bank? I'm sixty-eight years old, Larry. I got no children, nothing. What for I put in bank? (*Suddenly, reminded, he turns back to* RAYMOND, *pointing at the floor scale*). Why them goddam mice nobody does nothing?

RAYMOND (*alarmed by* GUS's *incipient anger*). Gus, I want you to go upstairs! (PATRICIA *enters from toilet.*)

GUS (*at the scale*). Twenty-two years them goddam mice! That's very bad, Raymond, so much mice! (*He starts rocking the scale*). Look at them goddam mice! (PATRICIA *screams as mice come running out from under the scale. A mêlée of shouts begins, everyone dodging mice or swinging brooms and boxes at them.* RAYMOND *is pulling* GUS *away from the scale, yelling at him to stop it.* AGNES *rushes in and, seeing the mice, screams and rushes out.* JERRY *and* WILLY *rush in and join in chasing the mice, laughing.* PATRICIA, *wearing leggins, is helped onto the packing table by* LARRY, *and* GUS *shouts up at her*). Come with me Atlantic City, Patricia! (*He pulls out the wad*). Five thousand dollars I got for my wife!

PATRICIA. You rotten thing, you! You dirty rotten thing, Gus!

GUS. I make you happy, Patricia! I make you—(*Suddenly*

his hand goes to his head; he is dizzy. LARRY *goes to him, takes one look.*)

LARRY. Come, come on. (*He walks* GUS *into the toilet.*)

PATRICIA (*out of the momentary silence*). Oh, that louse! Did you see what he did, that louse? (*She gets down off the table, and, glancing angrily toward the toilet, she goes out.*)

RAYMOND. All right, fellas, what do you say, heh? Let's get going. (*Work proceeds—the going and coming.*)

TOM (*as* RAYMOND *passes him*). I tried talking to him a couple of times, Ray, but he's got no will power! There's nothing you can do if there's no will power, y'know?

RAYMOND. Brother! It's a circus around here. Every Monday morning! I never saw anything like . . . (*He is gone.* KENNETH *is packing.* TOM *works at his desk.* JIM *comes and, leaving goods on the packing table, goes to the toilet, peeks in, then goes out, studying an order.* BERT *enters with goods.*)

KENNETH. There's one thing you have to say for the Civil Service; it seals the fate and locks the door. A man needn't wonder what he'll do with his life any more. (*JERRY enters with goods.*)

BERT (*glancing at the toilet door*). Gee, I never would've thought Gus liked his wife, would you? (*TOM, studying a letter, goes out.*)

JERRY (*looking up and out the window*). Jesus!

BERT (*not attending to* JERRY). I thought he always hated his wife—

JERRY. Jesus, boy!

KENNETH (*to* JERRY). What're you doin'? What's—?

JERRY. Look at the girls up in there. One, two, three, four windows—full a girls, look at them! Them two is naked! (*WILLY enters with goods.*)

KENNETH. Oh, my God!

WILLY (*rushing to the windows*). Where? Where?

KENNETH. Well, what're you gawkin' at them for! (GUS *and* LARRY *enter from the toilet.*)

JERRY. There's another one down there! Look at her on the bed! What a beast!

WILLY (*overjoyed*). It's a cathouse! Gus! A whole cathouse moved in! (WILLY *and* JERRY *embrace and dance around wildly;* GUS *stands with* LARRY, *staring out, as does* BERT.)

KENNETH. Aren't you ashamed of yourself!! (TOM *enters with his letter.*)

TOM. Hey, fellas, Eagle's here.

JERRY (*pointing out*). There's a new cathouse, Tommy! (TOM *goes and looks out the windows.*)

KENNETH. Oh, that's a terrible thing to be lookin' at, Tommy! (AGNES *enters;* KENNETH *instantly goes to her to get her out*). Oh, Agnes, you'd best not be comin' back here any more now—

AGNES. What? What's the matter? (JERRY *has opened a window, and he and* WILLY *whistle sharply through their fingers.* AGNES *looks out.*)

KENNETH. Don't, Agnes, don't look at that!

AGNES. Well, for heaven's sake! What are all those women doing there?

GUS. That's whorehouse, Aggie.

KENNETH. Gus, for God's sake! (*He walks away in pain.*)

AGNES. What are they sitting on the beds like that for?

TOM. The sun is pretty warm this morning—probably trying to get a little tan.

AGNES. Oh, my heavens. Oh, Bert, it's good you're leaving! (*She turns to them*). You're not all going, are you? (GUS *starts to laugh, then* TOM, *then* JERRY *and* WILLY, *then* LARRY, *and she is unstrung and laughing herself, but shocked*). Oh, my heavens! (*She is gone, as* JIM *enters with goods.*)

KENNETH. All right, now, clear off, all of you. I can't be

workin' with a lot of sex maniacs blockin' off me table!

GUS. Look, Jim! (JIM *looks out*.)

JIM. Oh, nice.

JERRY. How about it, fellas? Let's all go lunchtime! What do you say, Kenny? I'll pay for you! (GUS *goes to the desk, drags the chair over to the window*.)

KENNETH. I'd sooner roll meself around in the horse manure of the gutter!

JERRY. I betcha you wouldn't even know what to do!

KENNETH (*bristling, fists shut*). I'll show you what I do! I'll show you right now! (*Enter* RAYMOND, *furious*.)

RAYMOND. What the hell is this? What's going on here?

GUS (*sitting in his chair, facing the windows*). Whorehouse. (RAYMOND *looks out the windows*.)

KENNETH. You'd better pass a word to Mr. Eagle about this, Raymond, or the corporation's done for. Poor Agnes, she's all mortified, y'know.

RAYMOND. Oh, my God! (*To all*). All right, break it up, come on, break it up, Eagle's here. (WILLY, JERRY, BERT, *and* JIM *disperse, leaving with orders*. TOMMY *returns to the desk*). What're you going to do, Gus? You going to sit there? (GUS *doesn't answer; sits staring out thoughtfully*). What's going on with you? Gus! Eagle's here! All right, cook in your own juice. Sit there. (*He glances out the windows*). Brother, I needed this now! (*He goes out angrily*.)

LARRY. Give me the money, Gus, come on. I'll hold it for you.

GUS (*an enormous sadness is on him*). Go way. (*Enter* PATRICIA. *She glances at* LARRY *and* GUS, *then looks out the windows*.)

KENNETH (*wrapping*). Ah, Patricia, don't look out there. It's disgraceful.

TOM. It's only a lot of naked women.

KENNETH. Oh, Tommy, now! In front of a girl!

PATRICIA (*to* KENNETH). What's the matter? Didn't you ever see that before? (*She sees* GUS *sitting there*). Look at Kong, will ya? (*She laughs*). Rememberin' the old days, heh, Kong? (LARRY *is walking toward an exit at left.*)

GUS. Oh, shatap!

PATRICIA (*catching up with* LARRY *at the edge of the stage, quietly*). What's Ray sayin' about you sellin' the Auburn?

LARRY. Yeah, I'm kinda fed up with it. It's out of my class anyway.

PATRICIA. That's too bad. I was just gettin' to enjoy it.

LARRY (*very doubtfully*). Yeah?

PATRICIA. What're you mad at me for?

LARRY. Why should I be mad?

PATRICIA. You're married, what're you—?

LARRY. Let me worry about that, will you?

PATRICIA. Well, I gotta worry about it too, don't I?

LARRY. Since when do you worry about anything, Pat?

PATRICIA. Well, what did you expect me to do? How did I know you were serious? (GUS *goes to his coat, searches in a pocket.*)

LARRY. What did you think I was telling you all the time?

PATRICIA. Yeah, but Larry, anybody could say those kinda things.

LARRY. I know, Pat. But I never did. (*With a cool, hurt smile*). You know, kid, you better start believing people when they tell you something. Or else you're liable to end up in there. (*He points out the windows.*)

PATRICIA (*with quiet fury*). You take that back! (*He walks away; she goes after him*). You're going to take that back, Larry! (EAGLE *enters, nods to* LARRY *and* PATRICIA.)

EAGLE. Morning.

PATRICIA (*with a mercurial change to sunny charm*). Good

morning, Mr. Eagle! (*LARRY is gone, and she exits.* *EAGLE crosses, noticing GUS, who is standing beside his coat, drinking out of a pint whisky bottle.*)

EAGLE. Morning, Gus.

GUS (*lowering the bottle*). Good morning. (*EAGLE exits into the toilet.*)

TOM (*to GUS*). You gone nuts? (*GUS returns, holding the bottle, to his chair, where he sits, looking out the window. He is growing sodden and mean. BERT enters with goods.*)

KENNETH (*sotto voce*). Eagle's in there, and look at him. He'll get the back of it now for sure.

TOM (*going to GUS*). Gimme the bottle, Gus!

GUS. I goin' go someplace, Tommy. I goin' go cemetery. I wasn't one time in cemetery. I go see my Lilly. My Lilly die, I was in Staten Island. All alone she was in the house. Ts! (*JERRY enters with goods, sees him, and laughs.*)

BERT. Gus, why don't you give Tommy the bottle?

GUS. Twenty-two years I work here.

KENNETH (*to JERRY, who is staring out the window*). Will you quit hangin' around me table, please?

JERRY. Can't I look out the window? (*WILLY enters with goods.*)

WILLY. How's all the little pussies?

KENNETH. Now cut that out! (*They laugh at him.*)

TOM (*sotto voce*). Eagle's in there!

KENNETH. Is that all yiz know of the world—filthy women and dirty jokes and the ignorance drippin' off your faces? (*EAGLE enters from the toilet*). There's got to be somethin' done about this, Mr. Eagle. It's an awful humiliation for the women here. (*He points, and EAGLE looks*). I mean to say, it's a terrible disorganizing sight starin' a man in the face eight hours a day, sir.

EAGLE. Shouldn't have washed the windows, I guess. (*He glances down at* GUS *and his bottle and walks out.*)

KENNETH. Shouldn't have washed the windows, he says! (*They are laughing;* GUS *is tipping the bottle up.* JIM *enters with goods.*)

JERRY. What a donkey that guy is! (KENNETH *lunges for* JERRY *and grabs him by the tie, one fist ready.*)

KENNETH. I'll donkey you! (JERRY *starts a swing at him, and* BERT *and* TOM *rush to separate them as* RAYMOND *enters.*)

RAYMOND. Hey! Hey!

JERRY (*as they part*). All right, donkey, I'll see you later.

KENNETH. You'll see me later, all right—with one eye closed!

RAYMOND. Cut it out! (KENNETH, *muttering, returns to work at his table.* JERRY *rips an order off the hook and goes out.* WILLY *takes an order.* BERT *goes out with an order.* RAYMOND *has been looking down at* GUS, *who is sitting with the bottle*). You going to work, Gus? Or you going to do that? (GUS *gets up and goes to his coat, takes it off the hanger*). What're you doing?

GUS. Come on, Jim, we go someplace. Here—put on you coat.

RAYMOND. Where you going? It's half-past nine in the morning. (*Enter* AGNES.)

AGNES. What's all the noise here? (*She breaks off, seeing* GUS *dressing.*)

GUS. That's when I wanna go—half-past nine. (*He hands* JIM *his coat*). Here. Put on. Cold outside.

JIM (*quietly*). Maybe I better go with him, Ray. He's got all his money in— (BERT *enters with goods.*)

RAYMOND (*reasonably, deeply concerned*). Gus, now look; where you gonna go now? Why don't you lie down upstairs?

GUS (*swaying, to* BERT). Twenty-two years I was here.

BERT. I know, Gus. (LARRY *enters, watches.*)

GUS. I was here before you was born I was here.

BERT. I know.

GUS. Them mice was here before you was born. (BERT *nods uncomfortably, full of sadness*). When Mr. Eagle was in high school I was already here. When there was Winton Six I was here. When was Minerva car I was here. When was Stanley Steamer I was here, and Stearns Knight, and Marmon was good car; I was here all them times. I was here first day Raymond come; he was young boy; work hard be manager. When Agnes still think she was gonna get married I was here. When was Locomobile, and Model K Ford and Model N Ford—all them different Fords, and Franklin was good car, Jordan car, Reo car, Pierce Arrow, Cleveland car—all them was good cars. All them times I was here.

BERT. I know.

GUS. You don't know nothing. Come on, Jim. (*He goes and gets a fender.* JIM *gets the other*). Button up you coat, cold outside. Tommy? Take care everything good. (*He walks out with* JIM *behind him, each carrying a fender upright.* RAYMOND *turns and goes out, then* LARRY. AGNES *goes into the toilet. The lights lower as this movement takes place, until* BERT *is alone in light, still staring at the point where* GUS *left.*)

BERT. I don't understand;
I don't know anything:
How is it me that gets out?
I don't know half the poems Kenneth does,
Or a quarter of what Larry knows about an engine.
I don't understand how they come every morning,
Every morning and every morning,
And no end in sight.
That's the thing—there's no end!
Oh, there ought to be a statue in the park—
"To All the Ones That Stay."
One to Larry, to Agnes, Tom Kelly, Gus . . .
Gee, it's peculiar to leave a place—forever!

Still, I always hated coming here;
The same dried-up jokes, the dust;
Especially in spring, walking in from the sunshine,
Or any Monday morning in the hot days.

(*In the darkness men appear and gather around the packing table, eating lunch out of bags; we see them as ghostly figures, silent.*)

God, it's so peculiar to leave a place!
I know I'll remember them as long as I live,
As long as I live they'll never die,
And still I know that in a month or two
They'll forget my name, and mix me up
With another boy who worked here once,
And went. Gee, it's a mystery!

(*As full light rises* BERT *moves into the group, begins eating from a bag.*)

JERRY (*looking out the window*). You know what's a funny thing? It's a funny thing how you get used to that.

WILLY. Tommy, what would you say Cobb's average was for lifetime?

TOM. Cobb? Lifetime? (*He thinks. Pause.* KENNETH *sings.*)

KENNETH. "The minstrel boy to the war has gone—
    (PATRICIA *enters, crossing to toilet.*)
In the ranks of death you will find him."

PATRICIA. Is that an Irish song?

KENNETH. All Irish here, and none of yiz knows an Irish song! (*She laughs, exits into the toilet.*)

TOM. I'd say three-eighty lifetime for Ty Cobb. (*To* LARRY). You're foolish sellin' that car with all the work you put in it.

LARRY. Well, it was one of those crazy ideas. Funny how you get an idea, and then suddenly you wake up and you look at it and it's like—dead or something. I can't afford a car. (AGNES *enters, going toward the toilet.*)

AGNES. I think it's even colder today than yesterday. (RAY-MOND *enters.*)

RAYMOND. It's five after one, fellas; what do you say? (*They begin to get up as* JIM *enters in his overcoat and hat.*)

KENNETH. Well! The old soldier returns!

RAYMOND. Where's Gus, Jim? (AGNES *has opened the toilet door as* PATRICIA *emerges.*)

AGNES. Oh! You scared me. I didn't know you were in there!

JIM (*removing his coat*). He died, Ray.

RAYMOND. What? (*The news halts everyone—but one by one—in midair, as it were.*)

LARRY. He what?

AGNES. What'd you say?

JIM. Gus died.

KENNETH. Gus died!

BERT. Gus?

AGNES (*going to* JIM). Oh, good heavens. When? What happened?

LARRY. What'd you have an accident?

JIM. No, we—we went home and got the fenders on all right, and he wanted to go over and start at the bottom, and go right up Third Avenue and hit the bars on both sides. And we got up to about Fourteenth Street, in around there, and we kinda lost track of the car someplace. I have to go back there tonight, see if I can find—

AGNES. Well, what happened?

JIM. Well, these girls got in the cab, y'know, and we seen a lot of places and all that—we was to some real high-class places, forty cents for a cup of coffee and all that; and then he put me in another cab, and we rode around a while; and then he got another cab to follow us. Case one of our cabs got a flat, see? He just didn't want to be held up for a minute, Gus didn't.

LARRY. Where were you going?

JIM. Oh, just all over. And we stopped for a light, y'know, and I thought I'd go up and see how he was gettin' along, y'know, and I open his cab door, and—the girl was fast asleep, see—and he—was dead. Right there in the seat. It was just gettin' to be morning.

AGNES. Oh, poor Gus!

JIM. I tell ya, Agnes, he didn't look too good to me since she died, the old lady. I never knowed it. He—liked that woman.

RAYMOND. Where's his money?

JIM. Oh—(*with a wasting wave of the hand*)—it's gone, Ray. We was stoppin' off every couple minutes so he call long distance. I didn't even know it, he had a brother someplace in California. Called him half a dozen times. And there was somebody he was talkin' to in Texas someplace, somebody that was in the Navy with him. He was tryin' to call all the guys that was in the submarine with him, and he was callin' all over hell and gone— and givin' big tips, and he bought a new suit, and give the cab driver a wristwatch and all like that. I think he got himself too sweated. Y'know it got pretty cold last night, and he was all sweated up. I kept tellin' him, I says, "Gus," I says, "you're gettin' yourself all sweated, y'know, and it's a cold night," I says; and all he kept sayin' to me all night he says, "Jim," he says, "I'm gonna do it right, Jim." That's all he says practically all night. "I'm gonna do it right," he says. "I'm gonna do it right." (*Pause.* JIM *shakes his head*). Oh, when I open that cab door I knowed it right away. I takes one look at him and I knowed it. (*There is a moment of silence, and* AGNES *turns and goes into the toilet*). Oh, poor Agnes, I bet she's gonna cry now. (JIM *goes to the order hook, takes an order off, and, putting a cigar into his mouth, he goes out, studying the order.* RAYMOND *crosses and goes out; then* PATRICIA *goes.* WILLY *and* JERRY *exit in different directions with orders in their hands;* KENNETH *begins wrapping.* TOM *goes to his desk and sits, clasps his hands, and for a moment he prays.* BERT *goes and gets his jacket. He slowly puts it on. Enter* FRANK, *the truckdriver.*)

FRANK. Anything for West Bronx, Tommy?

TOM. There's some stuff for Sullivan's there.

FRANK. Okay. (*He pokes through the packages, picks some.*)

KENNETH. Gus died.

FRANK. No kiddin'!

KENNETH. Ya, last night.

FRANK. What do you know. Hm. (*He goes on picking packages out*). Is this all for West Bronx, Tom?

TOM. I guess so for now.

FRANK (*to* KENNETH). Died.

KENNETH. Yes, Jim was with him. Last night.

FRANK. Jesus. (*Pause. He stares, shakes his head*). I'll take Brooklyn when I get back, Tommy. (*He goes out, loaded with packages.* BERT *is buttoning his overcoat.* AGNES *comes out of the toilet.*)

BERT. Agnes?

AGNES (*seeing the coat on, the book in his hand*). Oh, you're leaving, Bert!

BERT. Yeah.

AGNES. Well. You're leaving.

BERT (*expectantly*). Yeah. (PATRICIA *enters.*)

PATRICIA. Agnes? Your switchboard's ringing. (JERRY *enters with goods.*)

AGNES. Okay! (PATRICIA *goes out*). Well, good luck. I hope you pass everything.

BERT. Thanks, Aggie. (*She walks across and out, wiping a hair across her forehead.* WILLY *enters with goods as* JERRY *goes out.* JIM *enters with goods.* BERT *seems about to say good-by to each of them, but they are en-*

grossed and he doesn't quite want to start a scene with them; but now JIM *is putting his goods on the table, so* BERT *goes over to him*). I'm leaving, Jim, so—uh—

JIM. Oh, leavin'? Heh! Well, that's—

TOM (*from his place at the desk, offering an order to* JIM). Jim? See if these transmissions came in yet, will ya? This guy's been ordering them all month.

JIM. Sure, Tom. (JIM *goes out past* BERT, *studying his order.* BERT *glances at* KENNETH, *who is busy wrapping. He goes to* TOM, *who is working at the desk.*)

BERT. Well, so long, Tommy.

TOM (*turning*). Oh, you goin', heh?

BERT. Yeah, I'm leavin' right now.

TOM. Well, keep up the will power, y'know. That's what docs it.

BERT. Yeah. I—uh—I wanted to—(RAYMOND *enters.*)

RAYMOND (*handing* TOM *an order*). Tommy, make this a special, will you? The guy's truck broke down in Peekskill. Send it out special today.

TOM. Right. (RAYMOND *turns to go out, sees* BERT, *who seems to expect some moment from him.*)

RAYMOND. Oh! 'By, Bert.

BERT. So long, Raymond, I—(RAYMOND *is already on his way, and he is gone.* JIM *enters with goods.* BERT *goes over to* KENNETH *and touches his back.* KENNETH *turns to him.* JIM *goes out as* WILLY *enters with goods—* JERRY *too, and this work goes on without halt*). Well, good-by, Kenny.

KENNETH (*he is embarrassed as he turns to* BERT). Well, it's our last look, I suppose, isn't it?

BERT. No, I'll come back sometime. I'll visit you.

KENNETH. Oh, not likely; it'll all be out of mind as soon as you turn the corner. I'll probably not be here anyway.

BERT. You made up your mind for Civil Service?

KENNETH. Well, you've got to keep movin', and—I'll move there, I guess. I done a shockin' thing last night, Bert; I knocked over a bar.

BERT. Knocked it over?

KENNETH. It's disgraceful, what I done. I'm standin' there, havin' a decent conversation, that's all, and before I know it I start rockin' the damned thing, and it toppled over and broke every glass in the place, and the beer spoutin' out of the pipes all over the floor. They took all me money; I'll be six weeks payin' them back. I'm for the Civil Service, I think; I'll get back to regular there, I think.

BERT. Well—good luck, Kenny. (*Blushing*). I hope you'll remember the poems again.

KENNETH (*as though they were unimportant*). No, they're gone, Bert. There's too much to do in this country for that kinda stuff. (WILLY *enters with goods.*)

TOM. Hey, Willy, get this right away; it's a special for Peekskill.

WILLY. Okay. (WILLY *takes the order and goes, and when* BERT *turns back to* KENNETH *he is wrapping again. So* BERT *moves away from the table.* JERRY *enters, leaves; and* JIM *enters, drops goods on the table, and leaves.* LARRY *enters with a container of coffee, goes to the order hook, and checks through the orders.* BERT *goes to him.*)

BERT. I'm goin', Larry.

LARRY (*over his shoulder*). Take it easy, kid. (PATRICIA *enters and crosses past* BERT, *looking out through the windows.* TOM *gets up and bumbles through a pile of goods on the table, checking against an order in his hand. It is as though* BERT *wished it could stop for a moment, and as each person enters he looks expectantly, but nothing much happens. And so he gradually moves —almost is moved—toward an exit, and with his book in*

his hand he leaves. Now KENNETH *turns and looks about,
sees* BERT *is gone. He resumes his work and softly sings.*)

KENNETH. "The minstrel boy to the war has gone!"
Tommy, I'll be needin' more crayon before the day is
out.

TOM (*without turning from the desk*). I'll get some for
you.

KENNETH (*looking at a crayon, peeling it down to a nub*).
Oh, the damn mice. But they've got to live too, I suppose. (*He marks a package and softly sings*):

". . . in the ranks of death you will find him.
His father's sword he has girded on,
And his wild harp slung behind him."

THE CURTAIN FALLS

THE BROWNING VERSION

by Terence Rattigan

CHARACTERS

JOHN TAPLOW

FRANK HUNTER

MILLIE CROCKER-HARRIS

ANDREW CROCKER-HARRIS

DR. FROBISHER

PETER GILBERT

MRS. GILBERT

THE BROWNING VERSION

SCENE. *The sitting-room in the Crocker-Harris's flat in a public school in the south of England. About 6:30 P.M. of a day in July.*

The building in which the flat is situated is large and Victorian, and at some fairly recent time has been converted into flats of varying size for masters, married and unmarried. The Crocker-Harris's have the ground floor and their sitting-room is probably the biggest—and gloomiest—room in the house. It boasts, however, access (through a stained glass door L.) to a small garden, and is furnished with chintzy and genteel cheerfulness. Another door, up R., leads into the hall and a third, up C., to the rest of the flat. The hall door is partially concealed by a screen. There is a large bay-window in the L. wall below the garden door. Near the window is a flat-topped desk with a swivel chair behind it and an upright chair on the other side. The fireplace is down R. Below it is an easy chair and a small table with a telephone. A settee stands in front of the fireplace at R.C. There is an oval dining-table with two chairs up C. R. of the door up C. is a sideboard; and against the wall L. of the door up R. is a hall-stand, in which some walking-sticks are kept. A small cupboard stands against the wall down R.

When the CURTAIN rises the room is empty. There are copies of "The Times" and the "Tatler" on the settee. We hear the front door opening and closing and immediately after there is a timorous knock on the door up R. After a pause the knock is repeated. The door opens and JOHN TAPLOW makes his appearance. He is a plain moon-faced boy of about sixteen, with glasses. He carries a book and an exercise-book. He is dressed in grey flannels, a dark blue coat and white scarf. He stands in doubt at the door for a moment, then goes back into the hall.

TAPLOW (*off; calling*). Sir! Sir! (*After a pause he comes back into the room, crosses to the garden door up L. and opens it. He calls).* Sir! *(There is no reply.* TAPLOW, *standing in the bright sunshine at the door, emits a plaintive sigh, then closes it firmly and comes down* R. *of the desk on which he places the book, the notebook and a pen. He sits in the chair* R. *of the desk. He looks round the room. On the table* C. *is a small box of chocolates, probably the Crocker-Harris's ration for the month.* TAP-LOW *rises, moves above the table and opens the box. He counts the number inside, and removes two. One of these he eats and the other, after a second's struggle, either with his conscience or his judgment of what he might be able to get away with, virtuously replaces in the box. He puts back the box on the table, and moves up* R. *to the hall-stand. He selects a walking-stick with a crooked handle, comes down* C., *and makes a couple of golf-swings, with an air of great concentration.* FRANK HUNTER *enters up* R. *and appears from behind the screen covering the door. He is a rugged young man—not perhaps quite as rugged as his deliberately-cultivated manner of ruthless honesty makes him appear, but wrapped in all the self-confidence of the popular master. He watches* TAPLOW, *whose back is to the door, making his swing.)*

FRANK *(coming down behind* TAPLOW*).* Roll the wrists away from the ball. Don't break them like that. *(He puts his large hands over the abashed* TAPLOW's*).* Now swing. *(*TAPLOW, *guided by* FRANK's *evidently expert hands, succeeds in hitting the carpet with more effect than before. He breaks away* R. *of* TAPLOW*).* Too quick. Slow back and stiff left arm. It's no good just whacking the ball as if you were the headmaster and the ball was you. It'll never go more than fifty yards if you do. Get a rhythm. A good golf swing is a matter of aesthetics, not of brute strength. *(*TAPLOW, *only half listening, is gazing at the carpet.)*

FRANK. What's the matter?

TAPLOW. I think we've made a tear in the carpet, sir. *(*FRANK *examines the spot perfunctorily.)*

FRANK (*taking the stick from* TAPLOW). Nonsense. That was there already. (*He crosses up* R. *and puts the stick in the hall-stand*). Do I know you? (*He comes down* L. *of the settee to* R. *of* TAPLOW.)

TAPLOW. No, sir.

FRANK. What's your name?

TAPLOW. Taplow.

FRANK. Taplow? No, I don't. You're not a scientist, I gather.

TAPLOW. No, sir. I'm still in the lower fifth. I can't specialize until next term—that's to say if I've got my remove all right.

FRANK. Don't you know yet if you've got your remove?

TAPLOW. No, sir. Mr. Crocker-Harris doesn't tell us the results like the other masters.

FRANK. Why not?

TAPLOW. Well, you know what he's like, sir.

FRANK (*moving away to the fireplace*). I believe there *is* a rule that form results should only be announced by the headmaster on the last day of term.

TAPLOW. Yes; but who else pays any attention to it—except Mr. Crocker-Harris?

FRANK. I don't, I admit—but that's no criterion. So you've got to wait until tomorrow to know your fate, have you?

TAPLOW. Yes, sir.

FRANK. Supposing the answer is favourable—what then?

TAPLOW. Oh—science sir, of course.

FRANK (*sadly*). Yes. We get all the slackers.

TAPLOW (*protestingly*). I'm extremely interested in science, sir.

FRANK. Are you? I'm not. Not at least in the science I have to teach.

TAPLOW (*moving above the desk*). Well, anyway, sir, it's a good deal more exciting than this muck. (*He indicates the book he put on the desk.*)

FRANK. What is this muck?

TAPLOW. Aeschylus, sir. *The Agamemnon*.

FRANK (*moving to the L. end of the couch*). And your considered view is that *The Agamemnon* of Aeschylus is muck, is it?

TAPLOW. Well, no, sir. I don't think the play is muck—exactly. I suppose, in a way, it's rather a good plot, really; a wife murdering her husband and having a lover and all that. I only meant the way it's taught to us—just a lot of Greek words strung together and fifty lines if you get them wrong.

FRANK. You sound a little bitter, Taplow.

TAPLOW. I am rather, sir.

FRANK. Kept in, eh?

TAPLOW. No, sir. Extra work.

FRANK. Extra work—on the last day of school?

TAPLOW. Yes, sir—and I might be playing golf. (*He moves into the window, upstage end*). You'd think *he'd* have enough to do anyway himself, considering he's leaving tomorrow for good—but oh no. I missed a day last week when I had 'flu—so here I am—and look at the weather, sir.

FRANK. Bad luck. Still there's one consolation. You're pretty well bound to get your remove tomorrow for being a good boy in taking extra work.

TAPLOW (*crossing to* C.). Well, I'm not so sure, sir. That would be true of the ordinary masters all right. They just wouldn't dare not give a chap a remove after his taking extra work—it would be such a bad advertisement for them. But those sort of rules don't apply to the Crock—Mr. Crocker-Harris. I asked him yesterday outright if he'd given me a remove and do you know what he said, sir?

FRANK. No. What?

TAPLOW (*mimicking a very gentle, rather throaty voice*).

"My dear Taplow, I have given you exactly what you deserve. No less; and certainly no more." Do you know, sir, I think he may have marked me down, rather than up, for taking extra work. I mean, the man's barely human. (*He breaks off quickly*). Sorry, sir. Have I gone too far?

FRANK (*sitting on the settee, L. end, and picking up "The Times"*). Yes. Much too far.

TAPLOW. Sorry, sir. I got sort of carried away.

FRANK. Evidently. (*He opens "The Times" and reads. TAPLOW moves to the chair R. of the desk and sits*). Er—Taplow.

TAPLOW. Yes, sir?

FRANK. What was that Mr. Crocker-Harris said to you? Just —er—repeat it, would you?

TAPLOW (*mimicking*). "My dear Taplow, I have given you exactly what you deserve. No less; and certainly no more." (FRANK *snorts, then looks stern.*)

FRANK. Not in the least like him. Read your nice Aeschylus and be quiet.

TAPLOW (*with weary disgust*). Aeschylus.

FRANK. Look, what time did Mr. Crocker-Harris tell you to be here?

TAPLOW. Six-thirty, sir.

FRANK. Well, he's ten minutes late. Why don't you cut? You could still get nine holes in before lock-up.

TAPLOW (*genuinely shocked*). Oh, no, I couldn't cut. Cut the Crock—Mr. Crocker-Harris? I shouldn't think it's ever been done in the whole time he's been here. God knows what would happen if I did. He'd probably follow me home, or something.

FRANK. I must admit I envy him the effect he seems to have on you boys in his form. You all seem scared to death of him. What does he do—beat you all, or something?

TAPLOW (*rising and moving to the* L. *end of the settee*). Good Lord, no. He's not a sadist, like one or two of the others.

FRANK. I beg your pardon?

TAPLOW. A sadist, sir, is someone who gets pleasure out of giving pain.

FRANK. Indeed? But I think you went on to say that some other masters . . .

TAPLOW. Well, of course they are, sir. I won't mention names, but you know them as well as I do. Of course I know most masters think we boys don't understand a thing—but dash it, sir, you're different. You're young—well comparatively anyway—and you're science and you canvassed for Labour in the last election. You must know what sadism is. (FRANK *stares for a moment at* TAPLOW, *then turns away.*)

FRANK. Good Lord! What are public schools coming to?

TAPLOW (*crossing to* R. *of the desk, below the chair, and leaning against it*). Anyway, the Crock isn't a sadist. That's what I'm saying. He wouldn't be so frightening if he were—because at least it would show he had some feelings. But he hasn't. He's all shrivelled up inside like a nut and he seems to hate people to like him. It's funny, that. I don't know any other master who doesn't like being liked.

FRANK. And I don't know any boy who doesn't trade on that very foible.

TAPLOW. Well, it's natural, sir. But not with the Crock.

FRANK (*making a feeble attempt at re-establishing the correct relationship*). Mr. Crocker-Harris.

TAPLOW. Mr. Crocker-Harris. The funny thing is that in spite of everything, I do rather like him. I can't help it. And sometimes I think he sees it and that seems to shrivel him up even more.

FRANK. I'm sure you're exaggerating.

TAPLOW. No, sir. I'm not. In form the other day he made

one of his little classical jokes. Of course nobody laughed
because nobody understood it, myself included. Still, I
knew he'd meant it as funny, so I laughed. Not out of
sucking-up, sir, I swear, but ordinary common politeness, and feeling a bit sorry for him having made a dud
joke. (*He moves round below the desk to* L. *of it*). Now
I can't remember what the joke was—but let's say it was
—(*mimicking*) Benedictus, benedicatur, benedictine . . .
Now, you laugh, sir. (FRANK *laughs formally.* TAPLOW
*looks at him over an imaginary pair of spectacles, and
then, very gently crooks his fore-finger to him in indication to approach the table.* FRANK *rises. He is genuinely
interested in the incident. In a gentle, throaty voice*).
Taplow—you laughed at my little pun, I noticed. I must
confess I am flattered at the evident advance your La-
tinity has made that you should so readily have understood what the rest of the form did not. Perhaps, now,
you would be good enough to explain it to them, so that
they too can share your pleasure. (*The door up* R. *is
pushed open and* MILLIE CROCKER-HARRIS *enters. She is a
thin woman in the late thirties, rather more smartly
dressed than the general run of school-masters' wives.
She is wearing a cape and carries a shopping basket.
She closes the door and then stands by the screen watching* TAPLOW *and* FRANK. *It is a few seconds before they
notice her*). Come along, Taplow. (FRANK *moves slowly
above the desk*). Do not be so selfish as to keep a good
joke to yourself. Tell the others . . . (*He breaks off suddenly, noticing* MILLIE). Oh Lord! (FRANK *turns quickly,
and seems infinitely relieved at seeing* MILLIE.)

FRANK. Oh, hullo.

MILLIE (*without expression*). Hullo. (*She comes down to
the sideboard and puts her basket on it.*)

TAPLOW (*moving up to* L. *of* FRANK; *whispering frantically*). Do you think she heard? (FRANK *shakes his head
comfortingly.* MILLIE *takes off her cape and hangs it on
the hall-stand*). I think she did. She was standing there

quite a time. If she did and she tells him, there goes my remove.

FRANK. Nonsense. (*He crosses to the fireplace.* MILLIE *takes the basket from the sideboard, moves above the table* C. *and puts the basket on it.*)

MILLIE (*to* TAPLOW). Waiting for my husband?

TAPLOW (*moving down* L. *of the table* C.). Er—yes.

MILLIE. He's at the Bursar's and might be there quite a time. If I were you I'd go.

TAPLOW (*doubtfully*). He said most particularly I was to come.

MILLIE. Well, why don't you run away for a quarter of an hour and come back? (*She unpacks some things from the basket.*)

TAPLOW. Supposing he gets here before me?

MILLIE (*smiling*). I'll take the blame. (*She takes a prescription out of the basket*). I tell you what—you can do a job for him. Take this prescription to the chemist and get it made up.

TAPLOW. All right, Mrs. Crocker-Harris. (*He crosses towards the door up* R.)

MILLIE. And while you're there you might as well slip into Stewart's and have an ice. Here. Catch. (*She takes a shilling from her bag and throws it to him.*)

TAPLOW (*turning and catching it*). Thanks awfully. (*He signals to* FRANK *not to tell, and moves to the door up* R.)

MILLIE. Oh, Taplow. (*She crosses to him.*)

TAPLOW (*turning on the step*). Yes, Mrs. Crocker-Harris.

MILLIE. I had a letter from my father today in which he says he once had the pleasure of meeting your mother.

TAPLOW (*uninterested but polite*). Oh, really?

MILLIE. Yes. It was at some fête or other in Bradford. My uncle—that's Sir William Bartop, you know—made a speech and so did your mother. My father met her afterwards at tea.

TAPLOW. Oh really?

MILLIE. He said he found her quite charming.

TAPLOW. Yes, she's jolly good at those sort of functions. (*Becoming aware of his lack of tact*). I mean—I'm sure she found him charming, too. So long. (*He goes out up* R.)

MILLIE (*coming down to the* L. *end of the settee*). Thank you for coming round.

FRANK. That's all right.

MILLIE. You're staying for dinner?

FRANK. If I may.

MILLIE. If you may! (*She crosses below the settee to him*). Give me a cigarette. (FRANK *takes out his case and extends it to her.* MILLIE *takes a cigarette. Indicating the case*). You haven't given it away yet, I see.

FRANK. Do you think I would?

MILLIE. Frankly, yes. Luckily it's a man's case. I don't suppose any of your girl friends would want it.

FRANK. Don't be silly.

MILLIE. Where have you been all this week?

FRANK (*sitting in the easy chair*). Correcting exam papers —making reports. You know what end of term is like.

MILLIE (*crossing below the settee and moving above the table* C.). I do know what end of term is like. But even Andrew has managed this last week to take a few hours off to say good-bye to people. (*She takes some packages out of the shopping basket.*)

FRANK. I really have been appallingly busy. Besides, I'm coming to stay with you in Bradford.

MILLIE. Not for over a month. Andrew doesn't start his new job until September first. That's one of the things I had to tell you.

FRANK. Oh. I had meant to be in Devonshire in September.

MILLIE (*quickly*). Who with?

FRANK. My family.

MILLIE. Surely you can go earlier, can't you? Go in August.

FRANK. It'll be difficult.

MILLIE. Then you'd better come to me in August.

FRANK. But Andrew will still be there. (*There is a pause.* MILLIE *crosses to* L. *of the desk, opens a drawer and takes out some scissors.*) I think I can manage September.

MILLIE (*shutting the drawer*). That'd be better—from every point of view. (*She moves below the table* C. *and puts down the scissors*). Except that it means I shan't see you for six weeks.

FRANK (*lightly*). You'll survive that, all right.

MILLIE. Yes, I'll survive it—(*she moves to the* L. *end of the settee*) but not as easily as you will. (FRANK *says nothing*). I haven't much pride, have I? (*She crosses to* FRANK *and stands above the easy chair*). Frank, darling —(*she sits on the arm of the chair and kisses him*) I love you so much. (FRANK *kisses her on the mouth, but a trifle perfunctorily, and then rises and breaks quickly away, as if afraid someone had come into the room. He moves below the settee. She laughs*). You're very nervous.

FRANK. I'm afraid of that screen arrangement. You can't see people coming in.

MILLIE. Oh yes. (*She rises and stands by the fireplace*). That reminds me. What were you and Taplow up to when I came in just now? Making fun of my husband?

FRANK. Afraid so. Yes.

MILLIE. It sounded rather a good imitation. I must get him to do it for me sometime. It was very naughty of you to encourage him.

FRANK. I know. It was.

MILLIE (*ironically*). Bad for discipline.

FRANK (*sitting on the settee*). Exactly. Currying favour

with the boys, too. My God, how easy it is to be popular. I've only been a master three years, but I've already slipped into an act and a vernacular that I just can't get out of. Why can't anyone ever be natural with the little blighters?

MILLIE. They probably wouldn't like it if you were. (*She crosses below the settee and moves above the table c. She picks up the scissors and a packet of luggage labels and cuts the latter one by one from the packet.*)

FRANK. I don't see why not. No one seems to have tried it yet, anyway. I suppose the trouble is—we're all too scared of them. Either one gets forced into an attitude of false and hearty and jocular bonhomie like myself, or into the sort of petty, soulless tyranny which your husband uses to protect himself against the lower fifth.

MILLIE (*rather bored with this*). He'd never be popular—whatever he did.

FRANK. Possibly not. He ought never to have become a schoolmaster really. Why did he?

MILLIE. It was his vocation, he said. He was sure he'd make a big success of it, especially when he got his job here first go off. (*Bitterly*). Fine success he's made, hasn't he?

FRANK. You should have stopped him.

MILLIE. How was I to know? He talked about getting a house, then a headmastership.

FRANK (*rising*). The Crock a headmaster! That's a pretty thought.

MILLIE. Yes, it's funny to think of now, all right. Still, he wasn't always the Crock, you know. He had a bit more gumption once. At least I thought he had. Don't let's talk any more about him—(*she comes R. round the table to c.*) it's too depressing. (*She starts to move L.*)

FRANK. I'm sorry for him.

MILLIE (*stopping and turning; indifferently*). He's not sorry for himself, so why should you be? It's me you should be sorry for.

FRANK. I am.

MILLIE (*moving in a few steps towards* FRANK; *smiling*). Then show me. (*She stretches out her arms to him.* FRANK *moves to her and kisses her again quickly and lightly. She holds him hungrily. He has to free himself almost roughly.*)

FRANK (*crossing to the fireplace*). What have you been doing all day?

MILLIE. Calling on the other masters' wives—saying fond farewells. I've worked off twelve. I've another seven to do tomorrow.

FRANK. You poor thing! I don't envy you.

MILLIE (*moving above the desk to* L. *of it with some labels*). It's the housemasters' wives that are the worst. (*She picks up a pen and writes on the labels*). They're all so damn patronizing. You should have heard Betty Carstairs. "My dear—it's such terrible bad luck on you both—that your husband should get this heart trouble just when, if only he'd stayed on, he'd have been bound to get a house. I mean, he's considerably senior to my Arthur as it is, and they simply couldn't have gone on passing him over, could they?"

FRANK. There's a word for Betty Carstairs, my dear, that I would hesitate to employ before a lady.

MILLIE. She's got her eye on you, anyway.

FRANK. Betty Carstairs? What utter rot!

MILLIE. Oh yes, she has. I saw you at that concert. Don't think I didn't notice.

FRANK. Millie, darling! Really! I detest the woman.

MILLIE. Then what were you doing in her box at Lord's?

FRANK. Carstairs invited me. I went there because it was a good place to see the match from.

MILLIE. Yes, I'm sure it was. Much better than the grandstand, anyway.

FRANK (*remembering something suddenly*). Oh, my God!

MILLIE (*coming below the desk*). It's all right, my dear. Don't bother to apologize. We gave the seat away, as it happens.

FRANK. I'm most terribly sorry.

MILLIE. It's all right. (*She moves to* R. *of the desk*). We couldn't afford a box, you see.

FRANK (*moving a few steps towards* R. C.). It wasn't that. You know it wasn't that. It's just that I—well, I clean forgot.

MILLIE. Funny you didn't forget the Carstairs invitation.

FRANK. Millie—don't be a fool.

MILLIE. It's you who are the fool. (*Appealingly*). Frank—have you never been in love? I know you're not in love with me—but haven't you ever been in love with anyone? Don't you realize what torture you inflict on someone who loves you when you do a thing like that?

FRANK. I've told you I'm sorry—I don't know what more I can say.

MILLIE. Why not the truth?

FRANK. The truth is—I clean forgot.

MILLIE. The truth is—you had something better to do—and why not say it?

FRANK. All right. Believe that if you like. It happens to be a lie, but believe it all the same. Only for God's sake stop this. (*He turns and moves down* R.)

MILLIE. Then for God's sake show me some pity. Do you think it's any pleasanter for me to believe that you cut me because you forgot? Do you think that doesn't hurt either? (FRANK *turns away. She moves above the up* R. *corner of the desk and faces the door up* L.). Oh damn! I was so determined to be brave and not mention Lord's. Why did I? Frank, just tell me one thing. Just tell me you're not running away from me—that's all I want to hear.

FRANK. I'm coming to Bradford.

MILLIE (*turning to* FRANK). I think, if you don't, I'll kill myself.

FRANK (*turning and taking a few steps in towards* MILLIE). I'm coming to Bradford. (*The door up* R. *opens.* FRANK *stops at the sound.* MILLIE *recovers herself and crosses above the table* C. *to the sideboard.* ANDREW CROCKER-HARRIS *enters and appears from behind the screen. Despite the summer sun he wears a serge suit and a stiff collar. He carries a mackintosh and a rolled-up time-table and looks, as ever, neat, complacent and unruffled. He speaks in a very gentle voice which he rarely raises.*)

ANDREW (*hanging his mackintosh on the hall-stand*). Is Taplow here? (FRANK *eases towards the fireplace.*)

MILLIE. I sent him to the chemist to get your prescription made up.

ANDREW. What prescription?

MILLIE. Your heart medicine. Don't you remember? You told me this morning it had run out.

ANDREW. Of course I remember, my dear, but there was no need to send Taplow for it. If you had telephoned the chemist he would have sent it round in plenty of time. He knows the prescription. (*He comes down to the* L. *end of the settee*). Now Taplow will be late and I am so pressed for time I hardly know how to fit him in. (*He sees* FRANK). Ah, Hunter! How are you? (*He moves* R. *to* FRANK.)

FRANK. Very well, thanks. (*They shake hands.*)

ANDREW. Most kind of you to drop in, but, as Millie should have warned you, I am expecting a pupil for extra work and . . .

MILLIE. He's staying to dinner, Andrew.

ANDREW. Good. Then I shall see something of you. However, when Taplow returns I'm sure you won't mind . . .

FRANK (*making a move*). No, of course not. I'll make myself scarce now, if you'd rather—I mean, if you're busy . . . (*He turns away and moves* C.)

ANDREW. Oh no. There is no need for that. Sit down, do. Will you smoke? I don't, as you know, but Millie does. (*He crosses below the desk and moves up L. of it*). Millie, give our guest a cigarette.

MILLIE (*moving down to the table* C.). I haven't any, I'm afraid. I've had to cadge from him. (*She takes a copy of the "Tatler" from the basket.* ANDREW *opens the drawer that should contain the scissors.* FRANK *takes out his cigarette case, crosses to* R. *of the table* C., *and offers it to* MILLIE. *She exchanges a glance with him as she takes a cigarette.*)

ANDREW (*looking for the scissors*). We expected you at Lord's, Hunter.

FRANK. What? Oh yes. I'm most terribly sorry. I . . .

MILLIE (*crossing behind the settee*). He clean forgot, Andrew. Imagine.

ANDREW. Forgot?

MILLIE. Not everyone is blessed with your superhuman memory, you see.

FRANK. I really can't apologize enough.

ANDREW. Please don't bother to mention it. On the second day we managed to sell the seat to a certain Dr. Lambert, who wore, I regret to say, the colours of the opposing faction, but who otherwise seemed a passably agreeable person. (*He moves above the table* C.). You liked him, didn't you, Millie?

MILLIE (*looking at* FRANK). Very much indeed. I thought him quite charming.

ANDREW. A charming old gentleman. (*To* FRANK). You have had tea? (*He picks up the scissors.*)

FRANK. Yes—thank you.

ANDREW. Is there any other refreshment I can offer you?

FRANK. No, thank you.

ANDREW (*cutting the string round the time-table*). Would

it interest you to see the new time-table I have drafted for next term?

FRANK. Yes, very much. (*He moves up* R. *of* ANDREW. AN-DREW *opens out a long roll of paper, made by pasting pieces of foolscap together, and which is entirely covered by his meticulous writing.*) I never knew you drafted our time-tables.

ANDREW. Didn't you? I have done so for the last fifteen years. (MILLIE *wanders down* R. *of the settee*). Of course, they are always issued in mimeograph under the headmaster's signature. Now what form do you take? Upper fifth Science—there you are—that's the general picture; but on the back you will see each form specified under separate headings—there—that's a new idea of mine—Millie, this might interest you.

MILLIE (*sitting in the easy chair; suddenly harsh*). You know it bores me to death. (FRANK *looks up, surprised and uncomfortable.* ANDREW *does not remove his eyes from the time-table.*)

ANDREW. Millie has no head for this sort of work. There you see. Now here you can follow the upper fifth Science throughout every day of the week.

FRANK (*indicating the time-table*). I must say, I think this is a really wonderful job.

ANDREW. Thank you. It has the merit of clarity, I think. (*He starts to roll up the time-table.*)

FRANK. I don't know what they'll do without you.

ANDREW (*without expression*). They'll find somebody else, I expect. (*There is a pause.*)

FRANK. What sort of job is this you're going to?

ANDREW (*looking at* MILLIE *for the first time*). Hasn't Millie told you?

FRANK. She said it was a cr— a private school.

ANDREW. A crammer's—for backward boys. It is run by an old Oxford contemporary of mine who lives in Dorset. (*He moves round* L. *of the table* C. *and finishes rolling up the time-table*). The work will not be so arduous as here and my doctor seems to think I will be able to undertake it without—er danger.

FRANK (*with genuine sympathy*). It's the most rotten bad luck for you. I'm awfully sorry.

ANDREW (*raising his voice a little*). My dear Hunter, there is nothing whatever to be sorry for. I am looking forward to the change. (*There is a knock at the door up* R.). Come in. (*He crosses below the table to* C. TAPLOW *enters up* R., *a trifle breathless and guilty-looking. He carries a medicine bottle wrapped and sealed*). Ah, Taplow. Good. You have been running, I see.

TAPLOW. Yes, sir. (*He crosses to the* L. *end of the settee.*)

ANDREW. There was a queue at the chemist's, I suppose?

TAPLOW. Yes, sir.

ANDREW. And doubtless an even longer one at Stewart's?

TAPLOW. Yes, sir—I mean—no, sir—I mean—(*he looks at* MILLIE) yes, sir. (*He crosses below the settee to* MILLIE *and hands her the medicine.*)

MILLIE. You were late yourself, Andrew.

ANDREW. Exactly. And for that I apologize, Taplow.

TAPLOW. That's all right, sir.

ANDREW (*crossing below the desk and moving* L. *of it*). Luckily we have still a good hour before lock-up, so nothing has been lost. (*He puts the time-table on the desk.*)

FRANK (*moving to the door up* L.; *to* MILLIE). May I use the short cut? I'm going back to my digs. (ANDREW *sits at his desk and opens a book.*)

MILLIE (*rising and moving up* R. *of the settee*). Yes. Go ahead. Come back soon. If Andrew hasn't finished we can sit in the garden. (*She crosses above the table* C. *and picks up the shopping basket. She puts the medicine on the sideboard*). I'd better go and see about dinner. (*She goes out up* C.)

ANDREW (*to* FRANK). Taplow is desirous of obtaining a remove from my form, Hunter, so that he can spend the rest of his career here playing happily with the crucibles, retorts and bunsen burners of your science fifth.

FRANK (*turning at the door*). Oh. Has he?

ANDREW. Has he what?

FRANK. Obtained his remove?

ANDREW (*after a pause*). He has obtained exactly what he deserves. No less; and certainly no more. (TAPLOW *mutters an explosion of mirth.* FRANK *nods, thoughtfully, and goes out.* ANDREW *has caught sight of* TAPLOW's *contorted face, but passes no remark on it. He beckons* TAPLOW *across and signs to him to sit in the chair* R. *of the desk.* TAPLOW *sits.* ANDREW *picks up a copy of "The Agamemnon" and* TAPLOW *does the same.*) Line thirteen hundred and ninety-nine. Begin. (*He leans back.*)

TAPLOW (*reading slowly*). Chorus. We—are surprised at . . .

ANDREW (*automatically*). We marvel at.

TAPLOW. We marvel at—thy tongue—how bold thou art— that you . . .

ANDREW. Thou. (*His interruptions are automatic. His thoughts are evidently far distant.*)

TAPLOW. Thou—can . . .

ANDREW. Canst.

TAPLOW. Canst—boastfully speak . . .

ANDREW. Utter such a boastful speech.

TAPLOW. Utter such a boastful speech—over—(*in a sudden rush of inspiration*) the bloody corpse of the husband you have slain. (ANDREW *puts on his glasses and looks down at his text for the first time.* TAPLOW *looks apprehensive.*)

ANDREW (*after a pause*). Taplow—I presume you are using a different text from mine.

TAPLOW. No, sir.

ANDREW. That is strange, for the line as I have it reads: "heetis toiond ep andri compadzise logon." However diligently I search I can discover no "bloody"—no "corpse" —no "you have slain." Simply "husband".

TAPLOW. Yes, sir. That's right.

ANDREW. Then why do you invent words that simply are not there?

TAPLOW. I thought they sounded better, sir. More exciting. After all, she did kill her husband, sir. (*With relish*). She's just been revealed with his dead body and Cassandra's weltering in gore.

ANDREW. I am delighted at this evidence, Taplow, of your interest in the rather more lurid aspects of dramaturgy, but I feel I must remind you that you are supposed to be construing Greek, not collaborating with Aeschylus. (*He leans back.*)

TAPLOW (*greatly daring*). Yes, but still, sir, translator's licence, sir—I didn't get anything wrong—and after all it *is* a play and not just a bit of Greek construe.

ANDREW (*momentarily at a loss*). I seem to detect a note of end of term in your remarks. I am not denying that *The Agamemnon* is a play. It is perhaps the greatest play ever written. (*He leans forward.*)

TAPLOW (*quickly*). I wonder how many people in the form think that? (*He pauses; instantly frightened of what he has said*). Sorry, sir. Shall I go on? (ANDREW *does not answer. He sits motionless, staring at his book*). Shall I go on, sir? (*There is another pause.* ANDREW *raises his head slowly from his book.*)

ANDREW (*murmuring gently, not looking at* TAPLOW). When I was a very young man, only two years older than you are now, Taplow, I wrote, for my own pleasure, a translation of *The Agamemnon*—a very free translation—I remember—in rhyming couplets.

TAPLOW. The whole *Agamemnon*—in verse? That must have been hard work, sir.

ANDREW. It was hard work; but I derived great joy from it. The play had so excited and moved me that I wished to communicate, however imperfectly, some of that emotion to others. When I had finished it, I remember, I thought it very beautiful—almost more beautiful than the original. (*He leans back.*)

TAPLOW. Was it ever published, sir?

ANDREW. No. Yesterday I looked for the manuscript while I was packing my papers. I was unable to find it. I fear it is lost—like so many other things. Lost for good.

TAPLOW. Hard luck, sir. (ANDREW *is silent again.* TAPLOW *steals a timid glance at him*). Shall I go on, sir? (AN-DREW, *with a slight effort, lowers his eyes again to his text.*)

ANDREW (*leaning forward; raising his voice slightly*). No. Go back and get that last line right. (TAPLOW, *out of* ANDREW'S *vision, as he thinks, makes a disgusted grimace in his direction.*)

TAPLOW. That—thou canst utter such a boastful speech over thy husband.

ANDREW. Yes. And now, if you would be so kind, you will do the line again, without the facial contortion which you just found necessary to accompany it. (TAPLOW *is about to begin the line again.* MILLIE *enters up* C., *hurriedly. She is wearing an apron.* TAPLOW *rises.*)

MILLIE. The headmaster's just coming up the drive. Don't tell him I'm in. The fish pie isn't in the oven yet. (*She exits up* C.)

TAPLOW (*turning hopefully to* ANDREW). I'd better go, hadn't I, sir? I mean—I don't want to be in the way.

ANDREW. We do not yet know that it is I the headmaster wishes to see. Other people live in this building. (*There is a knock at the door up* R.). Come in. (DR. FROBISHER *enters up* R. *He looks more like a distinguished diplomat than a doctor of literature and a classical scholar. He is in the middle fifties and goes to a very good tailor.* AN- DREW *rises.*)

FROBISHER. Ah, Crocker-Harris, I've caught you in. I'm so glad. (*He crosses behind the settee and comes down* L. *of it*). I hope I'm not disturbing you?

ANDREW. I have been taking a pupil in extra work. (TAP- LOW *eases below the table* C.)

FROBISHER. On the penultimate day of term? That argues either great conscientiousness on your part or considerable backwardness on his.

ANDREW. Perhaps a combination of both.

FROBISHER. Quite so, but as this is my only chance of speaking to you before tomorrow, I think that perhaps your pupil will be good enough to excuse us. (*He turns politely to* TAPLOW.)

TAPLOW. Oh yes, sir. That's really quite all right. (*He grabs his books off* ANDREW'S *desk.*)

ANDREW (*crossing to* TAPLOW). I'm extremely sorry, Taplow. You will please explain to your father exactly what occurred over this lost hour and tell him that I shall in due course be writing to him to return the money involved. (FROBISHER *moves below the settee to the fireplace.*)

TAPLOW (*hurriedly*). Yes, sir. But please don't bother, sir. (*He dashes to the door up* R.). I know it's all right, sir. Thank you, sir. (*He darts out.*)

FROBISHER (*idly picking up an ornament on the mantelpiece*). Have the Gilberts called on you yet? (*He turns to* ANDREW.)

ANDREW (*moving* C.). The Gilberts, sir? Who are they?

FROBISHER. Gilbert is your successor with the lower fifth. He is down here today with his wife, and as they will be taking over this flat I thought perhaps you wouldn't mind if they came in to look it over.

ANDREW. Of course not.

FROBISHER. I've told you about him, I think. He is a very brilliant young man and won exceptionally high honours at Oxford.

ANDREW. So I understand, sir.

FROBISHER. Not, of course, as high as the honours you yourself won there. He didn't, for instance, win the Chancellor's prize for Latin verse or the Gainsford.

ANDREW. He won the Hertford Latin, then?

FROBISHER (*replacing the ornament*). No. (*Mildly surprised*). Did you win that, too? (ANDREW *nods*). It's sometimes rather hard to remember that you are perhaps the most brilliant classical scholar we have ever had at the school.

ANDREW. You are very kind.

FROBISHER (*urbanely correcting his gaffe*). Hard to remember, I mean—because of your other activities—your brilliant work on the school time-table, for instance, and also for your heroic battle for so long and against such odds with the soul-destroying lower fifth.

ANDREW. I have not found that my soul has been destroyed by the lower fifth, Headmaster.

FROBISHER. I was joking, of course.

ANDREW. Oh. I see.

FROBISHER. Is your wife in?

ANDREW. Er—no. Not at the moment.

FROBISHER. I shall have a chance of saying good-bye to her tomorrow. (*He moves in a few steps below the settee*). I am rather glad I have got you to myself. I have a delicate matter—two rather delicate matters—to broach.

ANDREW (*moving in slightly; indicating the settee*). Please sit down. (*He stands at the* L. *end of the settee.*)

FROBISHER. Thank you. (*He sits*). Now you have been with us, in all, eighteen years, haven't you? (ANDREW *nods*). It is extremely unlucky that you should have had to retire at so comparatively early an age and so short a time before you would have been eligible for a pension. (*He is regarding his nails, as he speaks, studiously avoiding meeting* ANDREW's *gaze.* ANDREW *crosses below the settee to the fireplace and stands facing it.*)

ANDREW (*after a pause*). You have decided, then, not to award me a pension?

FROBISHER. Not I, my dear fellow. It has nothing at all to do with me. It's the governors who, I'm afraid, have been forced to turn down your application. I put your case to them as well as I could—— (ANDREW *turns and faces* FROBISHER.)—but they decided with great regret, that they couldn't make an exception to the rule.

ANDREW. But I thought—my wife thought, that an exception was made some five years ago . . .

FROBISHER. Ah! In the case of Buller, you mean? True. But the circumstances with Buller were quite remarkable. It was, after all, in playing rugger against the school that he received that injury.

ANDREW. Yes. I remember.

FROBISHER. And then the governors received a petition from boys, old boys and parents, with over five hundred signatures.

ANDREW. I would have signed that petition myself, but through some oversight I was not asked.

FROBISHER. He was a splendid fellow, Buller. Splendid. Doing very well, too, now, I gather.

ANDREW. I'm delighted to hear it.

FROBISHER. Your own case, of course, is equally deserving. If not more so—for Buller was a younger man. Unfortunately—rules are rules—and are not made to be broken every few years; at any rate that is the governors' view.

ANDREW. I quite understand.

FROBISHER. I knew you would. Now might I ask you a rather impertinent question?

ANDREW. Certainly.

FROBISHER. You have, I take it, private means?

ANDREW. My wife has some.

FROBISHER. Ah, yes. Your wife has often told me of her family connexions. I understand her father has a business in—Bradford—isn't it?

ANDREW. Yes. He runs a men's clothing shop in the Arcade.

FROBISHER. Indeed? Your wife's remarks had led me to imagine something a little more—extensive.

ANDREW. My father-in-law made a settlement on my wife at the time of our marriage. She has about three hundred a year of her own. I have nothing. Is that the answer to your question, Headmaster?

FROBISHER. Yes. Thank you for your frankness. Now, this private school you are going to . . .

ANDREW. My salary at the crammer's is to be two hundred pounds a year.

FROBISHER. Quite so. With board and lodging, of course?

ANDREW. For eight months of the year.

FROBISHER. Yes, I see. (*He ponders a second*). Of course, you know, there is the School Benevolent Fund that deals with cases of actual hardship.

ANDREW. There will be no actual hardship, Headmaster.

FROBISHER. No. I am glad you take that view. I must admit, though, I had hoped that your own means had proved a little more ample. Your wife had certainly led me to suppose . . .

ANDREW. I am not denying that a pension would have been very welcome, Headmaster, but I see no reason to quarrel with the governors' decision. What is the other delicate matter you have to discuss?

FROBISHER. Well, it concerns the arrangements at prize-giving tomorrow. You are, of course, prepared to say a few words?

ANDREW. I had assumed you would call on me to do so.

FROBISHER. Of course. It is always done, and I know the boys appreciate the custom.

ANDREW (*crossing to the upstage end of the desk*). I have already made a few notes of what I am going to say. Perhaps you would care . . .

FROBISHER. No, no. That isn't necessary at all. I know I can trust your discretion—not to say your wit. It will be, I know, a very moving moment for you—indeed for us all—but, as I'm sure you realize, it is far better to keep these occasions from becoming too heavy and distressing. You know how little the boys appreciate sentiment.

ANDREW. I do.

FROBISHER. That is why I've planned my own reference to you at the end of my speech to be rather more light and jocular than I would otherwise have made it.

ANDREW. I quite understand. (*He moves to L. of the desk, puts on his glasses and picks up his speech*). I too have prepared a few little jokes and puns for my speech. One—a play of words on *vale*, farewell and Wally, the Christian name of a backward boy in my class, is, I think, rather happy.

FROBISHER. Yes. (*He laughs belatedly*). Very neat. That should go down extremely well.

ANDREW. I'm glad you like it.

FROBISHER (*rising and crossing to R. of the desk*). Well, now—there is a particular favour I have to ask of you in connexion with the ceremony, and I know I shall not have to ask in vain. Fletcher, as you know, is leaving too.

ANDREW. Yes. He is going into the city, they tell me.

FROBISHER. Yes. Now he is, of course, considerably junior to you. He has only been here—let me see—five years. But, as you know, he has done great things for our cricket—positive wonders, when you remember what doldrums we were in before he came.

ANDREW. Our win at Lord's this year was certainly most inspiriting.

FROBISHER. Exactly. (*He moves above the desk*). Now I'm sure that tomorrow the boys will make the occasion of his farewell speech a tremendous demonstration of gratitude. The applause might go on for minutes—you know what the boys feel about Lord's—and I seriously doubt my ability to cut it short or even, I admit, the propriety of trying to do so. Now, you see the quandary in which I am placed?

ANDREW. Perfectly. You wish to refer to me and for me to make my speech before you come to Fletcher?

FROBISHER. It's extremely awkward, and I feel wretched about asking it of you—but it's more for your own sake than for mine or Fletcher's that I do. After all, a climax is what one must try to work up to on these occasions.

ANDREW. Naturally, Headmaster, I wouldn't wish to provide an anti-climax.

FROBISHER. You really mustn't take it amiss, my dear fellow. The boys, in applauding Fletcher for several minutes and yourself say—for—well, for not quite so long—won't be making any personal demonstration between you. It will be quite impersonal—I assure you—quite impersonal.

ANDREW. I understand.

FROBISHER (*patting* ANDREW's *shoulder; warmly*). I knew you would (*he looks at his watch*) and I can hardly tell you how wisely I think you have chosen. Well now —as that is all my business, I think perhaps I had better be getting along. (*He crosses to* R. *of the table* C.). This has been a terribly busy day for me—for you too, I imagine.

ANDREW. Yes. (MILLIE *enters up* C. *She has taken off her apron, and tidied herself up. She comes to* L. *of* FROBISHER.)

MILLIE (*in her social manner*). Ah, Headmaster. How good of you to drop in.

FROBISHER (*more at home with her than with* ANDREW).
Mrs. Crocker-Harris. How are you? (*They shake hands*).
You're looking extremely well, I must say. (*To* ANDREW).
Has anyone ever told you, Crocker-Harris, that you have
a very attractive wife?

ANDREW. Many people, sir. But then I hardly need to be
told.

MILLIE. Can I persuade you to stay a few moments and
have a drink, Headmaster? It's so rarely we have the
pleasure of seeing you.

FROBISHER. Unfortunately, dear lady, I was just on the
point of leaving. I have two frantic parents waiting for
me at home. You are dining with us tomorrow—both of
you, aren't you?

MILLIE. Yes, indeed—and so looking forward to it. (FRO-
BISHER *and* MILLIE *move to the door up* R.)

FROBISHER. I'm so glad. We can say our sad farewells then.
(*To* ANDREW). Au revoir, Crocker-Harris, and thank you
very much. (*He opens the door.* ANDREW *gives a slight
bow.* MILLIE *holds the door open.* FROBISHER *goes out.*)

MILLIE (*to* ANDREW). Don't forget to take your medicine,
dear, will you? (*She goes out.*)

ANDREW. No.

FROBISHER (*off*). Lucky invalid! To have such a very
charming nurse.

MILLIE (*off*). I really don't know what to say to all these
compliments, Headmaster. I don't believe you mean a
word of them. (ANDREW *turns and looks out of the
window.*)

FROBISHER (*off*). Every word. Till tomorrow, then? Good-
bye. (*The outer door is heard to slam.* ANDREW *is staring out of the window.* MILLIE *enters up* R.)

MILLIE. Well? Do we get it? (*She stands on the step.*)

ANDREW (*turning and moving below the chair* L. *of his
desk; absently*). Get what?

MILLIE. The pension, of course. Do we get it?

ANDREW. No.

MILLIE (*crossing above the settee to* c.). My God! Why not?

ANDREW (*sitting at his desk*). It's against the rules.

MILLIE. Buller got it, didn't he? Buller got it? What's the idea of giving it to him and not to us?

ANDREW. The governors are afraid of establishing a precedent.

MILLIE. The mean old brutes! My God, what I wouldn't like to say to them! (*She moves above the desk and rounds on* ANDREW). And what did you say? Just sat there and made a joke in Latin, I suppose?

ANDREW. There wasn't very much I could say, in Latin or any other language.

MILLIE. Oh, wasn't there? I'd have said it all right. I wouldn't just have sat there twiddling my thumbs and taking it from that old phoney of a headmaster. But, then, of course, I'm not a man. (ANDREW *is turning the pages of "The Agamemnon," not looking at her*). What do they expect you to do? Live on my money, I suppose.

ANDREW. There has never been any question of that. I shall be perfectly able to support myself.

MILLIE. Yourself? Doesn't the marriage service say something about the husband supporting his wife? (*She leans on the desk*). Doesn't it? You ought to know.

ANDREW. Yes, it does.

MILLIE. And how do you think you're going to do that on two hundred a year?

ANDREW. I shall do my utmost to save some of it. You're welcome to it, if I can.

MILLIE. Thank you for precisely nothing. (ANDREW *underlines a word in the text he is reading*). What else did the old fool have to say? (*She moves to* R. *of the chair*, R. *of the desk*.)

ANDREW. The headmaster? He wants me to make my speech tomorrow before instead of after Fletcher.

MILLIE (*sitting* R. *of the desk*). Yes. I knew he was going to ask that.

ANDREW (*without surprise*). You knew?

MILLIE. Yes. He asked my advice about it a week ago. I told him to go ahead. I knew you wouldn't mind, and as there isn't a Mrs. Fletcher to make *me* look a fool, I didn't give two hoots. (*There is a knock on the door up* R.). Come in. (MR. *and* MRS. GILBERT *enter up* R. *He is about twenty-two, and his wife a year or so younger.* MILLIE *rises and stands at the downstage corner of the desk.*)

GILBERT. Mr. Crocker-Harris?

ANDREW. Yes. (*He rises*). Is it Mr. and Mrs. Gilbert? The headmaster told me you might look in.

MRS. GILBERT (*crossing above the settee to* C.). I do hope we're not disturbing you. (GILBERT *follows* MRS. GILBERT *and stands down stage of, and slightly behind, her.*)

ANDREW. Not at all. This is my wife.

MRS. GILBERT. How do you do?

ANDREW. Mr. and Mrs. Gilbert are our successors to this flat, my dear.

MILLIE. Oh yes. (*She moves to* L. *of* MRS. GILBERT). How nice to meet you both.

GILBERT. How do you do? We really won't keep you more than a second—my wife thought as we were here you wouldn't mind us taking a squint at our future home.

MRS. GILBERT (*unnecessarily*). This is the drawing-room, I suppose? (GILBERT *crosses to the fireplace. He looks for a moment at the picture above the mantelpiece, then turns and watches the others.*)

MILLIE. Well, it's really a living-room. Andrew uses it as a study.

MRS. GILBERT. How charmingly you've done it!

MILLIE. Oh, do you think so? I'm afraid it isn't nearly as nice as I'd like to make it—but a schoolmaster's wife has to think of so many other things besides curtains and covers. Boys with dirty books and a husband with leaky fountain pens, for instance.

MRS. GILBERT. Yes, I suppose so. Of course, I haven't been a schoolmaster's wife for very long, you know.

GILBERT. Don't swank, darling. You haven't been a schoolmaster's wife at all yet.

MRS. GILBERT. Oh yes, I have—for two months. You were a schoolmaster when I married you.

GILBERT. Prep school doesn't count.

MILLIE. Have you only been married two months?

MRS. GILBERT. Two months and sixteen days.

GILBERT. Seventeen.

MILLIE (*sentimentally*). Andrew, did you hear? They've only been married two months.

ANDREW. Indeed? Is that all?

MRS. GILBERT (*crossing above* MILLIE *to the window*). Oh, look, darling. They've got a garden. It is yours, isn't it?

MILLIE. Oh, yes. It's only a pocket handkerchief, I'm afraid, but it's very useful to Andrew. He often works out there, don't you, dear?

ANDREW. Yes, indeed. I find it very agreeable.

MILLIE (*moving to the door up* C.). Shall I show you the rest of the flat? It's a bit untidy, I'm afraid, but you must forgive that. (*She opens the door.*)

MRS. GILBERT (*moving up to* L. *of* MILLIE). Oh, of course.

MILLIE. And the kitchen is in a terrible mess. I'm in the middle of cooking dinner.

MRS. GILBERT (*breathlessly*). Oh, do you cook?

MILLIE. Oh, yes. I have to. We haven't had a maid for five years.

MRS. GILBERT. Oh! I do think that's wonderful of you. I'm scared stiff of having to do it for Peter—I know the first dinner I have to cook for him will wreck our married life.

GILBERT. Highly probable. (MRS. GILBERT *exits up* C.)

MILLIE (*following* MRS. GILBERT). Well, these days we've all got to try and do things we weren't really brought up to do. (*She goes out, closing the door.*)

ANDREW (*to* GILBERT). Don't you want to see the rest of the flat?

GILBERT (*crossing to* C.). No. I leave all that sort of thing to my wife. She's the boss. I thought perhaps you could tell me something about the lower fifth.

ANDREW. What would you like to know?

GILBERT. Well, sir, quite frankly, I'm petrified.

ANDREW. I don't think you need to be. May I give you some sherry? (*He comes down* L. *to the cupboard.*)

GILBERT. Thank you.

ANDREW. They are mostly boys of about fifteen or sixteen. They are not very difficult to handle. (*He takes out a bottle and a glass.*)

GILBERT. The headmaster said you ruled them with a rod of iron. He called you "the Himmler of the lower fifth."

ANDREW (*turning, bottle and glass in hand*). Did he? "The Himmler of the lower fifth." I think he exaggerated. I hope he exaggerated. "The Himmler of the lower fifth." (*He puts the bottle on the desk, then fills the glass.*)

GILBERT (*puzzled*). He only meant that you kept the most wonderful discipline. I must say I do admire you for that. I couldn't even manage that with eleven-year-olds, so what I'll be like with fifteens and sixteens I shudder to think. (*He moves below the chair* R. *of the desk.*)

ANDREW. It is not so difficult. (*He hands* GILBERT *the glass*). They aren't bad boys. Sometimes a little wild and unfeeling, perhaps—but not bad. "The Himmler of the lower fifth." Dear me! (*He turns to the cabinet with the bottle.*)

GILBERT. Perhaps I shouldn't have said that. I've been tactless, I'm afraid.

ANDREW. Oh no. (*He puts the bottle in the cupboard*). Please sit down. (*He stands by the downstage end of the desk.*)

GILBERT. Thank you, sir. (*He sits* R. *of the desk.*)

ANDREW. From the very beginning I realized that I didn't possess the knack of making myself liked—a knack that you will find you do possess.

GILBERT. Do you think so?

ANDREW. Oh yes. I am quite sure of it. (*He moves up* L. *of the desk*). It is not a quality of great importance to a schoolmaster though, for too much of it, as you may also find, is as great a danger as the total lack of it. Forgive me lecturing, won't you?

GILBERT. I want to learn.

ANDREW. I can only teach you from my own experience. For two or three years I tried very hard to communicate to the boys some of my own joy in the great literature of the past. Of course I failed, as you will fail, nine hundred and ninety-nine times out of a thousand. But a single success can atone, and more than atone, for all the failure in the world. And sometimes—very rarely, it is true—but sometimes I had that success. That was in the early years.

GILBERT (*eagerly listening*). Please go on, sir.

ANDREW. In early years too, I discovered an easy substitute for popularity. (*He picks up his speech*). I had of course acquired—we all do—many little mannerisms and tricks of speech, and I found that the boys were beginning to laugh at me. I was very happy at that, and encouraged the boys' laughter by playing up to it. It made our relationship so very much easier. They didn't like me as a man, but they found me funny as a character, and you can teach more things by laughter than by earnestness—for I never did have much sense of humour. So, for a time, you see, I was quite a success as a school-master . . . (*He stops*). I fear this is all very personal and embarrassing to you. Forgive me. You need have no fears about the lower fifth. (*He puts the speech into his pocket and turns to the window.* GILBERT *rises and moves above the desk.*)

GILBERT (*after a pause*). I'm afraid I said something that hurt you very much. It's myself you must forgive, sir. Believe me, I'm desperately sorry.

ANDREW (*turning down stage and leaning slightly on the back of the swivel chair*). There's no need. You were merely telling me what I should have known for myself. Perhaps I did in my heart, and hadn't the courage to acknowledge it. I knew, of course, that I was not only not liked, but now positively disliked. I had realized too that the boys—for many long years now—had ceased to laugh at me. I don't know why they no longer found me a joke. Perhaps it was my illness. No, I don't think it was that. Something deeper than that. Not a sickness of the body, but a sickness of the soul. At all events it didn't take much discernment on my part to realize I had become an utter failure as a schoolmaster. Still, stupidly enough, I hadn't realized that I was also feared. "The Himmler of the lower fifth." I suppose that will become my epitaph. (GILBERT *is now deeply embarrassed and rather upset, but he remains silent. He sits on the upstage end of the window seat. With a mild laugh*). I cannot for the life of me imagine why I should choose to unburden myself to you—a total stranger—when I have been silent to others for so long. Perhaps it is because my very unworthy mantle is about to fall on your shoulders. If that is so I shall take a prophet's privilege and foretell that you will have a very great success with the lower fifth.

GILBERT. Thank you, sir. I shall do my best.

ANDREW. I can't offer you a cigarette, I'm afraid. I don't smoke.

GILBERT. That's all right, sir. Nor do I.

MRS. GILBERT (*off*). Thank you so much for showing me round. (MILLIE *and* MRS. GILBERT *enter up* C. ANDREW *rises.* MILLIE *comes down* R. *of the table* C., *picks up the papers on the settee and puts them on the fender down* R. MRS. GILBERT *comes down* L. *of the table* C. *to* R. *of* GILBERT.)

ANDREW. I trust your wife has found no major snags in your new flat.

MR. GILBERT. No. None at all.

MRS. GILBERT. Just imagine, Peter. Mr. and Mrs. Crocker-Harris first met each other on a holiday in the Lake District. Isn't that a coincidence?

GILBERT (*a little distrait*). Yes. Yes, it certainly is. On a walking tour, too? (ANDREW *turns and looks out of the window.*)

MILLIE. Andrew was on a walking tour. No walking for me. I can't abide it. I was staying with my uncle—that's Sir William Bartop, you know—you may have heard of him. (GILBERT *and* MRS. GILBERT *try to look as though they had heard of him constantly. She moves below the settee*). He'd taken a house near Windermere—quite a mansion it was really—rather silly for an old gentleman living alone—and Andrew knocked on our front door one day and asked the footman for a glass of water. So my uncle invited him in to tea.

MRS. GILBERT (*moving* C.). Our meeting wasn't quite as romantic as that.

GILBERT. I knocked her flat on her face. (*He moves behind* MRS. GILBERT *and puts his hands on her shoulders.*)

MRS. GILBERT. Not with love at first sight. With the swing doors of our hotel bar. So of course then he apologized and . . . (ANDREW *turns and faces into the room.*)

GILBERT (*brusquely*). Darling. The Crocker-Harrises, I'm sure, have far more important things to do than to listen to your detailed but inaccurate account of our very sordid little encounter. Why not just say I married you for your money and leave it at that? Come on, we must go.

MRS. GILBERT (*moving above the settee; to* MILLIE). Isn't he awful to me?

MILLIE (*moving round the* R. *end of the settee to the door up* R.). Men have no souls, my dear. My husband is just as bad.

MRS. GILBERT. Good-bye, Mr. Crocker-Harris.

ANDREW (*with a slight bow*). Good-bye.

MRS. GILBERT (*moving to the door up* R.; *to* MILLIE). I think your idea about the dining-room is awfully good —if only I can get the permit . . . (MILLIE *and* MRS. GILBERT *go out.* GILBERT *has dallied to say good-bye alone to* ANDREW.)

GILBERT. Good-bye, sir.

ANDREW (*crossing* C. *to* L. *of* GILBERT). Er—you will, I know, respect the confidences I have just made to you.

GILBERT. I should hate you to think I wouldn't.

ANDREW. I am sorry to have embarrassed you. I don't know what came over me. I have not been very well, you know. Good-bye, my dear fellow, and my best wishes.

GILBERT. Thank you. The very best of good luck to you too, sir, in your future career.

ANDREW. My future career? Yes. Thank you.

GILBERT. Well, good-bye, sir. (*He crosses up* R. *and goes out.* ANDREW *moves to the chair* R. *of the desk and sits. He picks up a book and looks idly at it.* MILLIE *enters up* R. *She crosses above the table* C., *picks up the box of chocolates and eats one as she speaks.*)

MILLIE. Good-looking couple.

ANDREW. Very.

MILLIE. He looks as if he'd got what it takes. I should think he'll be a success all right.

ANDREW. That's what I thought.

MILLIE. I don't think it's much of a career, though—a schoolmaster—for a likely young chap like that.

ANDREW. I know you don't.

MILLIE (*crossing down to the desk and picking up the luggage labels*). Still, I bet when he leaves this place it won't be without a pension. It'll be roses, roses all the way, and tears and cheers and good-bye, Mr. Chips.

ANDREW. I expect so.

MILLIE. What's the matter with you?

ANDREW. Nothing.

MILLIE. You're not going to have another of your attacks, are you? You look dreadful.

ANDREW. I'm perfectly all right.

MILLIE (*indifferently*). You know best. Your medicine's there, anyway, if you want it. (*She goes out up C.* ANDREW, *left alone, continues for a time staring at the text he has been pretending to read. Then he puts one hand over his eyes. There is a knock on the door up* R.)

ANDREW. Come in. (TAPLOW *enters up* R. *and appears timidly from behind the screen. He is carrying a small book behind his back. Sharply*). Yes, Taplow? What is it?

TAPLOW. Nothing, sir.

ANDREW. What do you mean, nothing?

TAPLOW (*timidly*). I just came back to say good-bye, sir.

ANDREW. Oh. (*He puts down the book and rises.*)

TAPLOW (*moving* C.). I didn't have a chance with the head here. I rather dashed out, I'm afraid. I thought I'd just come back and—wish you luck, sir.

ANDREW. Thank you, Taplow. That's good of you.

TAPLOW. I—er—thought this might interest you, sir. (*He quickly thrusts the small book towards* ANDREW.)

ANDREW (*taking out his glasses and putting them on*). What is it?

TAPLOW. Verse translation of *The Agamemnon*, sir. The Browning version. It's not much good. I've been reading it in the Chapel gardens.

ANDREW (*taking the book*). Very interesting, Taplow. (*He seems to have a little difficulty in speaking. He clears his throat and then goes on in his level, gentle voice*). I know the translation, of course. It has its faults, I agree, but I think you will enjoy it more when you get used to the metre he employs. (*He hands the book to* TAPLOW.)

TAPLOW (*brusquely thrusting the book back to* ANDREW). It's for you, sir.

ANDREW. For me?

TAPLOW. Yes, sir. I've written in it. (ANDREW *opens the fly-leaf and reads whatever is written there.*)

ANDREW. Did you buy this?

TAPLOW. Yes, sir. It was only second-hand.

ANDREW. You shouldn't have spent your pocket-money this way.

TAPLOW. That's all right, sir. It wasn't very much. (*Suddenly appalled*). The price isn't still inside, is it? (ANDREW *carefully wipes his glasses and puts them on again.*)

ANDREW (*at length*). No. Just what you've written. Nothing else.

TAPLOW. Good. I'm sorry you've got it already. I thought you probably would have.

ANDREW. I haven't got it already. I may have had it once. I can't remember. But I haven't got it now.

TAPLOW. That's all right, then. (ANDREW *continues to stare at* TAPLOW'S *inscription on the fly-leaf. Suspiciously*). What's the matter, sir? Have I got the accent wrong on "eumenose"?

ANDREW. No. The perispomenon is perfectly correct. (*His hands are shaking. He lowers the book and turns away above the chair* R. *of the desk*). Taplow, would you be good enough to take that bottle of medicine, which you so kindly brought in, and pour me out one dose in a glass which you will find in the bathroom?

TAPLOW (*seeing something is wrong*). Yes, sir. (*He moves up to the sideboard and picks up the bottle.*)

ANDREW. The doses are clearly marked on the bottle. I usually put a little water with it.

TAPLOW. Yes, sir. (*He darts out up* C. ANDREW, *the moment he is gone, breaks down and begins to sob uncontrollably. He sits in the chair* L. *of the desk and makes a desperate attempt, after a moment, to control himself, but when* TAPLOW *comes back his emotion is still very apparent.* TAPLOW *re-enters with the bottle and a glass, comes to the upstage end of the desk and holds out the glass.*)

ANDREW (*taking the glass*). Thank you. (*He drinks, turning his back on* TAPLOW *as he does so*). You must forgive this exhibition of weakness, Taplow. The truth is I have been going through rather a strain lately.

TAPLOW (*putting the bottle on the desk*). Of course, sir. I quite understand. (*He eases towards* C. *There is a knock on the door upper* L.)

ANDREW. Come in. (FRANK *enters up* L.)

FRANK. Oh, sorry. I though you'd be finished by now. (*He moves to* L. *of* TAPLOW.)

ANDREW. Come in, Hunter, do. It's perfectly all right. Our lesson was over some time ago, but Taplow most kindly came back to say good-bye. (FRANK, *taking in* TAPLOW's *rather startled face and* ANDREW's *obvious emotion, looks a little puzzled.*)

FRANK. Are you sure I'm not intruding?

ANDREW. No, no. I want you to see this book that Taplow has given me, Hunter. Look. A translation of *The Agamemnon,* by Robert Browning. (*He rises*). Do you see the inscription he has put into it? (*He hands the book open to* FRANK *across the desk.*)

FRANK (*glancing at the book*). Yes, but it's no use to me, I'm afraid. I never learnt Greek.

ANDREW. Then we'll have to translate it for him, won't we, Taplow? (*He recites by heart*). "ton kratownta malthecose theos prosothen eumenose prosdirkati." That means —in a rough translation: "God from afar looks graciously upon a gentle master." It comes from a speech of Agamemnon's to Clytaemnestra.

FRANK. I see. Very pleasant and very apt. (*He hands the book back to* ANDREW.)

ANDREW. Very pleasant. But perhaps not, after all, so very apt. (*He turns quickly away from both of them as emotion once more seems about to overcome him.* FRANK *brusquely jerks his head to the bewildered* TAPLOW *to get out.* TAPLOW *nods.*)

TAPLOW. Good-bye, sir, and the best of luck.

ANDREW. Good-bye, Taplow, and thank you very much. (TAPLOW *flees quickly up* R. *and goes out.* FRANK *watches* ANDREW's *back with a mixture of embarrassment and sympathy.*)

ANDREW (*turning at length, slightly recovered*). Dear me, what a fool I made of myself in front of that boy. And in front of you, Hunter. (*He moves in to the desk*). I can't imagine what you must think of me.

FRANK. Nonsense.

ANDREW. I am not a very emotional person, as you know, but there was something so very touching and kindly about his action, and coming as it did just after . . . (*He stops, then glances at the book in his hand*). This is a very delightful thing to have, don't you think?

FRANK. Delightful.

ANDREW. The quotation, of course, he didn't find entirely by himself. I happened to make some little joke about the line in form the other day. But he must have remembered it all the same to have found it so readily— and perhaps he means it.

FRANK. I'm sure he does, or he wouldn't have written it. (MILLIE *enters up* C. *with a tray of supper things. She puts the tray on the sideboard. She puts table napkins, mats and bread on the table.* ANDREW *turns and looks out of the window.*)

MILLIE. Hullo, Frank. I'm glad you're in time. Lend me a cigarette. I've been gasping for one for an hour. (FRANK *moves up* L. *of the table* C. *and once more extends his case.* MILLIE *takes a cigarette.*)

FRANK. Your husband has just had a very nice present.

MILLIE. Oh? Who from?

FRANK. Taplow. (*He comes down* L. *of the table.*)

MILLIE (*coming down* R. *of the table; smiling*). Oh, Taplow. (FRANK *lights* MILLIE's *cigarette.*)

ANDREW (*moving above the desk to the chair* R. *of it*). He bought it with his own pocket-money, Millie, and wrote a very charming inscription inside.

FRANK. "God looks kindly upon a gracious master."

ANDREW. No—not gracious—gentle, I think. "ton kratownta malthecose"—yes, I think gentle is the better translation. I would rather have had this present, I think, than almost anything I can think of. (*There is a pause.* MILLIE *laughs suddenly.*)

MILLIE (*holding out her hand*). Let's see it. The artful little beast. (ANDREW *hands the book across to* MILLIE. MILLIE *opens it.*)

FRANK (*urgently*). Millie. (MILLIE *looks at* ANDREW.)

ANDREW. Artful? (MILLIE *looks at* FRANK). Why artful? (FRANK *stares meaningly at* MILLIE. MILLIE *looks at* ANDREW). Why artful, Millie? (MILLIE *laughs again, quite lightly.*)

MILLIE. My dear, because I came into this room this afternoon to find him giving an imitation of you to Frank here. Obviously he was scared stiff I was going to tell you, and you'd ditch his remove or something. I don't blame him for trying a few bobs' worth of appeasement.

(She gives the book to ANDREW, *then moves up* R. *of the table to the sideboard, where she stubs out her cigarette, picks up some cutlery and starts to lay the table.* ANDREW *stands quite still, looking down at the book.)*

ANDREW *(after a pause; nodding).* I see. *(He puts the book gently on the desk, picks up the bottle of medicine and moves up* L. *of the table to the door up* C.)

MILLIE. Where are you going, dear? Dinner's nearly ready.

ANDREW *(opening the door).* Only to my room for a moment. I won't be long.

MILLIE. You've just had a dose of that, dear. I shouldn't have another, if I were you.

ANDREW. I am allowed two at a time.

MILLIE. Well, see it is two and no more, won't you? *(*ANDREW *meets her eye for a moment, then goes out quietly.* MILLIE *moves to* L. *of the table and lays the last knife and fork. She looks at* FRANK *with an expression half defiant and half ashamed.)*

FRANK *(with a note of real repulsion in his voice).* Millie! My God! How could you?

MILLIE. Well, why not? *(She crosses above the table and comes down* L. *of the settee).* Why should he be allowed his comforting little illusions? I'm not.

FRANK *(advancing on her).* Listen. You're to go to his room now and tell him that was a lie.

MILLIE. Certainly not. It wasn't a lie.

FRANK. If you don't, I will.

MILLIE. I shouldn't, if I were you. It'll only make things worse. He won't believe you.

FRANK *(moving up* R. *of the table* C.). We'll see about that.

MILLIE. Go ahead. See what happens. He knows I don't lie to him. He knows what I told him was the truth, and he won't like your sympathy. He'll think you're making fun of him, like Taplow. *(*FRANK *hesitates, then comes* *slowly down* C. *again.* MILLIE *watches him, a little frightened.*)

FRANK (*after a pause*). We're finished, Millie—you and I.

MILLIE (*laughing*). Frank, really! Don't be hysterical.

FRANK. I'm not. I mean it.

MILLIE (*lightly*). Oh yes, you mean it. Of course you mean it. Now just sit down, dear, and relax and forget all about artful little boys and their five bob presents, and talk to me. (*She pulls at his coat.*)

FRANK (*pulling away*). Forget? If I live to be a hundred I shall never forget that little glimpse you've just given me of yourself.

MILLIE. Frank—you're making a frightening mountain out of an absurd little molehill.

FRANK. Of course, but the mountain I'm making in my imagination is so frightening that I'd rather try to forget both it and the repulsive little molehill that gave it birth. But as I know I never can, I tell you, Millie—from this moment you and I are finished.

MILLIE (*quietly*). You can't scare me, Frank. (*She turns away towards the fireplace*). I know that's what you're trying to do, but you can't do it.

FRANK (*quietly*). I'm not trying to scare you, Millie. I'm telling you the simple truth. I'm not coming to Bradford. (*There is a pause.*)

MILLIE (*turning to face* FRANK; *with an attempt at bravado*). All right, my dear, if that's the way you feel about it. Don't come to Bradford.

FRANK. Right. Now I think you ought to go to your room and look after Andrew. (*He crosses towards the door up* L.). I'm leaving.

MILLIE (*following* FRANK). What is this? Frank, I don't understand, really I don't. What have I done?

FRANK. I think you know what you've done, Millie. Go and look after Andrew.

MILLIE (*moving to the* L. *end of the settee*). Andrew? Why this sudden concern for Andrew?

FRANK. Because I think he's just been about as badly hurt as a human being can be; and as he's a sick man and in a rather hysterical state it might be a good plan to go and see how he is.

MILLIE (*scornfully*). Hurt? Andrew hurt? You can't hurt Andrew. He's dead.

FRANK (*moving to* R. *of* MILLIE). Why do you hate him so much, Millie?

MILLIE. Because he keeps me from you.

FRANK. That isn't true.

MILLIE. Because he's not a man at all.

FRANK. He's a human being.

MILLIE. You've got a fine right to be so noble about him, after deceiving him for six months.

FRANK. Twice in six months—at your urgent invitation. (MILLIE *slaps his face, in a violent paroxysm of rage*). Thank you for that. I deserved it. (*He crosses to the chair* R. *of the desk*). I deserve a lot worse than that, too.

MILLIE (*running to him*). Frank, forgive me—I didn't mean it.

FRANK (*quietly*). You'd better have the truth, Millie, it had to come some time. (*He turns to face* MILLIE). I've never loved you. I've never told you I loved you.

MILLIE. I know, Frank, I know. (*She backs away slightly*). I've always accepted that.

FRANK. You asked me just now if I was running away from you. Well, I was.

MILLIE. I knew that, too.

FRANK. But I was coming to Bradford. It was going to be the very last time I was ever going to see you and at Bradford I would have told you that.

MILLIE. You wouldn't. You wouldn't. You've tried to tell me that so often before—(*she crosses to the fireplace*) and I've always stopped you somehow—somehow. I would have stopped you again.

FRANK (*quietly*). I don't think so, Millie. Not this time.

MILLIE (*crossing to* R. *of the table* C.). Frank, I don't care what humiliations you heap on me. I know you don't give two hoots for me as a person. I've always known that. I've never minded so long as you cared for me as a woman. And you do, Frank. You do. You do, don't you? (FRANK *is silent. He crosses slowly to the fireplace*). It'll be all right at Bradford, you see. It'll be all right, there.

FRANK. I'm not coming to Bradford, Millie. (*The door up* C. *opens slowly and* ANDREW *enters. He is carrying the bottle of medicine. He hands it to* MILLIE *and passes on crossing down* L. *below the desk.* MILLIE *holds the bottle up to the light.*)

ANDREW (*gently*). You should know me well enough by now, my dear, to realize how unlikely it is that I should ever take an overdose. (MILLIE, *without a word, puts the bottle on the sideboard and goes out up* C. AN-DREW *goes to the cupboard down* L. *and takes out the sherry and one glass.*)

FRANK. I'm not staying to dinner, I'm afraid.

ANDREW. Indeed? I'm sorry to hear that. You'll have a glass of sherry?

FRANK. No, thank you.

ANDREW. You will forgive me if I do.

FRANK. Of course. Perhaps I'll change my mind. (*He crosses to* C. ANDREW *takes out a second glass and fills both of them*). About Taplow . . .

ANDREW. Oh yes?

FRANK. It *is* perfectly true that he was imitating you. I, of course, was mostly to blame in that, and I'm very sorry.

ANDREW. That is perfectly all right. Was it a good imitation?

FRANK. No.

ANDREW. I expect it was. Boys are often very clever mimics.

FRANK. We talked about you, of course, before that. (*He moves in to* R. *of the desk*). He said—you probably won't believe this, but I thought I ought to tell you—he said he liked you very much. (ANDREW *smiles slightly*.)

ANDREW. Indeed? (*He drinks.*)

FRANK. I can remember very clearly his exact words. He said: "He doesn't seem to like people to like him—but in spite of that, I do—very much." (*Lightly*). So you see it looks after all as if the book might not have been a mere question of—appeasement.

ANDREW. The book? (*He picks it up*). Dear me! What a lot of fuss about a little book—and a not very good little book at that. (*He drops it on the desk.*)

FRANK. I would like you to believe me.

ANDREW. Possibly you would, my dear Hunter; but I can assure you I am not particularly concerned about Taplow's views of my character: or about yours either, if it comes to that.

FRANK (*hopelessly*). I think you should keep that book all the same. You may find it'll mean something to you after all.

ANDREW (*turning to the cupboard and pouring himself another sherry*). Exactly. It will mean a perpetual reminder to myself of the story with which Taplow is at this very moment regaling his friends in the House. "I gave the Crock a book, to buy him off, and he blubbed. The Crock blubbed. I tell you I was there. I saw it. The Crock blubbed." My mimicry is not as good as his, I fear. Forgive me. (*He moves up* L. *of the desk*). And now let us leave this idiotic subject and talk of more pleasant things. Do you like this sherry? I got it on my last visit to London.

FRANK. If Taplow ever breathes a word of that story to anyone at all, I'll murder him. But he won't. And if you think I will you greatly underestimate my character as well as his. (*He drains his glass and puts it on the desk. He moves to the door up* L. ANDREW *comes down* L., *puts his glass on the cupboard, and stands facing down stage*). Good-bye.

ANDREW. Are you leaving so soon? Good-bye, my dear fellow. (FRANK *stops. He takes out his cigarette case and places it on the* L. *end of the table* C.)

FRANK. As this is the last time I shall probably ever see you, I'm going to offer you a word of advice.

ANDREW (*politely*). I shall be glad to listen to it.

FRANK. Leave your wife. (*There is a pause.* ANDREW *looks out of the window.*)

ANDREW. So that you may the more easily carry on your intrigue with her?

FRANK (*moving in to the upstage end of the desk*). How long have you known that?

ANDREW. Since it first began.

FRANK. How did you find out?

ANDREW. By information.

FRANK. By whose information?

ANDREW. By someone's whose word I could hardly discredit. (*There is a pause.*)

FRANK (*slowly, with repulsion*). No! That's too horrible to think of.

ANDREW (*turning to* FRANK). Nothing is ever too horrible to think of, Hunter. It is simply a question of facing facts.

FRANK. She might have told you a lie. Have you faced that fact?

ANDREW. She never tells me a lie. In twenty years she has never told me a lie. Only the truth.

FRANK. This was a lie.

ANDREW (*moving up* L. *of* FRANK). No, my dear Hunter. Do you wish me to quote you dates?

FRANK (*still unable to believe it*). And she told you six months ago?

ANDREW (*moving down* L.). Isn't it seven?

FRANK (*savagely*). Then why have you allowed me inside your home? Why haven't you done something—reported me to the governors—anything—made a scene, knocked me down?

ANDREW. Knocked you down?

FRANK. You didn't have to invite me to dinner.

ANDREW. My dear Hunter, if, over the last twenty years, I had allowed such petty considerations to influence my choice of dinner guests I would have found it increasingly hard to remember which master to invite and which to refuse. You see, Hunter, you mustn't flatter yourself you are the first. My information is a good deal better than yours, you understand. It's authentic. (*There is a pause.*)

FRANK. She's evil.

ANDREW. That's hardly a kindly epithet to apply to a lady whom, I gather, you have asked to marry.

FRANK. Did she tell you that?

ANDREW. She's a dutiful wife. She tells me everything.

FRANK. That, at least, was a lie.

ANDREW. She never lies.

FRANK (*leaning on the desk*). That was a lie. Do you want the truth? Can you bear the truth?

ANDREW. I can bear anything. (*He crosses to the fireplace.*)

FRANK (*turning to face* ANDREW). What I did I did cold-bloodedly out of weakness and ignorance and crass stupidity. I'm bitterly, bitterly ashamed of myself, but, in a sense, I'm glad you know (*he moves* C.) though I'd rather a thousand times that you'd heard it from me than from your wife. I won't ask you to forgive me. I can only tell you, with complete truth, that the only emotion she has ever succeeded in arousing in me she aroused in me for the first time ten minutes ago—an intense and passionate disgust.

ANDREW. What a delightfully chivalrous statement.

FRANK (*moving below the settee*). Forget chivalry, Crock, for God's sake. Forget all your fine mosaic scruples. You must leave her—it's your only chance.

ANDREW. She's my wife, Hunter. You seem to forget that. As long as she wishes to remain my wife, she may.

FRANK. She's out to kill you.

ANDREW. My dear Hunter, if that was indeed her purpose, you should know by now that she fulfilled it long ago.

FRANK. Why won't you leave her?

ANDREW. Because I wouldn't wish to add another grave wrong to one I have already done her.

FRANK. What wrong have you done her?

ANDREW. To marry her. (*There is a pause.* FRANK *stares at him in silence*). You see, my dear Hunter, she is really quite as much to be pitied as I. We are both of us interesting subjects for your microscope. (*He sits on the fender*). Both of us needing from the other something that would make life supportable for us, and neither of us able to give it. Two kinds of love. Hers and mine. Worlds apart as I know now, though when I married her I didn't think they were incompatible. In those days I hadn't thought that her kind of love—the love she requires and which I was unable to give her—was so important that its absence would drive out the other kind of love—the kind of love that I require and which I thought, in my folly, was by far the greater part of love. (*He rises*). I may have been, you see, Hunter, a brilliant classical scholar, but I was woefully ignorant of the facts of life. I know better now, of course. I know that in both of us, the love that we should have borne each other has turned to bitter hatred. That's all the problem is. Not a very unusual one, I venture to think—nor nearly as tragic as you seem to imagine. Merely the problem of an unsatisfied wife and a henpecked husband. You'll find it all over the world. It is usually, I believe, a subject for farce. (*He turns to the mantelpiece and adjusts the hands of the clock*). And now, if you have to leave us, my dear fellow, please don't let me detain you any longer. (FRANK *makes no move to go.*)

FRANK. Don't go to Bradford. Stay here, until you take up your new job.

ANDREW. I think I've already told you I'm not interested in your advice.

FRANK. Leave her. It's the only way.

ANDREW (*violently*). Will you please go!

FRANK. All right. I'd just like you to say good-bye to me, properly, though. Will you? I shan't see you again. I know you don't want my pity, but, I would like to be of some help. (ANDREW *turns and faces* FRANK.)

ANDREW. If you think, by this expression of kindness, Hunter, that you can get me to repeat the shameful exhibition of emotion I made to Taplow a moment ago, I must tell you that you have no chance. My hysteria over that book just now was no more than a sort of reflex action of the spirit. The muscular twitchings of a corpse. It can never happen again.

FRANK. A corpse can be revived.

ANDREW. I don't believe in miracles.

FRANK. Don't you? Funnily enough, as a scientist, I do.

ANDREW (*turning to the fireplace*). Your faith would be touching, if I were capable of being touched by it.

FRANK. You are, I think. (*He moves behind* ANDREW. *After a pause*). I'd like to come and visit you at this crammer's.

ANDREW. That is an absurd suggestion.

FRANK. I suppose it is rather, but all the same I'd like to do it. May I?

ANDREW. Of course not.

FRANK (*sitting on the settee*). Your term begins on the first of September, doesn't it? (*He takes out a pocket diary.*)

ANDREW. I tell you the idea is quite childish.

FRANK. I could come about the second week.

ANDREW. You would be bored to death. So, probably, would I.

FRANK (*glancing at his diary*). Let's say Monday the twelfth, then.

ANDREW (*turning to face* FRANK, *his hands beginning to tremble*). Say anything you like, only please go. Please go, Hunter.

FRANK (*writing in his book and not looking at* ANDREW). That's fixed, then. Monday, September the twelfth. Will you remember that?

ANDREW (*after a pause; with difficulty*). I suppose I'm at least as likely to remember it as you are.

FRANK. That's fixed, then. (*He rises, slips the book into his pocket and puts out his hand*). Good bye, until then. (*He moves in to* ANDREW. ANDREW *hesitates, then shakes his hand.*)

ANDREW. Good-bye.

FRANK. May I go out through your garden? (*He crosses to* C.)

ANDREW (*nodding*). Of course.

FRANK. I'm off to have a quick word with Taplow. By the way, may I take him a message from you?

ANDREW. What message?

FRANK. Has he or has he not got his remove?

ANDREW. He has.

FRANK. May I tell him?

ANDREW. It is highly irregular. Yes, you may.

FRANK. Good. (*He turns to go, then turns back*). Oh, by

the way, I'd better have the address of that crammer's. *He moves below the settee, takes out his diary, and points his pencil, ready to write.* MILLIE *enters up* C. *She carries a casserole on three plates.*)

MILLIE (*coming above the table* C.). Dinner's ready. You're staying, Frank, aren't you? (*She puts the casserole and plates on the table.*)

FRANK (*politely*). No. I'm afraid not. (*To* ANDREW). What's that address?

ANDREW (*after great hesitation*). The Old Deanery, Malcombe, Dorset.

FRANK. I'll write to you and you can let me know about trains. Good-bye. (*To* MILLIE). Good-bye. (*He crosses to the door up* L. *and goes out.* MILLIE *is silent for a moment. Then she laughs.*)

MILLIE. That's a laugh, I must say.

ANDREW. What's a laugh, my dear?

MILLIE. You inviting him to stay with you.

ANDREW. I didn't. He suggested it.

MILLIE (*moving to the* L. *end of the settee*). He's coming to Bradford.

ANDREW. Yes. I remember your telling me so.

MILLIE. He's coming to Bradford. He's not going to you.

ANDREW. The likeliest contingency is, that he's not going to either of us.

MILLIE. He's coming to Bradford.

ANDREW. I expect so. Oh, by the way, I'm not. I shall be staying here until I go to Dorset.

MILLIE (*indifferently*). Suit yourself. What makes you think I'll join you there?

ANDREW. I don't.

MILLIE. You needn't expect me.

ANDREW. I don't think either of us has the right to expect anything further from the other. (*The telephone rings*). Excuse me. (*He moves to the table down* R. *and lifts the receiver*). Hullo . . . (*While he is speaking* MILLIE *crosses to* L. *of the table* C. *About to sit, she sees the cigarette case. She picks it up, fingers it for a moment, and finally drops it into her pocket*). Yes, Headmaster . . . The time-table? . . . It's perfectly simple. The middle fourth B division will take a ten-minute break on Tuesdays and a fifteen-minute break on alternate Wednesdays; while exactly the reverse procedure will apply to the lower Shell, C division. I thought I had sufficiently explained that on my chart . . . Oh, I see . . . Thank you, that is very good of you . . . Yes. I think you will find it will work out quite satisfactorily . . . Oh by the way, Headmaster. I have changed my mind about the prize-giving ceremony. I intend to speak after, instead of before, Fletcher, as is my privilege . . . Yes, I quite understand, but I am now seeing the matter in a different light . . . I know, but I am of opinion that occasionally an anti-climax can be surprisingly effective. Good-bye. (*He replaces the receiver, crosses to* R. *of the table* C., *and sits*). Come along, my dear. We mustn't let our dinner get cold. (*He unrolls his table napkin.* MILLIE *sits* L. *of the table and unrolls her table napkin.* ANDREW *offers her the bread. She ignores it. He takes a piece. She removes the lid of the casserole as—*

THE CURTAIN FALLS.

27 WAGONS FULL OF COTTON

by Tennessee Williams

CHARACTERS

JAKE MEIGHAN, *a cotton-gin owner.*
FLORA MEIGHAN, *his wife.*
SILVA VICARRO, *superintendent of the Syndicate Plantation.*

All of the action takes place on the front porch of the Meighans' residence near Blue Mountain, Mississippi.

27 WAGONS FULL OF COTTON

SCENE: *The front porch of the Meighans' cottage near Blue Mountain, Mississippi. The porch is narrow and rises into a single narrow gable. There are spindling white pillars on either side supporting the porch roof and a door of Gothic design and two Gothic windows on either side of it. The peaked door has an oval of richly stained glass, azure, crimson, emerald and gold. At the windows are fluffy white curtains gathered coquettishly in the middle by baby-blue satin bows. The effect is not unlike a doll's house.*

SCENE I

It is early evening and there is a faint rosy dusk in the sky. Shortly after the curtain rises, JAKE MEIGHAN, *a fat man of sixty, scrambles out the front door and races around the corner of the house carrying a gallon can of coal-oil. A dog barks at him. A car is heard starting and receding rapidly in the distance. A moment later* FLORA *calls from inside the house.*

FLORA. Jake! I've lost m' white kid pursel (*closer to the door*) Jake? Look'n see 'f uh laid it on th' swing. (*There is a pause*). Guess I could've left it in th' Chevy? (*She comes up to screen door*). Jake. Look'n see if uh left it in th' Chevy. Jake? (*She steps outside in the fading rosy dusk. She switches on the porch light and stares about, slapping at gnats attracted by the light. Locusts provide the only answering voice.* FLORA *gives a long nasal call*). Ja-ay—a-a-ake! (*A cow moos in the distance with the same inflection. There is a muffled explosion somewhere about half a mile away. A strange flickering glow appears, the reflection of a burst of flame. Distant voices are heard exclaiming.*)

VOICES (*shrill, cackling like hens*).
You heah that noise?

Yeah! Sound like a bomb went off!

Oh, look!

Why, it's a fire!

Where's it at? You tell?

Th' Syndicate Plantation!

Oh, my God! Let's go! (*A fire whistle sounds in the distance.*)

Henry! Start th' car! You all wanta go with us?

Yeah, we'll be right out!

Hurry, honey! (*A car can be heard starting up.*)

Be right there!

Well, hurry.

VOICE (*just across the dirt road*). Missus Meighan?

FLORA. Ye-ah?

VOICE. Ahn't you goin' th' fire?

FLORA. I wish I could but Jake's gone off in th' Chevy.

VOICE. Come awn an' go with us, honey!

FLORA. Oh, I cain't an' leave th' house wide open! Jake's gone off with th' keys. What do you all think it is on fire?

VOICE. Th' Syndicate Plantation!

FLORA. Th' Syndicate Plan-*ta*-tion? (*The car starts off and recedes*). Oh, my Go-od! (*She climbs laboriously back up on the porch and sits on the swing which faces the front. She speaks tragically to herself*). Nobody! Nobody! Never! Never! Nobody! (*Locusts can be heard. A car is heard approaching and stopping at a distance back of house. After a moment Jake ambles casually up around the side of the house.*)

FLORA (*in a petulant babyish tone*). Well!

JAKE. Whatsamatter, Baby?

FLORA. I never known a human being could be that mean an' thoughtless!

JAKE. Aw, now, that's a mighty broad statement fo' you to make, Mrs. Meighan. What's the complaint this time?

FLORA. Just flew out of the house without even sayin' a word!

JAKE. What's so bad about that?

FLORA. I told you I had a headache comin' on an' had to have a dope, there wassen a single bottle lef' in th' house, an' you said, Yeah, get into yuh things 'n' we'll drive in town right away! So I get into m' things an' I cain't find m' white kid purse. Then I remember I left it on th' front seat of th' Chevy. I come out here t' git it. Where are you? Gone off! Without a word! Then there's a big explosion! Feel my heart!

JAKE. Feel my baby's heart? (*He puts a hand on her huge bosom.*)

FLORA. Yeah, just you feel it, poundin' like a hammer! How'd I know what happened? You not here, just disappeared somewhere!

JAKE (*sharply*). Shut up! (*He pushes her head roughly.*)

FLORA. Jake! What did you do that fo'?

JAKE. I don't like how you holler! Holler ev'ry thing you say!

FLORA. What's the matter with you?

JAKE. Nothing's the matter with me.

FLORA. Well, why did you go off?

JAKE. I didn' go off!

FLORA. You certainly *did* go off! Try an' tell me that you never went off when I just now seen an' heard you drivin' back in th' car? What uh you take me faw? No sense a-tall?

JAKE. If you got sense you keep your big mouth shut!

FLORA. Don't talk to me like that!

JAKE. Come on inside.

FLORA. I won't. Selfish an' inconsiderate, that's what you are! I told you at supper, There's not a bottle of Coca-Cola left on th' place. You said, Okay, right after supper we'll drive on over to th' White Star drugstore an' lay in a good supply. When I come out of th' house—

JAKE (*he stands in front of her and grips her neck with both hands*). Look here! Listen to what I tell you!

FLORA. *Jake!*

JAKE. Shhh! Just listen, Baby.

FLORA. Lemme go! G'damn you, le' go my throat!

JAKE. Jus' try an' concentrate on what I tell yuh!

FLORA. Tell me what?

JAKE. I ain't been off th' po'ch.

FLORA. Huh!

JAKE. I ain't been off th' front po'ch! Not since supper! Understand that, now?

FLORA. Jake, honey, you've gone out of you' mind!

JAKE. Maybe so. Never you mind. Just get that straight an' keep it in your haid. I ain't been off the porch of this house since supper.

FLORA. But you sure as God *was* off it! (*He twists her wrist*). Ouuuu! Stop it, stop it, stop it!

JAKE. Where have I been since supper?

FLORA. Here, here! On th' porch! Fo' God's sake, quit that twistin'!

JAKE. Where have I been?

FLORA. Porch! Porch! Here!

JAKE. Doin' what?

FLORA. *Jake!*

JAKE. Doin' what?

FLORA. Lemme go! Christ, Jake! Let loose! Quit twisting, you'll break my wrist!

JAKE (*laughing between his teeth*). Doin' what? What doin'? Since supper?

FLORA (*crying out*). How in hell do I know!

JAKE. 'Cause you was right here with me, all the time, for every second! You an' me, sweetheart, was sittin' here together on th' swing, just swingin' back an' forth every minute since supper! You got that in your haid good now?

FLORA (*whimpering*). Le'-go!

JAKE. Got it? In your haid good now?

FLORA. Yeh, yeh, yeh—leggo!

JAKE. What was I doin', then?

FLORA. Swinging! For Christ's sake—swingin'! (*He releases her. She whimpers and rubs her wrist but the impression is that the experience was not without pleasure for both parties. She groans and whimpers. He grips her loose curls in his hand and bends her head back. He plants a long wet kiss on her mouth.*)

FLORA (*whimpering*). Mmmm-hmmm! Mmmm! Mmmm!

JAKE (*huskily*). Tha's my swee' baby girl.

FLORA. Mmmmm! Hurt! Hurt!

JAKE. Hurt?

FLORA. Mmmm! Hurt!

JAKE. Kiss?

FLORA. Mmmm!

JAKE. Good?

FLORA. Mmmm . . .

JAKE. Good! Make little room.

FLORA. Too hot!

JAKE. Go on, make little room.

FLORA. Mmmmm . . .

JAKE. Cross patch?

FLORA. Mmmmmm.

JAKE. Whose baby? Big? Sweet?

FLORA. Mmmmm! Hurt!

JAKE. Kiss! (*He lifts her wrist to his lips and makes gobbling sounds.*)

FLORA (*giggling*). Stop! Silly! Mmmm!

JAKE. What would I do if you was a big piece of cake?

FLORA. Silly.

JAKE. Gobble! Gobble!

FLORA. Oh, you—

JAKE. What would I do if you was angel food cake? Big white piece with lots of nice thick icin'?

FLORA (*giggling*). Quit!

JAKE. Gobble, gobble, gobble!

FLORA (*squealing*). Jake!

JAKE. Huh?

FLORA. You *tick*-le!

JAKE. Answer little question!

FLORA. Wh-at?

JAKE. Where I been since supper?

FLORA. Off in the Chevy! (*He instantly seizes the wrist again. She shrieks.*)

JAKE. Where've I been since supper?

FLORA. Po'ch! Swing!

JAKE. Doin' what?

FLORA. *Swingin'!* Oh, Christ, Jake, let loose!

JAKE. Hurt?

FLORA. Mmmmm . . .

JAKE. Good?

FLORA (*whimpering*). Mmmmm . . .

JAKE. Now you know where I been an' what I been doin' since supper?

FLORA. Yeah . . .

JAKE. Case anybody should ask?

FLORA. Who's going to ast?

JAKE. Never mind who's goin' t' ast, just you know the answers! Uh-huh?

FLORA. Uh-huh. (*Lisping babyishly*). This is where you been. Settin' on th' swing since we had supper. Swingin' —back an' fo'th—back an' fo'th. . . . You didn' go off in th' Chevy. (*Slowly*). An' you was awf'ly surprised w'en th' syndicate fire broke out! (JAKE *slaps her*). Jake!

JAKE. Everything you said is awright. But don't you get ideas.

FLORA. Ideas?

JAKE. A woman like you's not made to have ideas. Made to be hugged an' squeezed!

FLORA (*babyishly*). Mmmm. . . .

JAKE. But not for ideas. So don't you have ideas. (*He rises*). Go out an' get in th' Chevy.

FLORA. *We goin' to th' fire?*

JAKE. No. We ain' goin' no fire. We goin' in town an' get us a case a dopes because we're hot an' thirsty.

FLORA (*vaguely, as she rises*). I lost m' white—kid—purse . . .

JAKE. It's on the seat of th' Chevy whe' you left it.

FLORA. Whe' *you* goin'?

JAKE. I'm goin' in t' th' toilet. I'll be right out. (*He goes inside, letting the screen door slam.* FLORA *shuffles to the edge of the steps and stands there with a slight idiotic smile. She begins to descend, letting herself down each time with the same foot, like a child just learning to walk. She stops at the bottom of the steps and stares at the sky, vacantly and raptly, her fingers closing gently around the bruised wrist.* JAKE *can be heard singing inside.*)

> 'My baby don' care fo' rings
> or other expensive things—
> My baby just cares—fo'—me!'

CURTAIN

SCENE II

It is just after noon. The sky is the color of the satin bows on the window curtains—a translucent, innocent blue. Heat devils are shimmering over the flat Delta country and the peaked white front of the house is like a shrill exclamation. JAKE'S *gin is busy; heard like a steady pulse across the road. A delicate lint of cotton is drifting about in the atmosphere.*

JAKE *appears, a large and purposeful man with arms like hams covered with a fuzz of fine blond hair. He is followed by* SILVA VICARRO *who is the Superintendent of the Syndicate Plantation where the fire occurred last night.* VICARRO *is a rather small and wiry man of dark Latin looks and nature. He wears whipcord breeches, laced boots, and a white undershirt. He has a Roman Catholic medallion on a chain about his neck.*

JAKE (*with the good-natured condescension of a very large man for a small one*). Well, suh, all I got to say is you're a mighty lucky little fellow.

VICARRO. Lucky? In what way?

JAKE. That I can take on a job like this right now! Twenty-seven wagons full of cotton's a pretty big piece of bus'-ness, Mr. Vicarro. (*Stopping at the steps*). Baby! (*He bites off a piece of tobacco plug*). What's yuh firs' name?

VICARRO. Silva.

JAKE. How do you spell it?

VICARRO. S-I-L-V-A.

JAKE. Silva! Like a silver lining! Ev'ry cloud has got a silver lining. What does that come from? The Bible?

VICARRO (*sitting on the steps*). No. The Mother Goose Book.

JAKE. Well, suh, you sure are lucky that I can do it. If I'd been busy like I was two weeks ago I would've turned it down. *BABY! COME OUT HERE A MINUTE!* (*There is a vague response from inside.*)

VICARRO. Lucky. Very lucky. (*He lights a cigarette.* FLORA *pushes open the screen door and comes out. She has on her watermelon pink silk dress and is clutching against*

*her body the big white kid purse with her initials on it
in big nickel plate.*)

JAKE (*proudly*). Mr. Vicarro—I want you to meet Mrs.
Meighan. Baby, this is a very down-at-the-mouth young
fellow I want you to cheer up fo' me. He thinks he's out
of luck because his cotton gin burnt down. He's got
twenty-seven wagons full of cotton to be ginned out on a
hurry-up order from his most impo'tant customers in
Mobile. Well, suh, I said to him, Mr. Vicarro, you're to
be congratulated—not because it burnt down, but because I happen to be in a situation to take the business
over. Now you tell him just how lucky he is!

FLORA (*nervously*). Well, I guess he don't see how it was
lucky to have his gin burned down.

VICARRO (*acidly*). No, ma'am.

JAKE (*quickly*). Mr. Vicarro. Some fellows marry a girl
when she's little an' tiny. They like a small figure. See?
Then, when the girl gets comfo'tably settled down—what
does she do? Puts on flesh—of cou'se!

FLORA (*bashfully*). Jake!

JAKE. Now then! How do they react? Accept it as a matter of cou'se, as something which 'as been ordained by
nature? Nope! No, suh, not a bit! They sta't to feeling
abused. They think that fate must have a grudge
against them because the little woman is not so little as
she used to be. Because she's gone an' put on a matronly
figure. Well, suh, that's at the root of a lot of domestic
trouble. However, Mr. Vicarro, I never made that mistake. When I fell in love with this baby-doll I've got
here, she was just the same size then that you see her
today.

FLORA (*crossing shyly to porch rail*). Jake . . .

JAKE (*grinning*). A woman not large but tremendous!
That's how I liked her—tremendous! I told her right off,
when I slipped th' ring on her finger, one Satiddy night
in a boathouse on Moon Lake—I said to her, Honey, if

you take off one single pound of that body—I'm going to quit yuh! I'm going to quit yuh, I said, the minute I notice you've started to take off weight!

FLORA. Aw, Jake—please!

JAKE. I don't want nothing little, not in a woman. I'm not after nothing *petite*, as the Frenchmen call it. This is what I wanted—and what I *got!* Look at her, Mr. Vicarro. Look at her blush! (*He grips the back of* FLORA's *neck and tries to turn her around.*)

FLORA. Aw, quit, Jake! Quit, will yuh?

JAKE. See what a doll she is? (FLORA *turns suddenly and spanks him with the kid purse. He cackles and runs down the steps. At the corner of the house, he stops and turns*). Baby, you keep Mr. Vicarro comfo'table while I'm ginnin' out that twenty-seven wagons full of cotton. Th' good-neighbor policy, Mr. Vicarro. You do me a good turn an' I'll do you a good one! Be see'n' yuh! So long, Baby! (*He walks away with an energetic stride.*)

VICARRO. The good-neighbor policy! (*He sits on the porch steps.*)

FLORA (*sitting on the swing*). Izzen he out-ray-juss! (*She laughs foolishly and puts the purse in her lap.* VICARRO *stares gloomily across the dancing brilliance of the fields. His lip sticks out like a pouting child's. A rooster crows in the distance.*)

FLORA. I would'n' dare to expose myself like that.

VICARRO. Expose? To what?

FLORA. The sun. I take a terrible burn. I'll never forget the burn I took one time. It was on Moon Lake one Sunday before I was married. I never did like t' go fishin' but this young fellow, one of the Peterson boys, insisted that we go fishin'. Well, he didn't catch nothin' but jus' kep' fishin' an' fishin' an' I set there in th' boat with all that hot sun on me. I said, Stay under the willows. But he would'n' lissen to me, an' sure enough I took such an awful burn I had t' sleep on m' stummick th' nex' three nights.

VICARRO (*absently*). What did you say? You got sunburned?

FLORA. Yes. One time on Moon Lake.

VICARRO. That's too bad. You got over it all right?

FLORA. Oh, yes. Finally. Yes.

VICARRO. That must've been pretty bad.

FLORA. I fell in the lake once, too. Also with one of the Peterson boys. On another fishing trip. That was a wild bunch of boys, those Peterson boys. I never went out with 'em but something happened which made me wish I hadn't. One time, sunburned. One time, nearly drowned. One time—poison ivy! Well, lookin' back on it, now, we had a good deal of fun in spite of it, though.

VICARRO. The good-neighbor policy, huh? (*He slaps his boot with the riding crop. Then he rises from steps.*)

FLORA. You might as well come up on th' po'ch an' make you'self as comfo'table as you can.

VICARRO. Uh-huh.

FLORA. I'm not much good at—makin' conversation.

VICARRO (*finally noticing her*). Now don't you bother to make conversation for my benefit, Mrs. Meighan. I'm the type that prefers a quiet understanding. (FLORA *laughs uncertainly*). One thing I always notice about you ladies . . .

FLORA. What's that, Mr. Vicarro?

VICARRO. You always have something in your hands—to hold onto. Now that kid purse . . .

FLORA. My purse?

VICARRO. You have no reason to keep that purse in your hands. You're certainly not afraid that I'm going to snatch it!

FLORA. Oh, God, no! I wassen afraid of that!

VICARRO. That wouldn't be the good-neighbor policy,

would it? But you hold onto that purse because it gives you something to get a grip on. Isn't that right?

FLORA. Yes. I always like to have something in my hands.

VICARRO. Sure you do. You feel what a lot of uncertain things there are. Gins burn down. The volunteer fire department don't have decent equipment. Nothing is any protection. The afternoon sun is hot. It's no protection. The trees are back of the house. They're no protection. The goods that dress is made of—is no protection. So what do you do, Mrs. Meighan? You pick up the white kid purse. It's solid. It's sure. It's certain. It's something to hold *on* to. You get what I mean?

FLORA. Yeah, I think I do.

VICARRO. It gives you a feeling of being attached to something. The mother protects the baby? No, no, no—the baby protects the mother! From being lost and empty and having nothing but lifeless things in her hands! Maybe you think there isn't much connection!

FLORA. You'll have to excuse me from thinking. I'm too lazy.

VICARRO. What's your name, Mrs. Meighan?

FLORA. Flora.

VICARRO. Mine is Silva. Something not gold but—Silva!

FLORA. Like a silver dollar?

VICARRO. No, like a silver dime! It's an Italian name. I'm a native of New Orleans.

FLORA. Then it's not sun-burn. You're natcherally dark.

VICARRO (*raising his undershirt from his belly*). Look at this!

FLORA. Mr. Vicarro!

VICARRO. Just as dark as my arm is!

FLORA. You don't have to show me! I'm not from Missouri!

VICARRO (*grinning*). Excuse me.

FLORA (*she laughs nervously*). Whew! I'm sorry to say we don't have a coke in the house. We meant to get a case

of cokes las' night, but what with all the excitement going on—

VICARRO. What excitement was that?

FLORA. Oh, the fire and all.

VICARRO (*lighting a cigarette*). I shouldn't think you all
would of been excited about the fire.

FLORA. A fire is always exciting. After a fire, dogs an' chickens don't sleep. I don't think our chickens got to sleep
all night.

VICARRO. No?

FLORA. They cackled an' fussed an' flopped around on the
roost—took on something awful! Myself, I couldn't sleep
neither. I jus' lay there an' sweated all night long.

VICARRO. On account of th' fire?

FLORA. An' the heat an' mosquitoes. And I was mad at
Jake.

VICARRO. Mad at Mr. Meighan? What about?

FLORA. Oh, he went off an' left me settin' here on this ole
po'ch last night without a Coca-Cola on the place.

VICARRO. Went off an' left you, did he?

FLORA. Yep. Right after supper. An' when he got back the
fire 'd already broke out an' instead of drivin' in to town
like he said, he decided to go an' take a look at your
burnt-down cotton gin. I got smoke in my eyes an' my
nose an' throat. It hurt my sinus an' I was in such a
wo'n out, nervous condition, it made me cry. I cried like
a baby. Finally took two teaspoons of paregoric. Enough
to put an elephant to sleep. But still I stayed awake an'
heard them chickens carryin' on out there!

VICARRO. It sounds like you passed a very uncomfortable
night.

FLORA. Sounds like? Well, it *was*.

VICARRO. So Mr. Meighan—you say—disappeared after supper? (*There is a pause while* FLORA *looks at him
blankly.*)

FLORA. Huh?

VICARRO. You say Mr. Meighan was out of the house for a while after supper? (*Something in his tone makes her aware of her indiscretion.*)

FLORA. Oh—uh—just for a moment.

VICARRO. Just for a moment, huh? How long a moment? (*He stares at her very hard.*)

FLORA. What are you driving at, Mr. Vicarro?

VICARRO. Driving at? Nothing.

FLORA. You're looking at me so funny.

VICARRO. He disappeared for a moment! Is that what he did? How long a moment did he disappear for? Can you remember, Mrs. Meighan?

FLORA. What difference does that make? What's it to you, anyhow?

VICARRO. Why should you mind me asking?

FLORA. You make this sound like I was on trial for something!

VICARRO. Don't you like to pretend like you're a witness?

FLORA. Witness of what, Mr. Vicarro?

VICARRO. Why—for instance—say—a case of arson!

FLORA (*wetting her lips*). Case of—? What is—arson?

VICARRO. The willful destruction of property by fire. (*He slaps his boots sharply with the riding crop.*)

FLORA (*startled*). Oh! (*She nervously fingers the purse*). Well, now, don't you go and be getting any—funny ideas.

VICARRO. Ideas about what, Mrs. Meighan?

FLORA. My husband's disappearin'—after supper. I can explain that.

VICARRO. Can you?

FLORA. Sure I can.

VICARRO. Good! How do you explain it? (*He stares at her. She looks down*). What's the matter? Can't you collect your thoughts, Mrs. Meighan?

FLORA. No, but—

VICARRO. Your mind's a blank on the subject?

FLORA. Look here, now— (*She squirms on the swing.*)

VICARRO. You find it impossible to remember just what your husband disappeared for after supper? You can't imagine what kind of errand it was that he went out on, can you?

FLORA. No! No, I can't!

VICARRO. But when he returned—let's see . . . The fire had just broken out at the Syndicate Plantation?

FLORA. Mr. Vicarro, I don't have the slightest idear what you could be driving at.

VICARRO. You're a very unsatisfactory witness, Mrs. Meighan.

FLORA. I never can think when people—stare straight at me.

VICARRO. Okay. I'll look away, then. (*He turns his back to her*). Now does that improve your memory any? Now are you able to concentrate on the question?

FLORA. Huh . . .

VICARRO. No? You're not? (*He turns around again, grinning evilly*). Well . . . shall we drop the subject?

FLORA. I sure do wish you would.

VICARRO. It's no use crying over a burnt-down gin. This world is built on the principle of tit for tat.

FLORA. What do you mean?

VICARRO. Nothing at all specific. Mind if I . . . ?

FLORA. What?

VICARRO. You want to move over a little an' make some room? (FLORA *edges aside on the swing. He sits down with her*). I like a swing. I've always liked to sit an' rock on a swing. Relaxes you . . . You relaxed?

FLORA. Sure.

VICARRO. No, you're not. Your nerves are all tied up.

FLORA. Well, you made me feel kind of nervous. All of them questions you ast me about the fire.

VICARRO. I didn' ask you questions about the fire. I only asked you about your husband's leaving the house after supper.

FLORA. I explained that to you.

VICARRO. Sure. That's right. You did. The good-neighbor policy. That was a lovely remark your husband made about the good-neighbor policy. I see what he means by that now.

FLORA. He was thinking about President Roosevelt's speech. We sat up an' lissened to it one night last week.

VICARRO. No, I think that he was talking about something closer to home, Mrs. Meighan. You do me a good turn and I'll do you one, that was the way that he put it. You have a piece of cotton on your face. Hold still—I'll pick it off. (*He delicately removes the lint*). There now.

FLORA (*nervously*). Thanks.

VICARRO. There's a lot of fine cotton lint floating round in the air.

FLORA. I know there is. It irritates my nose. I think it gets up in my sinus.

VICARRO. Well, you're a delicate woman.

FLORA. Delicate? Me? Oh, no. I'm too big for that.

VICARRO. Your size is part of your delicacy, Mrs. Meighan.

FLORA. How do you mean?

VICARRO. There's a lot of you, but every bit of you is delicate. Choice. Delectable, I might say.

FLORA. Huh?

VICARRO. I mean you're altogether lacking in any—coarseness. You're soft. Fine-fibered. And smooth.

FLORA. Our talk is certainly taking a personal turn.

VICARRO. Yes. You make me think of cotton.

FLORA. Huh?

VICARRO. Cotton!

FLORA. Well! Should I say thanks or something?

VICARRO. No, just smile, Mrs. Meighan. You have an attractive smile. Dimples!

FLORA. No . . .

VICARRO. Yes, you have! Smile, Mrs. Meighan! Come on—smile! (FLORA *averts her face, smiling helplessly*). There now. See? You've got them! (*He delicately touches one of the dimples.*)

FLORA. Please don't touch me. I don't like to be touched.

VICARRO. Then why do you giggle?

FLORA. Can't help it. You make me feel kind of hysterical, Mr. Vicarro. Mr. Vicarro—

VICARRO. Yes?

FLORA. I hope you don't think that Jake was mixed up in that fire. I swear to goodness he never left the front porch. I remember it perfeckly now. We just set here on the swing till the fire broke out then we drove in town.

VICARRO. To celebrate?

FLORA. No, no, no.

VICARRO. Twenty-seven wagons full of cotton's a pretty big piece of business to fall in your lap like a gift from the gods, Mrs. Meighan.

FLORA. I thought you said that we would drop the subjeck.

VICARRO. You brought it up that time.

FLORA. Well, please don't try to mix me up any more. I swear to goodness the fire had already broke out when he got back.

VICARRO. That's not what you told me a moment ago.

FLORA. You got me all twisted up. We went in town. The fire broke out an' we didn't know about it.

VICARRO. I thought you said it irritated your sinus.

FLORA. Oh, my God, you sure put words in my mouth. Maybe I'd better make us some lemonade.

VICARRO. Don't go to the trouble.

FLORA. I'll go in an' fix it direckly, but right at this moment I'm too weak to get up. I don't know why, but I can't hardly hold my eyes open. They keep falling shut. . . . I think it's a little too crowded, two on a swing. Will you do me a favor an' set back down over there?

VICARRO. Why do you want me to move?

FLORA. It makes too much body heat when we're crowded together.

VICARRO. One body can borrow coolness from another.

FLORA. I always heard that bodies borrowed heat.

VICARRO. Not in this case. I'm cool.

FLORA. You don't seem like it to me.

VICARRO. I'm just as cool as a cucumber. If you don't believe it, touch me.

FLORA. Where?

VICARRO. Anywhere.

FLORA (*rising with great effort*). Excuse me. I got to go in. (*He pulls her back down*). What did you do that for?

VICARRO. I don't want to be deprived of your company yet.

FLORA. Mr. Vicarro, you're getting awf'ly familiar.

VICARRO. Haven't you got any fun-loving spirit about you?

FLORA. This isn't fun.

VICARRO. Then why do you giggle?

FLORA. I'm ticklish! Quit switching me, will yuh?

VICARRO. I'm just shooing the flies off.

FLORA. Leave 'em be, then, please. They don't hurt nothin'.

VICARRO. I think you like to be switched.

FLORA. I don't. I wish you'd quit.

VICARRO. You'd like to be switched harder.

FLORA. No, I wouldn't.

VICARRO. That blue mark on your wrist—

FLORA. What about it?

VICARRO. I've got a suspicion.

FLORA. Of what?

VICARRO. It was twisted. By your husband.

FLORA. You're crazy.

VICARRO. Yes, it was. And you liked it.

FLORA. I certainly didn't. Would you mind moving your arm?

VICARRO. Don't be so skittish.

FLORA. Awright. I'll get up then.

VICARRO. Go on.

FLORA. I feel so weak.

VICARRO. Dizzy?

FLORA. A little bit. Yeah. My head's spinning round. I wish you would stop the swing.

VICARRO. It's not swinging much.

FLORA. But even a little's too much.

VICARRO. You're a delicate woman. A pretty big woman, too.

FLORA. So is America. Big.

VICARRO. That's a funny remark.

FLORA. Yeah. I don't know why I made it. My head's so buzzy.

VICARRO. Fuzzy?

FLORA. Fuzzy an'—buzzy . . . Is something on my arm?

VICARRO. No.

FLORA. Then what're you brushing?

VICARRO. Sweat off.

FLORA. Leave it alone.

VICARRO. Let me wipe it. (*He brushes her arm with a handkerchief.*)

FLORA (*laughing weakly*). No, please, don't. It feels funny.

VICARRO. How does it feel?

FLORA. It tickles me. All up an' down. You cut it out now. If you don't cut it out I'm going to call.

VICARRO. Call who?

FLORA. I'm going to call that nigger. The nigger that's cutting the grass across the road.

VICARRO. Go on. Call, then.

FLORA (*weakly*). Hey! Hey, boy!

VICARRO. Can't you call any louder?

FLORA. I feel so funny. What is the matter with me?

VICARRO. You're just relaxing. You're big. A big type of woman. I like you. Don't get so excited.

FLORA. I'm not, but you—

VICARRO. What am I doing?

FLORA. Suspicions. About my husband and ideas you have about me.

VICARRO. Such as what?

FLORA. He burnt your gin down. He didn't. And I'm not a big piece of cotton. (*She pulls herself up*). I'm going inside.

VICARRO (*rising*). I think that's a good idea.

FLORA. I said I was. Not you.

VICARRO. Why not me?

FLORA. Inside it might be crowded, with you an' me.

VICARRO. Three's a crowd. We're two.

FLORA. You stay out. Wait here.

VICARRO. What'll you do?

FLORA. I'll make us a pitcher of nice cold lemonade.

VICARRO. Okay. You go on in.

FLORA. What'll you do?

VICARRO. I'll follow.

FLORA. That's what I figured you might be aiming to do. We'll both stay out.

VICARRO. In the sun?

FLORA. We'll sit back down in th' shade. (*He blocks her*). Don't stand in my way.

VICARRO. You're standing in mine.

FLORA. I'm dizzy.

VICARRO. You ought to lie down.

FLORA. How can I?

VICARRO. Go in.

FLORA. You'd follow me.

VICARRO. What if I did?

FLORA. I'm afraid.

VICARRO. You're starting to cry.

FLORA. I'm afraid!

VICARRO. What of?

FLORA. Of you.

VICARRO. I'm little.

FLORA. I'm dizzy. My knees are so weak they're like water. I've got to sit down.

VICARRO. Go in.

FLORA. I can't.

VICARRO. Why not?

FLORA. You'd follow.

VICARRO. Would that be so awful?

FLORA. You've got a mean look in your eyes and I don't like the whip. Honest to God he never. He didn't, I swear!

VICARRO. Do what?

FLORA. The fire . . .

VICARRO. Go on.

FLORA. Please don't!

VICARRO. Don't what?

FLORA. Put it down. The whip, please put it down. Leave it out here on the porch.

VICARRO. What are you scared of?

FLORA. You.

VICARRO. Go on. (*She turns helplessly and moves to the screen. He pulls it open.*)

FLORA. Don't follow. Please don't follow! (*She sways uncertainly. He presses his hand against her. She moves inside. He follows. The door is shut quietly. The gin pumps slowly and steadily across the road. From inside the house there is a wild and despairing cry. A door is slammed. The cry is repeated more faintly.*)

CURTAIN

SCENE III

It is about nine o'clock the same evening. Although the sky behind the house is a dusky rose color, a full September moon of almost garish intensity gives the front of the house a ghostly brilliance. Dogs are howling like demons across the prostrate fields of the Delta.

The front porch of the MEIGHANS *is empty.*

After a moment the screen door is pushed slowly open and FLORA MEIGHAN *emerges gradually. Her appearance is ravaged. Her eyes have a vacant limpidity in the moonlight, her lips are slightly apart. She moves with her hands stretched gropingly before her till she has reached a pillar of the porch. There she stops and stands moaning a little. Her hair hangs loose and disordered. The upper part of her body is unclothed except for a torn pink band about her breasts. Dark streaks are visible on the bare shoulders and arms and there is a large discoloration along one cheek. A dark trickle, now congealed, descends from one corner of her mouth. These more apparent tokens she covers with one hand when* JAKE *comes up on the porch. He is now heard approaching, singing to himself.*

JAKE. By the light—by the light—by the light—Of the silvery mo-o-on! (*Instinctively* FLORA *draws back into the sharply etched shadow from the porch roof.* JAKE *is too tired and triumphant to notice her appearance*). How's a baby? (FLORA *utters a moaning grunt*). Tired? Too tired t' talk? Well, that's how I feel. Too tired t' talk. *Too goddam tired t'speak a friggin' word!* (*He lets himself down on the steps, groaning and without giving* FLORA *more than a glance*). Twenty-seven wagons full of cotton. That's how much I've ginned since ten this mawnin'. A man-size job.

FLORA (*huskily*). Uh-huh. . . . A man-size—job. . . .

JAKE. *Twen*-ty *sev*-en *wa*-gons *full* of *cot*-ton!

FLORA (*senselessly repeating*). *Twen*-ty *sev*-en *wa*-gons *full* of *cot*-ton! (*A dog howls.* FLORA *utters a breathless laugh.*)

JAKE. What're you laughin' at, honey? Not at me, I hope.

FLORA. No. . . .

JAKE. That's good. The job that I've turned out is nothing to laugh at. I drove that pack of niggers like a mule-skinner. They don't have a brain in their bodies. All they got is bodies. You got to drive, drive, drive. I don't even see how niggers eat without somebody to tell them to put the food in their moufs! (*She laughs again, like water spilling out of her mouth*). Huh! You got a laugh like a—Christ. A terrific day's work I finished.

FLORA (*slowly*). I would'n' brag—about it. . . .

JAKE. I'm not braggin' about it, I'm just sayin' I done a big day's work, I'm all wo'n out an' I want a little appreciation, not cross speeches. Honey. . . .

FLORA. I'm not—(*she laughs again*) —makin' cross speeches.

JAKE. To take on a big piece of work an' finish it up an' mention the fack that it's finished I wouldn't call braggin'.

FLORA. You're not the only one's—done a big day's—work.

JAKE. Who else that you know of? (*There is a pause.*)

FLORA. Maybe you think that I had an easy time. (*Her laughter spills out again.*)

JAKE. You're laughin' like you been on a goddam jag. (FLORA *laughs*). What did you get pissed on? Roach poison or citronella? I think I make it pretty easy for you, workin' like a mule-skinner so you can hire you a nigger to do the wash an' take the house-work on. An elephant woman who acks as frail as a kitten, that's the kind of a woman I got on m' hands.

FLORA. Sure. . . . (*She laughs*). You make it easy!

JAKE. I've yet t' see you lift a little finger. Even gotten too lazy t' put you' things on. Round the house ha'f naked all th' time. Y' live in a cloud. All you can think of is "Give me a Coca-Cola!" Well, you better look out. They got a new bureau in the guvamint files. It's called U.W. Stands for Useless Wimmen. Tha's secret plans on foot t' have 'em shot! (*He laughs at his joke.*)

FLORA. Secret—plans—on foot?

JAKE. T' have 'em *shot.*

FLORA. That's good. I'm glad t' hear it. (*She laughs again.*)

JAKE. I come home tired an' you cain't wait t' peck at me. What're you cross about now?

FLORA. I think it was a mistake.

JAKE. What was a mistake?

FLORA. Fo' you t' fool with th' Syndicate—Plantation. . . .

JAKE. I don't know about that. We wuh kind of up-against it, honey. Th' Syndicate buyin' up all th' lan' aroun' here an' turnin' the ole croppers off it without their wages —mighty near busted ev'ry mercantile store in Two Rivers County! An' then they build their own gin to gin their own cotton. It looked for a while like I was stuck up high an' dry. But when the gin burnt down an' Mr. Vicarro decided he'd better throw a little bus'ness my way—I'd say the situation was much improved!

FLORA (*she laughs weakly*). Then maybe you don't understand th' good-neighbor—policy.

JAKE. Don't understand it? Why, I'm the boy that invented it.

FLORA. Huh-huh! What an—*invention!* All I can say is—

I hope you're satisfied now that you've ginned out—twenty-seven wagons full of—cotton.

JAKE. Vicarro was pretty well pleased w'en he dropped over.

FLORA. Yeah. He was—pretty well—pleased.

JAKE. How did you all get along?

FLORA. We got along jus' fine. Jus' fine an'—dandy.

JAKE. He didn't seem like a such a bad little guy. He takes a sensible attitude.

FLORA (*laughing helplessly*). He—sure—does!

JAKE. I hope you made him comfo'table in the house?

FLORA (*giggling*). I made him a pitcher—of nice cold —lemonade!

JAKE. With a little gin in it, huh? That's how you got pissed. A nice cool drink don't sound bad to me right now. Got any left?

FLORA. Not a bit, Mr. Meighan. We drank it *a-a-ll* up! (*She flops onto the swing.*)

JAKE. So you didn't have such a tiresome time after all?

FLORA. No. Not tiresome a bit. I had a nice conversation with Mistuh—Vicarro. . . .

JAKE. What did you all talk about?

FLORA. Th' good-neighbor policy.

JAKE. (*chuckling*). How does he feel about th' good-neighbor policy?

FLORA. Oh—(*She giggles*).—He thinks it's a—good idea! He says—

JAKE. Huh? (FLORA *laughs weakly*). Says what?

FLORA. Says—(*She goes off into another spasm of laughter.*)

JAKE. What ever he said must've been a panic!

FLORA. He says—(*controlling her spasm*)—he don't think he'll build him a new cotton gin any more. He's gonna let you do a-a-lll his ginnin'—fo' him!

JAKE. I told you he'd take a sensible attitude.

FLORA. Yeah. Tomorrow he plans t' come back—with lots more cotton. Maybe another twenty-seven wagons.

JAKE. Yeah?

FLORA. An' while you're ginnin' it out—he'll have me entertain him with—nice lemonade! (*She has another fit of giggles.*)

JAKE. The more I hear about that lemonade the better I like it. Lemonade highballs, huh? Mr. Thomas Collins?

FLORA. I guess it's—gonna go on fo'—th' rest of th'—summer. . . .

JAKE (*rising and stretching happily*). Well, it'll . . . it'll soon be fall. Cooler nights comin' on.

FLORA. I don't know that that will put a—stop to it—though. . . .

JAKE (*obliviously*). The air feels cooler already. You shouldn't be settin' out here without you' shirt on, honey. A change in the air can give you a mighty bad cold.

FLORA. I couldn't stan' nothin' on me—nex' to my—skin.

JAKE. It ain't the heat that gives you all them hives, it's too much liquor. Crog blossoms, that's what you got! I'm goin' inside to the toilet. When I come out—(*He opens the screen door and goes in*).—we'll drive in town an' see what's at th' movies. You go hop in the Chevy! (FLORA *laughs to herself. She slowly opens the huge kid purse and removes a wad of Kleenex. She touches herself tenderly here and there, giggling breathlessly.*)

FLORA (*aloud*). I really oughtn't' have a white kid purse. It's wadded full of—Kleenex—to make it big—like a baby! Big—in my arms—like a baby!

JAKE (*from inside*). What did you say, Baby?

FLORA (*dragging herself up by the chain of the swing*). I'm not—Baby. Mama! Ma! That's—me. . . . (*Cradling the big white purse in her arms, she advances slowly and tenderly to the edge of the porch. The moon shines full on her smiling and ravaged face. She begins to rock and sway gently, rocking the purse in her arms and crooning.)*

Rock-a-bye Baby—in uh treetops!

If a wind blows—a cradle will rock! (*She descends a step*).

If a bough bends—a baby will fall! (*She descends another step*).

Down will come Baby—cradle—an'—all! (*She laughs and stares raptly and vacantly up at the moon.*)

CURTAIN

SORRY, WRONG NUMBER

by Lucille Fletcher

CHARACTERS

MRS. STEVENSON

1ST OPERATOR

1ST MAN

2ND MAN

CHIEF OPERATOR

2ND OPERATOR

3RD OPERATOR

4TH OPERATOR

5TH OPERATOR

INFORMATION

HOSPITAL RECEPTIONIST

WESTERN UNION

SERGEANT DUFFY

A LUNCH ROOM COUNTER ATTENDANT

SORRY, WRONG NUMBER

SCENE: *As curtain rises, we see a divided stage, only the center part of which is lighted and furnished as* MRS. STEVENSON'S *bedroom. Expensive, rather fussy furnishings. A large bed, on which* MRS. STEVENSON, *clad in bed-jacket, is lying. A night-table close by, with phone, lighted lamp, and pill bottles. A mantel, with clock,* R. *A closed door,* R. *A window, with curtains closed, rear. The set is lit by one lamp on night-table. It is enclosed by three flats. Beyond this central set, the stage, on either side, is in darkness.*

MRS. STEVENSON *is dialling a number on phone, as curtain rises. She listens to phone, slams down receiver in irritation. As she does so, we hear sound of a train roaring by in the distance. She reaches for her pill bottle, pours herself a glass of water, shakes out pill, swallows it, then reaches for phone again, dials number nervously.* SOUND: *Number being dialled on phone: Busy signal.*

MRS. STEVENSON (*a querulous, self-centered neurotic*). Oh—dear! (*Slams down receiver. Dials* OPERATOR). (SCENE: *A spotlight,* L. *of side flat, picks up out of peripheral darkness, figure of* 1ST. OPERATOR, *sitting with headphones at small table. If spotlight not available, use flashlight, clicked on by* 1ST OPERATOR, *illumining her face.*)

OPERATOR. Your call, please?

MRS. STEVENSON. Operator? I have been dialling Murray Hill 4-0098 now for the last three-quarters of an hour, and the line is always busy. But I don't see how it *could* be busy that long. Will you try it for me, please?

OPERATOR. Murray Hill 4-0098? One moment, please. (SCENE: *She makes gesture of plugging in call through a switchboard.*)

MRS. STEVENSON. I don't see how it could be busy all this time. It's my husband's office. He's working late tonight, and I'm all alone here in the house. My health is very poor—and I've been feeling so nervous all day. . . .

OPERATOR. Ringing Murray Hill 4-0098. . . . (SOUND: *Phone buzz. It rings three times. Receiver is picked up at other end*). (SCENE: *Spotlight picks up figure of a heavy-set man, seated at desk with phone on* R. *side of dark periphery of stage. He is wearing a hat. Picks up phone, which rings three times.*)

MAN. Hello.

MRS. STEVENSON. Hello . . . ? (*a little puzzled*). Hello. Is Mr. Stevenson there?

MAN (*into phone, as though he had not heard*). Hello. . . . (*Louder*). Hello. (SCENE: *Spotlight on* L. *now moves from* OPERATOR *to another man,* GEORGE. *A killer type, also wearing hat, but standing as in a phone booth. A three-sided screen may be used to suggest this.*)

2ND MAN (*slow heavy quality, faintly foreign accent*). Hello.

1ST MAN. Hello. George?

GEORGE. Yes, sir.

MRS. STEVENSON (*louder and more imperious, to phone*). Hello. Who's this? What number am I calling, please?

1ST MAN. We have heard from our client. He says the coast is clear for tonight.

GEORGE. Yes, sir.

1ST MAN. Where are you now?

GEORGE. In a phone booth.

1ST MAN. Okay. You know the address. At eleven o'clock the private patrolman goes around to the bar on Second Avenue for a beer. Be sure that all the lights downstairs are out. There should be only one light visible from the street. At eleven-fifteen a subway train crosses the bridge. It makes a noise in case her window is open, and she should scream.

MRS. STEVENSON (*shocked*). Oh—HELLO! What number is this, please?

GEORGE. Okay. I understand.

1ST MAN. Make it quick. As little blood as possible. Our client does not wish to make her suffer long.

GEORGE. A knife okay, sir?

1ST MAN. Yes. A knife will be okay. And remember—remove the rings and bracelets, and the jewelry in the bureau drawer. Our client wishes it to look like simple robbery.

GEORGE. Okay—I get—— (SCENE: *Spotlight suddenly goes out on* GEORGE.) (SOUND: *A bland buzzing signal*). (SCENE: *Spotlight goes off on* 1ST MAN.)

MRS. STEVENSON (*clicking phone*). Oh . . . ! (*Bland buzzing signal continues. She hangs up*). How awful! How unspeakably . . . (SCENE: *She lies back on her pillows, overcome for a few seconds, then suddenly pulls herself together, reaches for phone*). (SOUND: *Dialling. Phone buzz*). (SCENE: *Spotlight goes on at* 1ST OPERATOR's *switchboard.* 1ST *and* 2ND MAN *exit as unobtrusively as possible, in darkness.*)

OPERATOR. Your call, please?

MRS. STEVENSON (*unnerved and breathless, into phone*). Operator. I—I've just been cut off.

OPERATOR. I'm sorry, madam. What number were you calling?

MRS. STEVENSON. Why—it was supposed to be Murray Hill 4-0098, but it wasn't. Some wires must have crossed—I was cut into a wrong number—and—I've just heard the most dreadful thing—a—a murder—and—(*Imperiously*). Operator, you'll simply have to retrace that call at once.

OPERATOR. I beg your pardon, madam—I don't quite——

MRS. STEVENSON. Oh—I know it was a wrong number, and I had no business listening—but these two men—they were cold-blooded fiends—and they were going to murder somebody—some poor innocent woman—who was all alone—in a house near a bridge. And we've got to stop them—we've got to——

OPERATOR (*patiently*). What number were you calling, madam?

MRS. STEVENSON. That doesn't matter. This was a *wrong* number. And *you* dialled it. And we've got to find out what it was—immediately!

OPERATOR. But—madam——

MRS. STEVENSON. Oh—why are you so stupid? Look—it was obviously a case of some little slip of the finger. I told you to try Murray Hill 4-0098 for me—you dialled it but your finger must have slipped—and I was connected with some other number—and I could hear them, but they couldn't hear me. Now, I simply fail to see why you couldn't make that same mistake again—on purpose—why you couldn't *try* to dial Murray Hill 4-0098 in the same careless sort of way. . . .

OPERATOR (*quickly*). Murray Hill 4-0098? I will try to get it for you, madam.

MRS. STEVENSON (*sarcastically*). *Thank* you. (SCENE: *She bridles, adjusts herself on her pillows, reaches for handkerchief, wipes forehead, glancing uneasily for a moment toward window, while still holding phone*). (*Sound of ringing: Busy signal.*)

OPERATOR. I am sorry. Murray Hill 4-0098 is busy.

MRS. STEVENSON (*frantically clicking receiver*). Operator. Operator.

OPERATOR. Yes, Madam.

MRS. STEVENSON (*angrily*). You *didn't* try to get that wrong number at all. I asked explicitly. And all you did was dial correctly.

OPERATOR. I am sorry. What number were you calling?

MRS. STEVENSON. Can't you, for once, forget what number I was calling, and do something specific? Now I want to trace that call. It's my civic duty—it's *your* civic duty

—to trace that call . . . and to apprehend those dangerous killers—and if *you* won't . . .

OPERATOR (*glancing around wearily*). I will connect you with the Chief Operator.

MRS. STEVENSON. *Please!* (*Sound of ringing*). (SCENE: OPERATOR *puts hand over mouthpiece of phone, gestures into darkness. A half whisper:*

OPERATOR. Miss Curtis. Will you pick up on 17, please? (MISS CURTIS, *Chief Operator, enters. Middle-aged, efficient type, pleasant. Wearing headphones.*)

MISS CURTIS. Yes, dear. What's the trouble?

OPERATOR. Somebody wanting a call traced. I can't make head nor tail of it. . . .

MISS CURTIS (*sitting down at desk, as* OPERATOR *gets up*). Sure, dear. 17? (*She makes gesture of plugging in her headphone, coolly and professionally*). This is the Chief Operator.

MRS. STEVENSON. Chief Operator? I want you to trace a call. A telephone call. Immediately. I don't know where it came from, or who was making it, but it's absolutely necessary that it be tracked down. Because it was about a murder. Yes, a terrible, cold-blooded murder of a poor innocent woman—tonight—at eleven-fifteen.

CHIEF OPERATOR. I see.

MRS. STEVENSON (*high-strung, demanding*). Can you trace it for me? Can you track down those men?

CHIEF OPERATOR. It depends, madam.

MRS. STEVENSON. Depends on what?

CHIEF OPERATOR. It depends on whether the call is still going on. If it's a live call, we can trace it on the equipment. If it's been disconnected, we can't.

MRS. STEVENSON. Disconnected?

CHIEF OPERATOR. If the parties have stopped talking to each other.

MRS. STEVENSON. Oh—but—but of course they must have

stopped talking to each other by *now*. That was at least five minutes ago—and they didn't sound like the type who would make a long call.

CHIEF OPERATOR. Well, I can try tracing it. (SCENE: *She takes pencil out of her hair-do*). Now—what is your name, madam?

MRS. STEVENSON. Mrs. Stevenson. Mrs. Elbert Stevenson. But—listen——

CHIEF OPERATOR (*writing it down*). And your telephone number?

MRS. STEVENSON (*more irritated*). Plaza 4-2295. But if you go on wasting all this time—— (SCENE: *She glances at clock on mantel.*)

CHIEF OPERATOR. And what is your reason for wanting this call traced?

MRS. STEVENSON. My reason? Well—for Heaven's sake—isn't it obvious? I overhear two men—they're killers—they're planning to murder this woman—it's a matter for the police.

CHIEF OPERATOR. Have you told the police?

MRS. STEVENSON. No. How could I?

CHIEF OPERATOR. You're making this check into a private call purely as a private individual?

MRS. STEVENSON. Yes. But meanwhile——

CHIEF OPERATOR. Well, Mrs. Stevenson—I seriously doubt whether we could make this check for you at this time just on your say-so as a private individual. We'd have to have something more official.

MRS. STEVENSON. Oh—for Heaven's sake! You mean to tell me I can't report a murder without getting tied up in all this redtape? Why—it's perfectly idiotic. All right, then. I *will* call the police. (*She slams down receiver*). (SCENE: *Spotlight goes off on two* OPERATORS). Ridiculous! (*Sound of dialling*). (SCENE: MRS. STEVENSON *dials numbers on phone, as two* OPERATORS *exit unobtrusively in darkness.*) (*On* R. *of stage, spotlight picks up a* 2ND OPERATOR, *seated like first, with headphones at table* [*same one vacated by* 1ST MAN].)

2ND OPERATOR. Your call, please?

MRS. STEVENSON (*very annoyed*). The Police Department —*please.*

2ND OPERATOR. Ringing the Police Department. (*Ring twice. Phone is picked up*). (SCENE: L. *stage, at table vacated by* 1ST *and* CHIEF OPERATOR, *spotlight now picks up* SERGEANT DUFFY, *seated in a relaxed position. Just entering beside him is a young man in cap and apron, carrying a large brown paper parcel, delivery boy for a local lunch counter. Phone is ringing.*)

YOUNG MAN. Here's your lunch, Sarge. They didn't have no jelly doughnuts, so I give you French crullers. Okay, Sarge?

S. DUFFY. French crullers. I got ulcers. Whyn't you make it apple pie? (*Picks up phone, which has rung twice*). Police department. Precinct 43. Duffy speaking. (SCENE: LUNCH ROOM ATTENDANT, *anxiously.* We don't have no apple pie, either, Sarge—)

MRS. STEVENSON. Police Department? Oh. This is Mrs. Stevenson—Mrs. Elbert Smythe Stevenson of 53 North Sutton Place. I'm calling up to report a murder. (SCENE: DUFFY *has been examining lunch, but double-takes suddenly on above.*)

DUFFY. Eh?

MRS. STEVENSON. I mean—the murder hasn't been committed yet. I just overheard plans for it over the telephone . . . over a wrong number that the operator gave me. (SCENE: DUFFY *relaxes, sighs, starts taking lunch from bag*). I've been trying to trace down the call myself, but everybody is so stupid—and I guess in the end you're the only people who could *do* anything.

DUFFY (*not too impressed*). (SCENE: ATTENDANT, *who exits*). Yes, ma'am.

MRS. STEVENSON (*trying to impress him*). It was a perfectly *definite* murder. I heard their plans distinctly. (SCENE: DUFFY *begins to eat sandwich, phone at his ear*). Two men were talking, and they were going to murder some woman at eleven-fifteen tonight—she lived in a house near a bridge.

DUFFY. Yes, ma'am.

MRS. STEVENSON. And there was a private patrolman on the street. He was going to go around for a beer on Second Avenue. And there was some third man—a client, who was paying to have this poor woman murdered— they were going to take her rings and bracelets—and use a knife . . . well, it's unnerved me dreadfully—and I'm not well. . . .

DUFFY. I see. (SCENE: *Having finished sandwich, he wipes mouth with paper napkin*). When was all this, ma'am?

MRS. STEVENSON. About eight minutes ago. Oh . . . (*Relieved*). Then you *can* do something? You *do* understand—

DUFFY. And what is your name, ma'am? (SCENE: *He reaches for pad.*)

MRS. STEVENSON (*impatiently*). Mrs. Stevenson. Mrs. Elbert Stevenson.

DUFFY. And your address?

MRS. STEVENSON. 53 North Sutton Place. *That's* near a bridge. The Queensboro Bridge, you know—and *we* have a private patrolman on *our* street—and Second Avenue——

DUFFY. And what was that number you were calling?

MRS. STEVENSON. Murray Hill 4-0098. (SCENE: DUFFY *writes it down.*) But—that wasn't the number I overheard. I mean Murray Hill 4-0098 is my husband's office. (SCENE: DUFFY, *in exasperation, holds pencil poised.*) He's working late tonight, and I was trying to reach him to ask him to come home. I'm an invalid, you know —and it's the maid's night off—and I *hate* to be alone—

even though he says I'm perfectly safe as long as I have the telephone right beside my bed.

DUFFY (*stolidly*). (SCENE: *He has put pencil down, pushes pad away*). Well—we'll look into it, Mrs. Stevenson— and see if we can check it with the telephone company.

MRS. STEVENSON (*getting impatient*). But the telephone company said they couldn't check the call if the parties had stopped talking. I've already taken care of *that*.

DUFFY. Oh—yes? (SCENE: *He yawns slightly.*)

MRS. STEVENSON (*high-handed*). Personally I feel you ought to do something far more immediate and drastic than just check the call. What good does checking the call do, if they've stopped talking? By the time you track it down, they'll already have committed the murder.

DUFFY (SCENE: *He reaches for paper cup of coffee*). Well —we'll take care of it, lady. Don't worry. (SCENE: *He begins to take off paper top of coffee container.*)

MRS. STEVENSON. I'd say the whole thing calls for a search —a complete and thorough search of the whole city. (SCENE: DUFFY *puts down phone for a moment, to work on cup, as her voice continues*). I'm very near a bridge, and I'm not far from Second Avenue. And I know I'd feel a whole lot better if you sent around a radio car to *this* neighborhood at once.

DUFFY (SCENE: *Picks up phone again, drinks coffee*). And what makes you think the murder's going to be committed in your neighborhood, ma'am?

MRS. STEVENSON. Oh—I don't know. The coincidence is so horrible. Second Avenue—the patrolman—the bridge . . .

DUFFY (SCENE: *He sips coffee*). Second Avenue is a very long street, ma'am. And do you happen to know how many bridges there are in the city of New York alone? Not to mention Brooklyn, Staten Island, Queens, and the Bronx? And how do you know there isn't some little house out on Staten Island—on some little Second Avenue you never heard about? (SCENE: *A long gulp of coffee*). How do you know they were even talking about New York at all?

MRS. STEVENSON. But I heard the call on the New York dialling system.

DUFFY. How do you know it wasn't a long distance call you overheard? Telephones are funny things. (SCENE: *He sets down coffee*). Look, lady, why don't you look at it this way? Supposing you hadn't broken in on that telephone call? Supposing you'd got your husband the way you always do? Would this murder have made any difference to you then?

MRS. STEVENSON. I suppose not. But it's so inhuman—so cold-blooded . . .

DUFFY. A lot of murders are committed in this city every day, ma'am. If we could do something to stop 'em, we would. But a clue of this kind that's so vague isn't much more use to us than no clue at all.

MRS. STEVENSON. But, surely——

DUFFY. Unless, of course, you have some reason for thinking this call is phoney—and that someone may be planning to murder *you*?

MRS. STEVENSON. *Me*? Oh—no—I hardly think so. I—I mean —why should anybody? I'm alone all day and night— I see nobody except my maid Eloise—she's a big two-hundred-pounder—she's too lazy to bring up my breakfast tray—and the only other person is my husband Elbert—he's crazy about me—adores me—waits on me hand and foot—he's scarcely left my side since I took sick twelve years ago——

DUFFY. Well—then—there's nothing for you to worry about, is there? (SCENE: LUNCH COUNTER ATTENDANT *has entered. He is carrying a piece of apple pie on a plate. Points it out to* DUFFY *triumphantly*). And now—if you'll just leave the rest of this to us——

MRS. STEVENSON. But what will you *do*? It's so late—it's nearly eleven o'clock.

DUFFY (*firmly*). (SCENE: *He nods to* ATTENDANT, *pleased*). We'll take care of it, lady.

MRS. STEVENSON. Will you broadcast it all over the city? And send out squads? And warn your radio cars to watch out—especially in suspicious neighborhoods like mine? (SCENE: ATTENDANT, *in triumph, has put pie down in front of* DUFFY. *Takes fork out of his pocket, stands at attention, waiting.*)

DUFFY (*more firmly*). Lady, I *said* we'd take care of it. (SCENE: *Glances at pie*). Just now I've got a couple of other matters here on my desk that require my immediate——

MRS. STEVENSON. Oh! (*She slams down receiver hard*). Idiot. (SCENE: DUFFY, *listening at phone, hangs up. Shrugs. Winks at* ATTENDANT *as though to say, "What a crazy character!" Attacks his pie as spotlight fades out*). (MRS. STEVENSON, *in bed, looking at phone nervously*). Now—why did I do that? Now—he'll think I *am* a fool. (SCENE: *She sits there tensely, then throws herself back against pillows, lies there a moment, whimpering with self-pity*). Oh—why doesn't Elbert come home? *Why* doesn't he? (SCENE: *We hear sound of train roaring by in the distance. She sits up reaching for phone*). (*Sound of dialling operator*). (SCENE: *Spotlight picks up* 2ND OPERATOR, *seated* R.)

OPERATOR. Your call, please?

MRS. STEVENSON. Operator—for Heaven's sake—will you ring that Murray Hill 4-0098 number again? I can't think what's keeping him so long.

OPERATOR. Ringing Murray Hill 4-0098. (*Rings. Busy signal*). The line is busy. Shall I——

MRS. STEVENSON (*nastily*). I can hear it. You don't have to tell me. I know it's busy. (*Slams down receiver*). (SCENE: *Spotlight fades off on* 2ND OPERATOR). (SCENE: MRS. STEVENSON *sinks back against pillows again, whimpering to herself fretfully. She glances at clock, then turning, punches her pillows up, trying to make herself comfortable. But she isn't. Whimpers to herself as she squirms restlessly in bed).* If I could only get out of this bed for a little while. If I could get a breath of fresh air—or just lean out the window—and see the street. . . . (SCENE: *She sighs, reaches for pill bottle, shakes out a pill. As she does so:) (The phone rings. She darts for it instantly).* Hello. Elbert? Hello. Hello. Hello. Oh—what's the *matter* with this phone? HELLO? HELLO? (*Slams down the receiver).* (SCENE: *She stares at it, tensely).* (*The phone rings again. Once. She picks it up).* Hello? Hello. . . . Oh—for Heaven's sake —who *is* this? Hello. Hello. HELLO. (*Slams down receiver. Dials operator).* (SCENE: *Spotlight comes on* L., *showing* 3RD OPERATOR, *at spot vacated by* DUFFY.

3RD OPERATOR. Your call, please?

MRS. STEVENSON (*very annoyed and imperious).* Hello. Operator. I don't know what's the matter with this telephone tonight, but it's positively driving me crazy. I've never seen such inefficient, miserable service. Now, look. I'm an invalid, and I'm very nervous, and I'm *not* supposed to be annoyed. But if this keeps on much longer . . .

3RD OPERATOR (*a young sweet type).* What seems to be the trouble, madam?

MRS. STEVENSON. Well—everything's wrong. The whole world could be murdered, for all you people care. And now—my phone keeps ringing. . . .

OPERATOR. Yes, madam?

MRS. STEVENSON. Ringing and ringing and ringing every five seconds or so, and when I pick it up, there's no one there.

OPERATOR. I am sorry, madam. If you will hang up, I will test it for you.

MRS. STEVENSON. I don't want you to test it for me. I want you to put through that call—whatever it is—at once.

OPERATOR (*gently*). I am afraid that is not possible, madam.

MRS. STEVENSON (*storming*). Not possible? And why—may I ask?

OPERATOR. The system is automatic, madam. If someone is trying to dial your number, there is no way to check whether the call is coming through the system or not —unless the person who is trying to reach you complains to his particular operator——

MRS. STEVENSON. Well, of all the stupid, complicated . . . ! And meanwhile *I've* got to sit here in my bed, *suffering* every time that phone rings—imagining everything. . . .

OPERATOR. I will try to check it for you, madam.

MRS. STEVENSON. Check it! Check it! That's all anybody can do. Of all the stupid, idiotic . . . !(*She hangs up*). Oh—what's the use . . . (SCENE: 3RD OPERATOR *fades out of spotlight, as*) (*Instantly* MRS. STEVENSON'S *phone rings again. She picks up receiver. Wildly*). Hello. HELLO. Stop ringing, do you hear me? Answer me? What do you want? Do you realize you're driving me crazy? (SCENE: *Spotlight goes on* R. *We see a* MAN *in eye-shade and shirt-sleeves, at desk with phone and telegrams*). Stark, staring . . .

MAN (*dull flat voice*). Hello. Is this Plaza 4-2295?

MRS. STEVENSON (*catching her breath*). Yes. Yes. This is Plaza 4-2295.

WESTERN UNION. This is Western Union. I have a telegram here for Mrs. Elbert Stevenson. Is there anyone there to receive the message?

MRS. STEVENSON (*trying to calm herself*). I am Mrs. Stevenson.

WESTERN UNION (*reading flatly*). The telegram is as follows: "Mrs. Elbert Stevenson. 53 North Sutton Place, New York, New York. Darling. Terribly sorry. Tried to get you for last hour, but line busy. Leaving for

Boston eleven p. m. tonight on urgent business. Back to-morrow afternoon. Keep happy. Love. Signed. Elbert."

MRS. STEVENSON (*breathlessly, aghast, to herself*). Oh . . . no . . .

WESTERN UNION. That is all, madam. Do you wish us to deliver a copy of the message?

MRS. STEVENSON. No—no, thank you.

WESTERN UNION. Thank you, madam. Good night. (*He hangs up phone.*) (SCENE: *Spotlight on* WESTERN UNION *immediately out.*)

MRS. STEVENSON (*mechanically, to phone*). Good night. (*She hangs up slowly. Suddenly bursting into*). No—no —it isn't true! He couldn't do it! Not when he knows I'll be all alone. It's some trick—some fiendish . . . (SCENE: *We hear sound of train roaring by outside. She half rises in bed, in panic, glaring toward curtains. Her movements are frenzied. She beats with her knuckles on bed, then suddenly stops, and reaches for phone*). (*She dials operator*). (SCENE: *Spotlight picks up* 4TH OPERATOR, *seated* L.)

OPERATOR (*coolly*). Your call, please?

MRS. STEVENSON. Operator—try that Murray Hill 4-0098 number for me just once more, please.

OPERATOR. Ringing Murray Hill 4-0098. (*Call goes through. We hear ringing at other end. Ring after ring*). (SCENE: *If telephone noises are not used audibly, have* OPERATOR *say after a brief pause:* "They do not answer.")

MRS. STEVENSON. He's gone. Oh—Elbert, how could you? How could you . . . ? (*She hangs up phone, sobbing pityingly to herself, turning restlessly*). (SCENE: *Spotlight goes out on* 4TH OPERATOR). But I can't be alone tonight. I can't. If I'm alone one more second . . . (SCENE: *She runs hands wildly through hair*). I don't care what he says—or what the expense is—I'm a sick woman—I'm entitled . . . (SCENE: *With trembling fin-*

gers she picks up receiver again). (*She dials* INFORMA-
TION). (SCENE: *The spotlight picks up* INFORMATION
OPERATOR, *seated* R.)

INFORMATION. This is Information.

MRS. STEVENSON. I want the telephone number of Henchley Hospital.

INFORMATION. Henchley Hospital? Do you have the address, madam?

MRS. STEVENSON. No. It's somewhere in the 70's, though.
It's a very small, private and exclusive hospital where
I had my appendix out two years ago. Henchley. H-E-
N-C——

INFORMATION. One moment, please.

MRS. STEVENSON. Please—hurry. And please—what *is* the
time?

INFORMATION. I do not know, madam. You may find out
the time by dialling Meridan 7-1212.

MRS. STEVENSON (*irritated*). Oh—for Heaven's sake!
Couldn't you——?

INFORMATION. The number of Henchley Hospital is Butterfield 7-0105, madam.

MRS. STEVENSON. Butterfield 7-0105. (*She hangs up before she finishes speaking, and immediately dials number
as she repeats it*). (SCENE: *Spotlight goes out on* IN-
FORMATION). (*Phone rings*). (SCENE: *Spotlight picks
up* WOMAN *in nurse's uniform, seated at desk,* L.)

WOMAN (*middle-aged, solid, firm, practical*). Henchley
Hospital, good evening.

MRS. STEVENSON. Nurses' Registry.

WOMAN. Who was it you wished to speak to, please?

MRS. STEVENSON (*high-handed*). I want the Nurses' Registry at once. I want a trained nurse. I want to hire her
immediately. For the night.

WOMAN. I see. And what is the nature of the case, madam?

MRS. STEVENSON. Nerves. I'm very nervous. I need soothing—and companionship. My husband is away—and I'm——

WOMAN. Have you been recommended to us by any doctor in particular, madam?

MRS. STEVENSON. No. But I really don't see why all this catechizing is necessary. I want a trained nurse. I was a patient in your hospital two years ago. And after all, I *do* expect to *pay* this person——

WOMAN. We quite understand that, madam. But registered nurses are very scarce just now—and our superintendent has asked us to send people out only on cases where the physician in charge feels it is absolutely necessary.

MRS. STEVENSON (*growing hysterical*). Well—it *is* absolutely necessary. I'm a sick woman. I—I'm very upset. Very. I'm alone in this house—and I'm an invalid—and tonight I overheard a telephone conversation that upset me dreadfully. About a murder—a poor woman who was going to be murdered at eleven-fifteen tonight—in fact, if someone doesn't come at once—I'm afraid I'll go out of my mind. . . . (*Almost off handle by now.*)

WOMAN (*calmly*). I see. Well—I'll speak to Miss Phillips as soon as she comes in. And what is your name, madam?

MRS. STEVENSON. Miss Phillips. And when do you expect her in?

WOMAN. I really don't know, madam. She went out to supper at eleven o'clock.

MRS. STEVENSON. Eleven o'clock. But it's not eleven yet. (*She cries out*). Oh, my clock *has* stopped. I thought it was running down. What time is it? (SCENE: WOMAN *glances at wristwatch.*)

WOMAN. Just fourteen minutes past eleven. . . . (*Sound of phone receiver being lifted on same line as* MRS. STEVENSON's. *A click.*)

MRS. STEVENSON (*crying out*). What's *that*?

WOMAN. What was what, madam?

MRS. STEVENSON. That—that click just now—in my own telephone? As though someone had lifted the receiver off the hook of the extension phone downstairs. . . .

WOMAN. I didn't hear it, madam. Now—about this . . .

MRS. STEVENSON (*scared*). But I *did*. There's someone in this house. Someone downstairs in the kitchen. And they're listening to me now. They're . . . (SCENE: *She puts hand over her mouth*). (*Hangs up phone*). (SCENE: *She sits there, in terror, frozen, listening*). (*In a suffocated voice*). I won't pick it up, I won't let them hear me. I'll be quiet—and they'll think . . . (*With growing terror*). But if I don't call someone now—while they're still down there—there'll be no time. . . . (*She picks up receiver. Bland buzzing signal. She dials operator. Ring twice*). (SCENE: *On second ring, spotlight goes on* R. *We see* 5TH OPERATOR.)

OPERATOR (*fat and lethargic*). Your call, please?

MRS. STEVENSON (*a desperate whisper*). Operator—I—I'm in desperate trouble . . . I——

OPERATOR. I cannot hear you, madam. Please speak louder.

MRS. STEVENSON (*still whispering*). I don't dare. I—there's someone listening. Can you hear me now?

OPERATOR. Your call, please? What number are you calling, madam?

MRS. STEVENSON (*desperately*). You've got to hear me. Oh —please. You've got to help me. There's someone in this house. Someone who's going to murder me. And you've got to get in touch with the . . . (*Click of receiver being put down on* MRS. STEVENSON's *line. Bursting out wildly*). Oh—there it is . . . he's put it down . . . he's coming . . . (*She screams.*) he's coming up the stairs . . . (SCENE: *She thrashes in bed, phone cord catching in lamp wire, lamp topples, goes out. Darkness*). (*Hoarsely*). Give me the Police Department. . . . (SCENE: *We see on the dark* C. *stage, the shadow of*

door opening). (Screaming). The police! . . . (SCENE:
*On stage, swift rush of a shadow, advancing to bed—
sound of her voice is choked out, as)*

OPERATOR. Ringing the Police Department. (*Phone is rung.
We hear sound of a train beginning to fade in. On second ring,* MRS. STEVENSON *screams again, but roaring of
train drowns out her voice. For a few seconds we hear
nothing but roaring of train, then dying away, phone
at police headquarters ringing).* (SCENE: Spotlight goes
on DUFFY, L. *stage.*)

DUFFY. Police Department. Precinct 43. Duffy speaking.
(*Pause*). (SCENE: *Nothing visible but darkness on* C.
stage). Police Department. Duffy speaking. (SCENE: *A
flashlight goes on, illuminating open phone to one side
of* MRS. STEVENSON's *bed. Nearby, hanging down, is her
lifeless hand. We see the second man,* GEORGE, *in black
gloves, reach down and pick up phone. He is breathing
hard.*)

GEORGE. Sorry. Wrong number. (*Hangs up*). (SCENE: *He
replaces receiver on hook quietly, exits, as* DUFFY *hangs
up with a shrug, and* CURTAIN FALLS.)

GLORY IN THE FLOWER

by William Inge

GLORY IN THE FLOWER

The play is set inside a small roadhouse called the Paradise, close to a Midwestern town. It is a totally unpretentious sort of place, yet there has been a serious attempt, in the decor, to create, successfully or not, an atmosphere of gayety. A kewpie doll, wearing a Hawaiian grass skirt, stands on the shelf behind the bar, and the walls have been painted with amateur murals depicting some fantasized seashore, edged by swaying palm trees, topped by a crescent moon and a starry sky. The total effect, whether intended or not, is primitive. The bar is extreme R., *and the entrance extreme* L. *One can see the gaudy neon sign outside,* PARADISE. *At the back are an enormous jukebox and a row of about six booths for customers. A gang of teen-agers fills the Paradise now, jiving and jitterbugging, making a background of noisy, zestful activity. There is one customer at the bar, a* SALESMAN, *a stout, weary man in his fifties who already has had a few too many drinks. His conversation to* HOWIE, *the bartender, is in a melancholy, nostalgic vein.*

SALESMAN (*to* HOWIE, *showing his drinks*). Nothing ever stays the same. Why *is* that?

HOWIE (*detached but human*). I couldn't say.

SALESMAN. It used t' be, when I came into this town, I'd leave it with . . . sometimes ten thousand dollars' worth of orders. Ten thousand!

HOWIE. I wouldn't doubt it.

SALESMAN. 'Course I did. Know what I do in this town now? I'm doin' good if I make my expenses. That's right. I'm doin' good if I make my expenses.

HOWIE. Is that a fact?

SALESMAN (*conscious of his repetitions*). I'm doin' good if I make my expenses. It don't hardly pay me any more to make this town. I might as well cut it outa my territory, cause I hardly make enough commission here to keep goin'.

HOWIE. Things is pretty bad all over, ain't they?

SALESMAN. Sure. Things is bad all over. I don't know why I stay on the road, Howie. The road's gone. (*Now* JACKIE *comes in from the outside. She is a woman nearing forty, but pretty, with a clear, fair skin and a pleasing fullness about the body, and a sweet, girlish smile that makes her attractive.* JACKIE *has tried to keep her youthful looks and succeeded. At this particular time, perhaps she has tried too hard, for her dress is quite frilly and fussy, there are flowers in her hair, and a little too much make-up. Only her sweetness and her seeming naïveté prevent her from seeming cheap. She hurries to the bar, radiating the excitement she feels, seeking* HOWIE.)

JACKIE. Howie, has Bus Riley been in here?

HOWIE. No, he hasn't, Jackie. You expectin' to meet Bus here?

JACKIE. Yes. I'm so excited. (*One of the teen-agers calls to* JACKIE. *He is* JOKER, *a husky, handsome kid of eighteen, a dynamo of youthful energy.*)

JOKER (*calling*). Hi, Miss Bowen!

JACKIE (*calling back*). Hi, Joker! (*To the others*). Hi, kids! (*And she sounds like a kid herself.*)

TEEN-AGERS. Hi! Hi, Miss Bowen!

JACKIE (*back to* HOWIE). I guess I'm a little early. I was so excited when Bus called, and I didn't wanta be late, so I hurried so much gettin' ready that here I am, ahead of time.

A GIRL (*to* JOKER, *teasing*). Jackie Bowen's in love with Joker. Jackie Bowen's in love with Joker.

JOKER. So what? Maybe I'm in love with her, too. (*The others all laugh.*)

BOY 1. No fool, Joker. I think she's got her eye on you.

JOKER (*embarrassed*). Cut it out, will you? She's a swell dame. Gives me a can of beer when I deliver the groceries, and we stand and talk sometimes. She always asks me about my school work . . . things like that . . . like she was really interested.

GIRL (*sarcastically*). I bet!

GIRL 2. My mother says she doesn't have a very good reputation, something that happened a long time ago.

JOKER. I don't care about her reputation. I *like* her.

JACKIE (*who has turned to the bartender—breathlessly*). Have you seen him, Howie?

HOWIE. Who? Bus?

JACKIE. Bus Riley was a *god*.

HOWIE. He never seemed like no god to me.

JACKIE. You just didn't like him.

HOWIE. No. I just didn't like him, and I know quite a few other people felt the same way I did.

JACKIE. They just didn't *know* Bus.

HOWIE. Anyway, I seen him. He was in here the other night, gettin' a load on.

JACKIE (*taken aback*). He was in here?

HOWIE. Yep!

JACKIE (*almost to herself*). Why he told me he hadn't been out of the house since he . . .

HOWIE. He come in here, wearin' a spiffy suit, full of big stories, just as ornery and bad natured as he ever was.

JACKIE. Bus really isn't like that, Howie. Not when you know him. Bus and I went steady, you know, for a long time. Of course, we were only kids then, but I think, lotsa times, a girl sees lots of very fine things about a boy . . . that other people . . . maybe just don't *wanta* see.

HOWIE. I think lotsa times a young girl, smitten on a boy, just sees lotsa "very fine things" in him that aren't there at all.

JACKIE (*giving thought*). Do you, Howie?

HOWIE. Kids! Kids get head-over-heels in love, and maybe even kill themselves for love, without even knowin' what they're in love with.

JACKIE (*trying to laugh it off*). Oh! You just wanta sound cynical, Howie. (JOKER *suddenly grabs* JACKIE *by the arm and pulls her out on the dance floor with him.*)

JOKER. C'mon and dance, Miss Bowen.

JACKIE (*while he drags her onto the floor*). Oh, Joker! You don't mean it. You don't wanta dance with *me*.

JOKER. Sure I do. I got an Oedipus complex. C'mon!

JACKIE (*trying to follow his jiving, sounding a little uncertain*). Well . . . I'll try . . .

HOWIE (*to the* SALESMAN). If you ask me, she's still a kid herself.

SALESMAN. Kinda pretty. S'pose she wants a little company?

HOWIE. No. Not Jackie. Not when Bus Riley's in town.

SALESMAN. That her husband?

HOWIE (*evasively*). No . . . Bus wasn't ever her husband. (*Now* JACKIE *comes back to the bar with* JOKER.)

JOKER. Miss Bowen, don't be a square.

JACKIE. Goodness, Joker, I can't do all those wild, crazy steps you kids do.

JOKER. Just get the swing and it's easy.

JACKIE. When I was your age, we used to like to dance . . . *soft* and *romantic* and dreamy.

HOWIE (*to* JOKER). You sure all your gang's eighteen and over?

JOKER (*kidding*). On my Boy Scout oath, Howie. (*Returns to his gang.*)

HOWIE (*eyeing a young couple in one of the back booths, the boy kissing the girl with youthful ardor. Calls to* JOKER). Now watch your behavior back there. (*A number of the young people are dancing with quick, spontaneous rhythm, very "hep."*)

JACKIE (*to* HOWIE, *a little self-consciously*). I've always been one of the best dancers in town, haven't I, Howie? Remember when I did the tango in the American Legion show?

HOWIE. Sure, Jackie.

JACKIE (*recalling a bit of a tango step, executing it just to make sure she remembers it*). I just loved the tango. Remember that black-haired fellow that did it with me? I heard he got run outta town, for passing bad checks.

HOWIE. Don't remember. What're you gonna have, Jackie?

JACKIE. I'll have a Tom Collins, Howie. Very sweet. (*Starts off*). If Bus comes, tell him I'll be out in a minute. (*She disappears behind a door marked* DOLLS, *at the back of the dance floor, opposite a door marked* GUYS.)

HOWIE. When them mines was operatin', this was the wealthiest town in the whole darn Midwest . . . *per capita*. That's what people said.

SALESMAN. Oh, this was a fine town in its day. No doubt about it.

HOWIE. The college professors had come here to look at them mines, and they told us they didn't run very deep. Folks didn't pay any attention.

SALESMAN. Well, who's gonna b'lieve a college professor?

HOWIE. Seems like folks b'lieve pretty much what they *wanta* b'lieve.

SALESMAN. But this was sure a fine town while . . . while it *was* a fine town.

HOWIE. I got no objection to it *now*. It's no *utopia* . . . or anything, but the wife and I got friends here, I like my work. Shoot! You can't expect . . . well you can't expect *paradise* until you *die*.

SALESMAN (*has not been listening*). It used t' be, I'd drive my car into town . . . I had a Buick then . . . and park in front of the hotel and there'd be a porter right there, waiting to take my things inside. And then when I got inside, he'd have a couple bottles waitin' for me

. . . they had Prohibition then . . . and I'd have my customers up and offer 'em a few drinks. Then I'd take 'em out to dinner.

HOWIE. Oh, those were the days, all right.

SALESMAN. Now I drive into town, pull up at the hotel and have to wake 'em up so they'll let me register. I carry my bags up to my room, myself, cause there ain't any porter, and I eat my dinner alone. (*Shakes his head sadly*). You can't even get a good meal in this town any more. (BUS RILEY *enters. He is a handsome man of thirty-nine or forty, but still young-looking, with a boyish face that has become somewhat hard and bitter. His dress is sharp, rather dapper. His physique is powerful and finely proportioned, with broad shoulders and slim waist. His walk and his manner are a little arrogant, a little disdainful. He goes straight to the bar.*)

BUS (*to* HOWIE). Jackie Bowen been here?

HOWIE (*nods at door marked* DOLLS). Be out in a minute, Bus. Sit down and make yourself at home.

BUS (*sitting*). Draw me a beer. Jigger of whiskey on the side.

HOWIE (*reaching for a glass*). One boiler-maker! This your first trip home in quite a while, ain't it, Bus?

BUS. It's gonna be my last one, too.

HOWIE. Don't the old home town look very good to you?

BUS. This *snob* town? Why should I come back here? I'd like to *tell* a few jerks in this town . . . I'd like to *show* 'em. People aren't like they are here *every*where. Out in Hollywood, I can go to places like *Ciro's*, and the *Mocambo* . . . places the hicks in this town never even heard of, places that've got *class*.

HOWIE (*unimpressed but interested*). That right, Bus? You have yourself a good time out there, do you?

BUS (*taking out his wallet, producing a snapshot*). See her? She's a starlet . . . one of the biggest studios out there. Drives around in a Jaguar. Every night we go off dancin' at *Ciro's* . . . or some place like that. I should waste my time comin' back to this jerk town!

HOWIE. You still in the ring, Bus?

BUS. Won a fight last November. I had the slob on the mat in three rounds.

HOWIE. You're gettin' a little old to fight, aren't you, Bus? You're gonna have to start lookin' for a new job soon, aren't you?

BUS. What're you talkin' about? (*Doubles a fist to display before* HOWIE). See that? That's still hard as a rock, and it's gonna stay that way. I can still dish it out, and I'll always be able to. Know why? Cause I got fight in *here*. (*Pounds his fist over his chest.*)

HOWIE. All the same, Bus, when a man gets past thirty-five, he begins to slow up, and . . .

BUS. Not me. I got it in here. I got fight in here. (*He pounds his heart*). And I'm never givin' up.

SALESMAN (*who has been studying the picture of the star-let*). They tell me those Hollywood girls are . . . pretty hot stuff.

BUS. They're all right. (*It's not in his self-image to show too much enthusiasm.*)

JACKIE (*suddenly appears at Bus's side. Her face is almost beatific with the joy of seeing him*). Bus! Bus Riley!

BUS (*turning quickly. He feels some true joy in seeing her*). Jackie! How ya, Doll? (*He throws his arms around her.*)

JACKIE. Bus Riley! I just can't believe it.

BUS. You're lookin' swell, Jackie. Not a day older.

JACKIE. You're still the best-lookin' guy I ever saw.

BUS (*more cautiously*). You're . . . you're not sore at me?

JACKIE (*thinks a moment*). No. Of course not, Bus.

BUS (*relieved*). Sit down, Doll, and have yourself a drink.

JACKIE (*picking up her Tom Collins*). I got one already.

I was so surprised when you called. Someone told me you were in town, but I didn't believe it. I didn't believe Bus Riley would ever come back to town without calling me.

BUS. I wasn't too sure you'd *wanta* see me, Doll.

JACKIE (*still in a personal voice*). Oh, Bus! you *knew* I did. I never blamed you for anything, Bus. Of course I wanted to see you.

BUS. Well . . . the old man, Jackie . . .

JACKIE (*seriously*). I heard about it, Bus. How is he?

BUS. I guess he's all right now. But when they wired me, they thought he was done for. I had to come back and give him some blood. See, I got the same type he has. He's gonna pull through now.

JACKIE. I'm glad, Bus.

BUS. So tomorrow morning, I'm pullin' out.

JACKIE. Tomorrow?

BUS (*trying to relieve tension*). I can't get over how swell you look, Doll. Hey, tell you what, I'll take you back to California with me and put you in movies. How ya like that? (*They laugh together*). Don't think I couldn't. I gotta lotta pull out there. Yah, I had dinner just the other night at *Ciro's* . . . with some very big people. *Very* big.

JACKIE (*thrilled. This is her dream man*). Oh, Bus! Thanks, just the same.

BUS. How 'bout a little dance, Doll?

JACKIE. That's what I've been waiting for all day. When you called, my heart began to swell out like a balloon and I was afraid it was gonna pop. And I told myself, "Tonight I'll be dancing with Bus again. After all these years."

BUS (*laughs, slaps her on the fanny*). You're a silly dame. (*They stand by the bar and talk before dancing*). Hey, we had some great times together, didn't we?

JACKIE. Yes . . . we did.

BUS. It don't seem so long ago. Remember the Senior Picnic?

JACKIE. Of course I do.

BUS. Remember the Thanksgiving game at Midwest?

JACKIE. You made all the touchdowns, and I was so proud to be your girl. Sure I remember.

BUS. The Commencement dance?

JACKIE. I . . . I remember everything, Bus. Everything.

BUS. And remember the English class we had together!

JACKIE. Yes. Miss Carson was the teacher.

BUS. That her name? Remember when she accused me of cribbin' off your test paper?

JACKIE. I told you she'd suspect something if you quoted the same lines a poetry I did.

BUS. But I had to write *some*thing.

JACKIE. She asked us to quote some poetry by William Wordsworth, and I wrote . . . I even remember the lines.

BUS. Yah?

JACKIE.

"Though nothing can bring back the hour
Of splendour in the grass, glory in the flower,
We will grieve not, rather find
Strength in what remains behind."

BUS (*impressed*). Well, what'ya know about that?

JACKIE. Sometimes . . . lines a poetry just stay with me. I don't know why.

BUS (*feeling awkward*). I never knew much about poetry . . . stuff like that.

JACKIE. I never did either . . . except for certain lines that I'd remember . . . just like songs I'd hear . . . (*Brightly, snapping back to the present*). Oh, I'm a longhair now. Honest!

BUS. You used to play the hottest piano in town.

JACKIE. Oh, I still like to play ragtime and popular stuff, but I got out some of my old music a few years ago, the things I studied when I was a kid. (*Laughs*). Chopin and Schubert and Brahms, they didn't make any sense to me then, but I started playing them again, and I couldn't believe it. They seemed . . . so beautiful and . . . and . . . Well, I wondered, where have I been all these years that I thought this stuff was dull.

BUS. Well, you're not too highbrow to dance to the jukebox now, are you?

JACKIE (*laughs*). Don't be silly.

BUS. . . . cause I never dance very well to . . . to Brahms. (*The jukebox now has turned sentimental. A recording of "Stardust" has turned up. It is a straight playing of the piece, simple, sweet, and tender.*)

JACKIE (*clutches* BUS's *arm*). Listen! It's "Stardust," Bus. You and I remember when that piece first came out, don't we?

BUS. Yah!

JACKIE. Kids have been dancing to that piece ever since, but we danced to it when it was *new*. I was dancing with you the first time I heard it played. Oh, Bus, let's . . . let's dance to it again.

BUS (*stretching out his arms to her*). Here's my arms, Doll. Just crawl into 'em again. (*He folds her into his arms and they dance softly together.*)

SALESMAN (*with the wonder of recall*). It used to be, I'd come into town, come in on the Northeast highway, over the new white bridge, and all the way down Elm Street, there was them fine big houses on both sides of the street. *Mansions!* Them high trees overhead, they was like a big green, leafy canopy, that let the sunlight through. And all the lawns was trimmed and smooth, and there was always a shiny big car sitting in the driveway . . .

HOWIE. Yah. When this town had it, we really *had* it.

SALESMAN. Them's all rooming houses now, ain't they?

HOWIE. The old Forester home's a business college.

SALESMAN. It . . . it just don't seem right. All them houses with the big trees, and the big cars sittin' out in front . . . they was so dern beautiful. Why couldn't they stay that way? Can you tell me that? Why couldn't they have stayed that way?

HOWIE. Don't ask *me*.

SALESMAN. There oughta be a law to keep things the way they are. Goll darn it, there oughta be a law. (JACKIE *and* BUS *are dancing.*)

JACKIE. Are you still fighting, Bus?

BUS. You said it, Doll. I'm still in there sluggin'. I've still got the hardest punch in . . .

JACKIE (*naïvely*). Maybe you'll be champion someday, huh?

BUS (*a little embarrassed*). Naw. I don't go in for championship bouts. I just fight once in a while now, when I feel like it. And I do a little movie work, too. Sure. When I feel like it. Yah, I been in quite a few pictures. Just small parts, of course. I never take parts where I have to speak lines. You have to study to do that, and I don't wanta be a star or anything. I just like to take a few parts once in a while . . . just for the fun of it. It's kind of a hobby with me, when I'm not fightin'. (*They stop dancing as music stops. They are* L. *near the window and front door.*)

JACKIE. I always knew you'd get someplace, Bus.

BUS (*you can fool some of the people and still feel embarrassed about it*). Yah . . . Well . . . (*Hurrying to change the subject*). Tell me about *you*, Doll. I thought I'd come back and find you an old married woman.

JACKIE (*now it is her turn to feel embarrassed*). No. I never got married, Bus.

BUS (*his face now turns serious. Something has been recalled*). Oh . . .

JACKIE (*quick to reassure him*). Oh, but I *could* have, Bus. Lotsa times. I dated Bunny Byram after you left . . .

BUS. Old Bunny?

JACKIE. He wanted to marry me, but he drank so much.

BUS. Yah. You stayed outa trouble there.

JACKIE. And I went with Dick Parsons a while, but I never really cared for him . . . much. And I got a boy friend now. Yes. His name is Gerald Baker. He sells dental supplies. I met him once in Dr. Millard's office, and he called me for a date that night. He's an awful nice fellow and a peck of fun. He wants to marry me . . . and I've been thinking it over. He . . . he's . . . well, he's nothing like *you*, Bus. But I seem to like him *more* every time we go out together. He . . . he seems to . . . to really like me. (*She gives a little laugh of embarrassment.*)

BUS (*feeling a little morose*). Well . . . I used to wonder about you at times . . . *you* know.

JACKIE. People really were very nice about it, Bus. After a while. At first they weren't. I mean . . . when I first came back to town, lotsa people wouldn't speak to me, and I didn't go to church or anything because I knew how all the women would look at me, but I got busy right away. I teach piano lessons. That was the only thing I knew how to do very well, was play the piano, and I had to earn a living. I didn't have many pupils at first, but people soon forgot and now I got all the pupils I can take care of, and no one ever tries to remind me . . .

BUS (*this is very hard for him to ask*). What . . . what ever happened to . . .

JACKIE. It was a little girl, Bus. I never saw her. I figured the best thing I could do for her was to give her to that place in Chicago. They see that the babies are adopted by nice families and . . . Well, they took her from me the very first thing. The nurse said it would be easier that way, if I never saw her. So I never did.

BUS (*completely inadequate to the situation*). Yah . . . well . . . you did the right thing. Sure. You did the right thing. (*Now the music has changed. The rhythm is high and fast and exciting. Teen-agers start dancing, their young bodies full of quickness and zest, their faces smiling and full of life.*)

BUS. Let's go back to the bar, Doll. What d'ya say? (*They go to the bar and* BUS *calls out to* HOWIE). Set 'em up for us again, Howie.

HOWIE. O.K. (*There is a long pause between* JACKIE *and* BUS. *They sit together at the bar now with their own private thoughts. Finally* JACKIE *speaks, in a very private voice.*)

JACKIE. Bus?

BUS. Yah, Doll?

JACKIE (*gives a little laugh*). I just can't get used to having you call me "Doll." I mean . . .

BUS. Out in L.A. that's all you ever hear. *Doll.*

JACKIE. I know, but . . . Well, when we were kids, you called me other things . . . like "honey," or "sweetie-pie," or "precious."

BUS. Well, what's wrong with *doll?*

JACKIE. Nothing's wrong with it. I . . . I just can't get used to it, that's all.

BUS. Every girl I see . . . I call "doll."

JACKIE. Oh.

BUS. . . . but you're a special doll, Jackie, cause you're the first doll I was ever really gone on. (JACKIE *smiles wistfully*). And how 'bout me, Doll? You were pretty gone on me, weren't you?

JACKIE. Yes . . . yes, Bus. I *was*.

BUS. . . . and I'm just sayin' this cause it's true, Doll, but right now I don't think you're so bad, either.

JACKIE (*of course she is thrilled to hear him say this*). Oh, Bus! when you say that, I . . . I feel just as thrilled

and excited as I did . . . when you said it before, all
those times you said it, you could say it to me a hundred
times a day, and each time, I'd feel thrilled . . . quiver
inside like a bird.

BUS (*laughs and throws a bearlike arm around her*). You're
O.K., Jackie. You're O.K.

JACKIE (*drawing from him for she has serious things to
say*). Bus . . . I was in love with you.

BUS (*not knowing for sure how to respond to her serious-
ness*). Well . . . after all, Doll . . .

JACKIE. I was in love with you. There. I've said it. And
I've wanted to say it all these years.

BUS (*unequal to the situation*). Yah? Well . . .

JACKIE. We were just kids then, and it's hard for kids to
say . . . "I love you." So I never said it . . . in so many
words, even though you musta known it.

BUS. I guess I did.

JACKIE. Then after you were gone . . .

BUS. Look, Jackie, the only thing for me to do was leave.
You know that. This town was flat. I couldn't find a job.

JACKIE. I never blamed you for leaving, Bus.

BUS (*his guilt is within himself*). Well . . . I just wondered . . .

JACKIE. But after you'd gone, and I . . . I had to go away
. . . you know . . . I missed you so, Bus, I wanted you
so bad, I thought my heart was gonna pound its way
out of my bosom . . .

BUS (*embarrassed*). Jackie!

JACKIE. Then after I'd got the baby taken care of and
come back home . . . I felt so empty inside, I . . . I
wanted to die. I almost . . .

BUS. Jackie! you didn't.

JACKIE. I . . . I did try. Finally Dr. Henry, that's
Bernice's father, he knew I didn't have any money so

he and Bernice took me up to Kansas City to see a psychiatrist.

BUS. Those guys don't know anything.

JACKIE. Anyway, I talked with him a few times and it helped. I came back home then and got to work.

BUS. Golly, Jackie, I wish you didn't have to bring all this up.

JACKIE. I've *got* to, Bus. You've got to know how I felt. 'Cause I was in love with you, and if you love someone and he's gone, and you can't say you love him, it all begins to hurt inside and it's gotta come out when it *can*.

BUS. O.K., Doll. Shoot!

JACKIE. Well . . . I guess I've said it now. Anyway, when I came back, Bernice Henry was the only friend I could count on. She used to take me riding of an evening. She did that for more'n a year. Every evening, I'd ask her to drive by your house. She said it was just making things worse, but I couldn't resist. I just wanted to see the places where I knew you'd been. I used to look up in your window and remember all the times I used to see your face in it. And I used to look at the old hot-rod in the back yard, and remember all the joy rides we had . . .

BUS (*here's a chance to lift the pressure*). Hey, it's still there. Was I ever surprised to find the old hot-rod in the back yard?

JACKIE. . . . and I . . . Now don't laugh, Bus . . . I used to pray for you. I did.

BUS. Pray for me?

JACKIE. You always seemed so discontent in lots of ways, and I used to pray that you'd pass American History and graduate, and then get a good job that'd keep you happy and . . .

BUS (*his belligerence returns*). Think anyone in this snob town'd give a job to a miner's son?

JACKIE. Bus, they *would* have. You imagined most of those things.

BUS. Oh yah! Oh sure! I *imagined* there wasn't any decent jobs around. I just imagined I had to dig ditches . . .

JACKIE. You'da got something better, if you'd been patient.

BUS (*going on, paying no attention*). I just *imagined* that the old lady had to take in washings. I just *imagined* that the old man used to come home drunk and beat up all his kids just to get his exercise . . .

JACKIE. I knew what it was like for you. I knew all the time.

BUS. And I suppose I'm to come back home now and *smile* at people and be *nice*.

JACKIE. Bus, there's *no* one can ever arrange things in his own life, when he's a kid anyway, to suit himself. You . . . you gotta make peace sometime with the life you were born with . . .

BUS. Not me, Doll!

JACKIE. But you got to, Bus, if you ever really make your life any better.

BUS. My life's a lot better.

JACKIE. I mean . . . to keep from going on . . . hating people . . . blaming other people . . . for things they couldn't help . . . or didn't mean . . .

BUS (*gritting his teeth*). It makes you feel strong . . . to *hate*.

JACKIE (*pained*). Oh, Bus!

BUS. Yah! It makes you feel strong.

JACKIE. . . . and I did know a time . . . when . . . sometimes . . . you *did* smile at people. I did know times you could be nice. There were even times when . . . Oh, you were sweet, Bus. You were very sweet.

BUS. A guy don't stay smiling . . . and nice . . . and sweet. A guy's gotta *fight*.

JACKIE. It hurts, Bus, to hear you talk like that. I can't tell you how it hurts.

BUS (*now he forces himself back into a party mood*). Hey, Doll! Fer cryin' out loud, let's stop it! Get that lost look off your face. We're out to celebrate tonight. Order another round of drinks. I wanta make a phone call. Be back in two seconds. (*He hurries off to the telephone booth.* JACKIE *sits at the bar, her face in her hands, a heavy sadness upon her.* HOWIE *and the* SALESMAN *resume their conversation, the latter has become a little more plastered than before.*)

SALESMAN. You know, sometimes I think about givin' up the road. The wife wants me to. She wants me to buy a little chicken farm, close to St. Louis. We'll never get rich that way, I tell her. She says we're not gettin' rich *this* way, and she's right. I know we could make a good living on the farm, but . . . but a man . . . always wants . . . somethin' *better*.

HOWIE. Take my brother Elmo. He's makin' big money up in Kansas City now, used-car business. He says to me, "Howie! ya gonna be a bartender all your life? Let me get you started in Kansas City and I'll have you drivin' around in a Cadillac." (*Chuckles*). Yah! that's my brother Elmo. He's got his fourteenth Cadillac now and his third wife. 'Course . . . I'm not sayin' that tendin' bar is the greatest job in the world . . . but I kinda like it. I take a kind of pride in doin' my work well . . . (*Suddenly sniffs something in the air, then hollers back at the teen-agers*). Hey! who's smokin' that stuff back there? (*He rushes back to the gang*). I don't allow that in here. You kids know I don't. I'm disgusted with you. Now who's got it? (*The kids are mum*). I don't wanta have to run you *all* out. (*Finally one boy steps forward. His name is* BRONCO.)

BRONCO. Aw, fer cryin' out loud, Howie. Let a guy have a little fun, will you?

HOWIE (*worked up about it*). Was it you, Bronco? Anyone else?

JOKER. No one else, Howie.

HOWIE. You swear to that, Joker? The rest of you kids swear to it, you weren't smokin' that weed?

THE GANG. Honest, Howie! Give us the benefit of the doubt. Honest. No one else had any.

HOWIE (*taking* BRONCO *by the collar*). Now look, Bronco! I don't like to spoil anyone's fun, but there's just certain kinds of fun I can't allow you to have here. And if that's the only kinda fun you enjoy, well . . . I personally feel darn sorry for you, kid, but I gotta force you to have your fun someplace else. That's all.

BRONCO (*straightening up*). You can't order me around like that. I'm not gonna take orders from you.

HOWIE. Look, boy, some day you're gonna have to take orders from *someone*.

BRONCO (*belligerent*). No one's gonna tell me what to do.

HOWIE. Yes, they are, kid. I can feel it in my bones. Someday you're gonna force 'em to. And if you force a man to tell you what to do, then you got a pretty unholy kinda man that's not gonna let you do *anything*. Now beat it.

BRONCO. I was goin' anyway. I don't enjoy this two-bit dump.

HOWIE. Just beat it, Bronco. Just beat it. (BRONCO *thrusts his hands into his hip pockets and strides arrogantly out.* HOWIE *returns to behind bar*). I don't know what's got into kids today. If I didn't watch 'em, they'd turn this place into an opium den.

SALESMAN. But I'll never give up the road. I know I'll never give it up, even if I don't make a dime.

HOWIE. Kids today *beat* me. Every one of them kids in there knows more'n *I* knew when I was thirty. They throw orgies that'd surprise a Roman emperor, but they go home to their folks and their folks still wanta read 'em bedtime stories. I don't know what's gonna happen to 'em. They're all ambitious but they all wanta be movie stars or bandleaders or disc-jockeys. They're too *good* for plain, ordinary, everyday work. And what's gonna happen to us if everyone becomes a bandleader, I'd like to know.

SALESMAN (*Who has been immersed in his own liquid thoughts*). What's that, Howie?

HOWIE. Oh . . . nothin', I guess. Nothin'.

SALESMAN. You know, Howie, I'll never give up the road 'cause I keep tellin' myself *some* day it's gonna come back.

HOWIE. Maybe it will, for all *I* know.

SALESMAN. I don't think so. (*Now* BUS *comes hurrying back to* JACKIE's *side. He is worked up about something. He whispers to her privately.*)

BUS. Hey, Jackie! What ya say, Doll? I just called Fred Beamis. Remember old Fred? His wife's gone. Yah! He's got the whole house there to himself. He says you and me can take it over and . . . Well, how 'bout it, Jackie?

JACKIE (*as though coming out of a dream*). Fred Beamis?

BUS. Yah! his wife's gone, Doll. Look, Doll, I'm lonesome. What ya say? It's your old boy friend Bus talkin' to you, Doll. Yah!

JACKIE. Bus . . . you been in town a whole week now and you . . . you never even called me till today.

BUS (*squirming a little*). Yah. Well, I told you how it was at home, Doll, there with the family, first time I've seen 'em in all these years, and the old man sick and the old lady about to blow a gasket . . .

JACKIE. You . . . you coulda *called,* Bus. You coulda called up and said, "Hi, Jackie! How are you?"

BUS. O.K., I didn't call. I tell you, I had a lotta things on my mind.

JACKIE (*without rancor*). It just didn't occur to you to call . . . until tonight . . . when you began to feel "lonesome" . . . and you knew Fred Beamis' wife was gone . . .

BUS. Aw, come off it, Jackie. Fer cryin' out loud!

JACKIE. No, Bus. I'm not goin' with you.

BUS (*all his plans wrecked*). Jackie!

JACKIE (*quietly but firmly*). No, Bus, I'm not goin' with you.

BUS (*this is a blow to his ego he can hardly counter*). Well, I'll be a . . .

JACKIE (*standing*). I guess I may as well go home now.

BUS (*bitterly mocking her previous claims of affection*). I was in *love* with you, Bus. I never loved anyone else, in quite the same way. Oh, you were the only one, Bus. I used to pray for you, Bus.

JACKIE (*this is too much for her. She covers her face with her hands*). Don't! Don't!

BUS. All I gotta say is, if you're so nuts about me, you gotta darn funny way of showin' it.

JACKIE (*she sounds strong but not vengeful*). I'm not *nuts* about you, Bus. Not any more. And I can say it now and feel like I'd just shed a heavy mantle that'd been weighing me down for years. (*Now* BUS *jumps off his stool and grabs* JACKIE *in his arms and kisses her fiercely, with a kiss he always had complete confidence in to get him what he wanted.*)

BUS. You can't go off and leave Bus. You *know* you can't. You know you're *nuts* about me. You still are. Yah. I seen it in your eyes when I first come into this joint. You're *nuts* about me.

JACKIE. No, Bus. I'm really not. You gotta believe me. I'm not nuts about you. I'm not any more. I got no hard feelings . . . I'm just not nuts about you.

BUS (*now he has to get mad*). Who do you think you are to turn me down? You're a small town pick-up, that's what, and you earn fifty dollars a week, maybe, givin' piano lessons. Out in Hollywood, I got girls that have got class. Yah! If I wanta doll, all I have to do is drop a dime in the telephone. Yah! I can have myself a different doll every night.

JACKIE. So long, Bus. (*She starts slowly out.*)

HOWIE (*from behind her, to* BUS). Now look here, Bus Riley, I ain't gonna let no one talk to Jackie Bowen that way in my bar.

BUS. And *who's* gonna stop me?

JACKIE (*turning back*). It's all right, Howie. It didn't mean anything at all. (*Out.*)

BUS (*over the bar*). Gimme another boiler-maker.

SALESMAN (*to himself*). Man, this was a pretty town in its day. That long street with all them high elm trees, the Country Club . . . that nice, big colonial house with the big columns . . . all the big, high-powered automobiles ridin' around in the street . . .

BUS. Hey, Howie! whatever happened to Zelma Buckley? Remember her?

HOWIE. Zelma, she got married a while back and moved to Oklahoma.

BUS. That right? (*Thinks again*). How about Dorothy Pierson? She around?

HOWIE. No, Bus. Dorothy got herself a big radio job up in Kansas City. Makin' good money. Just comes home once in a while to show off her mink coats.

BUS. Oh, a big-time girl, huh?

SALESMAN (*reduced to childish murmuring*). No. I'll never give up the road. I don't wanta start life on any chicken farm. You can't ever tell. The road might come back someday. (JACKIE *reappears, coming slowly back to the bar.* HOWIE *is the first to see her.*)

HOWIE. Leave something behind, Jackie?

JACKIE (*going to* BUS). No, Howie, I . . . I . . . (BUS *lifts his head and looks at her*). Bus, I . . .

BUS. I s'pose you had to come back to gimme hell.

JACKIE. No, Bus, I can't leave you feeling that way. You've

got to understand, I . . . I want to remember you with no hard feelings. Please, Bus.

BUS (*finally*). O.K., Jackie.

JACKIE. . . . and I hope we can always be friends.

BUS. Sure, Jackie. Shake. (*They shake hands on it. Then* JACKIE *hurries off. She gets to the door when* JOKER *catches up with her, his feet jiggling with rhythm, his arms extended to her.*)

JOKER. Hey, Miss Bowen, wanta try again?

JACKIE. No, Joker. You young people have your own dances. I'm not gonna try again. (*She takes the roses out of her hair as if suddenly she felt they didn't belong.*)

JOKER. Aw, come on. You're only as old as you feel.

JACKIE. Right now, I feel very old, and I'm kinda proud.

JOKER. Don't you like me? (*He winks at her, a little devilishly.*)

JACKIE (*maybe placing a fond hand on his cheek while she speaks*). Yes, Joker, I *do* like you. You're a vision of life itself, boy, with a face like a lamp and a lively spring in your step like you was attached to a current. How could I help but like you, Joker-boy?

JOKER (*putting an arm around her, trying to coax her to dance*). C'mon. Let's dance.

JACKIE (*holding him off*). But all that life you got, all that energy and pep, they're no good just in themselves . . . you gotta grow up, Joker-boy.

JOKER. Hey, I'm nineteen next month. I can lift a hundred pounds over my head.

JACKIE. I mean *really* grow up, not just in your body but in the way you think and feel. *Really* grow up, Joker.

JOKER (*sober*). I know what you mean. It's hard.

JACKIE. Yes, boy. It's awful hard. It takes some people half their lives . . . (*She throws her roses on the floor, disgustedly.*) and some people never do. Good-by, boy. (*She hurries out.* JOKER, *rather mystified, returns to his gang and sits thoughtfully in the midst of their dancing.*)

BUS. Gimme another, Howie.

HOWIE. Look, Bus. I've served you four of those boiler-makers already, and I don't like to serve you another.

BUS (*in the most belligerent voice*). Who's askin' you what you like? (*The* SALESMAN *is asleep now. His head lies on his arm, curved on the bar. He snores loudly.*)

HOWIE. O.K. If you wanta knock yourself out, I'm not stoppin' you. (*Sets the jigger of whiskey and the glass of beer before* BUS). One boiler-maker!

CURTAIN

HANDS ACROSS THE SEA

by Noel Coward

HANDS ACROSS THE SEA

The SCENE *is the drawing-room of the* GILPINS' *flat in London. The time is about 6 P.M. The room is nicely furnished and rather untidy.*

When the CURTAIN *rises the telephone is ringing.* WALTERS, *a neat parlourmaid, enters* R., *and answers it.*

WALTERS (*at the telephone*). Hallo . . . Yes . . . No, her ladyship's not back yet . . . She said she'd be in at five, so she ought to be here at any minute now . . . What name, please . . . Rawlingson . . . Mr. and Mrs. Rawlingson . . . (*She scribbles on the pad*). Yes . . . I'll tell her . . . (*She hangs up the receiver and goes out* R. *There is the sound of voices in the hall and* LADY MAUREEN GILPIN *enters, followed at a more leisurely pace by her husband,* PETER GILPIN. MAUREEN, *nicknamed* PIGGIE *by her intimates, is a smart, attractive woman in the thirties.* PETER *is tall and sunburned and reeks of the Navy.*)

PIGGIE (*as she comes in*). . . . and you can send the car back to me at eleven-thirty. It's quite simple, darling. I wish you wouldn't be so awfully complicated about everything.

PETER. What happens if my damned dinner goes on longer than that and I get stuck?

PIGGIE (*puts her hat on the telephone table*). You just get stuck, darling, and then you get unstuck and get a taxi——

PETER (*grumbling*). I shall be in uniform, clinking with medals——

PIGGIE. If you take my advice you'll faint dead away at eleven o'clock and then you can come home in the car and change and have time for everything——

PETER (*gets a cigarette from the cocktail table*). I can't faint dead away under the nose of the C.-in-C.

PIGGIE. You can feel a little poorly, can't you? Anybody has the right to feel a little poorly—— (*She sees the telephone-pad*). My God!

PETER. What is it?

PIGGIE. The Rawlingsons.

PETER. Who the hell are they? (*He crosses* c.)

PIGGIE. I'd forgotten all about them—I must get Maud at once—— (*She sits on the back upstage end of the sofa and dials a number.*)

PETER. Who are the Rawlingsons?

PIGGIE. Maud and I stayed with them in Samolo, I told you about it, that time when we had to make a forced landing—they practically saved our lives—— (*At the telephone*). Hullo—Maud—darling, the Rawlingsons are on us . . . What . . . the RAWLINGSONS—yes I asked them to-day and forgot all about it . . . You must come at once . . . But, darling, you *must* . . . Oh, dear . . . No, no, that was the Frobishers; these are the ones we stayed with. (PETER *sits in the armchair* R.C.). Mother and father and daughter—you must remember—pretty girl with bad legs . . . No . . . They didn't have a son . . . We swore we'd give them a lovely time when they came home on leave . . . I know they didn't have a son, that was those other people in Penang . . . Oh, all right . . . You'll have to do something about them, though . . . Let me ask them to lunch with you to-morrow . . . All right . . . one-thirty . . . I'll tell them . . . (*She hangs up*). She can't come. (*She goes down* L.)

PETER. You might have warned me that a lot of Colonial strangers were coming trumpeting into the house——

PIGGIE. I tell you I'd forgotten——

PETER. That world trip was a grave mistake——

PIGGIE. Who can I get that's celebrated (*she crosses* R.)— to give them a thrill?

PETER. Why do they have to have a thrill?

PIGGIE (*runs over to the telephone*). I'll get Clare, anyway—— (*She dials another number.*)

PETER. She'll frighten them to death.

PIGGIE. Couldn't you change early and come in in your
uniform? That would be better than nothing——

PETER. Perhaps they'd like to watch me having my bath!

PIGGIE (*at the telephone*). I want to speak to Mrs. Wedderburn, please . . . Yes . . . (*To* PETER). I do wish
you'd be a little helpful——

PETER. I wish you wouldn't attack me.

PIGGIE (*at the telephone*). Clare? . . . This is Piggie . . .
I want you to come round at once and help me with the
Rawlingsons . . . No, I know you haven't, but that
doesn't matter . . . Mother, father and daughter—very
sweet—I'm repaying hospitality . . . Maud's having
them to lunch to-morrow and Peter's going to take them
over the dockyard . . .

PETER (*jumps up*). I'm not going to do any such thing——

PIGGIE. Shut up. I just thought of that and it's a *very* good
idea—— (*At the telephone*). All right, darling—as soon as
you can . . . (*She hangs up*). I must go and change——
(*She picks up her hat.*)

PETER. You know perfectly well I haven't time to take
mothers and fathers and daughters with bad legs over
the dockyard——

PIGGIE. It wouldn't take a minute; they took us all over
their rubber plantations. (*She crosses to* PETER *above
the sofa.*)

PETER. It probably served you right.

PIGGIE. You're so disobliging, darling; you really should try
to conquer it. It's something to do with being English,
I think—as a race I'm ashamed of us—no sense of hospitality. The least we can do when people are kind to
us in far-off places is to be a little gracious in return.

PETER. They weren't kind to me in far-off places.

PIGGIE. You know there's a certain grudging, sullen streak in your character—I've been very worried about it lately —it's spreading like a forest fire——

PETER. Why don't you have them down for the week-end?

PIGGIE. Don't be so idiotic, how can I possibly? There's no room to start with, and even if there were they'd be utterly wretched——

PETER. I don't see why.

PIGGIE. They wouldn't know anybody—they probably wouldn't have the right clothes—they'd keep on huddling about in uneasy little groups—— (*She lights a cigarette from the box on the telephone table.*)

PETER. The amount of groups that three people can huddle about in is negligible. (ALASTAIR CORBETT *saunters into the room from* R. *He is good looking and also distinctly naval in tone.*)

ALLY. Hallo, chaps.

PIGGIE. Ally darling—how lovely—we're in trouble. Peter'll tell you all about it—— (*The telephone rings and she goes to it. The following conversations occur simultaneously.*)

ALLY. What trouble?

PETER. More of Piggie's beach friends.

ALLY. Let's have a drink.

PETER. Cocktail?

ALLY. No, a long one—whisky and soda.

PETER (*going to the drink table*). All right.

ALLY. What beach friends?

PETER. People Maud and Piggie picked up in the East.

PIGGY (*at the telephone*). Hulloh . . . Yes—Robert dear— how lovely! . . . It's Robert . . .

ALLY. Piggie ought to stay at home more. (PETER *mixes a whisky and soda.*)

PIGGIE (*on the telephone*). Where are you?

PETER. That's what I say!

PIGGIE. Oh, what a shame . . . No—Peter's going to sea on Thursday—I'm going down on Saturday.

ALLY. Rubber, I expect. Everybody in the East's rubber.

PIGGIE (*on the telephone*). No—nobody particular—just Clare and Bogey, and I think Pops, but he thinks he's got an ulcer or something and might not be able to come!

PETER. We thought you might be a real friend and take them over the dockyard.

ALLY. What on earth for?

PETER. Give them a thrill.

PIGGIE (*on the telephone*). All right—I'll expect you . . . No, I don't think it can be a very big one—he looks as bright as a button.

ALLY. Why don't you take them over the dockyard?

PETER. I shall be at sea Thursday—exercises!

PIGGIE (*on the telephone*). No, darling, what is the use of having her—she only depresses you . . . Oh, all right! (*She hangs up*). Oh dear——

PETER. It's quite easy for you—you can give them lunch on board——

ALLY. We're in dry dock.

PETER. They won't mind. What is it?

PIGGIE. Robert—plunged in gloom—he's got to do a course at Greenwich—he ran into a tram in Devonport—and he's had a row with Molly. He wants me to have her for the week-end so that they can make it up all over everybody. Have you told Ally about the Rawlingsons?

PETER. Yes, he's taking them over the dockyard, lunching them on board and then he's going to show them a submarine——

PIGGIE. Marvellous. You're an angel, Ally. I must take off these clothes, I'm going mad—— (*She goes out of the room up* L.C. *at a run. There is the sound of the front-door bell.*)

PETER. Let's go into my room—I can show you the plans——

ALLY. Already? They've been pretty quick with them.

PETER. I made a few alterations—there wasn't enough deck space. She ought to be ready by October. I shall have her sent straight out to Malta——

ALLY. Come on, we shall be caught—— (*They go off up* L.C. *as* WALTERS *ushers in* MR. *and* MRS. WADHURST *on the* R. *The* WADHURSTS *are pleasant, middle-aged people; their manner is a trifle timorous.*)

WALTERS. Her ladyship is changing; I'll tell her you are here.

MRS. WADHURST. Thank you.

MR. WADHURST. Thank you very much. (WALTERS *goes up* L.C. *The* WADHURSTS *look round the room,* C.)

MRS. WADHURST. It's a very nice flat.

MR. WADHURST. Yes—yes, it is.

MRS. WADHURST (*crosses* L., *scrutinizing a photograph on the piano*). That must be him.

MR. WADHURST. Who?

MRS. WADHURST. The Commander. (WALTERS *enters up* L.C., *crosses and exits* R.)

MR. WADHURST. Yes I expect it is.

MRS. WADHURST. Sailors always have such nice open faces, don't they?

MR. WADHURST. Yes, I suppose so.

MRS. WADHURST (*comes* C.). Clean-cut and look-you-straight-in-the-eye—I like men who look you straight in the eye. (*She crosses up* R.)

MR. WADHURST. Yes, it's very nice. (*He follows her.*)

MRS. WADHURST (*at another photograph on the half-moon table up* R.). This must be her sister—I recognize her from "The Tatler"—look. She was Lady Hurstley, you know, then she was Lady Macfadden, and I don't know who she is now.

MR. WADHURST. Neither do I. (*His back to the audience.*)

MRS. WADHURST. What a dear little boy—such a sturdy little fellow—look at the way he's holding his engine.

MR. WADHURST. Is that his engine?

MRS. WADHURST. He has rather a look of Donald Hotchkiss, don't you think?

MR. WADHURST. Yes, dear.

MRS. WADHURST. I must say they have very nice things—— Oh, dear, how lovely to be well off—— I must write to the Brostows by the next mail and tell them all about it.

MR. WADHURST. Yes, you must.

MRS. WADHURST. Don't you think we'd better sit down?

MR. WADHURST. Why not?

MRS. WADHURST. You sit in that chair and I'll sit on the sofa.

MR. WADHURST. Yes, dear. (*She sits on the sofa. He sits in the armchair.*)

MRS. WADHURST. I wish you wouldn't look quite so uncomfortable, Fred, there's nothing to be uncomfortable about. (*He puts his elbow on the arm of the chair.*)

MR. WADHURST. She does expect us, doesn't she?

MRS. WADHURST. Oh yes, I talked to her myself on the telephone last Wednesday; she was perfectly charming and said that we were to come without fail and that it would be divine.

MR. WADHURST. I still feel we should have telephoned again just to remind her. People are always awfully busy in London.

MRS. WADHURST. I do hope Lady Dalborough will be here too—I should like to see her again—she was so nice.

MR. WADHURST. She was the other one, wasn't she?

MRS. WADHURST (*irritably*). What do you mean, the other one?

MR. WADHURST. I mean not this one.

MRS. WADHURST. She's the niece of the Duke of Frensham, her mother was Lady Merrit, she was a great traveller too—I believe she went right across the Sahara dressed as an Arab. In those days that was a very dangerous thing to do.

MR. WADHURST. I shouldn't think it was any too safe now. (WALTERS *enters* R., *and ushers in* MR. BURNHAM, *a nondescript young man, carrying a longish roll of cardboard.*)

WALTERS. The Commander will be here in a minute.

MR. BURNHAM. Thanks—thanks very much. (WALTERS *goes out.* MR. WADHURST *rises.*)

MRS. WADHURST (*after a slightly awkward silence*). How do you do.

MR. BURNHAM. How do you do.

MRS. WADHURST (*with poise*). This is my husband.

MR. BURNHAM. How do you do.

MR. WADHURST. How do you do. (*They shake hands.*)

MRS. WADHURST (*vivaciously*). Isn't this a charming room? —so—so lived in.

MR. BURNHAM. Yes.

MR. WADHURST. Are you in the Navy too?

MR. BURNHAM. No.

MRS. WADHURST (*persevering*). It's so nice to be home again—we come from Malaya, you know.

MR. BURNHAM. Oh—Malaya.

MRS. WADHURST. Yes, Lady Maureen and Lady Dalborough visited us there—my husband has a rubber plantation up country—there's been a terrible slump, of course, but we're trying to keep our heads above water—aren't we, Fred?

MR. WADHURST. Yes, dear, we certainly are.

MRS. WADHURST. Have you ever been to the East?

MR. BURNHAM. No.

MRS. WADHURST. It's very interesting really, although the climate's rather trying until you get used to it, and of course the one thing we do miss is the theatre——

MR. BURNHAM. Yes—of course.

MRS. WADHURST. There's nothing my husband and I enjoy so much as a good play, is there, Fred?

MR. WADHURST. Nothing.

MRS. WADHURST. And all we get is films, and they're generally pretty old by the time they come out to us—— (*She laughs gaily.*)

MR. WADHURST. Do you go to the theatre much?

MR. BURNHAM. No. (*There is a silence, which is broken by the telephone ringing. Everybody jumps.*)

MRS. WADHURST. Oh, dear—do you think we ought to answer it?

MR. WADHURST. I don't know. (*The telephone continues to ring.* CLARE WEDDERBURN *comes in* R. *She is middle aged, well dressed and rather gruff. She is followed by* "BOGEY" GOSLING, *a Major in the Marines, a good-looking man in the thirties. He mixes cocktails.*)

CLARE. Hallo—where's the old girl?

MRS. WADHURST (*nervously*). I—er—I'm afraid I—— (CLARE *crosses and puts her gloves on the piano.* MR. BURNHAM *crosses* L. *and sits on the chair below the piano.*)

CLARE (*going to the telephone*). Mix a cocktail, Bogey—I'm a stretcher case—— (*At the telephone*). Hallo—no, it's me—Clare . . . God knows, dear . . . Shall I tell her to call you back . . . All right . . . No, it was bloody, darling—a gloomy dinner at the Embassy, then the worst play I've ever sat through, and then the Café de Paris and that awful man who does things with a duck . . . I've already seen him six times, darling . . . Oh, you know, he pinches its behind and it quacks "Land of Hope and Glory" . . . I don't know whether it hurts it or not —I minded at first, but I'm past caring now; after all, it's not like performing dogs; I mind about performing dogs terribly . . . All right . . . Good-bye . . . (*She hangs up and turns to* MRS. WADHURST). Ducks are pretty bloody, anyway, don't you think? (*She takes a cigarette from her case.*)

MRS. WADHURST. I don't know very much about them.

CLARE. The man swears it's genuine talent, but I think it's the little nip that does it.

MRS. WADHURST. It sounds rather cruel.

CLARE. It's a gloomy form of entertainment, anyhow, particularly as I've always hated "Land of Hope and Glory——"

BOGEY. Cocktail? (*Bringing one for* CLARE *and* MRS. WADHURST.)

CLARE. Thank God! (BOGEY *hands round cocktails. The* WADHURSTS *and* MR. BURNHAM *accept them and sip them in silence.*)

BOGEY (*going back to the cocktail table*). I suppose Piggie's in the bath.

CLARE. Go and rout her out. (*She takes off her hat and puts it on the piano.*)

BOGEY. Wait till I've had a drink.

CLARE (*to* MRS. WADHURST). Is Peter home or is he still darting about the Solent?

MRS. WADHURST. I'm afraid I couldn't say. You see——

BOGEY. I saw him last night with Janet——

CLARE. Hasn't she had her baby yet?

BOGEY. She hadn't last night.

CLARE. That damned baby's been hanging over us all for months—— (*The telephone rings—*CLARE *answers it. Sitting on the telephone table*). Hallo—yes—hallo, darling . . . No, it's Clare . . . Yes, he's here . . . No, I really couldn't face it . . . Yes, if I were likely to go to India I'd come, but I'm not likely to go to India . . . I think Rajahs bumble up a house-party so terribly . . . Yes, I know *he's* different, but the other one's awful . . . Angela had an agonizing time with him—all the dining-room chairs had to be changed because they were

leather and his religion prevented him sitting on them—
all the dogs had to be kept out of the house because
they were unclean, which God knows was true of the
Bedlington, but the other ones were clean as whistles—
and then to round everything off he took Laura Merst-
ham in his car and made passes at her all the way to
Newmarket . . . All right, darling, here he is . . . (*To*
BOGEY). It's Nina, she wants to talk to you—— (*She
hands the telephone to* BOGEY, *who reaches for it and
lifts the wire so that it just misses* MRS. WADHURST'S *hat.
It isn't quite long enough, so he has to bend down to
speak with his face practically touching her.*)

BOGEY. Excuse me. (*At the telephone*). Hallo, Nin . . .
I can't on Wednesday. I've got a Guest Night . . . It's
a hell of a long way, it'd take hours . . . (CLARE *crosses
to the stool by the cocktail table and sits.* PIGGIE *comes
in* L.C. *with a rush.*)

PIGGIE. I am so sorry—— (*She comes below the sofa and
up* C.)

CLARE. Shhh!

BOGEY. Shut up, I can't hear . . .

PIGGIE (*in a shrill whisper*). Who is it? (PIGGIE *shakes
hands with* MRS. WADHURST—*at the top of the sofa.*)

CLARE. Nina.

BOGEY (*at the telephone*). Well, you can tell George to
leave it for me—and I can pick it up . . .

PIGGIE. How lovely to see you again.

BOGEY. No—I shan't be leaving till about ten—so if he leaves
it by nine-thirty—I'll get it all right . . .

PIGGIE. My husband will be here in a minute—he has to go
to sea on Thursday, but he's arranged for you to be
taken over the dockyard at Portsmouth——

BOGEY. Give the old boy a crack on the jaw . . .

PIGGIE. It's the most thrilling thing in the world— You see
how the torpedoes are made!—millions of little wheels

inside, all clicking away like mad—and they cost thousands of pounds each——

BOGEY. No—I saw her last night . . . Not yet, but at any moment now—I should think . . . All right—call me at Chatham . . . If I can get away I shall have to bring Mickie too——

PIGGIE. How much do torpedoes cost——

CLARE. God knows, darling—something fantastic—ask Bogey——

PIGGIE. Bogey——

BOGEY. What?

PIGGIE. How much do torpedoes cost each?

BOGEY. What? . . . (*At the telephone*). . . . wait a minute, Piggie's yelling at me . . .

PIGGIE. Torpedoes—— (*She makes a descriptive gesture.*)

BOGEY. Oh, thousands and thousands—terribly expensive things—ask Peter—— (*At the telephone*). . . . If I do bring him you'll have to be frightfully nice to him, he's been on the verge of suicide for weeks . . . (PIGGIE *reaches for the cigarette box over the sofa and offers them to* MRS. WADHURST *and* MR. WADHURST.)

PIGGIE. Don't let her go, I must talk to her——

BOGEY (*at the telephone*). Hold on a minute, Piggie wants to talk to you . . . All right—I'll let you know . . . Here she is . . . (PIGGIE *leans over the sofa and takes the telephone from* BOGEY, *who steps over the wire and stumbles over* MRS. WADHURST). I'm most awfully sorry——

MRS. WADHURST. Not at all——

PIGGIE (*to* MRS. WADHURST, *sitting at the lower end of the sofa*). It's so lovely you being in England—— (*At the telephone*). . . . Darling—what was the meaning of that sinister little invitation you sent me?

BOGEY. You know what Mickey is.

PIGGIE. No, dear, I really can't . . . I always get so agitated.

CLARE. Well, why does he go on like that? It's so tiresome.

PIGGIE. I'll come if Clare will . . . (*To* CLARE). Are you going to Nina's Indian ding-dong?

CLARE. Not without an anæsthetic. (*She puts her bag on the floor.*)

PIGGIE (*at the telephone*). She's moaning a bit, but I'll persuade her . . . What happens after dinner? . . . The man with the duck from the Café de Paris . . . (*To the room in general*). She's got that sweet duck from the Café de Paris——

CLARE. Give me another cocktail, Bogey, I want to get so drunk that I just can't hear any more——

PIGGIE (*at the telephone*). But, darling, do you think it's quite *wise* . . . I mean, Maharajahs are terribly touchy and there's probably something in their religion about ducks being mortal sin or something . . . You know how difficult they are about cows and pigs . . . Just a minute . . . (*To the* WADHURSTS). *You* can tell us, of course—— (*She points to* MR. WADHURST *with the 'phone.*)

MR. WADHURST. I beg your pardon.

PIGGIE. Do Indians mind ducks?

MR. WADHURST. I—I don't think so——

BOGEY. Do you come from India?

MRS. WADHURST. No, Malaya.

PIGGIE. It's the same sort of thing, though, isn't it—if they don't mind them in Malaya it's *unlikely* that they'd mind them in India—— (*At the telephone*). . . . It'll probably be all right, but you'd better get Douglas Byng as a standby.

CLARE. There might be something in their religion about Douglas Byng. (*She eats an olive.*)

PIGGIE. Everyone's making such a noise. The room's

filled with the most dreadful people. (*Looking at* MR.
BURNHAM). Darling, it is definitely Waterloo Station. (*At
the telephone.*) No, I'm almost sure he can't—he's going
to sea on Thursday . . . Don't be silly, dear, you can't be
in the Navy without going to sea *sometimes* . . . (PETER
enters, up L.C., *followed by* ALLY. *At the telephone*).
Here he is now, you can ask him yourself . . . (*To*
PETER). Peter, it's Nina, she wants to talk to you—— (*To
the* WADHURSTS). This is my husband and Lieutenant-
Commander Corbett—he's been longing to meet you and
thank you for being so sweet to us—I told him all about
your heavenly house and the plantation—— (*She is up*
C.)

MRS. WADHURST (*bridling—to* ALLY). It was most delightful, I assure you, to have Lady Maureen with us—

PIGGIE. Not him, him—that's the wrong one——

MRS. WADHURST. Oh, I'm so sorry——

PETER (*shaking hands with* MRS. WADHURST). It was so
kind of you—my wife has talked of nothing else——

PIGGIE (*grabbing him*). Here—Nina's yelling like a ban-
shee—— (*She crosses* R. *for the cigarette-box on the
cocktail table and then moves up* C.)

PETER. Excuse me. (*He takes the telephone*). Hallo, Nin
. . . What for? . . . No, I can't, but Piggie probably
can . . . (*To* PIGGIE). Can you go to Nina's party for the
Rajahs?

PIGGIE. We've been through all that—— (*She offers the cigarettes to the* WADHURSTS.)

PETER. All right—I didn't know—— (*At the telephone*).
. . . No, I shall be at sea for about three days—it isn't
tiresome at all, I like it . . .

PIGGIE (*to* MRS. WADHURST). How's your daughter? (*She
fails to light* MR. WADHURST'S *cigarette.*)

MRS. WADHURST (*surprised*). She's a little better, thank
you.

PIGGIE. Oh, has she been ill? I'm so sorry.

MR. WADHURST (*gently*). She's been ill for five years.

PIGGIE (*puzzled*). How dreadful for you—are you happy with that cocktail, or would you rather have tea? (*She pushes* MR. WADHURST *into the armchair, and sits on the pouffe herself.*)

MRS. WADHURST. This is delicious, thank you. (*She picks up her cocktail and takes a sip.*)

PETER (*at the telephone*). . . . I honestly can't do anything about that, Nina—you might be able to find out from the Admiral . . . Well, if his mother was mad too, that is an extenuating circumstance . . . He'll probably be sent home . . . (*To* CLARE). Did you know that Freda Bathurst had once been in an asylum?

CLARE. No, but it explains a lot.

PIGGIE. Why?

PETER. Her son went mad in Hong-Kong.

CLARE. What did he do?

PETER. I don't know, but Nina's in a state about it.

PIGGIE. I don't see what it's got to do with Nina——

PETER. He's a relation of some sort——

PIGGIE. See what he did. (*She rises.*)

PETER (*at the telephone*). What did he do, Nina? . . . Oh . . . Oh, I see . . . Oh . . . Well, he'll certainly be sent home, and a good job too—we can't have that sort of thing in the Service . . . If I were you I'd keep well out of it . . . All right . . . Good-bye. (*He hangs up.*)

PIGGIE. What was it? (*She sits on the top arm of the sofa.*)

PETER. I couldn't possibly tell you. (*He takes a cigarette from the box on the telephone table.*)

PIGGIE. Poor boy, I expect the climate had something to do with it—the climate's awful in Hong-Kong—look at poor old Wally Smythe——

ALLY (*to the* WADHURSTS). Did you ever know Wally Smythe?

MRS. WADHURST. No, I'm afraid not.

CLARE. You didn't miss much.

PIGGIE. I adored Wally, he was a darling.

CLARE. He kept on having fights all the time—I do hate people hitting people—— (*To* MRS. WADHURST.) Don't you?

MRS. WADHURST. Yes. (*There is suddenly a complete silence.* PIGGIE *breaks it with an effort.*)

PIGGIE (*vivaciously to the* WADHURSTS). Maud was so frightfully sorry that she couldn't come to-day—she's pining to see you again and she asked me to ask you if you'd lunch there to-morrow?

MRS. WADHURST. How very kind of her.

PIGGIE. She's got a divine little house hidden away in a mews, it's frightfully difficult to find—— (*The telephone rings.* PETER *picks up the telephone and hands it to* PIGGIE). I've got millions of questions I want to ask you, what happened to that darling old native who did a dance with a sword? (*At the telephone*). Hallo . . . (*Continuing to everyone in general*). It was the most exciting thing I've ever seen, all the villagers sat round in torchlight and beat—— (MR. BURNHAM *rises and tries to give* PETER *the plans, but he turns his back on them. At the telephone*). Hallo . . . Yes, speaking . . . (*Continuing*).—beat drums and the— (*At the telephone*). Hallo . . . Darling, I'd no idea you were back—(*to everybody*) and the old man tore himself to shreds in the middle, it was marvellous—— (*At the telephone*). I can't believe it. Where are you speaking from? . . . My dear, you're *not!* . . . (*To everybody*). It's Boodie, she got back last night and she's staying with Norman——

CLARE. Is Phyllis there? (PETER *crosses* C.)

PIGGIE (*at the telephone*). Hallo, darling, is Phyllis there? . . . She's away . . . (*To* CLARE). She's away.

PETER (*to* MR. WADHURST). That's the best joke I ever heard.

CLARE. It's made my entire season, that's all—it's just made it. (PETER *goes* R. *and talks to* CLARE *and* BOGEY.)

PIGGIE (*at the telephone*). You'd better come and dine tonight . . . I'm on a diet, so there's only spinach, but we can talk . . . Yes, she's here—absolutely worn out—we all are . . . Oh yes, it was pretty grim; it started all right and everything was going beautifully when Vera arrived, unasked, my dear, and more determined than Hitler . . . Of course there was the most awful scene— Alice flounced upstairs with tears cascading down her face and locked herself in the cook's bedroom . . . Clare tried to save the situation by dragging Lady Borrowdale on to the terrace . . .

CLARE (*sibilantly*). *That* was *afterwards!*—— (*She rises and crosses* C.)

PIGGIE (*at the telephone*). Anyhow, hell broke loose . . . You can imagine . . . Janet was there, of course, and we were all worried about her . . . No, it hasn't arrived yet, but the odds are mounting . . . (*To everybody*). She hasn't had it yet, has she, Peter?

PETER. If she has, it was born in the gramophone department at Harrods'—I left her there at four-thirty—— (*crosses* R.)

PIGGIE (*at the telephone*). . . . . No it's still what's known as on the way . . . I'll expect you about eight-thirty . . . I've got to do my feet and then I'm going to relax . . . All right . . . Yes, she's here . . . (*To* CLARE). Here, Clare, she wants to talk to you—— (*She crosses* R. *a second, then up* C. CLARE, *in order to reach the telephone comfortably, has to kneel on the sofa.*)

CLARE. Excuse me.

MRS. WADHURST. I'm so sorry.

CLARE (*at the telephone*). Darling—I'm dead with surprise . . .

PIGGIE (*to* MRS. WADHURST). Now you must tell me some more——

MRS. WADHURST. Well, really, I don't——

CLARE. Shhh! I can't hear a word—— (*At the telephone*). He what? . . . When? . . . He must be raving . . .

PIGGIE (*in a harsh whisper*). Have you still got that sweet dog? (*She sits on the pouffe.*)

MRS. WADHURST (*also whispering*). Yes, we've still got Rudolph.

PIGGIE (*to everybody*). Rudolph's an angel, I can never tell you how divine he was—he used to come in every morning with my breakfast-tray and jump on to the bed——

MRS. WADHURST (*horrified*). Oh, you never told me that. How very naughty of him. He's very seldom allowed in the house at all——

PIGGIE (*puzzled*). But—but——

MR. WADHURST. Perhaps you're thinking of some other dog, Lady Maureen—Rudolph is a Great Dane—— (*They laugh.*)

PIGGIE (*bewildered*). Oh, yes, of course, how idiotic of me——

CLARE (*at the telephone*). . . . . All right, darling . . . Call me in the morning . . . Lovely . . . Good-bye. (*She hangs up.*)

PIGGIE. Do sit down, Clare, and stop climbing about over everybody. (*To* MRS. WADHURST). You must forgive me —this is a madhouse—it's always like this—I can't think why——

CLARE (*in a whisper to* PETER, *having noticed* MR. BURN-HAM). Why's that man got a roll of music, is he going to sing? (*She crosses to* PETER, *then returns to sit on the sofa.*)

MRS. WADHURST. Have you been in London for the whole season?

PIGGIE. Yes, it's been absolutely frightful, but my husband is getting leave soon, so we shall be able to pop off somewhere——

ALLY (*to* MR. WADHURST). I suppose you've never run across a chap in Burma called Beckwith?

MR. WADHURST. No, I've never been to Burma.

ALLY. He's in rubber too, I believe—or tea—he's very amusing. (*There is a pause.*)

MRS. WADHURST (*to* PIGGIE). We did hope you'd come and lunch with us one day—but I expect you're terribly busy——

PIGGIE. My dear, I'd worship it—— (*The telephone rings*). Oh really, this telephone never stops for one minute—— (*Standing at the telephone*). Hallo . . . Yes, speaking . . . Who? . . . Mrs. Rawlingson . . . Oh, yes, yes, yes . . . (*She hands the telephone to* MRS. WADHURST). Here—it's for you—

MRS. WADHURST (*astonished*). For me? How very curious——

PIGGIE (*crosses* R.). Give me a cocktail, Bogey—I haven't had one at all yet and I'm exhausted—— (PETER *is up stage* C.)

MRS. WADHURST (*at the telephone*). Hallo . . . What . . . Who? . . . I'm afraid I don't quite understand . . .

BOGEY (*giving* PIGGIE *a cocktail*). Here you are—it's a bit weak——

MRS. WADHURST (*still floundering*). . . . I think there must be some mistake . . . Just a moment . . . (*To* PIGGIE). It's for you, Lady Maureen—a Mrs. Rawlingson——

PIGGIE (*laughing*). Now isn't that the most extraordinary coincidence—— (*She takes the telephone*). . . . Hallo . . . Yes—speaking . . . (*She listens and her face changes*). Oh yes . . . (PETER *goes* L. *of the telephone table. She looks hurriedly at the* WADHURSTS, *then at* PETER). I'm so awfully sorry, I only just came in . . . Oh, what a shame . . . No, no, no, it doesn't matter a bit . . . No—indeed you must call me up the first moment he gets over it . . . Yes . . . I expect it was . . .

Yes . . . Good-bye. (*She slowly hangs up the receiver, looking at the* WADHURSTS *in complete bewilderment. She makes a sign to* PETER *over* MRS. WADHURST'S *shoulder, but he only shakes his head. Brightly, but with intense meaning*). That was Mrs. Rawlingson.

PETER. Good God!

PIGGIE (*with purpose, sitting next to* MRS. WADHURST, *who is still seated on the sofa*). Did you ever meet the Rawlingsons out East?

MRS. WADHURST. No—I don't know them.

PIGGIE. Maud and I stayed with them too, you know.

MRS. WADHURST. Where?

PIGGIE. It was in Malaya somewhere, I think—I do get so muddled.

MRS. WADHURST. I think we should have heard of them if they lived in Malaya. (PETER *meanwhile has gone to the piano and started to strum idly—he begins to hum lightly at the same time*.)

PETER (*humming to a waltz refrain, slightly indistinctly, but clearly enough for* PIGGIE *to hear*). "If these are not them, who are they? Who are they? Who are they?" (PIGGIE *rises and saunters over to the piano*.)

PIGGIE (*up stage to* PETER). Play the other bit, dear, out of the second act—(*she hums*)—you know—"I haven't the faintest idea—oh, no—I haven't the faintest idea."

PETER (*changing tempo*). "Under the light of the moon, dear—you'd better find out pretty soon, dear."

CLARE. What on earth's that out of?

PIGGIE. Don't be silly, Clare—all I ask is that you shouldn't be *silly!* (*She moves up stage.*)

CLARE (*understanding*). Oh yes—I see. (*There is a silence except for* PETER'S *playing—everybody looks covertly at the* WADHURSTS. PIGGIE *goes over to* MR. WADHURST.)

PIGGIE (*with determination*). What ship did you come home in? (*At top of the sofa.*)

MR. WADHURST. The "Naldera."

ALLY. P. & O.?

MRS. WADHURST. Yes.

PIGGIE. I suppose you got on at Singapore?

MR. WADHURST. No, Penang.

PIGGIE (*the light breaking*). Penang! Of course, Penang.

MRS. WADHURST. Yes, we have some friends there, so we went by train from Singapore and stayed with them for a couple of days before catching the boat.

PIGGIE (*sunk again*). Oh, yes—yes, I see.

PETER (*at the piano, humming to a march time*). "When you hear those drums rat-a-plan—rat-a-plan—find out the name of the place if you can—la la la la, la la la la— (PIGGIE *moves down and up stage.*)

PIGGIE (*persevering*). How far is your house from the sea? Maud and I were arguing about it for hours the other day——

MR. WADHURST. It's right on the sea.

PIGGIE. That's exactly what I said, but you know Maud's so vague—she never remembers a thing——

CLARE. I suppose it's hell hot all the year round where you are?

MRS. WADHURST. Yes, the climate is a little trying, but one gets used to it.

BOGEY. Are you far from Kuala Lumpur.

MRS. WADHURST. Yes, a long way.

BOGEY. Oh, I knew some people in Kuala Lumpur once.

MR. WADHURST. What were their names?

BOGEY. Damn it, I've forgotten—something like Harrison——

PIGGIE (*helpfully*). Morrison?

BOGEY. No.

ALLY. Williamson?

BOGEY. No.

PETER. Lightfoot.

BOGEY. No, it's gone——

PIGGIE (*irritably*). Never mind—it couldn't matter less really, could it?

MRS. WADHURST (*rising*). I'm afraid we must really go now, Lady Maureen——

PIGGIE. Oh, no—please——

MRS. WADHURST. We have to dress because we're dining and going to the theatre—that's the one thing we do miss dreadfully in Pendarla—the theatre——

PIGGIE (*remembering everything—turns to* PETER, *who plays final chord*). Pendarla—— Oh dear, what a long way away it seems—— Dear Mrs. Wadhurst—(*she shoots a triumphant glance at* PETER)—it's been so lovely having this little peep at you—you and Mr. Wadhurst must come and dine quietly one night and we'll go to another theatre——

MRS. WADHURST. That would be delightful—Fred——

MR. WADHURST. Good-bye.

PIGGIE. Peter—come and say good-bye to Mr. and Mrs. Wadhurst.

PETER (*coming over* C. *and shaking hands*). Good-bye—I can never tell you how grateful I am to you for having been so kind and hospitable to my wife——

MRS. WADHURST. Next time, I hope you'll come and call on us too.

PETER. I should love to. (CLARE *rises*.)

MRS. WADHURST. Good-bye.

CLARE. Good-bye—— (*Everybody says good-bye and shakes hands.* PETER *opens the door* R. *for the* WAD-HURSTS *and they go out on a wave of popularity. He goes out into the hall with them, closing the door after him.* PIGGIE *collapses onto the sofa.*)

PIGGIE (*hysterically*). Oh, my God, that was the most awful half an hour I've ever spent——

CLARE. I thought it all went down like a dinner.

PIGGIE (*rising and moving about* C.). I remember it all now; we stayed one night with them on our way from Siam—a man in Bangkok had wired to them or something—— (*She sits on the sofa.*)

ALLY. That was a nice bit you did about the old native dancing with a sword——

PIGGIE. Oh dear, they must have thought I was drunk. (PETER *re-enters.*)

PETER. Next time you travel, my darling, I suggest you keep a diary——

PIGGIE. Wasn't it frightful—poor angels—I must ring up Maud—— (*She dials a number*). I think they had a heavenly time though, don't you—I mean they couldn't have noticed a thing——

PETER. Oh no, the whole affair was managed with the utmost subtlety—I congratulate you——

PIGGIE. Don't be sour, Peter—— (*At the telephone*). Hallo . . . Maud? . . . Darling, it's not the Rawlingsons at all, it's the Wadhursts . . . (*To everybody*). Good heavens, I never gave them Maud's address. (*At the telephone*). . . . I forgot to give them your address . . . How can you be so unkind, Maud, you ought to be ashamed of yourself . . . They're absolutely pets, both of them . . .

PETER. Come on, Ally, I've got to dress——

ALLY. All right——

CLARE. Shall I see you on Sunday?

ALLY. Yes—I'll be over——

PIGGIE (*at the telephone*). . . . They had a lovely time and everybody was divine to them . . .

CLARE (*picking up her bag, she moves over to the piano for her gloves and hat*). Come on, Bogey, we must go too——

PIGGIE. Wait a minute, don't leave me—I've got to do my

feet. (*At the telephone*). . . . No, I was talking to Clare . . . My dear, I know, she rang me up too—she's staying with Norman . . . Phyllis will be as sour as a quince . . . (PETER *and* ALLY *go off* L.C., *talking.*)

CLARE. Darling, I really *must* go——

PIGGIE. Wait a moment. (*At the telephone*). . . . All right—I'll try to get hold of them in the morning and put them off. I do think it's horrid of you, though. After all, they were frightfully sweet to us . . . I've done all I can . . . Well, there's no need to get into a rage, I'm the one to get into a rage . . . Yes, you are, I can hear you. Your teeth are chattering like dice in a box . . . Oh, all right! (*She hangs up*). Maud's impossible——

CLARE. Listen, Piggie——

PIGGIE. Wait just one minute, I've got to get the things to do my feet—— (*She rushes out of the room up* L.C.)

CLARE. I really don't see why we should all wait about—— (*She suddenly sees* MR. BURNHAM). Oh—hallo.

MR. BURNHAM (*nervously*). Hallo. (*He rises and pushes the plans into* CLARE'S *face.*)

CLARE. I thought you'd left with your mother and father.

MR. BURNHAM. They weren't my mother and father—I'm from Freeman's. I've brought the designs for the Commander's speed-boat. Mr. Driscoll couldn't come——

CLARE. Well, you'd better wait—he'll be back soon——

MR. BURNHAM. I'm afraid I can't wait much longer—I have to get back to the shop——

CLARE. You should have piped up before——

BOGEY. Listen, Clare, we must push off——

CLARE. All right. (MR. BURNHAM *retires again into the shadows as* PIGGIE *returns with several bottles, a towel and a pair of scissors. She sits on the sofa and takes her shoes and stockings off.*)

PIGGIE. The trouble with Maud is, she's too insular——

CLARE. Are you driving down on Saturday?

PIGGIE. Yes—I promised to stop off at Godalming and have a cutlet with Freda on the way—do you want to come?

CLARE. You know perfectly well I hate Freda's guts.

PIGGIE (*beginning on her feet*). All right, darling—I'll expect you in the afternoon—— (*The telephone rings*—PIGGIE *reaches for it with one hand and goes on painting her toe-nails with the other. At the telephone*). Hallo . . . Yes. Oh, David, I'm *so* sorry—I completely forgot . . . (CLARE *and* BOGEY *kiss good-bye at her. She waves to them, and they go out*). I couldn't help it, I had to be sweet to some people that Maud and I stayed with in Malaya . . . Oh, David darling, don't be so soured up . . . Yes, of course I do, don't be so silly . . . No, I'm quite alone doing my feet . . . Well, I can't help that, I happen to *like* them red . . . Well, after all, they are my feet; I suppose I can paint them blue if I want to . . . (MR. BURNHAM *takes a drink and begins to tiptoe out of the room; he leaves his roll of designs on the table.* PIGGIE *catches sight of him just as he is gingerly opening the door. To* MR. BURNHAM). Oh, good-bye— it's been absolutely lovely, you're the sweetest family I've ever met in my life——

CURTAIN

THE DEVIL AND DANIEL WEBSTER

by Stephen Vincent Benét

CHARACTERS

JABEZ STONE

MARY STONE

DANIEL WEBSTER

MR. SCRATCH

THE FIDDLER

JUSTICE HATHORNE

JUSTICE HATHORNE'S CLERK

KING PHILIP

TEACH

WALTER BUTLER

SIMON GIRTY

DALE

MEN AND WOMEN OF CROSS CORNERS, NEW HAMPSHIRE

SCENE—JABEZ STONE'S FARMHOUSE.

TIME—1841.

THE DEVIL AND DANIEL WEBSTER

The scene is the main room of a New Hampshire farm-house in 1841, a big comfortable room that hasn't yet developed the stuffiness of a front-parlor. A door, right, leads to the kitchen—a door, left, to the outside. There is a fireplace, right. Windows, in center, show a glimpse of summer landscape. Most of the furniture has been cleared away for the dance which follows the wedding of JABEZ *and* MARY STONE, *but there is a settle or bench by the fireplace, a table, left, with some wedding presents upon it, at least three chairs by the table, and a cider barrel on which the* FIDDLER *sits, in front of the table. Near the table, against the side-wall, there is a cupboard where there are glasses and a jug. There is a clock.*

A country wedding has been in progress—the wedding of JABEZ *and* MARY STONE. *He is a husky young farmer, around twenty-eight or thirty. The bride is in her early twenties. He is dressed in stiff, store clothes but not ridiculously—they are of good quality and he looks important. The bride is in a simple white or cream wedding-dress and may carry a small, stiff bouquet of country flowers.*

Now the wedding is over and the guests are dancing. The FIDDLER *is perched on the cider barrel. He plays and calls square-dance figures. The guests include the recognizable types of a small New England town, doctor, lawyer, storekeeper, old maid, schoolteacher, farmer, etc. There is an air of prosperity and hearty country mirth about the whole affair.*

At rise, JABEZ *and* MARY *are up left center, receiving the congratulations of a few last guests who talk to them and pass on to the dance. The others are dancing. There is a buzz of conversation that follows the tune of the dance-music.*

FIRST WOMAN. Right nice wedding.

FIRST MAN. Handsome couple.

SECOND WOMAN (*passing through crowd with dish of oyster-stew*). Oysters for supper!

SECOND MAN (*passing cake*). And layer-cake—layer-cake——

AN OLD MAN (*hobbling toward cider barrel*). Makes me feel young again! Oh, by jingo!

AN OLD WOMAN (*pursuing him*). Henry, Henry, you've been drinking cider!

FIDDLER. Set to your partners! Dosy-do!

WOMAN. Mary and Jabez.

MEN. Jabez and Mary.

A WOMAN. Where's the State Senator?

A MAN. Where's the lucky bride? (*With cries of "Mary— Jabez—strike it up, Fiddler—make room for the bride and groom," the* CROWD *drags* MARY *and* JABEZ, *pleased but embarrassed, into the center of the room and* MARY *and* JABEZ *do a little solo-dance, while the* CROWD *claps, applauds and makes various remarks.*)

A MAN. Handsome steppers!

A WOMAN. She's pretty as a picture.

A SECOND MAN. Cut your pigeon-wing, Jabez!

THE OLD MAN. Young again, young again, that's the way I feel! (*He tries to cut a pigeon-wing himself.*)

THE OLD WOMAN. Henry, Henry, careful of your rheumatiz!

A THIRD WOMAN. Makes me feel all teary—seeing them so happy. (*The solo-dance ends, the music stops for a moment.*)

THE OLD MAN (*gossiping to a neighbor*). Wonder where he got it all—Stones was always poor.

HIS NEIGHBOR. Ain't poor now—makes you wonder just a mite.

A THIRD MAN. Don't begrudge it to him—but I wonder where he got it.

THE OLD MAN (*starting to whisper*). Let me tell you something—

THE OLD WOMAN (*quickly*). Henry, Henry, don't you start to gossip. (*She drags him away.*)

FIDDLER (*cutting in*). Set to your partners! Scratch for corn! (*The dance resumes, but as it does so, the* CROWD *chants back and forth.*)

WOMEN. Gossip's got a sharp tooth.

MEN. Gossip's got a mean tooth.

WOMEN. She's a lucky woman. They're a lucky pair.

MEN. That's true as gospel. But I wonder where he got it.

WOMEN. Money, land and riches.

MEN. Just came out of nowhere.

WOMEN and MEN (*together*). Wonder where he got it all— But that's his business.

FIDDLER. Left and right—grand chain! (*The dance rises to a pitch of ecstasy with the final figure—the fiddle squeaks and stops. The dancers mop their brows.*)

FIRST MAN. Whew! Ain't danced like that since I was knee-high to a grasshopper!

SECOND MAN. Play us "The Portland Fancy," fiddler!

THIRD MAN. No, wait a minute, neighbor. Let's hear from the happy pair! Hey, Jabez!

FOURTH MAN. Let's hear from the State Senator! (*They crowd around* JABEZ *and push him up on the settle.*)

OLD MAN. Might as well. It's the last time he'll have the last word!

OLD WOMAN. Now, Henry Banks, you ought to be ashamed of yourself!

OLD MAN. Told you so, Jabez!

THE CROWD. Speech!

JABEZ (*embarrassed*). Neighbors—friends—I'm not much of a speaker—spite of your 'lecting me to State Senate——

THE CROWD. That's the ticket, Jabez. Smart man, Jabez. I voted for ye. Go ahead, Senator, you're doing fine.

JABEZ. But we're certainly glad to have you here—me and

MARY. And we want to thank you for coming and——

A VOICE. Vote the Whig ticket!

ANOTHER VOICE. Hooray for Daniel Webster!

JABEZ. And I'm glad Hi Foster said that, for those are my sentiments, too. Mr. Webster has promised to honor us with his presence here tonight.

THE CROWD. Hurray for Dan'l! Hurray for the greatest man in the U. S.!

JABEZ. And when he comes, I know we'll give him a real New Hampshire welcome.

THE CROWD. Sure we will—Webster forever and to hell with Henry Clay!

JABEZ. And meanwhile—well, there's Mary and me (*takes her hand*)—and, if you folks don't have a good time, well, we won't feel right about getting married at all. Because I know I've been lucky—and I hope she feels that way, too. And, well, we're going to be happy or bust a trace! (*He wipes his brow to terrific applause. He and* MARY *look at each other.*)

A WOMAN (*in kitchen doorway*). Come and get the cider, folks! (*The* CROWD *begins to drift away—a few to the kitchen—a few toward the door that leads to the outside. They furnish a shifting background to the next little scene, where* MARY *and* JABEZ *are left alone by the fireplace.*)

JABEZ. Mary.

MARY. Mr. Stone.

JABEZ. Mary.

MARY. My husband.

JABEZ. That's a big word, husband.

MARY. It's a good word.

JABEZ. Are you happy, Mary?

MARY. Yes. So happy, I'm afraid.

JABEZ. Afraid?

MARY. I suppose it happens to every girl—just for a minute. It's like spring turning into summer. You want it to be summer. But the spring was sweet. (*Dismissing the mood*). I'm sorry. Forgive me. It just came and went, like something cold. As if we'd been too lucky.

JABEZ. We can't be too lucky, Mary. Not you and me.

MARY (*rather mischievously*). If you say so, Mr. Stone. But you don't even know what sort of housekeeper I am. And Aunt Hepsy says——

JABEZ. Bother your Aunt Hepsy! There's just you and me and that's all that matters in the world.

MARY. And you don't know something else——

JABEZ. What's that?

MARY. How proud I am of you. Ever since I was a little girl. Ever since you carried my books. Oh, I'm sorry for women who can't be proud of their men. It must be a lonely feeling.

JABEZ (*uncomfortably*). A man can't always be proud of everything, Mary. There's some things a man does, or might do—when he has to make his way.

MARY (*laughing*). I know—terrible things—like being the best farmer in the county and the best State Senator——

JABEZ (*quietly*). And a few things, besides. But you remember one thing, Mary, whatever happens. It was all for you. And nothing's going to happen. Because he hasn't come yet—and he would have come if it was wrong.

MARY. But it's wonderful to have Mr. Webster come to us.

JABEZ. I wasn't thinking about Mr. Webster. (*He takes both her hands*). Mary, I've got something to tell you. I should have told you before, but I couldn't seem to bear it. Only, now that it's all right, I can. Ten years ago——

A VOICE (*from off stage*). Dan'l! Dan'l Webster! (JABEZ *drops* MARY's *hands and looks around. The* CROWD *be-*

gins to mill and gather toward the door. Others rush in from the kitchen.)

ANOTHER VOICE. Black Dan'l! He's come!

ANOTHER VOICE. Three cheers for the greatest man in the U. S.!

ANOTHER VOICE. Three cheers for Daniel Webster! (*And, to the cheering and applause of the crowd,* DANIEL WEBSTER *enters and stands for a moment upstage, in the familiar pose, his head thrown back, his attitude leonine. He stops the cheering of the crowd with a gesture.*)

WEBSTER. Neighbors—old friends—it does me good to hear you. But don't cheer me—I'm not running for President this summer. (*A laugh from the* CROWD). I'm here on a better errand—to pay my humble respects to a most charming lady and her very fortunate spouse. (*There is the twang of a fiddlestring breaking.*)

FIDDLER. 'Tarnation! Busted a string!

A VOICE. He's always bustin' strings. (WEBSTER *blinks at the interruption but goes on.*)

WEBSTER. We're proud of State Senator Stone in these parts—we know what he's done. Ten years ago he started out with a patch of land that was mostly rocks and mortgages and now—well, you've only to look around you. I don't know that I've ever seen a likelier farm, not even at Marshfield—and I hope, before I die, I'll have the privilege of shaking his hand as Governor of this State. I don't know how he's done it—I couldn't have done it myself. But I know this—Jabez Stone wears no man's collar. (*At this statement there is a discordant squeak from the fiddle and* JABEZ *looks embarrassed.* WEBSTER *knits his brows*). And what's more, if I know Jabez, he never will. But I didn't come here to talk politics—I came to kiss the bride. (*He does so among great applause. He shakes hands with* JABEZ). Congratulations, Stone—you're a lucky man. And now, if our friend in the corner will give us a tune on his fiddle——

(*The* CROWD *presses forward to meet the great man. He shakes hands with several.*)

A MAN. Remember me, Mr. Webster? Saw ye up at the State House at Concord.

ANOTHER MAN. Glad to see ye, Mr. Webster. I voted for ye ten times. (WEBSTER *receives their homage politely, but his mind is still on music.*)

WEBSTER (*a trifle irritated*). I said, if our friend in the corner would give us a tune on his fiddle——

FIDDLER (*passionately, flinging the fiddle down*). Hell's delight—excuse me, Mr. Webster. But the very devil's got into that fiddle of mine. She was doing all right up to just a minute ago. But now I've tuned her and tuned her and she won't play a note I want. (*And, at this point,* MR. SCRATCH *makes his appearance. He has entered, unobserved, and mixed with the crowd while all eyes were upon* DANIEL WEBSTER. *He is, of course, the devil—a New England devil, dressed like a rather shabby attorney but with something just a little wrong in clothes and appearance. For one thing, he wears black gloves on his hands. He carries a large black tin box, like a botanist's collecting-box, under one arm. Now he slips through the crowd and taps the* FIDDLER *on the shoulder.*)

SCRATCH (*insinuatingly*). Maybe you need some rosin on your bow, fiddler?

FIDDLER. Maybe I do and maybe I don't. (*Turns and confronts the stranger*). But who are you? I don't remember seeing you before.

SCRATCH. Oh, I'm just a friend—a humble friend of the bridegroom's. (*He walks toward* JABEZ. *Apologetically*). I'm afraid I came in the wrong way, Mr. Stone. You've improved the place so much since I last saw it that I hardly knew the front door. But, I assure you, I came as fast as I could.

JABEZ (*obviously shocked*). It—it doesn't matter. (*With a great effort*). Mary—Mr. Webster—this is a—a friend of mine from Boston—a legal friend. I didn't expect him today but——

SCRATCH. Oh, my dear Mr. Stone—an occasion like this—I wouldn't miss it for the world. (*He bows*). Charmed, Mrs. Stone. Delighted, Mr. Webster. But—don't let me break up the merriment of the meeting. (*He turns back toward the table and the* FIDDLER.)

FIDDLER (*with a grudge, to* SCRATCH). Boston lawyer, eh?

SCRATCH. You might call me that.

FIDDLER (*tapping the tin box with his bow*). And what have you got in that big tin box of yours? Lawpapers?

SCRATCH. Oh—curiosities for the most part. I'm a collector, too.

FIDDLER. Don't hold much with Boston curiosities, myself. And you know about fiddling too, do you? Know all about it?

SCRATCH. Oh—— (*A deprecatory shrug.*)

FIDDLER. Don't shrug your shoulders at me—I ain't no Frenchman. Telling me I needed more rosin!

MARY (*trying to stop the quarrel*). Isaac—please——

FIDDLER. Sorry, Mary—Mrs. Stone. But I been playing the fiddle at Cross Corners weddings for twenty-five years. And now here comes a stranger from Boston and tells me I need more rosin!

SCRATCH. But, my good friend——

FIDDLER. Rosin indeed! Here—play it yourself then and see what you can make of it! (*He thrusts the fiddle at* SCRATCH. *The latter stiffens, slowly lays his black collecting-box on the table, and takes the fiddle.*)

SCRATCH (*with feigned embarrassment*). But really, I—— (*He bows toward* JABEZ). Shall I—Mr. Senator? (JABEZ *makes a helpless gesture of assent.*)

MARY (*to* JABEZ). Mr. Stone—Mr. Stone—are you ill?

JABEZ. No—no—but I feel—it's hot——

WEBSTER (*chuckling*). Don't you fret, Mrs. Stone. I've got the right medicine for him. (*He pulls a flask from his pocket*). Ten-year-old Medford, Stone—I buy it by the keg down at Marshfield. Here—— (*He tries to give some of the rum to* JABEZ.)

JABEZ. No—(*he turns*)—Mary—Mr. Webster—— (*But he cannot explain. With a burst*). Oh, let him play—let him play! Don't you see he's bound to? Don't you see there's nothing we can do? (*A rustle of discomfort among the guests.* SCRATCH *draws the bow across the fiddle in a horrible discord.*)

FIDDLER (*triumphantly*). I told you so, stranger. The devil's in that fiddle!

SCRATCH. I'm afraid it needs special tuning. (*Draws the bow in a second discord*). There—that's better. (*Grinning*). And now for this happy—this very happy occasion—in tribute to the bride and groom—I'll play something appropriate—a song of young love——

MARY. Oh, Jabez—Mr. Webster—stop him! Do you see his hands? He's playing with gloves on his hands. (WEBSTER *starts forward, but, even as he does so,* SCRATCH *begins to play and all freeze as* SCRATCH *goes on with the extremely inappropriate song that follows. At first his manner is oily and mocking—it is not till he reaches the line "The devil took the words away" that he really becomes terrifying and the crowd starts to be afraid.*)

SCRATCH (*accompanying himself fantastically*).

> Young William was a thriving boy.
> (Listen to my doleful tale.)
> Young Mary Clark was all his joy.
> (Listen to my doleful tale.)
>
> He swore he'd love her all his life.
> She swore she'd be his loving wife.
>
> But William found a gambler's den
> And drank with livery-stable men.
>
> He played the cards, he played the dice.
> He would not listen to advice.

And when in church he tried to pray,
The devil took the words away.

(SCRATCH, *still playing, starts to march across the stage.*)

The devil got him by the toe
And so, alas, he had to go.

"Young Mary Clark, young Mary Clark,
I now must go into the dark."

(*These last two verses have been directed at* JABEZ, SCRATCH *continues, now turning on* MARY.)

Young Mary lay upon her bed.
"Alas my Will-i-am is dead."

He came to her a bleeding ghost——

(*He rushes at* MARY *but* WEBSTER *stands between them.*)

WEBSTER. Stop! Stop! You miserable wretch—can't you see that you're frightening Mrs. Stone? (*He wrenches the fiddle out of* SCRATCH'S *hands and tosses it aside*). And now, sir—out of this house!

SCRATCH (*facing him*). You're a bold man, Mr. Webster. Too bold for your own good, perhaps. And anyhow, it wasn't my fiddle. It belonged to—— (*He wheels and sees the* FIDDLER *tampering with the collecting-box that has been left on the table*). Idiot! What are you doing with my collecting-box? (*He rushes for the* FIDDLER *and chases him round the table, but the* FIDDLER *is just one jump ahead.*)

FIDDLER. Boston lawyer, eh? Well, I don't think so. I think you've got something in that box of yours you're afraid to show. And, by jingo—— (*He throws open the lid of the box. The lights wink and there is a clap of thunder. All eyes stare upward. Something has flown out of the box. But what?* FIDDLER, *with relief*). Why, 'tain't nothing but a moth.

MARY. A white moth—a flying thing.

WEBSTER. A common moth—*telea polyphemus*——

THE CROWD. A moth—just a moth—a moth——

FIDDLER (*terrified*). But it ain't. It ain't no common moth!

I seen it! And it's got a death's-head on it! (*He strikes at the invisible object with his bow to drive it away.*)

VOICE OF THE MOTH. Help me, neighbors! Help me!

WEBSTER. What's that? It wails like a lost soul.

MARY. A lost soul.

THE CROWD. A lost soul—lost—in darkness—in the darkness.

VOICE OF THE MOTH. Help me, neighbors!

FIDDLER. It sounds like Miser Stevens.

JABEZ. Miser Stevens!

THE CROWD. The Miser—Miser Stevens—a lost soul—lost.

FIDDLER (*frantically*). It sounds like Miser Stevens—and you had him in your box. But it can't be. He ain't dead.

JABEZ. He ain't dead—I tell you he ain't dead! He was just as spry and mean as a woodchuck Tuesday.

THE CROWD. Miser Stevens—soul of Miser Stevens—but he ain't dead.

SCRATCH (*dominating them*). Listen! (*A bell off stage begins to toll a knell, slowly, solemnly.*)

MARY. The bell—the church bell—the bell that rang at my wedding.

WEBSTER. The church bell—the passing bell.

JABEZ. The funeral bell.

THE CROWD. The bell—the passing bell—Miser Stevens—dead.

VOICE OF THE MOTH. Help me, neighbors, help me! I sold my soul to the devil. But I'm not the first or the last. Help me. Help Jabez Stone!

SCRATCH. Ah, would you! (*He catches the moth in his red bandanna, stuffs it back into his collecting-box, and shuts the lid with a snap.*)

VOICE OF THE MOTH (*fading*). Lost—lost forever, forever. Lost, like Jabez Stone. (*The* CROWD *turns on* JABEZ. *They read his secret in his face.*)

THE CROWD. Jabez Stone—Jabez Stone—answer us—answer us.

MARY. Tell them, dear—answer them—you are good—you are brave—you are innocent. (*But the* CROWD *is all pointing hands and horrified eyes.*)

THE CROWD. Jabez Stone—Jabez Stone. Who's your friend in black, Jabez Stone? (*They point to* SCRATCH.)

WEBSTER. Answer them, Mr. State Senator.

THE CROWD. Jabez Stone—Jabez Stone. Where did you get your money, Jabez Stone? (SCRATCH *grins and taps his collecting-box.* JABEZ *cannot speak.*)

JABEZ. I—I—— (*He stops.*)

THE CROWD. Jabez Stone—Jabez Stone. What was the price you paid for it, Jabez Stone?

JABEZ (*looking around wildly*). Help me, neighbors! Help me! (*This cracks the built-up tension and sends the* CROWD *over the edge into fanaticism.*)

A WOMAN'S VOICE (*high and hysterical*). He's sold his soul to the devil! (*She points to* JABEZ.)

OTHER VOICES. To the devil!

THE CROWD. He's sold his soul to the devil! The devil himself! The devil's playing the fiddle! The devil's come for his own!

JABEZ (*appealing*). But, neighbors—I didn't know—I didn't mean—oh, help me!

THE CROWD (*inexorably*) He's sold his soul to the devil!

SCRATCH (*grinning*). To the devil!

THE CROWD. He's sold his soul to the devil! There's no help left for him, neighbors! Run, hide, hurry, before we're caught! He's a lost soul—Jabez Stone—he's the devil's own! Run, hide, hasten! (*They stream across the stage like a flurry of bats, the cannier picking up the wedding-presents they have given to take along with them.* MR. SCRATCH *drives them out into the night, fiddle in hand, and follows them.* JABEZ *and* MARY *are left with* WEBSTER. JABEZ *has sunk into a chair, beaten, with his head in his hands.* MARY *is trying to comfort him.* WEBSTER *looks at them for a moment and shakes his head, sadly.*

As he crosses to exit to the porch, his hand drops for a moment on JABEZ's *shoulder, but* JABEZ *makes no sign.* WEBSTER *exits.* JABEZ *lifts his head.*)

MARY (*comforting him*). My dear—my dear——

JABEZ. I—it's all true, Mary. All true. You must hurry.

MARY. Hurry?

JABEZ. Hurry after them—back to the village—back to your folks. Mr. Webster will take you—you'll be safe with Mr. Webster. You see, it's all true and he'll be back in a minute. (*With a shudder*). The other one. (*He groans*). I've got until twelve o'clock. That's the contract. But there isn't much time.

MARY. Are you telling me to run away from you, Mr. Stone?

JABEZ. You don't understand, Mary. It's true.

MARY. We made some promises to each other. Maybe you've forgotten them. But I haven't. I said, it's for better or worse. It's for better or worse. I said, in sickness or in health. Well, that covers the ground, Mr. Stone.

JABEZ. But, Mary, you must—I command you.

MARY. "For thy people shall be my people and thy God my God." (*Quietly*). That was Ruth, in the Book. I always liked the name of Ruth—always liked the thought of her. I always thought—I'll call a child Ruth, some time. I guess that was just a girl's notion. (*She breaks*). But, oh, Jabez—why?

JABEZ. It started years ago, Mary. I guess I was a youngster then—guess I must have been. A youngster with a lot of ambitions and no way in the world to get there. I wanted city clothes and a big white house—I wanted to be State Senator and have people look up to me. But all I got on the farm was a crop of stones. You could work all day and all night but that was all you got.

MARY (*softly*). It was pretty—that hill-farm, Jabez. You could look all the way across the valley.

JABEZ. Pretty? It was fever and ague—it was stones and blight. If I had a horse, he got colic—if I planted garden-truck, the woodchucks ate it. I'd lie awake nights and try to figure out a way to get somewhere—but there wasn't any way. And all the time you were growing up, in the town. I couldn't ask you to marry me and take you to a place like that.

MARY. Do you think it's the place makes the difference to a woman? I'd—I'd have kept your house. I'd have stroked the cat and fed the chickens and seen you wiped your shoes on the mat. I wouldn't have asked for more. Oh, Jabez—why didn't you tell me?

JABEZ. It happened before I could. Just an average day—you know—just an average day. But there was a mean east wind and a mean small rain. Well, I was plowing, and the share broke clean off on a rock where there hadn't been any rock the day before. I didn't have money for a new one—I didn't have money to get it mended. So I said it and I said loud, "I'll sell my soul for about two cents," I said. (*He stops.* MARY *stares at him*). Well, that's all there is to it, I guess. He came along that afternoon—that fellow from Boston—and the dog looked at him and ran away. Well, I had to make it more than two cents, but he was agreeable to that. So I pricked my thumb with a pin and signed the paper. It felt hot when you touched it, that paper. I keep remembering that (*He pauses*). And it's all come true and he's kept his part of the bargain. I got the riches and I've married you. And, oh, God Almighty, what shall I do?

MARY. Let us run away! Let us creep and hide!

JABEZ. You can't run away from the devil—I've seen his horses. Miser Stevens tried to run away.

MARY. Let us pray—let us pray to the God of Mercy that He redeem us.

JABEZ. I can't pray, Mary. The words just burn in my heart.

MARY. I won't let you go! I won't! There must be someone who could help us. I'll get the judge and the squire——

JABEZ. Who'll take a case against old Scratch? Who'll face the devil himself and do him brown? There isn't a lawyer in the world who'd dare do that. (WEBSTER *appears in the doorway.*)

WEBSTER. Good evening, neighbors. Did you say something about lawyers——

MARY. Mr. Webster!

JABEZ. Dan'l Webster! But I thought——

WEBSTER. You'll excuse me for leaving you for a moment. I was just taking a stroll on the porch, in the cool of the evening. Fine summer evening, too.

JABEZ. Well, it might be, I guess, but that kind of depends on the circumstances.

WEBSTER. H'm. Yes. I happened to overhear a little of your conversation. I gather you're in trouble, Neighbor Stone.

JABEZ. Sore trouble.

WEBSTER (*delicately*). Sort of law case, I understand.

JABEZ. You might call it that, Mr. Webster. Kind of a mortgage case, in a way.

MARY. Oh, Jabez!

WEBSTER. Mortgage case. Well, I don't generally plead now, except before the Supreme Court, but this case of yours presents some very unusual features and I never deserted a neighbor in trouble yet. So, if I can be of any assistance——

MARY. Oh, Mr. Webster, will you help him?

JABEZ. It's a terrible lot to ask you. But—well, you see, there's Mary. And, if you could see your way to it——

WEBSTER. I will.

MARY (*weeping with relief*). Oh, Mr. Webster!

WEBSTER. There, there, Mrs. Stone. After all, if two New Hampshire men aren't a match for the devil, we might as well give the country back to the Indians. When is he coming, Jabez?

JABEZ. Twelve o'clock. The time's getting late.

WEBSTER. Then I'd better refresh my memory. The—er—mortgage was for a definite term of years?

JABEZ. Ten years.

WEBSTER. And it falls due——?

JABEZ. Tonight. Oh, I can't see how I came to be such a fool!

WEBSTER. No use crying over spilt milk, Stone. We've got to get you out of it, now. But tell me one thing. Did you sign this precious document of your own free will?

JABEZ. Yes, it was my own free will. I can't deny that.

WEBSTER. H'm, that's a trifle unfortunate. But we'll see.

MARY. Oh, Mr. Webster, can you save him? Can you?

WEBSTER. I shall do my best, madam. That's all you can ever say till you see what the jury looks like.

MARY. But even you, Mr. Webster—oh, I know you're Secretary of State—I know you're a great man—I know you've done wonderful things. But it's different—fighting the devil!

WEBSTER (*towering*). I've fought John C. Calhoun, madam. And I've fought Henry Clay. And, by the great shade of Andrew Jackson, I'd fight ten thousand devils to save a New Hampshire man!

JABEZ. You hear, Mary?

MARY. Yes. And I trust Mr. Webster. But—oh, there must be some way that I can help!

WEBSTER. There is one, madam, and a hard one. As Mr. Stone's counsel, I must formally request your withdrawal.

MARY. No.

WEBSTER. Madam, think for a moment. You cannot help Mr. Stone—since you are his wife, your testimony would be prejudiced. And frankly, madam, in a very few moments this is going to be no place for a lady.

MARY. But I can't—I can't leave him—I can't bear it!

JABEZ. You must go, Mary. You must.

WEBSTER. Pray, madam—you can help us with your prayers. Are the prayers of the innocent unavailing?

MARY. Oh, I'll pray—I'll pray. But a woman's more than a praying machine, whatever men think. And how do I know?

WEBSTER. Trust me, Mrs. Stone. (MARY *turns to go, and, with one hand on* JABEZ' *shoulder, as she moves to the door, says the following prayer:*)

MARY.

> Now may there be a blessing and a light betwixt thee and me, forever.
> For, as Ruth unto Naomi, so do I cleave unto thee.
> Set me as a seal upon thy heart, as a seal upon thine arm, for love is strong as death.
> Many waters cannot quench love, neither can the floods drown it.
> As Ruth unto Naomi, so do I cleave unto thee.
> The Lord watch between thee and me when we are absent, one from the other.
> Amen. Amen. (*She goes out.*)

WEBSTER. Amen.

JABEZ. Thank you, Mr. Webster. She ought to go. But I couldn't have made her do it.

WEBSTER. Well, Stone—I know ladies—and I wouldn't be surprised if she's still got her ear to the keyhole. But she's best out of this night's business. How long have we got to wait?

JABEZ (*beginning to be terrified again*). Not long—not long.

WEBSTER. Then I'll just get out the jug, with your permission, Stone. Somehow or other, waiting's wonderfully shorter with a jug. (*He crosses to the cupboard, gets out jug and glasses, pours himself a drink*). Ten-year-old Medford. There's nothing like it. I saw an inch-worm take a drop of it once and he stood right up on his hind legs and bit a bee. Come—try a nip.

JABEZ. There's no joy in it for me.

WEBSTER. Oh, come, man, come! Just because you've sold your soul to the devil, that needn't make you a teeto-taller. (*He laughs and passes the jug to* JABEZ *who tries to pour from it. But at that moment the clock whirs and begins to strike the three-quarters, and* JABEZ *spills the liquor.*)

JABEZ. Oh, God!

WEBSTER. Never mind—it's a nervous feeling, waiting for a trial to begin. I remember my first case——

JABEZ. 'Tain't that. (*He turns to* WEBSTER). Mr. Web-ster—Mr. Webster—for God's sake harness your horses and get away from this place as fast as you can!

WEBSTER (*placidly*). You've brought me a long way, neighbor, to tell me you don't like my company.

JABEZ. I've brought you the devil's own way. I can see it all, now. He's after both of us—him and his damn col-lecting-box! Well, he can have me, if he likes—I don't say I relish it but I made the bargain. But you're the whole United States! He can't get you, Mr. Webster—he mustn't get you!

WEBSTER. I'm obliged to you, Neighbor Stone. It's kindly thought of. But there's a jug on the table and a case in hand. And I never left a jug or a case half-finished in my life. (*There is a knock at the door.* JABEZ *gives a cry*). Ah, I thought your clock was a trifle slow, Neigh-bor Stone. Come in! (SCRATCH *enters from the night.*)

SCRATCH. Mr. Webster! This *is* a pleasure!

WEBSTER. Attorney of record for Jabez Stone. Might I ask your name?

SCRATCH. I've gone by a good many. Perhaps Scratch will do for the evening. I'm often called that in these regions. May I? (*He sits at the table and pours a drink from the jug. The liquor steams as it pours into the glass while* JABEZ *watches, terrified.* SCRATCH *grins, toasting* WEBSTER *and* JABEZ *silently in the liquor. Then he becomes businesslike. To* WEBSTER). And now I call upon you, as a law-abiding citizen, to assist me in taking possession of my property.

WEBSTER. Not so fast, Mr. Scratch. Produce your evidence, if you have it. (SCRATCH *takes out a black pocketbook and examines papers.*)

SCRATCH. Slattery—Stanley—Stone. (*Takes out a deed*). There, Mr. Webster. All open and above board and in due and legal form. Our firm has its reputation to consider—we deal only in the one way.

WEBSTER (*taking deed and looking it over*). H'm. This appears—I say, it appears—to be properly drawn. But, of course, we contest the signature. (*Tosses it back, contemptuously*).

SCRATCH (*suddenly turning on* JABEZ *and shooting a finger at him*). Is that your signature?

JABEZ (*wearily*). You know damn well it is.

WEBSTER (*angrily*). Keep quiet, Stone. (*To* SCRATCH). But that is a minor matter. This precious document isn't worth the paper it's written on. The law permits no traffic in human flesh.

SCRATCH. Oh, my dear Mr. Webster! Courts in every State in the Union have held that human flesh is property and recoverable. Read your Fugitive Slave Act. Or, shall I cite Brander versus McRae?

WEBSTER. But, in the case of the State of Maryland versus Four Barrels of Bourbon——

SCRATCH. That was overruled, as you know, sir. North Carolina versus Jenkins and Co.

WEBSTER (*unwillingly*). You seem to have an excellent acquaintance with the law, sir.

SCRATCH. Sir, that is no fault of mine. Where I come from, we have always gotten the pick of the Bar.

WEBSTER (*changing his note, heartily*). Well, come now, sir. There's no need to make hay and oats of a trifling matter when we're both sensible men. Surely we can settle this little difficulty out of court. My client is quite prepared to offer a compromise. (SCRATCH *smiles*). A very substantial compromise. (SCRATCH *smiles more broadly, slowly shaking his head*). Hang it, man, we offer ten thousand dollars! (SCRATCH *signs* "No"). Twenty thousand—thirty—name your figure! I'll raise it if I have to mortgage Marshfield!

SCRATCH. Quite useless, Mr. Webster. There is only one thing I want from you—the execution of my contract.

WEBSTER. But this is absurd. Mr. Stone is now a State Senator. The property has greatly increased in value!

SCRATCH. The principle of *caveat emptor* still holds, Mr. Webster. (*He yawns and looks at the clock*). And now, if you have no further arguments to adduce—I'm rather pressed for time—(*He rises briskly as if to take* JABEZ *into custody.*)

WEBSTER (*thundering*). Pressed or not, you shall not have this man. Mr. Stone is an American citizen and no American citizen may be forced into the service of a foreign prince. We fought England for that, in '12, and we'll fight all hell for it again!

SCRATCH. Foreign? And who calls me a foreigner?

WEBSTER. Well, I never yet heard of the dev—of your claiming American citizenship?

SCRATCH. And who with better right? When the first wrong was done to the first Indian, I was there. When the first slaver put out for the Congo, I stood on her deck. Am I not in your books and stories and beliefs, from the first settlements on? Am I not spoken of, still, in every church in New England? 'Tis true, the North claims me for a Southerner and the South for a Northerner, but I am neither. I am merely an honest American like yourself —and of the best descent—for, to tell the truth, Mr.

Webster, though I don't like to boast of it, my name is older in the country than yours.

WEBSTER. Aha! Then I stand on the Constitution! I demand a trial for my client!

SCRATCH. The case is hardly one for an ordinary jury— and indeed, the lateness of the hour——

WEBSTER. Let it be any court you choose, so it is an American judge and an American jury. Let it be the quick or the dead, I'll abide the issue.

SCRATCH. The quick or the dead! You have said it! (*He points his finger at the place where the jury is to appear. There is a clap of thunder and a flash of light. The stage blacks out completely. All that can be seen is the face of* SCRATCH, *lit with a ghastly green light as he recites the invocation that summons the* JURY. *As, one by one, the important* JURYMEN *are mentioned, they appear*).

I summon the jury Mr. Webster demands.
From churchyard mould and gallows grave,
Brimstone pit and burning gulf,
I summon them!
Dastard, liar, scoundrel, knave,
I summon them! Appear!
There's Simon Girty, the renegade,
The haunter of the forest glade
Who joined with Indian and wolf
To hunt the pioneer.
The stains upon his hunting-shirt
Are not the blood of the deer.
There's Walter Butler, the loyalist,
Who carried a firebrand in his fist
Of massacre and shame.
King Philip's eye is wild and bright.
They slew him in the great Swamp Fight,
But still, with terror and affright,
The land recalls his name.
Blackbeard Teach, the pirate fell,

Smeet the strangler, hot from hell,
Dale, who broke men on the wheel,
Morton, of the tarnished steel,
I summon them, I summon them
From their tormented flame!
Quick or dead, quick or dead,
Broken heart and bitter head,
True Americans, each one,
Traitor and disloyal son,
Cankered earth and twisted tree,
Outcasts of eternity,
Twelve great sinners, tried and true,
For the work they are to do!
I summon them, I summon them!
Appear, appear, appear!

(*The* JURY *has now taken its place in the box*—WALTER
BUTLER *in the place of foreman. They are eerily lit and
so made-up as to suggest the unearthly. They sit stiffly
in their box. At first, when one moves, all move, in stylized
gestures. It is not till the end of* WEBSTER's *speech that
they begin to show any trace of humanity. They speak
rhythmically, and, at first, in low, eerie voices.*)

JABEZ (*seeing them, horrified*). A jury of the dead!

JURY. Of the dead!

JABEZ. A jury of the damned!

JURY. Of the damned!

SCRATCH. Are you content with the jury, Mr. Webster?

WEBSTER. Quite content. Though I miss General Arnold
from the company.

SCRATCH. Benedict Arnold is engaged upon other business.
Ah, you asked for a justice, I believe. (*He points his
finger and* JUSTICE HATHORNE, *a tall, lean, terrifying
Puritan, appears, followed by his* CLERK). Justice Hathorne is a jurist of experience. He presided at the Salem
witch-trials. There were others who repented of the
business later. But not he, not he!

HATHORNE. Repent of such notable wonders and under-
takings? Nay, hang them, hang them all! (*He takes
his place on the bench. The* CLERK, *an ominous little
man with clawlike hands, takes his place. The room has
now been transformed into a courtroom.*)

CLERK (*in a gabble of ritual*). Oyes, oyes, oyes. All ye
who have business with this honorable court of special
session this night, step forward!

HATHORNE (*with gavel*). Call the first case.

CLERK. The World, the Flesh and the Devil versus Jabez
Stone.

HATHORNE. Who appears for the plaintiff?

SCRATCH. I, Your Honor.

HATHORNE. And for the defendant?

WEBSTER. I.

JURY. The case—the case—he'll have little luck with this
case.

HATHORNE. The case will proceed.

WEBSTER. Your Honor, I move to dismiss this case on the
grounds of improper jurisdiction.

HATHORNE. Motion denied.

WEBSTER. On the grounds of insufficient evidence.

HATHORNE. Motion denied.

JURY. Motion denied—denied. Motion denied.

WEBSTER. I will take an exception.

HATHORNE. There are no exceptions in this court.

JURY. No exceptions—no exceptions in this court. It's a
bad case, Daniel Webster—a losing case.

WEBSTER. Your Honor——

HATHORNE. The prosecution will proceed——

SCRATCH. Your Honor—gentlemen of the jury. This is a
plain, straightforward case. It need not detain us long.

JURY. Detain us long—it will not detain us long.

SCRATCH. It concerns one thing alone—the transference,

barter and sale of a certain piece of property, to wit, his soul, by Jabez Stone, farmer, of Cross Corners, New Hampshire. That transference, barter or sale is attested by a deed. I offer that deed in evidence and mark it Exhibit A.

WEBSTER. I object.

HATHORNE. Objection denied. Mark it Exhibit A. (SCRATCH *hands the deed—an ominous and impressive document— to the* CLERK *who hands it to* HATHORNE. HATHORNE *hands it back to the* CLERK *who stamps it. All very fast and with mechanical gestures.*)

JURY. Exhibit A—mark it Exhibit A. (SCRATCH *takes the deed from the* CLERK *and offers it to the* JURY, *who pass it rapidly among them, hardly looking at it, and hand it back to* SCRATCH). We know the deed—the deed—it burns in our fingers—we do not have to see the deed. It's a losing case.

SCRATCH. It offers incontestable evidence of the truth of the prosecutions's claim. I shall now call Jabez Stone to the witness-stand.

JURY (*hungrily*). Jabez Stone to the witness-stand, Jabez Stone. He's a fine, fat fellow, Jabez Stone. He'll fry like a batter-cake, once we get him where we want him.

WEBSTER. Your Honor, I move that this jury be discharged for flagrant and open bias!

HATHORNE. Motion denied.

WEBSTER. Exception.

HATHORNE. Exception denied.

JURY. His motion's always denied. He thinks himself smart and clever—lawyer Webster. But his motion's always denied.

WEBSTER. Your Honor! (*He chokes with anger.*)

CLERK (*advancing*). Jabez Stone to the witness-stand!

JURY. Jabez Stone—Jabez Stone. (WEBSTER *gives* JABEZ *an encouraging pat on the back, and* JABEZ *takes his place in the witness-stand, very scared.*)

CLERK (*offering a black book*). Do you solemnly swear—testify—so help you—and it's no good for we don't care what you testify?

JABEZ. I do.

SCRATCH. What's your name?

JABEZ. Jabez Stone.

SCRATCH. Occupation?

JABEZ. Farmer.

SCRATCH. Residence?

JABEZ. Cross Corners, New Hampshire. (*These three questions are very fast and mechanical on the part of* SCRATCH. *He is absolutely sure of victory and just going through a form.*)

JURY. A farmer—he'll farm in hell—we'll see that he farms in hell.

SCRATCH. Now, Jabez Stone, answer me. You'd better, you know. You haven't got a chance and there'll be a cooler place by the fire for you.

WEBSTER. I protest! This is intimidation! This mocks all justice!

HATHORNE. The protest is irrelevant, incompetent and immaterial. We have our own justice. The protest is denied.

JURY. Irrelevant, incompetent and immaterial—we have our own justice—oh, ho, Daniel Webster! (*The* JURY's *eyes fix upon* WEBSTER *for an instant, hungrily.*)

SCRATCH. Did you or did you not sign this document?

JABEZ. Oh, I signed it! You know I signed it. And, if I have to go to hell for it, I'll go! (*A sigh sweeps over the* JURY.)

JURY. One of us—one of us now—we'll save a place by the fire for you, Jabez Stone.

SCRATCH. The prosecution rests.

HATHORNE. Remove the prisoner.

WEBSTER. But I wish to cross-examine—I wish to prove——

HATHORNE. There will be no cross-examination. We have

our own justice. You may speak, if you like. But be brief.

JURY. Brief—be very brief—we're weary of earth—incompetent, irrelevant and immaterial—they say he's a smart man, Webster, but he's lost his case tonight—be very brief—we have our own justice here. (WEBSTER *stares around him like a baited bull. Can't find words*).

MARY'S VOICE (*from off stage*). Set me as a seal upon thy heart, as a seal upon thine arm, for love is strong as death——

JURY (*loudly*). A seal!—ha, ha—a burning seal!

MARY'S VOICE. Love is strong

JURY (*drowning her out*). Death is stronger than love. Set the seal upon Daniel Webster—the burning seal of the lost. Make him one of us—one of the damned—one with Jabez Stone! (*The* JURY's *eyes all fix upon* WEBSTER. *The* CLERK *advances as if to take him into* CUSTODY. *But* WEBSTER *silences them all with a great gesture.*)

WEBSTER.

Be still!

I was going to thunder and roar. I shall not do that.

I was going to denounce and defy. I shall not do that.

You have judged this man already with your abominable justice. See that you defend it. For I shall not speak of this man.

You are demons now, but once you were men. I shall speak to every one of you.

Of common things I speak, of small things and common.

The freshness of morning to the young, the taste of food to the hungry, the day's toil, the rest by the fire, the quiet sleep.

These are good things.

But without freedom they sicken, without freedom they are nothing.

Freedom is the bread and the morning and the risen sun.

It was for freedom we came in the boats and the ships. It was for freedom we came.

It has been a long journey, a hard one, a bitter one.

But, out of the wrong and the right, the sufferings and the starvations, there is a new thing, a free thing.

The traitors in their treachery, the wise in their wisdom, the valiant in their courage—all, all have played a part.

It may not be denied in hell nor shall hell prevail against it.

Have you forgotten this? (*He turns to the* JURY). Have you forgotten the forest?

GIRTY (*as in a dream*). The forest, the rustle of the forest, the free forest.

WEBSTER (*to* KING PHILIP). Have you forgotten your lost nation?

KING PHILIP. My lost nation—my fires in the wood—my warriors.

WEBSTER (*to* TEACH). Have you forgotten the sea and the way of ships?

TEACH. The sea—and the swift ships sailing—the blue sea.

JURY. Forgotten—remembered—forgotten yet remembered.

WEBSTER. You were men once. Have you forgotten?

JURY. We were men once. We have not thought of it nor remembered. But we were men.

WEBSTER.

Now here is this man with good and evil in his heart.

Do you know him? He is your brother. Will you take the law of the oppressor and bind him down?

It is not for him that I speak. It is for all of you.

There is sadness in being a man but it is a proud thing, too.

There is failure and despair on the journey—the endless journey of mankind.

We are tricked and trapped—we stumble into the pit—but, out of the pit, we rise again.

No demon that was ever foaled can know the inwardness of that—only men—bewildered men.

They have broken freedom with their hands and cast her out from the nations—yet shall she live while man lives.

She shall live in the blood and the heart—she shall live in the earth of this country—she shall not be broken.

When the whips of the oppressors are broken and their names forgotten and destroyed,

I see you, mighty, shining, liberty, liberty! I see free men walking and talking under a free star.

God save the United States and the men who have made her free.

The defense rests.

JURY (*exultantly*). We were men—we were free—we were men—we have not forgotten—our children—our children shall follow and be free.

HATHORNE (*rapping with gavel*). The jury will retire to consider its verdict.

BUTLER (*rising*). There is no need. The jury has heard Mr. Webster. We find for the defendant, Jabez Stone!

JURY. Not guilty!

SCRATCH (*in a screech, rushing forward*). But, Your Honor— (*But, even as he does so, there is a flash and a thunderclap, the stage blacks out again, and when the lights come on, JUDGE and JURY are gone. The yellow light of dawn lights the windows.*)

JABEZ. They're gone and it's morning—Mary, Mary!

MARY (*in doorway*). My love—my dear. (*She rushes to him. Meanwhile SCRATCH has been collecting his papers and trying to sneak out. But WEBSTER catches him.*)

WEBSTER. Just a minute, Mr. Scratch. I'll have that paper first, if you please. (*He takes the deed and tears it*). And, now, sir, I'll have *you!*

SCRATCH. Come, come, Mr. Webster. This sort of thing is ridic—ouch—is ridiculous. If you're worried about the costs of the case, naturally, I'd be glad to pay.

WEBSTER. And so you shall! First of all, you'll promise and covenant never to bother Jabez Stone or any other New Hampshire man from now till doomsday. For any hell we want to raise in this State, we can raise ourselves, without any help from you.

SCRATCH. Ouch! Well, they never did run very big to the barrel but—ouch—I agree!

WEBSTER. See you keep to the bargain! And then—well, I've got a ram named Goliath. He can butt through an iron door. I'd like to turn you loose in his field and see what he could do to you. (SCRATCH *trembles*). But that would be hard on the ram. So we'll just call in the neighbors and give you a shivaree.

SCRATCH. Mr. Webster—please—oh——

WEBSTER. Neighbors! Neighbors! Come in and see what a long-barrelled, slab-sided, lantern-jawed, fortune-telling note-shaver I've got by the scruff of the neck! Bring on your kettles and your pans! (*A noise and murmur outside*). Bring on your muskets and your flails!

JABEZ. We'll drive him out of New Hampshire!

MARY. We'll drive old Scratch away! (*The* CROWD *rushes in, with muskets, flails, brooms, etc. They pursue* SCRATCH *around the stage, chanting.*)

THE CROWD.

> We'll drive him out of New Hampshire!
> We'll drive old Scratch away!
> Forever and a day, boys,
> Forever and a day!

(*They finally catch* SCRATCH *between two of them and fling him out of the door, bodily*).

A MAN. Three cheers for Dan'l Webster!

ANOTHER MAN. Three cheers for Daniel Webster! He's licked the devil!

WEBSTER (*moving to center stage, and joining* JABEZ' *hands and* MARY's). And whom God hath joined let no man put asunder. (*He kisses* MARY *and turns, dusting his hands*). Well, that job's done. I hope there's pie for breakfast, Neighbor Stone. (*And, as some of the women, dancing, bring in pies from the kitchen*)

THE CURTAIN FALLS

THE HAPPY JOURNEY

by Thornton Wilder

CHARACTERS

THE STAGE MANAGER
MA KIRBY
ARTHUR (*thirteen*)
CAROLINE (*fifteen*)
PA (ELMER) KIRBY
BEULAH (*twenty-two*)

No scenery is required for this play. The idea is that no place is being represented. This may be achieved by a gray curtain back-drop with no side-pieces; a cyclorama; or the empty bare stage.

THE HAPPY JOURNEY

As the curtain rises the STAGE MANAGER *is leaning lazily against the proscenium pillar at the Left. He is smoking.* ARTHUR *is playing marbles down Center in pantomime.* CAROLINE *is way up Left talking to some girls who are invisible to us.* MA KIRBY *is anxiously putting on her hat (real) before an imaginary mirror up Right.*

MA. Where's your pa? Why isn't he here? I declare we'll never get started.

ARTHUR. Ma, where's my hat? I guess I don't go if I can't find my hat. (*Still playing marbles.*)

MA. Go out into the hall and see if it isn't there. Where's Caroline gone to now, the plagued child?

ARTHUR. She's out waitin' in the street talkin' to the Jones girls.—I just looked in the hall a thousand times, Ma, and it isn't there. (*He spits for good luck before a difficult shot and mutters:*) Come on, baby.

MA. Go and look again, I say. Look carefully. (ARTHUR *rises, reluctantly, crosses Right, turns around, returns swiftly to his game Center, flinging himself on the floor with a terrible impact and starts shooting an aggie.*)

ARTHUR. No, Ma, it's not there.

MA (*serenely*). Well, you don't leave Newark without that hat, make up your mind to that. I don't go no journeys with a hoodlum.

ARTHUR. Aw, Ma! (MA *comes down Right to the footlights, pulls up an imaginary window and talks toward the audience.*)

MA (*calling*). Oh, Mrs. Schwartz!

THE STAGE MANAGER (*down Left. Consulting his script*). Here I am, Mrs. Kirby. Are you going yet?

MA. I guess we're going in just a minute. How's the baby?

THE STAGE MANAGER. She's all right now. We slapped her on the back and she spat it up.

MA. Isn't that fine!—Well, now, if you'll be good enough to give the cat a saucer of milk in the morning and the evening, Mrs. Schwartz, I'll be ever so grateful to you.— Oh, good-afternoon, Mrs. Hobmeyer!

THE STAGE MANAGER. Good-afternoon, Mrs. Kirby, I hear you're going away.

MA (*modest*). Oh, just for three days, Mrs. Hobmeyer, to see my married daughter, Beulah, in Camden. Elmer's got his vacation week from the laundry early this year, and he's just the best driver in the world. (CAROLINE *comes down stage Right and stands by her mother.*)

THE STAGE MANAGER. Is the whole family going?

MA. Yes, all four of us that's here. The change ought to be good for the children. My married daughter was down-right sick a while ago——

THE STAGE MANAGER. Tchk—tchk—tchk! Yes. I remember you tellin' us.

MA (*with feeling*). And I just want to go down and see the child. I ain't seen her since then. I just won't rest easy in my mind without I see her. (*To* CAROLINE). Can't you say good-afternoon to Mrs. Hobmeyer?

CAROLINE (*lowers her eyes and says woodenly*). Good afternoon, Mrs. Hobmeyer.

THE STAGE MANAGER. Good-afternoon, dear.—Well, I'll wait and beat these rugs until after you're gone, because I don't want to choke you. I hope you have a good time and find everything all right.

MA. Thank you, Mrs. Hobmeyer, I hope I will.—Well, I guess that milk for the cat is all, Mrs. Schwartz, if you're sure you don't mind. If anything should come up, the key to the back door is hanging by the ice-box.

CAROLINE. Ma! Not so loud.

ARTHUR. Everybody can hear yuh.

MA. Stop pullin' my dress, children. (*In a loud whisper*).

The key to the back door I'll leave hangin' by the ice-box and I'll leave the screen door unhooked.

THE STAGE MANAGER. Now have a good trip, dear, and give my love to Beuhly.

MA. I will, and thank you a thousand times. (*She lowers the window, turns up stage and looks around.* CAROLINE *goes Left and vigorously rubs her cheeks.* MA *occupies herself with the last touches of packing*). What can be keeping your pa?

ARTHUR (*who has not left his marbles*). I can't find my hat, Ma. (*Enter* ELMER *holding a cap, up Right.*)

ELMER. Here's Arthur's hat. He musta left it in the car Sunday.

MA. That's a mercy. Now we can start.—Caroline Kirby, what you done to your cheeks?

CAROLINE (*defiant-abashed*). Nothin'.

MA. If you've put anything on 'em, I'll slap you.

CAROLINE. No, Ma, of course I haven't. (*Hanging her head*). I just rubbed 'm to make 'm red. All the girls do that at High School when they're goin' places.

MA. Such silliness I never saw. Elmer, what kep' you?

ELMER (*always even-voiced and always looking out a little anxiously through his spectacles*). I just went to the ga-rage and had Charlie give a last look at it, Kate.

MA. I'm glad you did. (*Collecting two pieces of imaginary luggage and starting for the door*). I wouldn't like to have no breakdown miles from anywhere. Now we can start. Arthur, put those marbles away. Anybody'd think you didn't want to go on a journey to look at yuh. (*They go out through the "hall."* MA *opens an imaginary door down Right.* PA, CAROLINE *and* ARTHUR *go through it.* MA *follows, taking time to lock the door, hang the key by the "ice-box." They turn up at an abrupt angle, go-ing up stage. As they come to the steps from the back porch, each arriving at a given point, starts bending his knees lower and lower to denote going downstairs, and find themselves in the street. The* STAGE MANAGER *moves from the Right the automobile. It is Right Center of the stage, seen partially at an angle, its front pointing down Center.)*

ELMER (*coming forward*). Here, you boys, you keep away from that car.

MA. Those Sullivan boys put their heads into everything. (*They get into the car.* ELMER's *hands hold an imaginary steering wheel and continually shift gears.* MA *sits beside him.* ARTHUR *is behind him and* CAROLINE *is behind* MA.)

CAROLINE (*standing up in the back seat, waving, self-consciously*). Good-bye, Mildred. Good-bye, Helen.

THE STAGE MANAGER (*having returned to his position by the Left proscenium*). Good-bye, Caroline. Good-bye, Mrs. Kirby. I hope y' have a good time.

MA. Good-bye, girls.

THE STAGE MANAGER. Good-bye, Kate. The car looks fine.

MA (*looking upward toward a window Right*). Oh, good-bye, Emma! (*Modestly*). We think it's the best little Chevrolet in the world.—(*Looking up toward the Left*). Oh, good-bye, Mrs. Adler!

THE STAGE MANAGER. What, are you going away, Mrs. Kirby?

MA. Just for three days, Mrs. Adler, to see my married daughter in Camden.

THE STAGE MANAGER. Have a good time. (*Now* MA, CAROLINE, *and the* STAGE MANAGER *break out into a tremendous chorus of good-byes. The whole street is saying good-bye.* ARTHUR *takes out his pea shooter and lets fly happily into the air. There is a lurch or two and they are off.)*

ARTHUR (*leaning forward in sudden fright*). Pa! Pa! Don't go by the school. Mr. Biedenbach might see us!

MA. I don't care if he does see us. I guess I can take my children out of school for one day without having to hide

down back streets about it. (ELMER *nods to a passerby.
Without sharpness*). Who was that you spoke to,
Elmer?

ELMER. That was the fellow who arranges our banquets
down to the Lodge, Kate.

MA. Is he the one who had to buy four hundred steaks?
(PA *nods*). I declare, I'm glad I'm not him.

ELMER. The air's getting better already. Take deep breaths,
children. (*They inhale noisily.*)

ARTHUR (*pointing to a sign and indicating that it gradually
goes by*). Gee, it's almost open fields already. "*Weber
and Heilbroner Suits for Well-dressed Men.*" Ma, can I
have one of them some day?

MA. If you graduate with good marks perhaps your father'll let you have one for graduation. (*Pause. General
gazing about, then sudden lurch.*)

CAROLINE (*whining*). Oh, Pa! do we have to wait while
that whole funeral goes by? (ELMER *takes off his hat.
MA cranes forward with absorbed curiosity.*)

MA (*not sharp and bossy*). Take off your hat, Arthur. Look
at your father.—Why, Elmer, I do believe that's a lodge-
brother of yours. See the banner? I suppose this is the
Elizabeth branch. (ELMER *nods.* MA *sighs: Tchk—tchk
—tchk. The children lean forward and all watch the funeral in silence, growing momentarily more solemnized.
After a pause,* MA *continues almost dreamily but not
sentimentally*): Well, we haven't forgotten the funeral
that we went on, have we? We haven't forgotten our
good Harold. He gave his life for his country, we mustn't
forget that. (*There is another pause; with cheerful resignation*). Well, we'll all hold up the traffic for a few
minutes some day.

THE CHILDREN (*very uncomfortable*). Ma!

MA (*without self-pity*). Well, I'm "ready," children. I hope
everybody in this car is "ready." And I pray to go first,
Elmer. Yes. (ELMER *touches her hand.*)

CAROLINE. Ma, everybody's looking at you.

ARTHUR. Everybody's laughing at you.

MA. Oh, hold your tongues! I don't care what a lot of silly people in Elizabeth, New Jersey, think of me.—Now we can go on. That's the last. (*There is another lurch and the car goes on.*)

CAROLINE (*looking at a sign and turning as she passes it*). "Fit-Rite Suspenders. The Working Man's Choice." Pa, why do they spell Rite that way?

ELMER. So that it'll make you stop and ask about it, Missy.

CAROLINE. Papa, you're teasing me.—Ma, why do they say *"Three Hundred Rooms Three Hundred Baths"*?

ARTHUR. *"Miller's Spaghetti: The Family's Favorite Dish."* Ma, why don't you ever have spaghetti?

MA. Go along, you'd never eat it.

ARTHUR. Ma, I like it now.

CAROLINE (*with gesture*). Yum-yum. It looked wonderful up there. Ma, make some when we get home?

MA (*dryly*). "The management is always happy to receive suggestions. We aim to please." (*The children scream with laughter. Even* ELMER *smiles.* MA *remains modest.*)

ELMER. Well, I guess no one's complaining, Kate. Everybody knows you're a good cook.

MA. I don't know whether I'm a good cook or not, but I know I've had practice. At least I've cooked three meals a day for twenty-five years.

ARTHUR. Aw, Ma, you went out to eat once in a while.

MA. Yes. That made it a leap year. (*The children laugh again.*)

CAROLINE (*in an ecstasy of well-being puts her arms around her mother*). Ma, I love going out in the country like this. Let's do it often, Ma.

MA. Goodness, smell that air, will you! It's got the whole ocean in it.—Elmer, drive careful over that bridge. This must be New Brunswick we're coming to.

ARTHUR (*after a slight pause*). Ma, when is the next comfort station?

MA (*unruffled*). You don't want one. You just said that to be awful.

CAROLINE (*shrilly*). Yes, he did, Ma. He's terrible. He says that kind of thing right out in school and I want to sink through the floor, Ma. He's terrible.

MA. Oh, don't get so excited about nothing, Miss Proper! I guess we're all yewman beings in this car, at least as far as I know. And, Arthur, you try and be a gentleman. —Elmer, don't run over that collie dog. (*She follows the dog with her eyes*). Looked kinda peaked to me. Needs a good honest bowl of leavings. Pretty dog, too. (*Her eyes fall on a billboard at the Right*). That's a pretty advertisement for Chesterfield cigarettes, isn't it? Looks like Beulah, a little.

ARTHUR. Ma?

MA. Yes.

ARTHUR (*"route" rhymes with "out"*). Can't I take a paper route with the Newark *Daily Post?*

MA. No, you cannot. No, sir. I hear they make the paper boys get up at four-thirty in the morning. No son of mine is going to get up at four-thirty every morning, not if it's to make a million dollars. Your *Saturday Evening Post* route on Thursday mornings is enough.

ARTHUR. Aw, Ma.

MA. No, sir. No son of mine is going to get up at four-thirty and miss the sleep God meant him to have.

ARTHUR (*sullenly*). Hhm! Ma's always talking about God. I guess she got a letter from Him this morning.

MA (*outraged*). Elmer, stop that automobile this minute. I don't go another step with anybody that says things like that. Arthur, you get out of this car. (ELMER *stops the car*). Elmer, you give him a dollar bill. He can go back to Newark by himself. I don't want him.

ARTHUR. What did I say? There wasn't anything terrible about that.

ELMER. I didn't hear what he said, Kate.

MA. God has done a lot of things for me and I won't have Him made fun of by anybody. Get out of this car this minute.

CAROLINE. Aw, Ma,—don't spoil the ride.

MA. No.

ELMER. We might as well go on, Kate, since we've got started. I'll talk to the boy to-night.

MA (*slowly conceding*). All right, if you say so, Elmer. (ELMER *starts the car.*)

ARTHUR (*frightened*). Aw, Ma, that wasn't so terrible.

MA. I don't want to talk about it. I hope your father washes your mouth out with soap and water.—Where'd we all be if I started talking about God like that, I'd like to know! We'd be in the speak-easies and night-clubs and places like that, that's where we'd be.

CAROLINE (*after a very slight pause*). What did he say, Ma? I didn't hear what he said.

MA. I don't want to talk about it. (*They drive on in silence for a moment, the shocked silence after a scandal.*)

ELMER. I'm going to stop and give the car a little water, I guess.

MA. All right, Elmer. You know best.

ELMER (*turns the wheel and stops; as to a garage hand*). Could I have a little water in the radiator—to make sure?

THE STAGE MANAGER (*in this scene alone he lays aside his script and enters into a rôle seriously*). You sure can. (*He punches the left front tire*). Air all right? Do you need any oil or gas? (*Goes up around car.*)

ELMER. No, I think not. I just got fixed up in Newark. (THE STAGE MANAGER *carefully pours some water into the hood.*)

MA. We're on the right road for Camden, are we?

THE STAGE MANAGER (*coming down on Right side of car*). Yes, keep straight ahead. You can't miss it. You'll be in Trenton in a few minutes. Camden's a great town, lady, believe me.

MA. My daughter likes it fine,—my married daughter.

THE STAGE MANAGER. Ye'? It's a great burg all right. I guess I think so because I was born near there.

MA. Well, well. Your folks still live there?

THE STAGE MANAGER (*standing with one foot on the rung of MA's chair. They have taken a great fancy to one another*). No, my old man sold the farm and they built a factory on it. So the folks moved to Philadelphia.

MA. My married daughter Beulah lives there because her husband works in the telephone company.—Stop pokin' me, Caroline!—We're all going down to see her for a few days.

THE STAGE MANAGER. Ye'?

MA. She's been sick, you see, and I just felt I had to go and see her. My husband and my boy are going to stay at the Y.M.C.A. I hear they've got a dormitory on the top floor that's real clean and comfortable. Have you ever been there?

THE STAGE MANAGER. No. I'm Knights of Columbus myself.

MA. Oh.

THE STAGE MANAGER. I used to play basketball at the Y though. It looked all right to me. (*He reluctantly moves away and pretends to examine the car again*). Well, I guess you're all set now, lady. I hope you have a good trip; you can't miss it.

EVERYBODY. Thanks. Thanks a lot. Good luck to you. (*Jolts and lurches.*)

MA (*with a sigh*). The world's full of nice people.—That's what I call a nice young man.

CAROLINE (*earnestly*). Ma, you oughtn't to tell 'm all everything about yourself.

MA. Well, Caroline, you do your way and I'll do mine.—
He looked kinda pale to me. I'd like to feed him up for
a few days. His mother lives in Philadelphia and I expect he eats at those dreadful Greek places.

CAROLINE. I'm hungry. Pa, there's a hot dog stand. K'n I
have one?

ELMER. We'll all have one, eh, Kate? We had such an
early lunch.

MA. Just as you think best, Elmer. (ELMER *stops the car.*)

ELMER. Arthur, here's half a dollar.—Run over and see
what they have. Not too much mustard either. (ARTHUR
descends from the car and goes off stage Right. MA *and*
CAROLINE *get out and walk a bit, up stage and to the
Left.* CAROLINE *keeps at her mother's Right.*)

MA. What's that flower over there?—I'll take some of those
to Beulah.

CAROLINE. It's just a weed, Ma.

MA. I like it.—My, look at the sky, wouldya! I'm glad I
was born in New Jersey. I've always said it was the best
state in the Union. Every state has something no other
state has got. (*Presently* ARTHUR *returns with his hands
full of imaginary hot dogs which he distributes. First
to his father, next to* CAROLINE, *who comes forward to
meet him, and lastly to his mother. He is still very much
cast down by the recent scandal, and as he approaches
his mother says falteringly*):

ARTHUR. Ma, I'm sorry. I'm sorry for what I said. (*He
bursts into tears.*)

MA. There. There. We all say wicked things at times. I
know you didn't mean it like it sounded. (*He weeps still
more violently than before*). Why, now, now! I forgive
you, Arthur, and to-night before you go to bed you . . .
(*She whispers*). You're a good boy at heart, Arthur, and
we all know it. (CAROLINE *starts to cry too.* MA *is suddenly joyously alive and happy*). Sakes alive, it's too
nice a day for us all to be cryin'. Come now, get in.

(*Crossing behind car to the right side, followed by the children*). Caroline, go up in front with your father. Ma wants to sit with her beau. (CAROLINE *sits in front with her father.* MA *lets* ARTHUR *get in car ahead of her; then she closes door*). I never saw such children. Your hot dogs are all getting wet. Now chew them fine, everybody.—All right, Elmer, forward march. (*Car starts.* CAROLINE *spits*). Caroline, whatever are you doing?

CAROLINE. I'm spitting out the leather, Ma.

MA. Then say: Excuse me.

CAROLINE. Excuse me, please. (*She spits again.*)

MA. What's this place? Arthur, did you see the post-office?

ARTHUR. It said Lawrenceville.

MA. Hhn. School kinda. Nice. I wonder what that big yellow house set back was.—Now it's beginning to be Trenton.

CAROLINE. Papa, it was near here that George Washington crossed the Delaware. It was near Trenton, Mama. He was first in war and first in peace, and first in the hearts of his countrymen.

MA (*surveying the passing world, serene and didactic*). Well the thing I like about him best was that he never told a lie. (*The children are duly cast down. There is a pause.* ARTHUR *stands up and looks at the car ahead*). There's a sunset for you. There's nothing like a good sunset.

ARTHUR. There's an Ohio license in front of us. Ma, have you ever been to Ohio?

MA. No. (*A dreamy silence descends upon them.* CAROLINE *sits closer to her father, toward the Left;* ARTHUR *closer to* MA *on the Right, who puts her arm around him, unsentimentally.*)

ARTHUR. Ma, what a lotta people there are in the world, Ma. There must be thousands and thousands in the United States. Ma, how many are there?

MA. I don't know. Ask your father.

ARTHUR. Pa, how many are there?

ELMER. There are a hundred and twenty-six million, Kate.

MA (*giving a pressure about* ARTHUR's *shoulder*). And they all like to drive out in the evening with their children beside 'm. Why doesn't somebody sing something? Arthur, you're always singing something; what's the matter with you?

ARTHUR. All right. What'll we sing? (*He sketches*)

"In the Blue Ridge Mountains of Virginia,
    On the . . ."

No, I don't like that any more. Let's do:

"I been workin' on de railroad
    (CAROLINE *joins in*).
All de liblong day.
    (MA *sings*).
I been workin' on de railroad
    (ELMER *joins in*).
Just to pass de time away.
Don't you hear de whistle blowin'," etc.

(MA *suddenly jumps up with a wild cry and a large circular gesture.*)

MA. Elmer, that signpost said Camden. I saw it.

ELMER. All right, Kate, if you're sure. (*Much shifting of gears, backing, and jolting.*)

MA. Yes, there it is. Camden—five miles. Dear old Beulah. (*The journey continues*). Now, children, you be good and quiet during dinner. She's just got out of bed after a big sorta operation, and we must all move around kinda quiet. First you drop me and Caroline at the door and just say hello, and then you men-folk go over to the Y.M.C.A. and come back for dinner in about an hour.

CAROLINE (*shutting her eyes and pressing her fists passionately against her nose*). I see the first star. Everybody make a wish.

Star light, star bright,
First star I seen to-night.
I wish I may, I wish I might
Have the wish I wish to-night.

(*Then solemnly*). Pins. Mama, you say "needles." (*She interlocks little fingers with her mother across back of seat.*)

MA. Needles.

CAROLINE. Shakespeare. Ma, you say "Longfellow."

MA. Longfellow.

CAROLINE. Now it's a secret and I can't tell it to anybody. Ma, you make a wish.

MA (*with almost grim humor*). No, I can make wishes without waiting for no star. And I can tell my wishes right out loud too. Do you want to hear them?

CAROLINE (*resignedly*). No, Ma, we know 'm already. We've heard 'm. (*She hangs her head affectedly on her left shoulder and says with unmalicious mimicry*). You want me to be a good girl and you want Arthur to be honest-in-word-and-deed.

MA (*majestically*). Yes. So mind yourself.

ELMER. Caroline, take out that letter from Beulah in my coat pocket by you and read aloud the places I marked with red pencil.

CAROLINE (*laboriously making it out*). "A few blocks after you pass the two big oil tanks on your left . . ."

EVERYBODY (*pointing backward*). There they are!

CAROLINE. ". . . you come to a corner where there's an A and P store on the left and a firehouse kitty-corner to it . . ." (*They all jubilantly identify these landmarks*). ". . . turn right, go two blocks and our house is Weyerhauser St. Number 471.*"

MA. It's an even nicer street than they used to live in. And right handy to an A and P.

CAROLINE (*whispering*). Ma, it's better than our street. It's richer than our street. Ma, isn't Beulah richer than we are?

MA (*looking at her with a firm and glassy eye*). Mind yourself, Missy. I don't want to hear anybody talking about rich or not rich when I'm around. If people aren't nice I don't care how rich they are. I live in the best street in the world because my husband and children live there. (*She glares impressively at* CAROLINE *a moment to let this lesson sink in, then looks up, sees* BEULAH *off left and waves*). There's Beulah standing on the steps looking for us. (BEULAH *enters from Left, also waving. They all call out: "Hello, Beulah—hello." Presently they are all getting out of the car, except* ELMER, *busy with brakes*.)

BEULAH. Hello, Mama. Well, lookit how Arthur and Caroline are growing.

MA. They're bursting all their clothes.

BEULAH (*crossing in front of them and kissing her father long and affectionately*). Hello, Papa. Good old papa. You look tired, Pa.

MA. Yes, your pa needs a rest. Thank Heaven, his vacation has come just now. We'll feed him up and let him sleep late. (ELMER *gets out of car and stands in front of it*). Pa has a present for you, Loolie. He would go and buy it.

BEULAH. Why, Pa, you're terrible to go and buy anything for me. Isn't he terrible? (STAGE MANAGER *removes automobile*.)

MA. Well, it's a secret. You can open it at dinner.

BEULAH (*puts her arm around his neck and rubs her nose against his temple*). Crazy old pa, goin' buyin' things! It's me that oughta be buyin' things for you, Pa.

ELMER. Oh, no! There's only one Loolie in the world.

BEULAH (*whispering, as her eyes fill with tears*). Are you glad I'm still alive, Pa? (*She kisses him abruptly and goes back to the house steps*.)

ELMER. Where's Horace, Loolie?

BEULAH. He was kep' over a little at the office. He'll be here any minute. He's crazy to see you all.

MA. All right. You men go over to the Y and come back in about an hour.

BEULAH. Go straight along, Pa, you can't miss it. It just stares at yuh. (ELMER *and* ARTHUR *exit down Right*). Well, come on upstairs, Ma, and take your things.—Caroline, there's a surprise for you in the back yard.

CAROLINE. Rabbits?

BEULAH. No.

CAROLINE. Chickins?

BEULAH. No. Go and see. (CAROLINE *runs off stage, down Left*). There are two new puppies. You be thinking over whether you can keep one in Newark.

MA. I guess we can. (MA *and* BEULAH *turn and walk way up stage Right.* THE STAGE MANAGER *pushes out a cot from the Left, and places it down left on a slant so that its foot is toward the Left.* BEULAH *and* MA *come down stage Center toward Left*). It's a nice house, Beulah. You just got a *lovely* home.

BEULAH. When I got back from the hospital, Horace had moved everything into it, and there wasn't anything for me to do.

MA. It's lovely. (BEULAH *sits on the cot, testing the springs.*)

BEULAH. I think you'll find this comfortable, Ma. (BEULAH *sits on down stage end of it.*)

MA (*taking off her hat*). Oh, I could sleep on a heapa shoes, Loolie! I don't have no trouble sleepin'. (*She sits down up stage of her*). Now let me look at my girl. Well, well, when I last saw you, you didn't know me. You kep' saying: *When's Mama comin'? When's Mama comin'?* But the doctor sent me away.

BEULAH (*puts her head on her mother's shoulder and weeps*). It was awful, Mama. It was awful. She didn't even live a few minutes, Mama. It was awful.

MA (*in a quick, light, urgent undertone*). God thought best, dear. God thought best. We don't understand why. We just go on, honey, doin' our business. (*Then almost *abruptly*). Well, now, (*stands up*) what are we giving the men to eat to-night?

BEULAH. There's a chicken in the oven.

MA. What time didya put it in?

BEULAH (*restraining her*). Aw, Ma, don't go yet. (*Taking her mother's hand and drawing her down beside her*). I like to sit here with you this way. You always get the fidgets when we try and pet yuh, Mama.

MA (*ruefully, laughing*). Yes, it's kinda foolish. I'm just an old Newark bag-a-bones. (*She glances at the backs of her hands.*)

BEULAH (*indignantly*). Why, Ma, you're good-lookin'! We always said you were good-lookin'.—And besides, you're the best ma we could ever have.

MA (*uncomfortable*). Well, I hope you like me. There's nothin' like bein' liked by your family.—(*Rises*). Now I'm going downstairs to look at the chicken. You stretch out here for a minute and shut your eyes. (*She helps BEULAH to a lying position*). Have you got everything laid in for breakfast before the shops close?

BEULAH. Oh, you know! Ham and eggs. (*They both laugh. MA puts an imaginary blanket over BEULAH.*)

MA. I declare I never could understand what men see in ham and eggs. I think they're horrible.—What time did you put the chicken in?

BEULAH. Five o'clock.

MA. Well, now, you shut your eyes for ten minutes. (*MA turns, walks directly up stage, then along the back wall to the Right as she absent-mindedly and indistinctly sings*):

"There were ninety and nine that safely lay
In the shelter of the fold . . ."

AND THE CURTAIN FALLS

HERE WE ARE

by Dorothy Parker

COPYRIGHT 1931 BY DOROTHY PARKER

From the story "Here We Are" from *THE PORTABLE DORO-THY PARKER*. All rights reserved on this version; no public reading or performances of any nature permitted without formal authorization from The Viking Press, Inc., 625 Madison Avenue, New York 22.

HERE WE ARE

SCENE: *A compartment in a Pullman car. He is storing the suitcases in the rack and hanging up coats. She is primping. He finishes disposing of the luggage and sits.*

HE. Well!

SHE. Well!

HE. Well, here we are.

SHE. Here we are, aren't we?

HE. Eeyop. I should say we are. Here we are.

SHE. Well!

HE. Well! Well! How does it feel to be an old married lady?

SHE. Oh, it's too soon to ask me that. At least—I mean. Well, I mean, goodness, we've only been married about three hours, haven't we?

HE. We have been married exactly two hours and twenty-six minutes.

SHE. My, it seems like longer.

HE. No, it isn't hardly half-past six yet.

SHE. It seems like later. I guess it's because it starts getting dark so early.

HE. It does, at that. The nights are going to be pretty long from now on. I mean. I mean—well, it starts getting dark early.

SHE. I didn't have any idea what time it was. Everything was so mixed up, I sort of don't know where I am, or what it's all about. Getting back from the church, and then all those people, and then changing all my clothes, and then everybody throwing things, and all. Goodness, I don't see how people do it every day.

HE. Do what?

SHE. Get married. When you think of all the people, all

over the world, getting married just as if it was nothing. Chinese people and everybody. Just as if it wasn't anything.

HE. Well, let's not worry about people all over the world. Let's don't think about a lot of Chinese. We've got something better to think about. I mean. I mean—well, what do we care about them?

SHE. I know, but I just sort of got to thinking of them, all of them, all over everywhere, doing it all the time. At least, I mean—getting married, you know. And it's—well, it's sort of such a big thing to do, it makes you feel queer. You think of them, all of them, all doing it just like it wasn't anything. And how does anybody know what's going to happen next?

HE. Let them worry, we don't have to. We know darn well what's going to happen next. I mean—well, we know it's going to be great. Well, we know we're going to be happy. Don't we?

SHE. Oh, of course. Only you think of all the people, and you have to sort of keep thinking. It makes you feel funny. An awful lot of people that get married, it doesn't turn out so well. And I guess they all must have thought it was going to be great.

HE. Aw, come on, now, this is no way to start a honeymoon, with all this thinking going on. Look at us—all married and everything done. I mean. The wedding all done and all.

SHE. Ah, it was nice, wasn't it? Did you really like my veil?

HE. You looked great, just great.

SHE. Oh, I'm terribly glad. Ellie and Louise looked lovely, didn't they? I'm terribly glad they did finally decide on pink. They looked perfectly lovely.

HE. Listen, I want to tell you something. When I was standing up there in that old church waiting for you to come up, and I saw those two bridesmaids, I thought to myself, I thought, "Well, I never knew Louise could look like that!" I thought she'd have knocked anybody's eye out.

SHE. Oh, really? Funny. Of course, everybody thought her dress and hat were lovely, but a lot of people seemed to think she looked sort of tired. People have been saying that a lot, lately. I tell them I think it's awfully mean of them to go around saying that about her. I tell them they've got to remember that Louise isn't so terribly young any more, and they've got to expect her to look like that. Louise can say she's twenty-three all she wants to, but she's a good deal nearer twenty-seven.

HE. Well, she was certainly a knockout at the wedding. Boy!

SHE. I'm terribly glad you thought so. I'm glad someone did. How did you think Ellie looked?

HE. Why, I honestly didn't get a look at her.

SHE. Oh, really? Well, I certainly think that's too bad. I don't suppose I ought to say it about my own sister, but I never saw anybody look as beautiful as Ellie looked today. And always so sweet and unselfish, too. And you didn't even notice her. But you never pay attention to Ellie, anyway. Don't think I haven't noticed it. It makes me feel just terrible. It makes me feel just awful that you don't like my own sister.

HE. I do so like her! I'm crazy for Ellie. I think she's a great kid.

SHE. Don't think it makes any difference to Ellie! Ellie's got enough people crazy about her. It isn't anything to her whether you like her or not. Don't flatter yourself she cares! Only, the only thing is, it makes it awfully hard for me you don't like her, that's the only thing. I keep thinking, when we come back and get in the apartment and everything, it's going to be awfully hard for me that you won't want all my family around. I know how you feel about my family. Don't think I haven't seen it. Only, if you don't ever want to see them, that's your loss. Not theirs. Don't flatter yourself!

HE. Oh, now, come on! What's all this talk about not wanting your family around? Why, you know how I feel
about your family. I think your old lady—I think your
mother's swell. And Ellie. And your father. What's all
this talk?

SHE. Well, I've seen it. Don't think I haven't. Lots of people
they get married, and they think it's going to be great
and everything, and then it all goes to pieces because
people don't like people's families, or something like that.
Don't tell me! I've seen it happen.

HE. Honey, what is all this? What are you getting all angry
about? Hey, look, this is our honeymoon. What are you
trying to start a fight for? Ah, I guess you're just feeling sort of nervous.

SHE. Me? What have I got to be nervous about? I mean.
I mean, goodness, I'm not nervous.

HE. You know, lots of times, they say that girls get kind of
nervous and yippy on account of thinking about—I
mean. I mean—well, it's like you said, things are all so
sort of mixed up and everything, right now. But afterwards, it'll be all right. I mean. I mean—well, look,
honey, you don't look any too comfortable. Don't you
want to take your hat off? And let's don't ever fight, ever.
Will we?

SHE. Ah, I'm sorry I was cross. I guess I did feel a little
bit funny. All mixed up, and then thinking of all those
people all over everywhere, and then being sort of 'way
off here, all alone with you. It's so sort of different. It's
sort of such a big thing. You can't blame a person for
thinking, can you? Yes, don't let's ever, ever fight. We
won't be like a whole lot of them. We won't fight or be
nasty or anything. Will we?

HE. You bet your life we won't.

SHE. I guess I will take this darned old hat off. It kind of
presses. Just put it up on the rack, will you, dear? Do
you like it, sweetheart?

HE. Looks good on you.

SHE. No, but I mean, do you really like it?

HE. Well, I'll tell you, I know this is the new style and everything like that, and it's probably great. I don't know anything about things like that. Only I like the kind of a hat like that blue hat you had. Gee, I like that hat.

SHE. Oh, really? Well, that's nice. That's lovely. The first thing you say to me, as soon as you get me off on a train away from my family and everything, is that you don't like my hat. The first thing you say to your wife is you think she has terrible taste in hats. That's nice, isn't it?

HE. Now, honey, I never said anything like that. I only said——

SHE. What you don't seem to realize is this hat cost twenty-two dollars. Twenty-two dollars. And that horrible old blue thing you think you're so crazy about, that cost three ninety-five.

HE. I don't give a darn what they cost. I only said—I said I liked that blue hat. I don't know anything about hats. I'll be crazy about this one as soon as I get used to it. Only it's kind of not like your other hats. I don't know about the new styles. What do I know about women's hats?

SHE. It's too bad you didn't marry somebody that would get the kind of hats you'd like. Hats that cost three ninety-five. Why didn't you marry Louise? You always think she looks so beautiful. You'd love her taste in hats. Why didn't you marry her?

HE. Ah, now, honey, for heaven's sakes!

SHE. Why didn't you marry her? All you've done, ever since we got on this train, is talk about her. Here I've sat and sat, and just listened to you saying how wonderful Louise is. I suppose that's nice, getting me off here all alone with you, and then raving about Louise right in front

of my face. Why didn't you ask her to marry you? I'm
sure she would have jumped at the chance. There aren't
so many people asking her to marry them. It's too bad
you didn't marry her. I'm sure you'd have been much
happier.

HE. Listen, baby, while you're talking about things like
that, why didn't you marry Joe Brooks? I suppose he
could have given you all the twenty-two-dollar hats you
wanted, I suppose!

SHE. Well, I'm not so sure I'm not sorry I didn't. There!
Joe Brooks wouldn't have waited until he got me all
off alone and then sneered at my taste in clothes. Joe
Brooks wouldn't ever hurt my feelings. Joe Brooks has
always been fond of me.

HE. Yeah, he's fond of you. He was so fond of you he didn't
even send a wedding present. That's how fond of you he
was.

SHE. I happen to know for a fact that he was away on
business, and as soon as he comes back he's going to
give me anything I want for the apartment.

HE. Listen, I don't want anything he gives you in our apartment. Anything he gives you, I'll throw right out the
window. That's what I think of your friend Joe Brooks.
And how do you know where he is and what he's going
to do, anyway? Has he been writing to you?

SHE. I suppose my friends can correspond with me. I didn't
hear there was any law against that.

HE. Well, I suppose they can't! And what do you think of
that? I'm not going to have my wife getting a lot of letters from cheap traveling salesmen!

SHE. Joe Brooks is not a cheap traveling salesman! He is not!
He gets a wonderful salary.

HE. Oh yeah? Where did you hear that?

SHE. He told me so himself.

HE. Oh, he told you so himself. I see. He told you so himself.

SHE. You've got a lot of right to talk about Joe Brooks. You and your friend Louise. All you ever talk about is Louise.

HE. Oh, for heaven's sakes! What do I care about Louise? I just thought she was a friend of yours, that's all. That's why I ever noticed her.

SHE. Well, you certainly took an awful lot of notice of her today. On our wedding day! You said yourself when you were standing there in the church you just kept thinking of her. Right up at the altar. Oh, right in the presence of God! And all you thought about was Louise.

HE. Listen, honey, I never should have said that. How does anybody know what kind of crazy things come into their heads when they're standing there waiting to get married? I was just telling you that because it was so kind of crazy. I thought it would make you laugh.

SHE. I know, I've been all sort of mixed up today, too. I told you that. Everything so strange and everything. And me all the time thinking about all those people all over the world, and now us here all alone, and everything. I know you get all mixed up. Only I did think, when you kept talking about how beautiful Louise looked, you did it with malice and forethought.

HE. I never did anything with malice and forethought! I just told you that about Louise because I thought it would make you laugh.

SHE. Well, it didn't.

HE. No, I know it didn't. It certainly did not. Ah, baby, and we ought to be laughing, too. Hell, honey lamb, this is our honeymoon. What's the matter?

SHE. I don't know. We used to squabble a lot when we were going together and then engaged and everything, but I thought everything would be so different as soon as you were married. And now I feel so sort of strange and everything. I feel so sort of alone.

HE. Well, you see, sweetheart, we're not really married yet.

I mean. I mean—well, things will be different afterwards. Oh, hell. I mean, we haven't been married very long.

SHE. No.

HE. Well, we haven't got much longer to wait now. I mean —well, we'll be in New York in about twenty minutes. Then we can have dinner, and sort of see what we feel like doing. Or, I mean—is there anything special you want to do tonight?

SHE. What?

HE. What I mean to say, would you like to go to a show or something?

SHE. Why, whatever you like. I sort of didn't think people went to theaters and things on their—I mean, I've got a couple of letters I simply must write. Don't let me forget.

HE. Oh, you're going to write letters tonight?

SHE. Well, you see, I've been perfectly terrible. What with all the excitement and everything. I never did thank poor old Mrs. Sprague for her berry spoon, and I never did a thing about those book ends the McMasters sent. It's just too awful of me. I've got to write them this very night.

HE. And when you've finished writing your letters, maybe I could get you a magazine or a bag of peanuts.

SHE. What?

HE. I mean, I wouldn't want you to be bored.

SHE. As if I could be bored with you! Silly! Aren't we married? Bored!

HE. What I thought, I thought when we got in, we could go right up to the Biltmore and anyway leave our bags, and maybe have a little dinner in the room, kind of quiet, and then do whatever we wanted. I mean. I mean —well, let's go right up there from the station.

SHE. Oh, yes, let's. I'm so glad we're going to the Biltmore. I just love it. The twice I've stayed in New York we've always stayed there, Papa and Mamma and Ellie and I, and I was crazy about it. I always sleep so well there. I go right off to sleep the minute I put my head on the pillow.

HE. Oh, you do?

SHE. At least, I mean, 'way up high it's so quiet.

HE. We might go to some show or other tomorrow night instead of tonight. Don't you think that would be better?

SHE. Yes, I think it might.

HE. Do you really have to write those letters tonight?

SHE. Well, I don't suppose they'd get there any quicker than if I wrote them tomorrow.

HE. And we won't ever fight any more, will we?

SHE. Oh, no. Not ever! I don't know what made me do like that. It all got so sort of funny, sort of like a nightmare, the way I got thinking of all those people getting married all the time; and so many of them, everything spoils on account of fighting and everything. I got all mixed up thinking about them. Oh, I don't want to be like them. But we won't be, will we?

HE. Sure we won't.

SHE. We won't go all to pieces. We won't fight. It'll all be different, now we're married. It'll all be lovely. Reach me down my hat, will you, sweetheart? It's time I was putting it on. Thanks. Ah, I'm sorry you don't like it.

HE. I do so like it!

SHE. You said you didn't. You said you thought it was perfectly terrible.

HE. I never said any such thing. You're crazy.

SHE. All right, I may be crazy. Thank you very much. But that's what you said. Not that it matters—it's just a little thing. But it makes you feel pretty funny to think you've gone and married somebody that says you have perfectly terrible taste in hats. And then goes and says you're crazy, besides.

HE. Now, listen here, nobody said any such thing. Why, I

love that hat. The more I look at it the better I like it. I think it's great.

SHE. That isn't what you said before.

HE. Honey, stop it, will you? What do you want to start all this for? I love the damned hat. I mean, I love your hat. I love anything you wear. What more do you want me to say?

SHE. Well, I don't want you to say it like that.

HE. I said I think it's great. That's all I said.

SHE. Do you really? Do you honestly? Ah, I'm so glad. I'd hate you not to like my hat. It would be—I don't know, it would be sort of such a bad start.

HE. Well, I'm crazy for it. Now we've got that settled, for heaven's sakes. Ah, baby. Baby lamb. We're not going to have any bad starts. Look at us—we're on our honeymoon. Pretty soon we'll be regular old married people. I mean. I mean, in a few minutes we'll be getting in to New York, and then we'll be going to the hotel, and then everything will be all right. I mean—well, look at us! Here we are married! Here we are!

SHE. Yes, here we are, aren't we?

CURTAIN

THE TRAVELER

by Marc Connelly

CHARACTERS

MR. MERCER

MORTON, THE PORTER

MR. BARCLAY, THE CONDUCTOR

SCENE

The smoking compartment of a Pullman Car.

THE TRAVELER

In the darkness, the voice of a Train Announcer is heard.

ANNOUNCER. Bo-o-ard! Twentieth Century Limited for Albany, Utica, Syracuse, Buffalo, Cleveland, and Chicago. First stop—One Hundred and Twenty-fifth Street. Bo-o-ard! (*The lights go up and we behold the smoking compartment of a Pullman Car. As it is about 6:30 of a March evening, nothing need be seen through the two windows upstage. The usual bench seat runs up and down stage, L., and the usual chair is to its R., facing D.R. At least one wash-basin should be shown U.L., and also the door to the toilet, which is not opened during the performance. The suggested corridor of the car runs R. and L., behind the curtain line. Standing in the compartment and holding several bundles, with an overcoat over his arm, is* MORTON, *the car's porter. He is looking off L.*)

MORTON (*cordially*). All right. This way, sir. This way to the various other parts inside the car. (KENNETH MERCER *enters.* MR. MERCER *is naturally excited as this is his first trip on a train in some time.*)

MERCER. Oh. So *here* you are. I was standing on the platform watching the different people get on board the train . . . the various types, you know.

MORTON. I guess you are a student of human nature.

MERCER (*modestly*). I just dabble at it.

MORTON. I understand. Now this is the smoking compartment. Would you like to sit in here?

MERCER. I have a choice?

MORTON. As a passenger you have the choice of sitting in here and smoking and chatting, or sitting in seat Number 7 in the body of the car.

MERCER (*with a grin of perplexity*). I hardly know which to choose.

MORTON. Why don't you stop in here temporarily and see how you feel about making a permanent choice later?

MERCER. Yes! That is my decision!

MORTON. Very good. I'll take these things of yours to seat Number 7, and then later we'll see how you feel.

MERCER. Good. Now I have the choice of any seat in here, I suppose?

MORTON (*who likes his little joke now and then*). Any seat that's not occupied.

MERCER (*the laugh being on him*). Very, very good. Whatever is your name?

MORTON. Morton, the porter.

MERCER. "Morton." All right, Morton. My name is Mr. Mercer. (*There is a pause as this sinks in; then* MERCER *darts like a panther to the seat in the corner next to the window*). And I choose this seat!

MORTON. Well, you've just chosen the very best seat in the smoking compartment, that's all!

MERCER. No fooling?

MORTON. I was never more serious. You see, if you'd chosen the chair, you'd be riding backwards, whereas this way, you are both riding forwards and have the use of the window as well.

MERCER (*scenting a trick*). Yes, but it's getting to be night-time, and there's nothing to see right now.

MORTON. Yes, but wait till the train starts passing through towns! Whizz!

MERCER. Oh, boy! Hey, Morton? (*He looks out of the window.* MORTON *joins him*). Ooh, look! It's starting! Good-bye, old Grand Central Station!

MORTON (*stolidly*). Yes, it's good-bye old Grand Central Station, sure enough. (MERCER *watches through the window for a second. Then, realizing the train is under way, he turns from the window in simple awe at the wonders of science.*)

MERCER. Gee, this is some trip! (MORTON *is glad* MR. MERCER *is happy, and stands waiting to be of further service*). By the way, Morton, who is the conductor on our train?

MORTON. Why, a Mr. Barclay is our conductor—pro tem.

MERCER. Is he congenial?

MORTON. He's just a peach! We porter chaps swear by him. I'll send him to you. (*Exits.* MR. MERCER *cautiously inspects the various parts of the compartment and finally walks over to a match-rack on the wall. He extracts a match and, full of the spirit of adventure, he lights it.* MR. BARCLAY, *the conductor, enters.* MR. MERCER *hastily blows out the match and places it in the cuspidor.* MR. BARCLAY *is jovial, yet dignified.*)

BARCLAY. I'm Mr. Barclay, the conductor. Are you the gentleman that's going to One Hundred and Twenty-fifth Street?

MERCER. I guess I'm the party.

BARCLAY. Well, I'm Mr. Barclay.

MERCER. Yes. Morton, the porter, was telling me about you. I'm Mr. Mercer. (*He is searching through his pocketbook*). I don't know whether I've a card here or not.

BARCLAY. Oh, that's all right. We have lots of passengers we don't know from Adam riding with us.

MERCER. Oh, I guess I haven't got a card. Being a stranger and all, I thought——

BARCLAY. That's all right, sir. This is a public conveyance and we must take care of you gentlemen whether we know you or not. Pray sit down. (MR. MERCER *sits in his seat in the corner.* MR. BARCLAY *sits facing him in the chair.*)

MERCER (*with a sly grin*). You're riding backwards.

BARCLAY. Well, I'm used to roughing it. This is your first trip on our lines, Mr. Mercer?

MERCER. Well, the first in a long time. You see, I usually

come up town via our subway system. Occasionally, if I'm feeling quite fatigued, I take a taxicab ride. But today, with Spring in the air and all, I sort of thought I'd take a railroad train.

BARCLAY. That's perfectly all right. I'm sure you'll never regret it. What's more, we'll get you there in jig time.

MERCER. Oh, I'm counting on you. Do you ever get around to my stamping ground, Mr. Barclay?

BARCLAY. Which stamping ground *is* that, Mr. Mercer?

MERCER. One Hundred and Twenty-fifth Street.

BARCLAY. To be sure. Not very often. You see, being a railroad man, I'm usually on my train. But when I was a boy, I often longed to visit One Hundred and Twenty-fifth Street. May I ask what prompted your question?

MERCER. I just thought you might know some people in my neck of the woods.

BARCLAY. I fear not. Er—wait a minute! I believe you have a gentleman up there named Mastbaum?

MERCER. You mean Mastbaum and Sons Furniture?

BARCLAY. I certainly do.

MERCER. Well, for heaven's sake! I should say we have! I know them very well! At least I know their store. Why, I pass it every day! Do you know the Mastbaums?

BARCLAY. Not personally, I fear. But I've seen their advertisements so often I feel as if I almost knew them.

MERCER. That's exactly the way I feel! Well, I'll be darned! You know about Mastbaums' store!

BARCLAY. Oh, Lordy, yes.

MERCER. I guess I've gone past Mastbaums' store a couple of hundred times.

BARCLAY. Well, for goodness' sakes! They certainly have attractive ads in the papers, don't they?

MERCER. Don't they though? Do you have very much time for reading in the—conducting game?

BARCLAY. Not very much, I must confess. They keep us hustling, you know. If it isn't collecting tickets, it's making new friends for the Company. You see, Mr. Mercer, each one of us conductors is really a contact man.

MERCER. Ummmm?

BARCLAY. Our President calls us "Ambassadors of Friendship."

MERCER. Beautiful motto. I wonder if you know a conductor by the name of George Whipple?

BARCLAY. George Whipple? No. I knew a George Galloway.

MERCER. This is George Whipple.

BARCLAY. I don't recall the name.

MERCER. A very interesting personality. My wife, Mrs. Mercer, and I met him on a trip through Sunny California last year. Happened to be out there. Young Whipple is in sole charge of the train between Los Angeles and San Francisco, and as luck would have it, we were on his train. That's how we happened to meet him.

BARCLAY (*musingly*). George Whipple. He sounds like quite a character. But I don't think I ever met him.

MERCER. That's a great pity.

BARCLAY. I meet very few fellows in this game. I dare say I don't meet up with one new conductor a month.

MERCER. Ah—you'd love Whipple.

BARCLAY (*again searching his memory*). I don't *think* I ever met him.

MERCER. Perhaps not. Say, this car reminds me of the old Tyrone. Is this the Tyrone?

BARCLAY. No, this car is the Waukesha.

MERCER. Well, now, it's mighty like the Tyrone.

BARCLAY. You have a keen eye, Mr. Mercer. But you will find the ash-tray is in a different place.

MERCER. Ah.

BARCLAY. I confess it's almost a sister car to the Tyrone.

MERCER. I did notice the resemblance, you see. Where is the Tyrone nowadays?

BARCLAY. Well, I had a letter from a fellow only last week. He had seen it in Pittsburgh, going towards Cleveland, as I recall.

MERCER. Probably on its way somewhere.

BARCLAY. Yes.

MERCER. It's a great old car, the Tyrone.

BARCLAY. One of the finest, we used to say.

MERCER. What other cars have you, Mr. Barclay, on this train?

BARCLAY. Well, now, up front, there's the Lindbrooke, the Ottawatomie, and—ah—the Barota. We had our hearts set on having the Manitoba, too, this trip, but of course they didn't give it to us. Mr. Davis, my engineer, is mad as a hornet. They practically promised him the Manitoba this trip—his favorite car! But—it wasn't to be.

MERCER. Sure tough on Davis.

BARCLAY. Office politics, Mr. Mercer. And it's a pity, too. Davis asks for very little in this world.

MERCER. Where is he now? Up in the locomotive?

BARCLAY. I'll say he is. He's there, chin up, keeping things going.

MERCER. I wonder if I ought to go up and speak to him.

BARCLAY. No, Mr. Mercer. Not while the train is in motion. You see, he has to keep his eye on it every minute. That prevents wrecks!

MERCER. Sounds to me like a fellow with back-bone.

BARCLAY. He's got plenty of it.

MERCER. Give him my best.

BARCLAY. I certainly will.

MERCER (*holding out package of cigarettes*). Do you indulge, Mr. Barclay?

BARCLAY. Very seldom, Mr. Mercer. One can't take chances with one's health in this man's game.

MERCER (*putting cigarettes away out of respect to* BARCLAY). Well, probably not. My grandfather wouldn't employ a man who smoked. He was quite a character.

BARCLAY. What was his name?

MERCER. He was christened Frederick. (*Laughing as he recalls the incident*). But we children used to call him "Grandpa."

BARCLAY (*laughing*). Isn't that just like a kid! I have a cousin by the name of Frederick.

MERCER. Living?

BARCLAY. Oh, yes. The little chap resides with his Aunt Carrie.

MERCER. Well, good for him! (*There is a pause*). I see we both wear black shoes.

BARCLAY. In ancient Rome they wore sandals.

MERCER. They probably had their reasons for doing so.

BARCLAY. I daresay. A strange people.

MERCER (*trying to be fair*). But very historic.

BARCLAY (*with a chuckle*). You can say that again.

MORTON (*appearing in the door to the compartment with coat over his arm and bundles in his hands*). You gentlemen getting along all right?

MERCER. Just fine, Morton.

MORTON. The passengers are prepared to give you their tickets now, Mr. Barclay.

BARCLAY. Excellent. Shall we begin with you, Mr. Mercer?

MERCER. We might as well, I guess. If a fellow's going to ride, he's got to pay the piper. Here you are.

BARCLAY. A one way ticket, eh?

MERCER. Well, look—I almost always come down town by subway.

BARCLAY. You've done nothing really criminal, Mercer. We'll forget it.

MERCER. I certainly want to play fair.

MORTON. And Mr. Davis is just nosin' us in to One Hundred and Twenty-fifth Street, sir.

MERCER. It's a good thing you came in here, Morton. We were so wrapped up in our talk, I'd have gone right on to One Hundred and Thirty-eighth Street. I hope we haven't seen the last of each other, Barclay. We ought to keep in touch by letter, anyway.

BARCLAY. That will be fine. Just address your communications to Conductor Joseph Barclay, via the Railroad. And now, I trust you will find your dear ones hale and hearty. Write me soon.

MERCER. I certainly will. Now, Morton——

MORTON. Yes, sir.

MERCER (*as* MORTON *helps him into his overcoat*). In connection with a little remembrance I want to give you, I will take care of you when we get off the steps of the train.

MORTON. That's all right, Mr. Mercer. You can present it to me when we say good-bye.

MERCER (*nervously looking about to see if he has forgotten anything*). Well, that will be fine. Well, good-bye, Mr. Barclay.

BARCLAY. Make it Joe.

MERCER. Thanks. Good-bye, Joe.

BARCLAY. Good-bye, old man. And good luck. (BARCLAY *suddenly senses that the train has stopped. He dashes to the window, looks out, then turns around, ready to do his duty as a conductor. He takes a deep breath. Before making his announcement, he glances at* MERCER). Excuse me. (*His head now goes forward again, as he calls out in a loud voice*). One Hundred and Twenty-fifth Street!

MERCER (*in awe*). That was fine. (*His excitement now returns*). Well, the same to you, Joe. Always. (*With great enthusiasm*). And I'll tell you what! We'll do the whole darn trip over again this summer! Good-bye and thanks.

BARCLAY. Good-bye.

MERCER. All right, Morton. (*Exits.* MR. BARCLAY *takes an address book from his pocket, and writes in it.*)

BARCLAY (*writing*). "Mr. Mercer." Another friend for our Company.

CURTAIN

THE STILL ALARM

by George S. Kaufman

CHARACTERS

ED
BOB
THE BELLBOY
A FIREMAN
ANOTHER FIREMAN

SCENE: *A hotel bedroom.*

THE STILL ALARM

VITAL NOTE: *It is important that the entire play should be acted calmly and politely, in the manner of an English drawing-room comedy. No actor ever raises his voice; every line must be read as though it were an invitation to a cup of tea. If this direction is disregarded, the play has no point at all. The Scene is a hotel bedroom. Two windows rear; door to the hall at the right, chair R.C. Bed between windows. 'Phone stand R., downstage end of bed. Dresser L.U. corner. Another door at left. Small table and chairs downstage L.C.*

ED *and* BOB *are on the stage.* ED *is getting into his overcoat as the curtain rises. Both are at R. door.*

ED. Well, Bob, it's certainly been nice to see you again.

BOB. It was nice to see *you.*

ED. You come to town so seldom, I hardly ever get the chance to——

BOB. Well, you know how it is. A business trip is always more or less of a bore.

ED. Next time you've got to come out to the house.

BOB. I want to come out. I just had to stick around the hotel this trip.

ED. Oh, I understand. Well, give my best to Edith.

BOB (*remembering something*). Oh, I say, Ed. Wait a minute.

ED. What's the matter?

BOB. I knew I wanted to show you something. (*Crosses L. to table. Gets roll of blueprints from drawer*). Did you know I'm going to build?

ED (*follows to R. of table*). A house?

BOB. You bet it's a house! (*Knock on R. door*). Come in! (*Spreads plans*). I just got these yesterday.

ED (*sits*). Well, that's fine! (*The knock is repeated—louder. Both men now give full attention to the door.*)

BOB. Come! Come in!

BELLBOY (*enters* R.). Mr. Barclay?

BOB. Well?

BELLBOY. I've a message from the clerk, sir. For Mr. Barclay personally.

BOB (*crosses to boy*). I'm Mr. Barclay. What is the message?

BELLBOY. The hotel is on fire, sir.

BOB. What's that?

BELLBOY. The hotel is on fire.

ED. This hotel?

BELLBOY. Yes, sir.

BOB. Well—is it bad?

BELLBOY. It looks pretty bad, sir.

ED. You mean it's going to burn down?

BELLBOY. We think so—yes, sir.

BOB (*a low whistle of surprise*). Well! We'd better leave.

BELLBOY. Yes, sir.

BOB. Going to burn down, huh?

BELLBOY. Yes, sir. If you'll step to the window you'll see. (BOB *goes to* R. *window.*)

BOB. Yes, that is pretty bad. H'm. (*To* ED). I say, you really ought to see this——

ED (*crosses up to* R. *window—peering out*). It's reached the floor right underneath.

BELLBOY. Yes, sir. The lower part of the hotel is about gone, sir.

BOB (*still looking out—looks up*). Still all right up above, though. (*Turns to boy*). Have they notified the Fire Department?

BELLBOY. I wouldn't know, sir. I'm only the bellboy.

BOB. Well, that's the thing to do, obviously—(*Nods head to each one as if the previous line was a bright idea*)—notify the Fire Department. Just call them up, give them the name of the hotel——

ED. Wait a minute. I can do better than that for you. (*To the boy*). Ring through to the Chief, and tell him that Ed Jamison told you to telephone him. (*To* BOB). We went to school together, you know.

BOB. That's fine. (*To the boy*). Now, get that right. Tell the Chief that Mr. Jamison said to ring him.

ED. *Ed* Jamison.

BOB. Yes, *Ed* Jamison.

BELLBOY. Yes, sir. (*Turns to go.*)

BOB. Oh! Boy! (*Pulls out handful of change; picks out a coin*). Here you are.

BELLBOY. Thank you, sir. (*Exit* BELLBOY. ED *sits* R. *of table, lights cigarette and throws match downstage, then steps on it. There is a moment's pause.*)

BOB. Well! (*Crosses and looks out* L. *window*). Say, we'll have to get out of here pretty soon.

ED (*going to window*). How is it—no better?

BOB. Worse, if anything. It'll be up here in a few moments.

ED. What floor *is* this?

BOB. Eleventh.

ED. Eleven. We couldn't jump, then.

BOB. Oh, no. You never could jump. (*Comes away from window to dresser*). Well, I've got to get my things together. (*Pulls out suitcase.*)

ED (*smoothing out the plans*). Who made these for you?

BOB. A fellow here—Rawlins. (*Turns a shirt in his hand*). I ought to call one of the other hotels for a room.

ED. Oh, you can get in.

BOB. They're pretty crowded. (*Feels something on the sole of his foot; inspects it*). Say, the floor's getting hot.

ED. I know it. It's getting stuffy in the room, too. Phew! (*He looks around, then goes to the 'phone*). Hello.—Ice water in eleven-eighteen. (*Crosses to* R. *of table.*)

BOB (*at bed*). That's the stuff. (*Packs*). You know, if I move to another hotel I'll never get my mail. Everybody thinks I'm stopping here.

ED. (*studying the plans*). Say, this isn't bad.

BOB (*eagerly*). Do you like it? (*Remembers his plight*). Suppose I go to another hotel and there's a fire there, too!

ED. You've got to take *some* chance.

BOB. I know, but here I'm sure. (*'Phone rings*). Oh, answer that, will you, Ed? (*To dresser and back.*)

ED (*crosses to 'phone*). Sure. (*At 'phone*). Hello— Oh, that's good. Fine. What?—Oh! Well, wait a minute. (*To* BOB). The firemen are downstairs and some of them want to come up to this room.

BOB. Tell them, of course.

ED (*at 'phone*). All right. Come right up. (*Hangs up, crosses and sits* R. *of table*). Now we'll get some action.

BOB (*looks out of window* L.). Say, there's an awful crowd of people on the street.

ED (*absently, as he pores over the plans*). Maybe there's been some kind of accident.

BOB (*peering out, suitcase in hand*). No. More likely they heard about the fire. (*A knock at the door* R.). Come in.

BELLBOY (*enters*). I beg pardon, Mr. Barclay, the firemen have arrived.

BOB. Show them in. (*Crosses to* R. *The door opens. In the doorway appear two* FIREMEN *in full regalia. The* FIRST FIREMAN *carries a hose and rubber coat; the* SECOND *has a violin case,* R.C.)

FIRST FIREMAN (*enters* R. *Very apologetically*). Mr. Barclay.

BOB. I'm Mr. Barclay.

FIRST FIREMAN. We're the firemen, Mr. Barclay. (*They remove their hats.*)

BOB. How de do?

ED. How de do?

BOB. A great pleasure, I assure you. Really must apologize for the condition of this room, but——

FIRST FIREMAN. Oh, that's all right. I know how it is at home.

BOB. May I present a friend of mine, Mr. Ed Jamison——

FIRST FIREMAN. How are you?

ED. How are you, boys? (SECOND FIREMAN *nods*). I know your Chief.

FIRST FIREMAN. Oh, is that so? He knows the Chief—dear old Chiefie. (SECOND FIREMAN *giggles.*)

BOB (*embarrassed*). Well, I guess you boys want to get to work, don't you?

FIRST FIREMAN. Well, if you don't mind. We would like to spray around a little bit.

BOB. May I help you?

FIRST FIREMAN. Yes, if you please. (BOB *helps him into his rubber coat. At the same time the* SECOND FIREMAN, *without a word, lays the violin case on the bed, opens it, takes out the violin, and begins tuning it.*)

BOB (*watching him*). I don't think I understand.

FIRST FIREMAN. Well, you see, Sid doesn't get much chance to practice at home. Sometimes, at a fire, while we're waiting for a wall to fall or something, why, a fireman doesn't really have anything to do, and personally I like to see him improve himself symphonically. I hope you don't resent it. You're not anti-symphonic?

BOB. Of course not—— (BOB *and* ED *nod understandingly; the* SECOND FIREMAN *is now waxing the bow.*)

FIRST FIREMAN. Well, if you'll excuse me—— (*To window* R. *Turns with decision toward the window. You feel that he is about to get down to business.*)

BOB (*crosses* L.). Charming personalities.

ED (*follows over to the window* R.). How *is* the fire?

FIRST FIREMAN (*feels the wall*). It's pretty bad right now. This wall will go pretty soon now, but it'll fall out that way, so it's all right. (*Peers out*). That next room is the place to fight it from. (*Crosses to door* L. BOB *shows ties as* ED *crosses*.)

ED (*sees ties*). Oh! Aren't those gorgeous!

FIRST FIREMAN (*to* BOB). Have you the key for this room?

BOB. Why, no. I've nothing to do with that room. I've just got this one. (*Folding a shirt as he talks*.)

ED. Oh, it's very comfortable.

FIRST FIREMAN. That's too bad, I had something up my sleeve. If I could have gotten in there. Oh, well, may I use your 'phone?

BOB. Please do. (*To* ED). Do you think you might hold this? (*Indicates the hose*.)

ED. How?

FIRST FIREMAN. Just crawl under it. (*As he does that*). Thanks. (*At 'phone*). Hello. Let me have the clerk, please. (*To* SECOND FIREMAN). Give us that little thing you played the night the Equitable Building burned down. (*Back to 'phone*). Are you there? This is one of the firemen. Oh, *you* know. I'm in a room—ah—— (*Looks at* BOB.)

BOB. Eleven-eighteen.

FIRST FIREMAN. Eleven-eighteen, and I want to get into the next room—— Oh, goody. Will you send someone up with the key? There's no one in there? Oh, super-goody! Right away. (*Hangs up*.)

BOB. That's fine. (*To* FIREMAN). Won't you sit down?

FIRST FIREMAN. Thanks.

ED. Have a cigar?

FIRST FIREMAN (*takes it*). Much obliged.

BOB. A light?

FIRST FIREMAN. If you please.

ED (*failing to find a match*). Bob, have you a match?

BOB (*crosses to* L.C.). I thought there were some here. (*Hands in pockets.*)

FIRST FIREMAN. Oh, never mind. (*He goes to* R. *window, leans out, and emerges with cigar lighted.* BOB *crosses* L. *to dresser; slams drawer. The* SECOND FIREMAN *taps violin with bow.*)

FIRST FIREMAN. Mr. Barclay, I think he's ready now.

BOB (*takes chair from* R. *table and sits* C.). Pardon me. (*They all sit. The* SECOND FIREMAN *takes center of stage, with all the manner of a concert violinist. He goes into "Keep the Home Fires Burning."* BOB, ED *and* FIRST FIREMAN *wipe brow as curtain falls slowly.*)

THE MOON OF
THE CARIBBEES
by Eugene O'Neill

CHARACTERS

YANK
DRISCOLL
OLSON
DAVIS — *Seamen of the British tramp steamer,*
COCKY — *Glencairn*
SMITTY
PAUL

LAMPS, *the lamptrimmer*
CHIPS, *the carpenter*
OLD TOM, *the donkeyman*

BIG FRANK
DICK
MAX — *Firemen on the Glencairn*
PADDY

BELLA
SUSIE
VIOLET — *West Indian Negresses*
PEARL

THE FIRST MATE

Two other seamen—SCOTTY and IVAN—and several other members of the stokehole-engine-room crew.

THE MOON OF THE CARIBBEES

SCENE—*A forward section of the main deck of the British tramp Steamer* Glencairn, *at anchor off an island in the West Indies. The full moon, halfway up the sky, throws a clear light on the deck. The sea is calm and the ship motionless.*

On the left two of the derrick booms of the foremast jut out at an angle of forty-five degrees, black against the sky. In the rear the dark outline of the port bulwark is sharply defined against a distant strip of coral beach, white in the moonlight, fringed with coco palms whose tops rise clear of the horizon. On the right is the forecastle with an open doorway in the center leading to the seamen's and firemen's compartments. On either side of the doorway are two closed doors opening on the quarters of the Bo'sun, the ship's carpenter, the messroom steward, and the donkeyman—what might be called the petty officers of the ship. Near each bulwark there is also a short stairway, like a section of fire escape, leading up to the forecastle head (the top of the forecastle)—the edge of which can be seen on the right.

In the center of the deck, and occupying most of the space, is the large, raised square of the number one hatch, covered with canvas, battened down for the night.

A melancholy negro chant, faint and far-off, drifts, crooning, over the water.

Most of the seamen and firemen are reclining or sitting on the hatch. PAUL *is leaning against the port bulwark, the upper part of his stocky figure outlined against the sky.* SMITTY *and* COCKY *are sitting on the edge of the forecastle head with their legs dangling over. Nearly all are smoking pipes or cigarettes. The majority are dressed in patched suits of dungaree. Quite a few are in their bare feet and some of them, especially the firemen, have nothing on but a pair of pants and an undershirt. A good many wear caps.*

There is the low murmur of different conversations going on in the separate groups as the curtain rises. This is followed by a sudden silence in which the singing from the land can be plainly heard.

DRISCOLL (*a powerfully built Irishman who is sitting on the edge of the hatch, front—irritably*). Will ye listen to them naygurs? I wonder now, do they call that keenin' a song?

SMITTY (*a young Englishman with a blond mustache. He is sitting on the forecastle head looking out over the water with his chin supported on his hands*). It doesn't make a chap feel very cheerful, does it? (*He sighs.*)

COCKY (*a wizened runt of a man with a straggling gray mustache—slapping SMITTY on the back*). Cheero, ole dear! Down't be ser dawhn in the marf, Duke. She loves yer.

SMITTY (*gloomily*). Shut up, Cocky! (*He turns away from COCKY and falls to dreaming again, staring toward the spot on shore where the singing seems to come from.*)

BIG FRANK (*a huge fireman sprawled out on the right of the hatch—waving a hand toward the land*). They bury somebody—py chiminy Christmas, I tink so from way it sound.

YANK (*a rather good-looking rough who is sitting beside DRISCOLL*). What d'yuh mean, bury? They don't plant 'em down here, Dutchy. They eat 'em to save fun'ral expenses. I guess this guy went down the wrong way an' they got indigestion.

COCKY. Indigestion! Ho yus, not 'arf! Down't yer know as them blokes 'as two stomacks like a bleedin' camel?

DAVIS (*a short, dark man seated on the right of hatch*). An' you seen the two, I s'pect, ain't you?

COCKY (*scornfully*). Down't be showin' yer igerance be tryin' to make a mock o' me what has seen more o' the world than yeself ever will.

MAX (*a Swedish fireman—from the rear of hatch*). Spin dat yarn, Cocky.

COCKY. It's Gawd's troof, what I tole yer. I 'eard it from a bloke what was captured pris'ner by 'em in the Solomon Islands. Shipped wiv 'im one voyage. 'Twas a rare treat to 'ear 'im tell what 'appened to 'im among 'em. (*Musingly*). 'E was a funny bird, 'e was—'ailed from Mile End, 'e did.

DRISCOLL (*with a snort*). Another lyin' Cockney, the loike av yourself!

LAMPS (*a fat Swede who is sitting on a camp stool in front of his door talking with* CHIPS). Where you meet up with him, Cocky?

CHIPS (*a lanky Scotchman—derisively*). In New Guinea, I'll lay my oath!

COCKY (*defiantly*). Yus! It *was* in New Guinea, time I was shipwrecked there. (*There is a perfect storm of groans and laughter at this speech.*)

YANK (*getting up*). Yuh know what we said yuh'd get if yuh sprung any of that lyin' New Guinea dope on us again, don't yuh? Close that trap if yuh don't want a duckin' over the side.

COCKY. Ow, I was on'y tryin' to edicate yer a bit. (*He sinks into dignified silence.*)

YANK (*nodding toward the shore*). Don't yuh know this is the West Indies, yuh crazy mut? There ain't no cannibals here. They're only common blacks.

DRISCOLL (*irritably*). Whativir they are, the divil take their cryin'. It's enough to give a man the jigs listenin' to 'em.

YANK (*with a grin*). What's the matter, Drisc? Yuh're as sore as a boil about somethin'.

DRISCOLL. I'm dyin' wid impatience to have a dhrink; an' that blarsted bumboat woman took her oath she'd bring back rum enough for the lot av us whin she came back on board to-night.

BIG FRANK (*overhearing this—in a loud eager voice*). You say the bumboat voman vill bring booze?

DRISCOLL (*sarcastically*). That's right—tell the Old Man about ut, an' the Mate, too. (*All of the crew have edged nearer to* DRISCOLL *and are listening to the conversation with an air of suppressed excitement.* DRISCOLL *lowers his voice impressively and addresses them all*). She said she cud snake ut on board in the bottoms av thim baskets av fruit they're goin' to bring wid 'em to sell to us for'ard.

THE DONKEYMAN (*an old gray-headed man with a kindly, wrinkled face. He is sitting on a camp stool in front of his door, right front*). She'll be bringin' some black women with her this time—or times has changed since I put in here last.

DRISCOLL. She said she wud—two or three—more, maybe, I dunno. (*This announcement is received with great enthusiasm by all hands.*)

COCKY. Wot a bloody lark!

OLSON. Py yingo, we have one hell of a time!

DRISCOLL (*warningly*). Remimber ye must be quiet about ut, ye scuts—wid the dhrink, I mane—ivin if the bo'sun is ashore. The Old Man ordered her to bring no booze on board or he wudn't buy a thing off av her for the ship.

PADDY (*a squat, ugly Liverpool Irishman*). To the divil wid him!

BIG FRANK (*turning on him*). Shud up, you tamn fool, Paddy! You vant make trouble? (*To Driscoll*). You und me, ve keep dem quiet, Drisc.

DRISCOLL. Right ye are, Dutchy. I'll split the skull av the first wan av ye starts to foight. (*Three bells are heard striking.*)

DAVIS. Three bells. When's she comin', Drisc?

DRISCOLL. She'll be here any minute now, surely. (*To* PAUL, *who has returned to his position by the bulwark after hearing* DRISCOLL'S *news*). D'you see 'em comin', Paul?

PAUL. I don't see anyting like bumboat. (*They all set themselves to wait, lighting pipes, cigarettes, and making themselves comfortable. There is a silence broken only by the mournful singing of the Negroes on shore.*)

SMITTY (*slowly—with a trace of melancholy*). I wish they'd stop that song. It makes you think of—well—things you ought to forget. Rummy go, what?

COCKY (*slapping him on the back*). Cheero, ole love! We'll be 'avin our rum in arf a mo', Duke. (*He comes down to the deck, leaving* SMITTY *alone on the forecastle head.*)

BIG FRANK. Sing someting, Drisc. Den ve don't hear dot yelling.

DAVIS. Give us a chanty, Drisc.

PADDY. Wan all av us knows.

MAX. We all sing in on chorus.

OLSON. "Rio Grande," Drisc.

BIG FRANK. No, ve don't know dot. Sing "Viskey Johnny."

CHIPS. "Flyin' Cloud."

COCKY. Now! Guv us "Maid o' Amsterdam."

LAMPS. "Santa Anna" iss good one.

DRISCOLL. Shut your mouths, all av you. (*Scornfully*). A chanty is ut ye want? I'll bet me whole pay day there's not wan in the crowd 'ceptin' Yank here, an' Ollie, an' meself, an' Lamps an' Cocky, maybe, wud be sailors enough to know the main from the mizzen on a windjammer. Ye've heard the names av chanties but divil a note av the tune or a loine av the words do ye know. There's hardly a rale deep-water sailor lift on the seas, more's the pity.

YANK. Give us "Blow The Man Down." We all know some of that. (*A chorus of assenting voices: Yes!—Righto!— Let 'er drive! Start 'er, Drisc! etc.*)

DRISCOLL. Come in then, all av ye. (*He sings*): As I was a-roamin' down Paradise Street—

ALL. Wa-a-ay, blow the man down!

DRISCOLL. As I was a-roamin' down Paradise Street—

ALL. Give us some time to blow the man down!

CHORUS

Blow the man down, boys, oh, blow the man down!
Wa-a-ay, blow the man down!
As I was a-roamin' down Paradise Street—
Give us some time to blow the man down!

DRISCOLL. A pretty young maiden I chanced for to meet.

ALL. Wa-a-ay, blow the man down!

DRISCOLL. A pretty young maiden I chanced for to meet.

ALL. Give us some time to blow the man down!

CHORUS

Blow the man down, boys, oh, blow the man down!
Wa-a-ay, blow the man down!
A pretty young maiden I chanced for to meet.
Give us some time to blow the man down!

PAUL (*just as* DRISCOLL *is clearing his throat preparatory to starting the next verse*). Hay, Drisc! Here she come, I tink. Some bumboat comin' dis way. (*They all rush to the side and look toward the land.*)

YANK. There's five or six of them in it—and they paddle like skirts.

DRISCOLL (*wildly elated*). "Hurroo, ye scuts! 'Tis thim right enough. (*He does a few jig steps on the deck.*)

OLSON (*after a pause during which all are watching the approaching boat*). Py yingo, I see six in boat, yes, sir.

DAVIS. I kin make out the baskets. See 'em there amid-ships?

BIG FRANK. Vot kind booze dey bring—viskey?

DRISCOLL. Rum, foine West Indy rum wid a kick in ut loike a mule's hoind leg.

LAMPS. Maybe she don't bring any; maybe skipper scare her.

DRISCOLL. Don't be throwin' cold water, Lamps. I'll skin her black hoide off av her if she goes back on her worrd.

YANK. Here they come. Listen to 'em gigglin'. (*Calling*). Oh, you kiddo! (*The sound of women's voices can be heard talking and laughing.*)

DRISCOLL (*calling*). Is ut you, Mrs. Old Black Joe?

A WOMAN'S VOICE. Ullo, Mike! (*There is loud feminine laughter at this retort.*)

DRISCOLL. Shake a leg an' come abord thin.

THE WOMAN'S VOICE. We're a-comin'.

DRISCOLL. Come on, Yank. You an' me'd best be goin' to give 'em a hand wid their truck. 'Twill put 'em in good spirits.

COCKY (*as they start off left*). Ho, you ain't 'arf a fox, Drisc. Down't drink it all afore we sees it.

DRISCOLL (*over his shoulder*). You'll be havin' yours, me sonny bye, don't fret. (*He and* YANK *go off left.*)

COCKY (*licking his lips*). Gawd blimey, I can do wiv a wet.

DAVIS. Me, too!

CHIPS. I'll bet there ain't none of us'll let any go to waste.

BIG FRANK. I could trink a whole barrel mineself, py chimminy Christmas!

COCKY. I 'opes all the gels ain't as bloomin' ugly as 'er. Looked like a bloody organ-grinder's monkey, she did. Gawd, I couldn't put up wiv the likes of 'er!

PADDY. Ye'll be lucky if any of thim looks at ye, ye squinteyed runt.

COCKY (*angrily*). Ho, yus? You ain't no bleedin' beauty prize yeself, me man. A 'airy ape, I calls yer.

PADDY (*walking toward him—truculently*). Whot's thot? Say ut again if ye dare.

COCKY (*his hand on his sheath knife—snarling*). 'Airy ape! That's wot I says! (PADDY *tries to reach him but the others keep them apart.*)

BIG FRANK (*pushing* PADDY *back*). Vot's the matter mit you, Paddy. Don't you hear vat Driscoll say—no fighting?

PADDY (*grumblingly*). I don't take no back talk from that deck-scrubbin' shrimp.

COCKY. Blarsted coal-puncher! (DRISCOLL *appears wearing a broad grin of satisfaction. The fight is immediately forgotten by the crowd who gather around him with exclamations of eager curiosity.* How is it, Drisc? Any luck? Vot she bring, Drisc? Where's the gels? *etc.*)

DRISCOLL (*with an apprehensive glance back at the bridge*). Not so loud, for the love av hivin! (*The clamor dies down*). Yis, she has ut wid her. She'll be here in a minute wid a pint bottle or two for each wan av ye—three shillin's a bottle. So don't be impashunt.

COCKY (*indignantly*). Three bob! The bloody cow!

SMITTY (*with an ironic smile*). Grand larceny, by God! (*They all turn and look up at him, surprised to hear him speak.*)

OLSON. Py yingo, we don't pay so much.

BIG FRANK. Tamn black tief!

PADDY. We'll take ut away from her and give her nothin'.

THE CROWD (*growling*). Dirty thief! Dot's right! Give her nothin'! Not a bloomin' 'apenny! etc.

DRISCOLL (*grinning*). Ye can take ut or lave ut, me sonny byes. (*He casts a glance in the direction of the bridge and then reaches inside his shirt and pulls out a pint bottle*). 'Tis foine rum, the rale stuff. (*He drinks*). I slipped this wan out av wan av the baskets whin they wasn't lookin'. (*He hands the bottle to* OLSON *who is nearest him*). Here ye are, Ollie. Take a small sup an' pass ut to the nixt. 'Tisn't much but 'twill serve to take the black taste out av your mouths if ye go aisy wid ut. An' there's buckets more av ut comin'. (*The bottle passes from hand to hand, each man taking a sip and smacking his lips with a deep "Aa-ah" of satisfaction.*)

DAVIS. Where's she now, Drisc?

DRISCOLL. Up havin' a worrd wid the skipper, makin' arrangements about the money, I s'pose.

DAVIS. An' where's the other gels?

DRISCOLL. Wid her. There's foive av thim she took aboard —two swate little slips av things, near as white as you an' me are, for that gray-whiskered auld fool, an' the mates—an' the engineers too, maybe. The rist av thim'll be comin' for'ard whin she comes.

COCKY. 'E ain't 'arf a funny ole bird, the skipper. Gawd blimey! 'Member when we sailed from 'ome 'ow 'e stands on the bridge lookin' like a bloody ole sky pilot? An' 'is missus dawn on the bloomin' dock 'owlin' fit to kill 'erself? An' 'is kids 'owlin' an' wavin' their 'andkerchiefs? (*With great moral indignation*). An' 'ere 'e is makin' up to a bleedin' black! There's a captain for yer! Gawd blimey! Bloody crab, I calls 'im!

DRISCOLL. Shut up, ye insect! Sure, it's not you should be talkin', an' you wid a woman an' childer weepin' for ye in iviry divil's port in the wide worrld, if we can believe your own tale av ut.

COCKY (*still indignant*). I ain't no bloomin' captain, I ain't. I ain't got no missus—reg'lar married, I means. I ain't——

BIG FRANK (*putting a huge paw over* COCKY'S *mouth*). You ain't going talk so much, you hear? (COCKY *wriggles away from him*). Say, Drisc, how ve pay dis voman for booze? Ve ain't got no cash.

DRISCOLL. It's aisy enough. Each girl'll have a slip av paper wid her an' whin you buy anythin' you write ut down and the price beside ut and sign your name. If ye can't write have some one who can do ut for ye. An' rimimber this: Whin ye buy a bottle av dhrink or (*With a wink*) somethin' else forbid, ye must write down tobaccy or fruit or somethin' the loike av that. Whin she laves the skipper'll pay what's owin' on the paper an' take ut out av your pay. Is ut clear to ye now?

ALL. Yes—Clear as day—Aw right, Drisc—Righto—Sure. etc.

DRISCOLL. An' don't forgit what I said about bein' quiet wid the dhrink, or the Mate'll be down on our necks an' spile the fun. (*A chorus of assent.*)

DAVIS (*looking aft*). Ain't this them comin'? (*They all look in that direction. The silly laughter of a woman is heard.*)

DRISCOLL. Look at Yank, wud ye, wid his arrm around the middle av wan av thim. That lad's not wastin' any toime. (*The four women enter from the left, giggling and whispering to each other. The first three carry baskets on their heads. The youngest and best-looking comes last.* YANK *has his arm about her waist and is carrying her basket in his other hand. All four are distinct negro types. They wear light-colored, loose-fitting clothes and have bright bandana handkerchiefs on their heads. They put down their baskets on the hatch and sit down beside them. The men crowd around, grinning.*)

BELLA (*she is the oldest, stoutest, and homeliest of the four—grinning back at them*). 'Ullo, boys.

THE OTHER GIRLS. 'Ullo, boys.

THE MEN. Hello, yourself—Evenin'—Hello—How are you? etc.

BELLA (*genially*). Hope you had a nice voyage. My name's Bella, this here's Susie, yander's Violet, and her there (*Pointing to the girl with* YANK) is Pearl. Now we all knows each other.

PADDY (*roughly*). Never mind the girls. Where's the dhrink?

BELLA (*tartly*). You're a hawg, ain't you? Don't talk so loud or your don't git any—you nor no man. Think I wants the ole captain to put me off the ship, do you?

YANK. Yes, nix on hollerin', you! D'yuh wanta queer all of us?

BELLA (*casting a quick glance over her shoulder*). Here! Some of you big strapping boys sit back of us on the hatch there so's them officers can't see what we're doin'.

(DRISCOLL *and several of the others sit and stand in back of the girls on the hatch.* BELLA *turns to* DRISCOLL). Did you tell 'em they gotter sign for what they gits—and *how* to sign?

DRISCOLL. I did—what's your name again—oh, yis—Bella, darlin'.

BELLA. Then it's all right; but you boys has gotter go inside the fo'castle when you gits your bottle. No drinkin' out here on deck. I ain't takin' no chances. (*An impatient murmur of assent goes up from the crowd*). Ain't that right, Mike?

DRISCOLL. Right as rain, darlin'. (BIG FRANK *leans over and says something to him in a low voice.* DRISCOLL *laughs and slaps his thigh*). Listen, Bella, I've somethin' to ask ye for my little friend here who's bashful. Ut has to do wid the ladies so I'd best be whisperin' ut to ye meself to kape them from blushin'. (*He leans over and asks her a question.*)

BELLA (*firmly*). Four shillin's.

DRISCOLL (*laughing*). D'you hear that, all av ye? Four shillin's ut is.

PADDY (*angrily*). To hell wid this talkin'. I want a dhrink.

BELLA. Is everything all right, Mike?

DRISCOLL (*after a look back at the bridge*). Sure. Let her droive!

BELLA. All right, girls. (*The girls reach down in their baskets in under the fruit which is on top and each pulls out a pint bottle. Four of the men crowd up and take the bottles*). Fetch a light, Lamps, that's a good boy. (LAMPS *goes to his room and returns with a candle. This is passed from one girl to another as the men sign the sheets of paper for their bottles*). Don't you boys forget to mark down cigarettes or tobacco or fruit, remember! Three shillin's is the price. Take it into the fo'-castle. For Gawd's sake, don't stand out here drinkin' in the moonlight. (*The four go into the forecastle. Four*

more take their places. PADDY *plants himself in front of*
PEARL *who is sitting by* YANK *with his arm still around
her.*)

PADDY (*gruffly*). Gimme thot! (*She holds out a bottle
which he snatches from her hand. He turns to go away.*)

YANK (*sharply*). Here, you! Where d'yuh get that stuff?
You ain't signed for that yet.

PADDY (*sullenly*). I can't write me name.

YANK. Then I'll write it for yuh. (*He takes the paper from
PEARL and writes*). There ain't goin' to be no welchin'
on little Bright Eyes here—not when I'm around, see?
Ain't I right, kiddo?

PEARL (*with a grin*). Yes, suh.

BELLA (*seeing all four are served*). Take it into the fo'-
castle, boys. (PADDY *defiantly raises his bottle and gulps
down a drink in the full moonlight.* BELLA *sees him*).
Look at 'im! Look at the dirty swine! (PADDY *slouches
into the forecastle*). Wants to git me in trouble. That
settles it! We all got to git inside, boys, where we won't
git caught. Come on, girls. (*The girls pick up their baskets and follow* BELLA. YANK *and* PEARL *are the last to
reach the doorway. She lingers behind him, her eyes
fixed on* SMITTY, *who is still sitting on the forecastle
head, his chin on his hands, staring off into vacancy.*)

PEARL (*waving a hand to attract his attention*). Come
ahn in, pretty boy. Ah likes you.

SMITTY (*coldly*). Yes; I want to buy a bottle, please. (*He
goes down the steps and follows her into the forecastle.
No one remains on deck but the* DONKEYMAN, *who sits
smoking his pipe in front of his door. There is the subdued babble of voices from the crowd inside but the
mournful cadence of the song from the shore can again
be faintly heard.* SMITTY *reappears and closes the door
to the forecastle after him. He shudders and shakes his
shoulders as if flinging off something which disgusted
him. Then he lifts the bottle which is in his hand to his*

lips and gulps down a long drink. THE DONKEYMAN *watches him impassively.* SMITTY *sits down on the hatch facing him. Now that the closed door has shut off nearly all the noise the singing from shore comes clearly over the moonlit water.*)

SMITTY (*listening to it for a moment*). Damn that song of theirs. (*He takes another big drink*). What do you say, Donk?

THE DONKEYMAN (*quietly*). Seems nice an' sleepy-like.

SMITTY (*with a hard laugh*). Sleepy! If I listened to it long—sober—I'd never go to sleep.

THE DONKEYMAN. 'Tain't sich bad music, is it? Sounds kinder pretty to me—low an' mournful—same as listenin' to the organ outside o' church of a Sunday.

SMITTY (*with a touch of impatience*). I didn't mean it was bad music. It isn't. It's the beastly memories the damn thing brings up—for some reason. (*He takes another pull at the bottle.*)

THE DONKEYMAN. Ever hear it before?

SMITTY. No; never in my life. It's just a something about the rotten thing which makes me think of—well—oh, the devil! (*He forces a laugh.*)

THE DONKEYMAN (*spitting placidly*). Queer things, mem'-ries. I ain't ever been bothered much by 'em.

SMITTY (*looking at him fixedly for a moment—with quiet scorn*). No, you wouldn't be.

THE DONKEYMAN. Not that I ain't had my share o' things goin' wrong; but I puts 'em out o' me mind, like, an' fergets 'em.

SMITTY. But suppose you couldn't put them out of your mind? Suppose they haunted you when you were awake and when you were asleep—what then?

THE DONKEYMAN (*quietly*). I'd git drunk, same's you're doin'.

SMITTY (*with a harsh laugh*). Good advice. (*He takes another drink. He is beginning to show the effects of the liquor. His face is flushed and he talks rather wildly).* We're poor little lambs who have lost our way, eh, Donk? Damned from here to eternity, what? God have mercy on such as we! True, isn't it, Donk?

THE DONKEYMAN. Maybe; I dunno. (*After a slight pause*). Whatever set you goin' to sea? You ain't made for it.

SMITTY (*laughing wildly*). My old friend in the bottle here, Donk.

THE DONKEYMAN. I done my share o' drinkin' in my time. (*Regretfully*). Them was good times, those days. Can't hold up under drink no more. Doctor told me I'd got to stop or die. (*He spits contentedly*). So I stops.

SMITTY (*with a foolish smile*). Then I'll drink one for you. Here's your health, old top! (*He drinks.*)

THE DONKEYMAN (*after a pause*). S'pose there's a gel mixed up in it someplace, ain't there?

SMITTY (*stiffly*). What makes you think so?

THE DONKEYMAN. Always is when a man lets music bother 'im. (*After a few puffs at his pipe*). An' she said she threw you over 'cause you was drunk; an' you said you was drunk 'cause she threw you over. (*He spits leisurely*). Queer thing, love, ain't it?

SMITTY (*rising to his feet with drunken dignity*). I'll trouble you not to pry into my affairs, Donkeyman.

THE DONKEYMAN (*unmoved*). That everybody's affair, what I said. I been through it many's the time. (*Genially*). I always hit 'em a whack on the ear an' went out and got drunker'n ever. When I come home again they always had somethin' special nice cooked fur me to eat. (*Puffing at his pipe*). That's the on'y way to fix 'em when they gits on their high horse. I don't s'pose you ever tried that?

SMITTY (*pompously*). Gentlemen don't hit women.

THE DONKEYMAN (*placidly*). No; that's why they has mem'-ries when they hears music. (SMITTY *does not deign to reply to this but sinks into a scornful silence.* DAVIS *and the girl* VIOLET *come out of the forecastle and close the door behind them. He is staggering a bit and she is laughing shrilly.*)

DAVIS (*turning to the left*). This way, Rose, or Pansy, or Jessamine, or black Tulip, or Violet, or whatever the hell flower your name is. No one'll see us back here. (*They go off left.*)

THE DONKEYMAN. There's love at first sight for you—an' plenty more o' the same in the fo'c's'tle. No mem'ries jined with that.

SMITTY (*really repelled*). Shut up, Donk. You're disgusting. (*He takes a long drink.*)

THE DONKEYMAN (*philosophically*). All depends on how you was brung up, I s'pose. (PEARL *comes out of the forecastle. There is a roar of voices from inside. She shuts the door behind her, sees* SMITTY *on the hatch, and comes over and sits beside him and puts her arm over his shoulder.*)

THE DONKEYMAN (*chuckling*). There's love for you, Duke.

PEARL (*patting* SMITTY's *face with her hand*). 'Ullo, pretty boy. (SMITTY *pushes her hand away coldly*). What you doin' out here all alone by yourself?

SMITTY (*with a twisted grin*). Thinking and,—(*He indicates the bottle in his hand*)—drinking to stop thinking. (*He drinks and laughs maudlinly. The bottle is three-quarters empty.*)

PEARL. You oughtn't drink so much, pretty boy. Don' you know dat? You have big, big headache come mawnin'.

SMITTY (*dryly*). Indeed?

PEARL. Tha's true. Ah knows what Ah say. (*Cooingly*). Why you run 'way from me, pretty boy? Ah likes you. Ah don' like them other fellahs. They act too rough. You ain't rough. You're a genelman. Ah knows. Ah can tell a genelman fahs Ah can see 'im.

SMITTY. Thank you for the compliment; but you're wrong,

you see. I'm merely—a ranker. (*He adds bitterly*). And a rotter.

PEARL (*patting his arm*). No, you ain't. Ah knows better. You're a genelman. (*Insinuatingly*). Ah wouldn't have nothin' to do with them other men, but (*She smiles at him enticingly*) you is diff'rent. (*He pushes her away from him disgustedly. She pouts*). Don' you like me, pretty boy?

SMITTY (*a bit ashamed*). I beg your pardon. I didn't mean to be rude, you know, really. (*His politeness is drunkenly exaggerated*). I'm a bit off color.

PEARL (*brightening up*). Den you do like me—little ways?

SMITTY (*carelessly*). Yes, yes, why shouldn't I? (*He suddenly laughs wildly and puts his arm around her waist and presses her to him*). Why not? (*He pulls his arm back quickly with a shudder of disgust, and takes a drink. PEARL looks at him curiously, puzzled by his strange actions. The door from the forecastle is kicked open and YANK comes out. The uproar of shouting, laughing and singing voices has increased in violence. YANK staggers over toward SMITTY and PEARL.*)

YANK (*blinking at them*). What the hell—oh, it's you, Smitty the Duke. I was goin' to turn one loose on the jaw of any guy'd cop my dame, but seein' it's you—— (*Sentimentally*). Pals is pals and any pal of mine c'n have anythin' I got, see? (*Holding out his hand*). Shake, Duke. (SMITTY *takes his hand and he pumps it up and down*). You'n me's frens. Ain't I right?

SMITTY. Right it is, Yank. But you're wrong about this girl. She isn't with me. She was just going back to the fo'c's'tle to you. (PEARL *looks at him with hatred gathering in her eyes.*)

YANK. Tha' right?

SMITTY. On my word!

YANK (*grabbing her arm*). Come on then, you, Pearl! Le's have a drink with the bunch. (*He pulls her to the en-*

trance where she shakes off his hand long enough to turn on SMITTY *furiously.*)

PEARL. You swine! You can go to hell! (*She goes in the forecastle, slamming the door.*)

THE DONKEYMAN (*spitting calmly*). There's love for you. They're all the same—white, brown, yeller 'n' black. A whack on the ear's the only thing'll learn 'em. (SMITTY *makes no reply but laughs harshly and takes another drink; then sits staring before him, the almost empty bottle tightly clutched in one hand. There is an increase in volume of the muffled clamor from the forecastle and a moment later the door is thrown open and the whole mob, led by* DRISCOLL, *pours out on deck. All of them are very drunk and several of them carry bottles in their hands.* BELLA *is the only one of the women who is absolutely sober. She tries in vain to keep the men quiet.* PEARL *drinks from* YANK'S *bottle every moment or so, laughing shrilly, and leaning against* YANK, *whose arm is about her waist.* PAUL *comes out last carrying an accordion. He staggers over and stands on top of the hatch, his instrument under his arm.*)

DRISCOLL. Play us a dance, ye square-head swab!—a rale, Godforsaken son av a turkey trot wid guts to ut.

YANK. Straight from the old Barbary Coast in Frisco!

PAUL. I don' know. I try. (*He commences tuning up.*)

YANK. Ataboy! Let 'er rip! (DAVIS *and* VIOLET *come back and join the crowd.* THE DONKEYMAN *looks on them all with a detached, indulgent air.* SMITTY *stares before him and does not seem to know there is any one on deck but himself.*)

BIG FRANK. Dance? I don't dance. I trink! (*He suits the action to the word and roars with meaningless laughter.*)

DRISCOLL. Git out av the way thin, ye big hulk, an' give us some room. (BIG FRANK *sits down on the hatch, right. All of the others who are not going to dance either follow his example or lean against the port bulwark.*)

BELLA (*on the verge of tears at her inability to keep them in the forecastle or make them be quiet now they are out*). For Gawd's sake, boys, don't shout so loud! Want to git me in trouble?

DRISCOLL (*grabbing her*). Dance wid me, me cannibal quane. (*Some one drops a bottle on deck and it smashes.*)

BELLA (*hysterically*). There they goes! There they goes! Captain'll hear that! Oh, my Lawd!

DRISCOLL. Be damned to him! Here's the music! Off ye go! (PAUL *starts playing "You Great Big Beautiful Doll" with a note left out every now and then. The four couples commence dancing—a jerk-shouldered version of the old Turkey Trot as it was done in the sailor-town dives, made more grotesque by the fact that all the couples are drunk and keep lurching into each other every moment. Two of the men start dancing together, intentionally bumping into the others.* YANK *and* PEARL *come around in front of* SMITTY *and, as they pass him,* PEARL *slaps him across the side of the face with all her might, and laughs viciously. He jumps to his feet with his fists clenched but sees who hit him and sits down again smiling bitterly.* YANK *laughs boisterously.*)

YANK. Wow! Some wallop! One on you, Duke.

DRISCOLL (*hurling his cap at* PAUL). Faster, ye toad! (PAUL *makes frantic efforts to speed up and the music suffers in the process.*)

BELLA (*puffing*). Let me go. I'm wore out with you steppin' on my toes, you clumsy Mick. (*She struggles but* DRISCOLL *holds her tight.*)

DRISCOLL. God blarst you for havin' such big feet, thin. Aisy, aisy, Mrs. Old Black Joe! 'Tis dancin'll take the blubber off ye. (*He whirls her around the deck by main force.* COCKY, *with* SUSIE, *is dancing near the hatch, right, when* PADDY, *who is sitting on the edge with* BIG FRANK, *sticks his foot out and the wavering couple stumble over it and fall flat on the deck. A roar of laughter goes up.* COCKY *rises to his feet, his face livid with rage, and springs at* PADDY, *who promptly knocks him down.* DRISCOLL *hits* PADDY *and* BIG FRANK *hits* DRISCOLL. *In a flash a wholesale fight has broken out and the deck is a surging crowd of drink-maddened men hitting out at each other indiscriminately, although the general idea seems to be a battle between seamen and firemen. The women shriek and take refuge on top of the hatch, where they huddle in a frightened group. Finally there is the flash of a knife held high in the moonlight and a loud yell of pain.*)

DAVIS (*somewhere in the crowd*). Here's the Mate comin'! Let's git out o' this! (*There is a general rush for the forecastle. In a moment there is no one left on deck but the little group of women on the hatch;* SMITTY, *still dazedly rubbing his cheek;* THE DONKEYMAN *quietly smoking on his stool; and* YANK *and* DRISCOLL, *their faces battered up considerably, their undershirts in shreds, bending over the still form of* PADDY, *which lies stretched out on the deck between them. In the silence the mournful chant from the shore creeps slowly out to the ship.*)

DRISCOLL (*quickly—in a low voice*). Who knoifed him?

YANK (*stupidly*). I didn't see it. How do I know? Cocky, I'll bet. (*The* FIRST MATE *enters from the left. He is a tall, strongly-built man dressed in a plain blue uniform.*)

THE MATE (*angrily*). What's all this noise about? (*He sees the man lying on the deck*). Hello! What's this? (*He bends down on one knee beside* PADDY.)

DRISCOLL (*stammering*). All av us—was in a bit av a harmless foight, sir,—an'—I dunno—— (*The* MATE *rolls* PADDY *over and sees a knife wound on his shoulder.*)

THE MATE. Knifed, by God. (*He takes an electric flash from his pocket and examines the cut*). Lucky it's only a flesh wound. He must have hit his head on deck when he fell. That's what knocked him out. This is only a scratch. Take him aft and I'll bandage him up.

DRISCOLL. Yis, sor. (*They take* PADDY *by the shoulders and feet and carry him off left. The* MATE *looks up and sees the women on the hatch for the first time.*)

THE MATE (*surprised*). Hello! (*He walks over to them*). Go to the cabin and get your money and clear off. If I had my way, you'd never—— (*His foot hits a bottle. He stoops down and picks it up and smells of it*). Rum, by God! So that's the trouble! I thought their breaths smelled damn queer. (*To the women, harshly*). You needn't go to the skipper for any money. You won't get any. That'll teach you to smuggle rum on a ship and start a riot.

BELLA. But, Mister——

THE MATE (*sternly*). You know the agreement—rum—no money.

BELLA (*indignantly*). Honest to Gawd, Mister, I never brung no——

THE MATE (*fiercely*). You're a liar! And none of your lip or I'll make a complaint ashore tomorrow and have you locked up.

BELLA (*subdued*). Please, Mister—

THE MATE. Clear out of this, now! Not another word out of you! Tumble over the side damn quick! The two others are waiting for you. Hop, now! (*They walk quickly—almost run—off to the left.* THE MATE *follows them, nodding to* THE DONKEYMAN, *and ignoring the oblivious* SMITTY. *There is absolute silence on the ship for a few moments. The melancholy song of the Negroes drifts crooning over the water.* SMITTY *listens to it intently for a time; then sighs heavily, a sigh that is half a sob.*)

SMITTY. God! (*He drinks the last drop in the bottle and throws it behind him on the hatch.*)

THE DONKEYMAN (*spitting tranquilly*). More mem'ries? (SMITTY *does not answer him. The ship's bell tolls four bells.* THE DONKEYMAN *knocks out his pipe*). I think I'll turn in. (*He opens the door to his cabin, but turns to look at* SMITTY—*kindly*). You can't hear it in the fo'c's'tle —the music, I mean—an' there'll likely be more drink in there, too. Good night. (*He goes in and shuts the door.*)

SMITTY. Good night, Donk. (*He gets wearily to his feet and walks with bowed shoulders, staggering a bit, to the forecastle entrance and goes in. There is silence for a second or so, broken only by the haunted, saddened voice of that brooding music, faint and far-off, like the mood of the moonlight made audible.*)

THE CURTAIN FALLS

THE MAKER OF DREAMS

by Oliphant Down

CHARACTERS

PIERROT

PIERRETTE

THE MANUFACTURER

THE MAKER OF DREAMS

Evening. A room in an old cottage, with walls of dark oak, lit only by the moonlight that peers through the long, low casement-window at the back, and the glow from the fire that is burning merrily on the spectator's left. A cobbled street can be seen outside, and a door to the right of the window opens directly on to it. Opposite the fire is a kitchen dresser with cups and plates twinkling in the firelight. A high-backed oak settle, as though afraid of the cold moonlight, has turned its back on the window and warms its old timbers at the fire. In the middle of the room stands a table with a red cover; there are chairs on either side of it. On the hob, a kettle is keeping itself warm; whilst overhead, on the hood of the chimney-piece, a small lamp is turned very low.

A figure flits past the window and, with a click of the latch, PIERRETTE *enters. She hangs up her cloak by the door, gives a little shiver and runs to warm herself for a moment. Then, having turned up the lamp, she places the kettle on the fire. Crossing the room, she takes a tablecloth from the dresser and proceeds to lay tea, setting out crockery for two. Once she goes to the window and, drawing aside the common red casement-curtains, looks out, but returns to her work, disappointed. She puts a spoonful of tea into the teapot, and another, and a third. Something outside attracts her attention; she listens, her face brightening. A voice is heard singing:*

> "Baby, don't wait for the moon,
>   She is caught in a tangle of boughs;
>   And mellow and musical June
>   Is saying 'Good-night' to the cows."

(The voice draws nearer and a conical white hat goes past the window. PIERROT *enters.)*

PIERROT *(throwing his hat to* PIERRETTE*)*. Ugh! How cold it is. My feet are like ice.

PIERRETTE. Here are your slippers. I put them down to warm. (*She kneels beside him, as he sits before the fire and commences to slip off his shoes.*)

PIERROT (*singing*).

"Baby, don't wait for the moon,
    She will put out her tongue and grimace;
And mellow and musical June
    Is pinning the stars in their place."

Isn't tea ready yet?

PIERRETTE. Nearly. Only waiting for the kettle to boil.

PIERROT. How cold it was in the market-place to-day! I don't believe I sang at all well. I can't sing in the cold.

PIERRETTE. Ah, you're like the kettle. He can't sing when he's cold either. Hurry up, Mr. Kettle, if you please.

PIERROT. I wish it were in love with the sound of its own voice.

PIERRETTE. I believe it is. Now it's singing like a bird. We'll make the tea with the nightingale's tongue. (*She pours the boiling water into the teapot*). Come along.

PIERROT (*looking into the fire*). I wonder. She had beauty, she had form, but had she soul?

PIERRETTE (*cutting bread and butter at the table*). Come and be cheerful, instead of grumbling there to the fire.

PIERROT. I was thinking.

PIERRETTE. Come and have tea. When you sit by the fire, thoughts only fly up the chimney.

PIERROT. The whole world's a chimney-piece. Give people a thing as worthless as paper, and it catches fire in them and makes a stir; but real thought, they let it go up with the smoke.

PIERRETTE. Cheer up, Pierrot. See how thick I've spread the butter.

PIERROT. You're always cheerful.

PIERRETTE. I try to be happy.

PIERROT. Ugh! (*He has moved to the table. There is a short silence, during which* PIERROT *sips his tea moodily.*)

PIERRETTE. Tea all right?

PIERROT. Middling.

PIERRETTE. Only middling! I'll pour you out some fresh.

PIERROT. Oh, it's all right! How you do worry a fellow!

PIERRETTE. Heigh-ho! Shall I chain up that big black dog?

PIERROT. I say, did you see that girl to-day?

PIERRETTE. Whereabouts?

PIERROT. Standing by the horse-trough. With a fine air, and a string of great beads.

PIERRETTE. I didn't see her.

PIERROT. I did, though. And she saw me. Watched me all the time I was singing, and clapped her hands like anything each time. I wonder if it is possible for a woman to have a soul as well as such beautiful colouring.

PIERRETTE. She was made up!

PIERROT. I'm sure she was not! And how do you know? You didn't see her.

PIERRETTE. Perhaps I *did* see her.

PIERROT. Now, look here, Pierrette, it's no good your being jealous. When you and I took on this show business, we arranged to be just partners and nothing more. If I see any one I want to marry, I shall marry 'em. And if you see any one who wants to marry you, *you* can marry 'em.

PIERRETTE. I'm not jealous! It's absurd!

PIERROT (*singing abstractedly*).

"Baby, don't wait for the moon,
    She has scratched her white chin on the gorse;
And mellow and musical June
    Is bringing the cuckoo remorse."

PIERRETTE. Did you see that girl after the show?

PIERROT. No. She had slipped away in the crowd. Here, I've had enough tea. I shall go out and try to find her.

PIERRETTE. Why don't you stay in by the fire? You could help me to darn the socks.

PIERROT. Don't try to chaff me. Darning, indeed! I hope life has got something better in it than darning.

PIERRETTE. I doubt it. It's pretty much the same all the world over. First we wear holes in our socks, and then we mend them. The wise ones are those who make the best of it, and darn as well as they can.

PIERROT. I say, that gives me an idea for a song.

PIERRETTE. Out with it, then.

PIERROT. Well, I haven't exactly formed it yet. This is what flashed through my mind as you spoke: (*He runs up on to the table, using it as a stage*).

> "Life's a ball of worsted,
> Unwind it if you can,
> You who oft have boasted

(*He pauses for a moment, then hurriedly, in order to gloss over the false accenting*).

> That you are a man."

Of course that's only a rough idea.

PIERRETTE. Are you going to sing it at the show?

PIERROT (*jumping down from the table*). You're always so lukewarm. A man of artistic ideas is as sensitively skinned as a baby.

PIERRETTE. Do stay in, Pierrot. It's so cold outside.

PIERROT. You want me to listen to your grumbling, I suppose.

PIERRETTE. Just now you said I was always cheerful.

PIERROT. There you are; girding at me again.

PIERRETTE. I'm sorry, Pierrot. But the market-place is dreadfully wet, and your shoes are awfully thin.

PIERROT. I tell you I will not stop in. I'm going out to find that girl. How do I know she isn't the very woman of my dreams?

PIERRETTE. Why are you always trying to picture an ideal
woman?

PIERROT. Don't *you ever* picture an ideal man?

PIERRETTE. No, I try to be practical.

PIERROT. Women are so unimaginative! They are such pa-
thetic, motherly things, and when they feel extra motherly they say, "I'm in love." All that is so sordid and
petty. I want a woman I can set on a pedestal, and just
look up at her and love her.

PIERRETTE (*speaking very fervently*).

> "Pierrot, don't wait for the moon,
>   There's a heart chilling cold in her rays;
> And mellow and musical June
>   Will only last thirty short days."

PIERROT. Oh, I should never make you understand! Well,
I'm off. (*As he goes out, he sings, sidelong, over his
shoulder in a mocking tone*, "Baby, don't wait for the
moon." PIERRETTE *listens for a moment to his voice dying away in the distance. Then she moves to the fireplace, and begins to stir the fire. As she kneels there, the
words of an old recitation form on her lips. Half uncon-
sciously she recites it again to an audience of laughing
flames and glowing, thoughtful coals.*

"There lives a maid in the big, wide world,
    By the crowded town and mart,
And people sigh as they pass her by;
    They call her Hungry Heart.

For there trembles that on her red rose lip
    That never her tongue can say,
And her eyes are sad, and she is not glad
    In the beautiful calm of day.

Deep down in the waters of pure, clear thought,
    The mate of her fancy lies;
Sleeping, the night is made fair by his light
    Sweet kiss on her dreaming eyes.

Though a man was made in the wells of time
Who could set her soul on fire,
Her life unwinds, and she never finds
This love of her heart's desire.
If you meet this maid of a hopeless love,
Play not a meddler's part.
Silence were best; let her keep in her breast
The dream of her hungry heart."

(*Overcome by tears, she hides her face in her hands. A slow, treble knock comes on the door;* PIERRETTE *looks up wonderingly. Again the knock sounds.*)

PIERRETTE. Come in. (*The door swings slowly open, as though of its own accord, and without, on the threshold, is seen* THE MANUFACTURER, *standing full in the moonlight. He is a curious, though kindly-looking, old man, and yet, with all his years, he does not appear to be the least infirm. He is the sort of person that children take to instinctively. He wears a quaintly cut, bottle-green coat, with silver buttons and large side-pockets, which almost hides his knee-breeches. His shoes have large buckles and red heels. He is exceedingly unlike a prosperous manufacturer, and, but for the absence of a violin, would be mistaken for a village fiddler. Without a word he advances into the room, and, again of its own accord, the door closes noiselessly behind him.*)

PIERRETTE (*jumping up and moving towards him*). Oh, I'm so sorry. I ought to have opened the door when you knocked.

MANUFACTURER. That's all right. I'm used to opening doors. And yours opens much more easily than some I come across. Would you believe it, some people positively nail their doors up, and it's no good knocking. But there, you're wondering who I am.

PIERRETTE. I was wondering if you were hungry.

MANUFACTURER. Ah, a woman's instinct. But, thank you, no. I am a small eater; I might say a very small eater. A smile or a squeeze of the hand keeps me going admirably.

PIERRETTE. At least you'll sit down and make yourself at home.

MANUFACTURER (*moving to the settle*). Well, I have a habit of making myself at home everywhere. In fact, most people think you can't make a *home* without *me*. May I put my feet on the fender? It's an old habit of mine. I always do it.

PIERRETTE. They say round here:

"Without feet on the fender
Love is but slender."

MANUFACTURER. Quite right. It is the whole secret of the domestic fireside. Pierrette, you have been crying.

PIERRETTE. I believe I have.

MANUFACTURER. Bless you, I know all about it. It's Pierrot. And so you're in love with him, and he doesn't care a little bit about you, eh? What a strange old world it is! And you cry your eyes out over him.

PIERRETTE. Oh, no, I don't often cry. But to-night he seemed more grumpy than usual, and I tried so hard to cheer him up.

MANUFACTURER. Grumpy, is he?

PIERRETTE. He doesn't mean it, though. It's the cold weather, and the show hasn't been paying so well lately. Pierrot wants to write an article about us for the local paper by way of an advertisement. He thinks the editor may print it if he gives him free passes for his family.

MANUFACTURER. Do you think Pierrot is worth your tears?

PIERRETTE. Oh, yes!

MANUFACTURER. You know, tears are not to be wasted. We only have a certain amount of them given to us just for keeping the heart moist. And when we've used them all up and haven't any more, the heart dries up, too.

PIERRETTE. Pierrot is a splendid fellow. You don't know

him as well as I do. It's true he's always discontented,
but it's only because he's not in love with any one. You
know, love does make a tremendous difference in a man.

MANUFACTURER. That's true enough. And has it made a
difference in you?

PIERRETTE. Oh, yes! I put Pierrot's slippers down to warm,
and I make tea for him, and all the time I'm happy because I'm doing something for him. If I weren't in love,
I should find it a drudgery.

MANUFACTURER. Are you sure it's real love?

PIERRETTE. Why, yes!

MANUFACTURER. Every time you think of Pierrot, do you
hear the patter of little bare feet? And every time he
speaks, do you feel little chubby hands on your breast
and face?

PIERRETTE (*fervently*). Yes! Oh, yes! That's just it!

MANUFACTURER. You've got it right enough. But why is it
that Pierrot can wake up all this poetry in you?

PIERRETTE. Because—oh, because he's just Pierrot.

MANUFACTURER. "Because he's just Pierrot." The same old
reason.

PIERRETTE. Of course, he is a bit dreamy. But that's his
soul. I am sure he could do great things if he tried. And
have you noticed his smile? Isn't it lovely! Sometimes,
when he's not looking, I want ever so much to try it on,
just to see how I should look in it. (*Pensively*). But I
wish he'd smile at me a little more often, instead of at
others.

MANUFACTURER. Ho! So he smiles at others, does he?

PIERRETTE. Hardly a day goes by but there's some fine lady
at the show. There was one there to-day, a tall girl with
red cheeks. He is gone to look for her now. And it is not
their faults. The poor things can't help being in love with
him. (*Proudly*). I believe every one is in love with
Pierrot.

MANUFACTURER. But supposing one of these fine ladies were to marry him?

PIERRETTE. Oh, they'd never do that. A fine lady would never marry a poor singer. If Pierrot were to get married, I think I should just . . . fade away . . . Oh, but I don't know why I talk to you like this. I feel as if I had known you for a long, long time. (*The* MANUFACTURER *rises from the settle and moves across to* PIERRETTE, *who is now folding up the white tablecloth.*)

MANUFACTURER (*very slowly*). Perhaps you *have* known me for a long, long time. (*His tone is so kindly and impressive that* PIERRETTE *forgets the table-cloth and looks up at him. For a moment or two he smiles back at her as she gazes, spellbound; then he turns away to the fire again, with the little chuckle that is never far from his lips.*)

PIERRETTE (*taking a small bow from his side-pocket*). Oh, look at this.

MANUFACTURER (*in mock alarm*). Oh, oh, I didn't mean you to see that. I'd forgotten it was sticking out of my pocket. I used to do a lot of archery at one time. I don't get much chance now. (*He takes it and puts it back in his pocket.*)

PIERROT (*singing in the distance*).

> "Baby, don't wait for the moon,
> She is drawing the sea in her net;
> And mellow and musical June
> Is teaching the rose to forget."

MANUFACTURER (*in a whisper as the voice draws nearer*). Who is that?

PIERRETTE. Pierrot. (*Again the conical white hat flashes past the window and* PIERROT *enters.*)

PIERROT. I can't find her anywhere. (*Seeing the* MANUFACTURER). Hullo! Who are you?

MANUFACTURER. I am a stranger to you, but Pierrette knew me in a moment.

PIERROT. An old flame perhaps?

MANUFACTURER. True, I am an old flame. I've lighted up the world for a considerable time. Yet when you say "old," there are many people who think I'm wonderfully well preserved for my age. How long do you think I've been trotting about?

PIERROT (*testily, measuring a length with his hands*). Oh, about that long.

MANUFACTURER. I suppose being funny all day *does* get on your nerves.

PIERRETTE. Pierrot, you needn't be rude.

MANUFACTURER (*anxious to be alone with* PIERROT). Pierrette, have you got supper in?

PIERRETTE. Oh, I must fly! The shops will all be shut. Will you be here when I come back?

MANUFACTURER (*bustling her out*). I can't promise, but I'll try, I'll try. (PIERRETTE *goes out. There is a silence, during which the* MANUFACTURER *regards* PIERROT *with amusement.*)

MANUFACTURER. Well, friend Pierrot, so business is not very brisk.

PIERROT. Brisk! If laughter meant business, it would be brisk enough, but there's no money. However, I've done one good piece of work to-day. I've arranged with the editor to put an article in the paper. That will fetch 'em. (*Singing*).

"Please come one day and see our house that's down among the trees,
But do not come at four o'clock for then we count the bees,
And bathe the tadpoles and the frogs, who splash the clouds with gold,
And watch the new-cut cucumbers perspiring with the cold."

That's a song I'm writing.

MANUFACTURER. Pierrot, if you had all the money in the world you wouldn't be happy.

PIERROT. Wouldn't I? Give me all the money in the world and I'll risk it. To start with, I'd build schools to educate the people up to high-class things.

MANUFACTURER. You dream of fame and wealth and empty ideals, and you miss all the best things there are. You are discontented. Why? Because you don't know how to be happy.

PIERROT (*reciting*).

> "Life's a running brooklet,
> Catch the fishes there,
> You who wrote a booklet
> On a woman's hair."

(*Explaining*). That's another song I'm writing. It's the second verse. Things come to me all of a sudden like that. I must run out a third verse, just to wind it up.

MANUFACTURER. Why don't you write a song without any end, one that goes on for ever?

PIERROT. I say, that's rather silly, isn't it?

MANUFACTURER. It all depends. For a song of that sort the singer must be always happy.

PIERROT. That wants a bit of doing in my line.

MANUFACTURER. Shall you and I transact a little business?

PIERROT. By all means. What seats would you like? There are the front rows covered in velvet, one shilling; wooden benches behind, sixpence; and, right at the back, the two-penny part. But, of course, you'll have shilling ones. How many shall we say?

MANUFACTURER. You don't know who I am.

PIERROT. That makes no difference. All are welcome, and we thank you for your courteous attention.

MANUFACTURER. Pierrot, I am a maker of dreams.

PIERROT. A what?

MANUFACTURER. I make all the dreams that float about this musty world.

PIERROT. I say, you'd better have a rest for a bit. I expect you're a trifle done up.

MANUFACTURER. Pierrot, Pierrot, your superior mind can't tumble to my calling. A child or one of the "people" would in a moment. I am a maker of dreams, little things that glide about into people's hearts and make them glad. Haven't you often wondered where the swallows go to in the autumn? They come to my workshop, and tell me who wants a dream, and what happened to the dreams they took with them in the spring.

PIERROT. Oh, I say, you can't expect me to believe that.

MANUFACTURER. When flowers fade, have you never wondered where their colours go to, or what becomes of all the butterflies in the winter? There isn't much winter about my workshop.

PIERROT. I had never thought of it before.

MANUFACTURER. It's a kind of lost property office, where every beautiful thing that the world has neglected finds its way. And there I make my celebrated dream, the dream that is called "love."

PIERROT. Ho! ho! Now we're talking.

MANUFACTURER. You don't believe it?

PIERROT. Yes, in a way. But it doesn't last. It doesn't last. If there is form, there isn't soul, and, if there is soul, there isn't form. Oh, I've tried hard enough to believe it, but, after the first wash, the colours run.

MANUFACTURER. You only got hold of a substitute. Wait until you see the genuine article.

PIERROT. But how is one to tell it?

MANUFACTURER. There are heaps of signs. As soon as you get the real thing, your shoulder-blades begin to tingle. That's love's wings sprouting. And, next, you want to soar up among the stars and sit on the roof of heaven and sing to the moon. Of course, that's because I put such a lot of the moon into my dreams. I break bits off until it's nearly all gone, and then I let it grow big again. It grows very quickly, as I dare say you've noticed. After a fortnight it is ready for use once more.

PIERROT. This is most awfully fascinating. And do the swallows bring all the dreams?

MANUFACTURER. Not always; I have other messengers. Every night when the big clock strikes twelve, a day slips down from the calendar, and runs away to my workshop in the Land of Long Ago. I give him a touch of scarlet and a gleam of gold, and say, "Go back, little Yesterday, and be a memory in the world." But my best dreams I keep for to-day. I buy babies, and fit them up with a dream, and then send them complete and carriage paid . . . in the usual manner.

PIERROT. I've been dreaming all my life, but they've always been dreams I made myself. I suppose I don't mix 'em properly.

MANUFACTURER. You leave out the very essence of them. You must put in a little sorrow, just to take away the over-sweetness. I found that out very soon, so I took a little of the fresh dew that made pearls in the early morning, and I sprinkled my dreams with the gift of tears.

PIERROT (*ecstatically*). The gift of tears! How beautiful! You know, I should rather like to try a real one. Not one of my own making.

MANUFACTURER. Well, there are plenty about, if you only look for them.

PIERROT. That is all very well, but who's going to look about for stray dreams?

MANUFACTURER. I once made a dream that would just suit you. I slipped it inside a baby. That was twenty years ago, and the baby is now a full-grown woman, with great blue eyes and fair hair.

PIERROT. It's a lot of use merely telling me about her.

MANUFACTURER. I'll do more. When I shipped her to the world, I kept the bill of lading. Here it is. You shall have it.

PIERROT. Thanks, but what's the good of it?

MANUFACTURER. Why, the holder of that is able to claim the goods; you will notice it contains a complete description, too. I promise you, you're in luck.

PIERROT. Has she red cheeks and a string of great beads?

MANUFACTURER. No.

PIERROT. Ah, then it is not she. Where shall I find her?

MANUFACTURER. That's for you to discover. All you have to do is to search.

PIERROT. I'll start at once. (*He moves as if to go.*)

MANUFACTURER. I shouldn't start out tonight.

PIERROT. But I want to find her soon. Somebody else may find her before me.

MANUFACTURER. Pierrot, there was once a man who wanted to gather mushrooms.

PIERROT (*annoyed at the commonplace*). Mushrooms!

MANUFACTURER. Fearing people would be up before him, he started out overnight. Morning came, and he found none, so he returned disconsolate to his house. As he came through the garden, he found a great mushroom had grown up in the night by his very door-step. Take the advice of one who knows, and wait a bit.

PIERROT. If that's your advice . . . But tell me this, do you think I shall find her?

MANUFACTURER. I can't say for certain. Would you consider yourself a fool?

PIERROT. Ah . . . of course . . . when you ask me a direct thing like that, you make it . . . er . . . rather awkward for me. But, if I may say so, as man to ma . . . I mean as man to . . . (*He hesitates.*)

MANUFACTURER (*waiving the point*). Yes, yes.

PIERROT. Well, I flatter myself that . . .

MANUFACTURER. Exactly. And that's your principal danger. Whilst you are striding along gazing at the stars, you may be treading on a little glowworm. Shall I give you a third verse for your song?

> "Life's a woman calling,
> Do not stop your ears,
> Lest, when night is falling,
> Darkness brings you tears."

(*The* MANUFACTURER's *kindly and impressive tone holds* PIERROT *as it had held* PIERRETTE *some moments before. Whilst the two are looking at each other, a little red cloak dances past the window, and* PIERRETTE *enters with her marketing.*)

PIERRETTE. Oh, I'm so glad you're still here.

MANUFACTURER. But I must be going now. I am a great traveller.

PIERRETTE (*standing against the door, so that he cannot pass*). Oh, you mustn't go yet.

MANUFACTURER. Don't make me fly out of the window. I only do that under very unpleasant circumstances.

PIERROT (*gaily, with mock eloquence*). Pierrette, regard our visitor. You little knew whom you were entertaining. You see before you the maker of the dreams that slip about the world like little fish among the rushes of a stream. He has given me the bill of lading of his great masterpiece, and it only remains for me to find her. (*Dropping to the commonplace*). I wish I knew where to look.

MANUFACTURER. Before I go, I will give you this little rhyme:

> "Let every woman keep a school,
> For every man is born a fool."

(*He bows, and goes out quickly and silently.*)

PIERRETTE (*running to the door, and looking out*). Why, how quickly he has gone! He's out of sight.

PIERROT. At last I am about to attain my great ideal. There

will be a grand wedding, and I shall wear my white coat
with the silver braid, and carry a tall gold-topped stick.
(*Singing.*)

"If we play any longer, I fear you will get
Such a cold in the head, for the grass is so wet.
But during the night, Margareta divine,
I will hang the wet grass up to dry on the line."

Pierrette, I feel that I am about to enter into a man's inheritance, a woman's love.

PIERRETTE. I wish you every happiness.

PIERROT (*singing teasingly*).

"We shall meet in our dreams, that's a thing understood;
You dream of the river, I'll dream of the wood.
I am visiting you, if the river it be;
If we meet in the wood, you are visiting me."

PIERRETTE. We must make lots of money, so that you can
give her all she wants. I'll dance and dance until I fall,
and the people will exclaim, "Why, she has danced herself to death."

PIERROT. You're right. We must pull the show together.
I'll do that article for the paper at once. (*He takes paper,
ink, etc., from the dresser, and, seating himself at the
table, commences to write*). "There has lately come to
this town a company of strolling players, who give a
show that is at once musical and droll. The audience is
enthralled by Pierrot's magnificent singing and dancing,
and . . . er . . . very much entertained by Pierrette's
homely dancing. Pierrette is a charming comedienne of
twenty, with . . ." what colour hair?

PIERRETTE. Fair, quite fair.

PIERROT. Funny how one can see a person every day and
not know the colour of their hair. "Fair hair and . . ."
eyes?

PIERRETTE. Blue, Pierrot.

PIERROT. "Fair hair and blue eyes." Fair! Blue! Oh, of
course it's nonsense, though.

PIERRETTE. What's nonsense?

PIERROT. Something I was thinking. Most girls have fair hair and blue eyes.

PIERRETTE. Yes, Pierrot, we can't all be ideals.

PIERROT. How musical your voice sounds! I can't make it out. Oh, but, of course, it *is* all nonsense! (*He takes the bill of lading from his pocket and reads it.*)

PIERRETTE. What's nonsense? . . . Pierrot, won't you tell me?

PIERROT. Pierrette, stand in the light.

PIERRETTE. Is anything the matter?

PIERROT. I almost believe that nothing matters. (*Reading and glancing at her*). "Eyes that say 'I love you'; arms that say 'I want you'; lips that say 'Why don't you?'" Pierrette, is it possible! I've never noticed before how beautiful you are. You don't seem a bit the same. I believe you have lost your real face, and have carved another out of a rose.

PIERRETTE. Oh, Pierrot, what is it?

PIERROT. Love! I've found it at last. Don't you understand it all?

> "I am a fool
> Who has learned wisdom in your school."

To think that I've seen you every day, and never dreamed . . . dreamed! Yes, ah yes, it's one of his beautiful dreams. That is why my heart seems full of the early morning.

PIERRETTE. Ah, Pierrot!

PIERROT. Oh, how my shoulders tingle! I want to soar up, up. Don't you want to fly up to the roof of heaven and sing among the stars?

PIERRETTE. I have been sitting on the moon ever so long, waiting for my lover. Pierrot, let me try on your smile. Give it to me in a kiss. (*With their hands outstretched behind them, they lean towards each other, till their lips meet in a long kiss.*)

PIERRETTE (*throwing back her head with a deep sigh of happiness*). Oh, I am so happy. This might be the end of all things.

PIERROT. Pierrette, let us sit by the fire and put our feet on the fender, and live happily ever after. (*They have moved slowly to the settle. As they sit there,* PIERROT *sings softly:*)

"Baby, don't wait for the moon,
   The stairs of the sky are so steep;
And mellow and musical June
   Is waiting to kiss you to sleep."

(*The lamp on the hood of the chimney-piece has burned down, leaving only the red glow from the fire upon their faces, as the curtain whispers down to hide them.*)

THE FLATTERING WORD

by George Kelly

CHARACTERS

THE REVEREND LORING RIGLEY, *Pastor of the East Hill-crest Grace Reformed Church of Youngstown, Ohio*

MARY, *his wife*

MRS. ZOOKER, *a church-worker*

LENA, *her daughter*

EUGENE TESH, *a prominent dramatic star*

SCENE—A room in the parsonage, on an afternoon in February,—about five o'clock.

THE FLATTERING WORD

When the curtain is well up, MRS. RIGLEY, *the minister's wife, a very nice, refined-looking woman of probably thirty, dressed in a one-piece dress of navy blue silk, relieved with collar and cuffs of white silk, and wearing her hair very plainly, hurries in through the door at the left and comes forward to the window, where, drawing aside the* portière *with which the window is hung, she looks out anxiously. At this point, there is a sudden burst of laughter out at the right, which causes her to turn and hurry across to the archway leading to the hall.*

RIGLEY (*out at the front door*). Well, you know, "He who loves the danger shall perish in it!" (*This quotation causes another outburst from the two ladies at the front door*). If you'll excuse me—(MRS. RIGLEY *glances out into the hallway; then, taking a folded telegram from the bosom of her dress, she steps back towards the center of the room and commences to read it rather excitedly.*)

MRS. ZOOKER (*out at the front door*). We know what you went through last November!

THE OTHER WOMAN (*at the front door, and speaking simultaneously*). Don't mention it, Doctor! Not at all, I'm sure.

RIGLEY. It's too much for me!

MRS. ZOOKER. I'll be right in, Reverend.

RIGLEY. You'd better, Mrs. Zooker! you know, "The good die young"! (*The ladies are again convulsed by the Doctor's brilliancy.*)

MRS. ZOOKER. Oh, ain't he terrible! (*The outer door is heard to close; and, immediately, Mr. Rigley comes laughing into the hallway and hangs his hat upon the hall-tree.*)

MARY (*advancing and taking the rather large, flat black book which he extends to her*). Is that Mrs. Zooker out there?

RIGLEY (*removing his overcoat*). Yes, she's talking with Mrs. Fox.

MARY (*hurriedly taking the book over to the little table at the left of the mantelpiece*). Are they coming in?

RIGLEY. Mrs. Zooker is, immediately, yes; she has one of my lists. (*Hangs his overcoat on the hall-tree.*)

MARY. Well, you haven't been standing out there in the cold, have you?

RIGLEY. I should say I haven't!

MARY (*coming back towards the hall door*). Well, listen, Loring!

RIGLEY (*coming in through the hall door, rubbing his hands*). It's gotten fearfully cold! (MR. RIGLEY *is a baldheaded blond, with a slightly pedantic manner of speech, and a dignity, at all times, far in excess of even the dignity of his calling. He is a trifle stout for his forty years, although the clerical garb is not unbecoming to him. He wears black, heavy-rimmed nose-glasses with a black tape over his right ear.*)

MARY (*handing him the telegram*). This telegram came a few minutes ago; and I've been terribly anxious till you'd get here. (*She touches an electric button at the right of the mantelpiece, and the room becomes illuminated— by means of the floor lamp over at the left. Then she starts across the room towards the window.*)

RIGLEY. Is it for me?

MARY. No, it's for me.

RIGLEY. Bad news?

MARY. No, it's from my brother Joe!

RIGLEY (*reading the telegram*). Eugene What?

MARY (*coming back to him*). Eugene Tesh. He's that boy you've heard me speak of that used to go to school with my brother Joe and me—back in Baltimore; we used to live next door to each other when we were children.

RIGLEY. What's this,—"plays Youngstown the twenty-ninth"?

MARY. Yes, that's to-night; that's the reason I've been so anxious till you'd get here. (*Looking over his left shoulder, and indicating a line with a finger of her left hand*). You see it says, "played Newark two weeks ago." (*To* RIGLEY). And Joe must have seen him; because it says, (*Indicating the telegram again*). "Asked about you—told him you were living in Youngstown—gave him your address—he is going to walk in on you when he plays Youngstown the twenty-seventh—thought I'd better tip you off." (*She straightens up and looks at* RIGLEY). And, you see, to-day is the twenty-seventh!

RIGLEY (*with a puzzled expression*). What does it mean,—he "*plays* Youngstown"?

MARY. He's on the stage! (RIGLEY *turns and looks at her as though she had just told him that she had decided to go on the stage herself*). He went on the stage shortly after he left school; it must be fifteen years ago.

RIGLEY. You mean that he is an actor?

MARY. Yes!—You've surely heard me speak of Eugene Tesh!

RIGLEY (*handing her back the telegram with a touch of state, as he passes in front of her and proceeds towards the little table at the left of the mantelpiece*). I can't say that I have.

MARY. Well, his name is always in the newspapers; he's a dramatic star.

RIGLEY (*picking up the black book and opening it, with a suggestion of ceremony*). I am not familiar with the names of dramatic stars.

MARY. I thought perhaps you might have seen his name on one of the theatrical bill-boards.

RIGLEY. I never look at theatrical bill-boards.

MARY (*coming a little forward at the right of the center*

table). I suppose Joe thought he'd better send me this wire so that I'd be sure and be in, in case Mr. Tesh comes.

RIGLEY (*closing the book, with a rather uninvolved expression*). Well, you can be in if you like. (*He looks at her, and she meets the look; then he starts for the door at the left.*)

MARY (*taking a step or two towards him*). Well, you'll see him if he comes, won't you, Loring? (*He stops and turns to her, then comes back a step or two.*)

RIGLEY. Isn't that rather a strange question to ask me?

MARY. Why so?

RIGLEY. You understand the opposition of our church to the theater?

MARY. But, this isn't the theater, Loring!

RIGLEY. Your friend is of it, isn't he?

MARY. Yes, of course.

RIGLEY. Very well, then. Besides, I think I have sufficiently emphasized my *personal* opposition to the theater; the life of the stage is not compatible with the life of a Christian, and I see nothing to be gained by association with its people.

MARY. Well, what can I do?

RIGLEY. You can do nothing very well, under the circumstances; but I *certainly* shouldn't care to have any of the members know that we were entertaining stage folk.

MARY. They needn't know anything about it.

RIGLEY. How could you prevent it, if he should walk in while Mrs. Zooker is here. (*He looks at his watch*). What time is he coming?

MARY. It doesn't say in this wire.

RIGLEY. It's eight minutes past five now.

MARY (*glancing at the clock on the mantelpiece*). Well, if he has to play to-night, I don't see how he's going to come out here, unless he comes before dinner.

RIGLEY (*replacing his watch, and starting for the door at the left*). Tell Mrs. Zooker to bring her list right into the study. (*He reaches the door and stops*). And-a- (*He turns to* MARY). If it should be necessary to introduce your friend to her, I should suggest that you refer to him as an acquaintance, rather than as an actor. And let me know when he's gone. (MARY *looks at him steadily; he turns and starts through the door*). You'd better put something around your shoulders—this room isn't any too warm. (MARY *stands for a second irresolute; then, suddenly, starts to follow him; but the voice of* MRS. ZOOKER *in the hallway—at the right—arrests her; so she replaces the telegram in the bosom of her dress and stands looking at the hall door.*)

MRS. ZOOKER (*in the hallway*). If you'll wait there for a second I'll call her. (*Appearing at the door leading into the hallway*). Why, there's a gentleman here to see you, Mrs. Rigley.

MARY. Oh, is there, Mrs. Zooker?

MRS. ZOOKER (*sidling in, and standing a little to the right of the door*). Yes, he's right out here at the door.

MARY (*glancing in the mirror over the mantelpiece, and touching her hair and dress*). Thanks, so much. Mr. Rigley said to go right into the study.

MRS. ZOOKER (*starting across towards the door at the left*). Oh, all right, I will.

MARY (*going out through the hall door*). Aren't you frozen?

MRS. ZOOKER. No, I don't seem to mind the cold very much.

MARY. You're lucky! (*Speaking to* TESH *at the front door*). Is this Eugene Tesh? (MRS. ZOOKER, *who is just leaving the room through the door at the left, pauses, and tiptoes back to the left of the mantelpiece; from which point she endeavors, by dint of divers peerings and strainings, to see what is going on at the front door. She's a poor old thing, this* MRS. ZOOKER, *with a wizened little*

*face and no teeth; and a get-up generally that is redo-
lent of rummage sales and vanished vogues. She wears
a skimpy coat of faded black—three-quarter length—and
a heavy gray skirt, quite full, and touching the floor all
the way around. Her hat is black—a little toque, rather
rusty, and trimmed with a dab of withered violets, from
whose center looms the remnant of a saffron-colored os-
trich tip. She has a very ratty muff, of nameless fur, de-
pending on a soiled and knotted cord; and, around her
neck, she wears a stringy scarf, one end of which is
thrown back over her shoulder.)*

TESH *(at the front door)*. Then, you have been expecting
me?

MARY. Only for the past fifteen minutes. I'm so glad to see
you again, Gene!

TESH. And I am certainly delighted to see you too, Mary!

MARY. You certainly have grown up! *(At the approach of
the voices,* MRS. ZOOKER *scurries through the door at the
left.)*

TESH. So have you!

MARY *(laughing, and appearing at the hall door; hanging
TESH's hat on the hall-tree)*. Have I?

TESH. Rather! *(The front door closes.)*

MARY *(coming into the room)*. Come right in, Gene. *(After taking a few steps forward and to the left, she
stops, and faces the hall door.* TESH *appears; and takes
the room in at a glance)*. I suppose we've been thinking of each other as we were at school.

TESH. Yes. *(He starts down towards the center table.
He is a dramatic star, of considerable reputation, with
a personality possessing that quality which has been
defined as stellar. He is tall and thin,—has a lot of soft-
looking black hair and is rather austerely pale; although
this latter characteristic is somewhat nullified by a certain charm of manner, and the suggestion of a twinkle
in his eye. He wears a long, beautifully tailored coat of*

excellent black, with a high, rolling collar; and, under it, a perfectly cut, double-breasted sack suit of the same material. He is quietly gloved and spatted; wears a gorgeous shawl scarf of steel-blue silk around his neck, and carries a snakewood cane, tipped with silver.)

MARY. I had this wire from Joe only fifteen minutes ago, saying that you were to play here to-night; otherwise I don't suppose I should *ever* have known that you were in town at all.

TESH (*standing just above the center table*). I had intended to walk in on you and surprise you.

MARY. Well, you certainly have!

TESH (*removing his gloves and tossing them on the table*). But Joe has given it away. (*He leans over to look at a small framed photograph on the table.*)

MARY (*standing to the left of the center table*). Well, I suppose he only did that to make sure that I'd be in, so that you wouldn't have your trip out here for nothing. Won't you take off your things, Gene?

TESH (*lifting his cane from his left arm*). I'll take off my cane.

MARY (*laughing a little, and indicating the back of the armchair at the right of the center table*). Put it there.

TESH (*holding the cane toward her*). You see I carry a cane now.

MARY. So I see. Is that the sign of age?

TESH (*turning to her, after having hung the cane on the back of the armchair*). Sign of an actor. You seem to be very nicely fixed here, Mary.

MARY. Yes, we're comfortable.

TESH. Joe tells me you married a minister.

MARY. Yes; Doctor Rigley.

TESH. How do you like him? (*Checking himself*). I mean, do you get along well with him?

MARY. Yes; very well.

TESH. You do?

MARY. Yes.

TESH (*commencing to remove his coat*). I've never been in a minister's house before.

MARY. Haven't you?

TESH. No; it's quite like other people's houses, isn't it?

MARY. You're quite like other people, Gene. (*He laughs.*)

TESH. You wouldn't have thought so if you'd seen the way that old woman stared at me out at the door. (*He folds his coat over the back of the armchair.*)

MARY. Who, Mrs. Zooker?

TESH (*removing his scarf*). The old woman that let me in.

MARY. Yes, that's Mrs. Zooker.

TESH. Does she work here?

MARY (*coming forward to the chair at the left of the center table*). No, she just helps my husband with the church work. Sit down, Gene.

TESH (*placing the scarf across the back of the chair, and moving around to the front of the chair*). I can't stay a moment, Mary; my train was two hours late.

MARY (*sitting at the left of the table*). Did you just get into town?

TESH (*sitting at the right of the table*). Ten minutes ago; I came out here in a taxi.

MARY. Well, you can sit down for a minute.

TESH. I haven't been to a hotel yet.

MARY (*resting her elbows on the table*). And, what have you been doing all these years, Gene?

TESH (*picking up the little framed photograph from the table*). Acting, all over the place. Is this your husband's picture?

MARY. No, that's Abraham Lincoln.

TESH (*setting down the picture, and picking up a little*

black book). And, what sort of a man is your husband, Mary?

MARY. Oh, like most ministers, I suppose.

TESH. But, I don't know any ministers. What book is this?

MARY. That's our church manual.

TESH. Very interesting, I suppose?

MARY. If you're a good church member.

TESH (*putting it down on the table, as he rises*). I'll have to get a copy. (MARY *laughs a little, and rises also.*)

MARY. I suppose you never go to church, do you, Gene?

TESH (*coming forward, as though he were approaching a window*). No, but I have a very intimate friend who has been there. Is this your church out here?

MARY. Yes; don't you think it's pretty?

TESH (*nodding his head slowly*). Hum-hum. I should say romantic.

MARY. Rather; we had three weddings in it last month.

TESH (*casually*). It isn't so innocent as it looks, is it?

MARY. Are you married, Gene?

TESH (*turning to her suddenly*). What?

MARY. I say, are you married?

TESH. Why, not this season. (*He resumes his observation of the church.*)

MARY (*turning away from him, laughing*). You're perfectly dreadful, Gene! (*Turning back to him*). Aren't you really married, Gene?

TESH. No, really, I'm not, Mary.

MARY. Why, I thought you'd have been married years ago.

TESH (*raising his hand in disapproval, and passing across her towards the window at the left*). I shouldn't care for it.

MARY (*crossing over back of the center table, and moving down to the right of it*). Well, how do you know whether you would or not?

TESH. I have played husbands so often that I am quite disillusioned.

MARY. Are you playing the part of a husband in this piece you're doing now?

TESH. Yes; he's one of those very good husbands; I'll be glad when the season is over. (*Coming away from the window*). By the way, Mary,—where is *your* husband?

MARY. In his study, I believe.

TESH. Does he know I'm here?

MARY. I haven't told him.

TESH. Going to?

MARY (*rather embarrassed, and smiling*). Not necessarily, Gene. (*He stops, inclines his head and raises his eyebrows comprehendingly.*)

TESH. Is he opposed to the theater?

MARY. Very much; our church is, you know.

TESH. Oh, really? Are you?

MARY. Indeed, I'm not! (TESH *laughs*). I'm crazy about the theater, and always have been.

TESH. Well, do you go?

MARY. I can't very well; he's so dreadfully opposed, personally.

TESH (*glancing over his shoulder towards the door at the left*). I suppose it's a lucky thing Mrs. Zooker didn't know that I was an actor a while ago, or she wouldn't have let me in at all.

MARY. I guess not. But, really, Gene, I haven't been to see a play since I've been married; and that's nearly seven years ago.

TESH (*sitting on the edge of the table*). Oh, dear me!

MARY. Can you imagine that!

TESH. No.

MARY. And you were playing in New York three years ago, while we were there—

TESH. Is that so?

MARY. Yes; and I did my level best to try and get to see you; but I simply couldn't manage it; and it nearly broke my heart, because I've always been dying to see you on the stage.

TESH. Well, we must try and manage it to-night, Mary.

MARY. I don't think we'll succeed. (TESH *thinks keenly for a second, then glances towards the door at the left.*)

TESH. Has your husband ever been on the stage?

MARY. Heavens, no!

TESH. You should have told him that he ought to have been; it invariably removes any prejudices.

MARY (*very much amused*). I'm afraid he'd shoot me, Gene!

TESH. Hah! Not the slightest danger, my dear girl; that is the flattering word; the one compliment that has never failed. Tell any man, woman or child that he should be on the stage,—and you'll find him quite as susceptible as a cat is to catnip.

MARY. Why is that, Gene?

TESH. Because every human being has, at some time or other in his life, experienced the desire to be on the stage. Of course, he may not admit it; but he has, just the same; and if he hasn't, all you've got to do is tell him he should be on the stage, and he *will* experience it. (*She laughs*). I tell you, Mary, that is the universal susceptibility. And very naturally so; the most fundamental instinct of human life is to express oneself; and the stage is perhaps the most complete form of self-expression; so that—when a person is stage-struck—he is simply struck with the desire to express himself more completely. If I were to tell Mrs. Zooker—or your husband—or anybody—from the minister to the mechanic—that he should be on the stage—why—the first thing you know he'd start inquiring about the fare to New York.

MARY (*laughing a little, and going up to the mantelpiece*).

Well, please don't tell my husband or Mrs. Zooker that they should have been on the stage while I'm in the room.

TESH. Why not?

MARY (*coming down at his left, carrying a little old-fashioned photograph in a black frame, which she has taken from the mantelpiece*). Because I'd never be able to keep my face straight. (TESH *laughs*). Here's a little picture of my husband; it's ages old, but it isn't a bad picture. He had it taken in Boston I think, a long time ago.

TESH. Does he look like this?

MRS. ZOOKER (*sidling through the door at the left*). You'll have to excuse me for bothering you, Mrs. Rigley— (MRS. RIGLEY *turns, and* TESH *rises.*)

MARY. Oh, are you going, Mrs. Zooker?

MRS. ZOOKER (*crossing towards the door leading into the hallway*). Yes, I've got to run along; it's after five. I told Mr. Rigley I'd be right over again after supper, to go over that other list. (*She has reached the hall door, and* TESH *has moved slowly towards the left.*)

MARY. Oh, Mrs. Zooker! (MRS. ZOOKER *turns*). I want you to meet Mr. Tesh. (TESH *turns.* MRS. ZOOKER *melts and shrinks, as* MARY *puts her arm around her waist and leads her slowly down to the right of the center table, talking as she comes*). This is a boy that I went to school with in Baltimore, nearly fifteen years ago.

MRS. ZOOKER. Oh, is that a fact, Mrs. Rigley!

MARY. And we haven't seen each other since. Mrs. Zooker, Gene.

TESH (*advancing very graciously, and crossing to the right in front of the center table*). How do you do, Mrs. Zooker?

MRS. ZOOKER. I'm pleased to meet you, I'm sure.

TESH. Thank you.

MRS. ZOOKER (*looking straight ahead*). You're welcome. (TESH *glances at her; then, after half-glancing over his left shoulder in the direction of* MARY, *who has gradually come down on the left of the center table, and is arranging the photograph of Abraham Lincoln, he turns back to* MRS. ZOOKER.)

TESH. What company are you here with, Mrs. Zooker? (MARY *looks up suddenly.*)

MRS. ZOOKER. Sir?

TESH. I say, what company are you playing here with?

MARY (*laying her hand on* TESH'S *arm*). Gene, Mrs. Zooker isn't on the stage!

TESH. Beg pardon?

MARY. I say, Mrs. Zooker isn't on the stage.

TESH (*turning back to* MRS. ZOOKER *in polite surprise*). Oh, isn't she?

MARY. No.

TESH (*turning slowly to* MARY). Why, I thought I understood you to say that Mrs. Zooker was in the profession?

MARY. No, I didn't, Gene.

TESH (*turning back to* MRS. ZOOKER, *rather amused*). Well, how extraordinary that I should have gotten that impression! (*He laughs faintly; and* MRS. ZOOKER, *not knowing what else to do, laughs a little too; then* TESH *turns back to* MARY). I was quite sure you said that Mrs. Zooker was in the profession. (*But* MARY *has slipped across back of him towards* MRS. ZOOKER.)

MRS. ZOOKER. What's he sayin'?

MARY (*placing her hand on* MRS. ZOOKER'S *arm*). Mr. Tesh thought you were an actress, dear.

MRS. ZOOKER. Who, me?

MARY. Yes.

MRS. ZOOKER (*turning suddenly away from* MARY, *to the right*). Good night! (*She breaks into a cackling, self-conscious laugh, and goes up to the hall door; and* MARY *crosses down to the extreme right.* MRS. ZOOKER *turns at the hall door and speaks directly to* MARY). I'll have to tell our Lena that!

MARY. Yes, you must.

MRS. ZOOKER (*coming slowly forward again at the right of the table*). I'm sure I don't know what there is about me that'd make anybody think that! (*She laughs again*). Oh, dear!—What made you think it, Mr. Tesh?

TESH. What did you say, Mrs. Zooker?

MRS. ZOOKER. I say,—what made you think I was an actress?

TESH. Well, I don't know that I could say exactly, Mrs. Zooker, but,—well, you gave me that impression.

MRS. ZOOKER. Is that a fact?

TESH. Yes.

MRS. ZOOKER (*turning to* MARY). What do you think of that! (*She laughs again; then settles her muff*). I guess it must have been my voice.

TESH. It may have been.

MRS. ZOOKER. Because I know when I was growing up,—people always used to say that I had quite a voice.

TESH. Well, you have appeared publicly, haven't you?

MRS. ZOOKER (*becoming a bit serious*). Well, not much these late years; but before I was married I used to go on quite a bit—

TESH (*raising his finger*). Ah!

MRS. ZOOKER. At the little affairs we used to have at the Sunday school.

TESH. You recited, didn't you?

MRS. ZOOKER. Yes.

TESH. Dramatic recitations?

MRS. ZOOKER. Very dramatic.

TESH. I should imagine you would do those best.

MRS. ZOOKER. Is that so?

TESH. Yes,—there is a distinctly dramatic quality in your voice, Mrs. Zooker.

MRS. ZOOKER. Is that a fact?

TESH. Distinctly.

MRS. ZOOKER (*turning to* MARY *and breaking into a laugh*). Now, what do you think of that! (*Turning back to* TESH). Well, now, that's a funny thing, because since I've been married, I've kinda give it up.

TESH. Ah, don't you think that was a mistake, Mrs. Zooker?

MRS. ZOOKER. Well, yes, I do, sometimes, Mr. Tesh; but, you see, my husband has always carried on so, whenever I've went on.

TESH. I see, I see.

MRS. ZOOKER. Of course, he has no talent of any kind himself, so I don't suppose he can understand how anybody else can have any. (*She nods rather vigorously at the conclusion of this remark, and* TESH *joins her in the nodding.*)

TESH. Yes, that's the way it goes, Mrs. Zooker.

MRS. ZOOKER. But, do you know, it's a funny thing, Mr. Tesh!—It just seems like the Irony of Fate—I have a daughter—

TESH. Ah, yes?

MRS. ZOOKER (*turning to* MARY). Our Lena—(MARY *smiles and nods*). Mrs. Rigley here has heard her—she'll be fifteen the twenty-first day of this coming May; and, do you know, she just seems to have *took* that from me.

TESH. You mean, her talent?

MRS. ZOOKER. Yes! (TESH *nods comprehendingly*). Now, last Thanksgiving Eve— (*Checking herself*). No, I'm telling a lie; it was New Year's Eve.

TESH. I was going to say—

MRS. ZOOKER. We were having a little entertainment down at the Guild; and she done that piece of Longfellow's, called, "Ring the Bells"—

TESH. Ah, yes, yes!

MRS. ZOOKER. And, do you know, she was just wonderful, really! And as I sat there watchin' her, goin' through her gestures, and takin' her part off so good,—I just began to realize what a fool I'd been to give it all up. (TESH *appreciates her tragedy, with a slow, serious nod*). And I made up my mind, then and there (*turning to* MARY) that if our Lena's cut out for the stage,— I'll never raise my voice to keep her from it!

TESH. You're a very sensible woman, Mrs. Zooker.

MRS. ZOOKER. Never! She can go to the heights, (*with a dramatic gesture*) and I'll never stand in her way! (*The clock strikes five-thirty.*)

TESH. You're a very sensible woman.

MRS. ZOOKER (*turning abruptly to* MARY). Well, I've got to run along—it's half-past five! (*She starts for the hall door, then remembers and steps back to* TESH). Well, I'm awful glad to have met you, Mr. Tesh, I'm sure.

TESH (*taking her hand*). Thank you, Mrs. Zooker; I'm sure I'm very pleased to have met you, too.

MRS. ZOOKER (*holding his hand*). I'm goin' to ast you an awful personal question, if it wouldn't be makin' too free?

TESH (*smiling*). Not at all, what is it?

MRS. ZOOKER. Ain't you an actor?

TESH. Yes.

MRS. ZOOKER (*turning suddenly to* MARY). Now, ain't that funny! I never set eyes on Mr. Tesh before in all my life; and yet, the minute I seen you at the door, I knowed you was an actor!

TESH (*amused*). Well, you know the old saying, Mrs. Zooker, "The eagle knows the eagle."

MRS. ZOOKER (*breaking into a laugh*). Well, I guess there's somethin' in that, too!

TESH. Indeed, I guess there is. (*He turns away slightly to hide his amusement*). Yes, indeed.

MRS. ZOOKER. My husband has been an eagle for twelve years. (TESH *moves to the window at the left*). Well, I've got to skip along. (*She goes up to the hall door and turns again.* MARY *has crossed back of her to the mantelpiece*). Do you show here to-night, Mr. Tesh?

TESH (*turning from the window*). Yes.

MRS. ZOOKER. How do you like Youngstown?

TESH. Oh, it's like New York, and the rest of them.

MRS. ZOOKER. Well, of course, we don't think there's no place in the world like Youngstown.

TESH. I've never seen anything just like it.

MRS. ZOOKER. I'm sorry Mr. Tesh couldn't have met our Lena.

MARY. Yes, it's too bad.

TESH. Is she the one who recites?

MRS. ZOOKER. Yes; she's not home this afternoon, or I'd have her come over, and do one or two of her little pieces for you.

TESH. That'd be lovely.

MRS. ZOOKER. She went to that lecture at the Guild.

MARY. Oh, did she?

MRS. ZOOKER. Yes; and I'm kinda anxious till she gets home to hear how it was. Good-by, Mr. Tesh.

TESH. Good-by, Mrs. Zooker.

MRS. ZOOKER. I guess my husband'll think I've eloped. (*She laughs, and they join her, out of courtesy; then she hurries out into the hallway.* MARY *stops at the hall door, and stands looking into the hallway after her,—and* TESH *takes a walk down around the settee and up again to the left-hand corner of the mantelpiece*). Now, don't come out here in this cold hallway with me!

MARY. I won't.

MRS. ZOOKER. That's the way people gets their death. I'll let myself out.

MARY. All right, Mrs. Zooker. (*The outer door is heard to*

close. MARY *turns and looks at* TESH, *then goes down to the right of the center table, laughing).* You're perfectly terrible, Gene!

TESH (*suddenly, and starting down at the left of the table towards her*). Listen! You don't think there's any danger of her bringing her daughter over here, do you?

MARY. I don't think she's home.

TESH. You know, I've heard a few child wonders in my time. (RIGLEY *appears at the left door.*)

MARY (*seeing him over* TESH's *shoulder, and starting up towards the mantelpiece*). What is it, Loring?

RIGLEY. Has Mrs. Zooker gone?

MARY. Yes, this minute; did you want to see her?

RIGLEY (*crossing in front of her to the hall door*). I did, yes; but it's unimportant; she'll be over again this evening.

MARY. Yes, she said she would. (MR. RIGLEY *glances out into the hallway, then turns and recrosses the room, giving* TESH *a penetrating and disapproving look as he goes.* TESH, *however, is occupied with an examination of the little photograph, which he still holds in his hands. Just as* RIGLEY *reaches the door at the left,* MARY *calls him*). Oh, Loring! (*He stops, and turns to her*). I want you to meet Mr. Tesh. (TESH *turns quietly and rests his fingers on the center table*). This is the Eugene Tesh that you've possibly heard me speak of—that I used to go to school with in Baltimore (*turning to* TESH *and half laughing*) I'm ashamed to say how many years ago. My husband, Gene.

TESH (*inclining his head pleasantly*). How do you do, Mr. Rigley?

RIGLEY. How do you do, sir?

TESH. I should have known you from your photograph.

MARY. I've just been showing Mr. Tesh that old picture you had taken in Boston.

RIGLEY. That's quite an old picture.

TESH. Taken before you entered the ministry, wasn't it, Mr. Rigley?

RIGLEY (*coming forward a little*). Oh, yes, yes.

TESH. I noticed you weren't wearing the frock.

MARY. I've always been trying to persuade him to have some new pictures taken, but he simply won't do it.

RIGLEY. That's quite a good picture.

MARY. But it's ages old, Loring! And, besides, it isn't very ministerial-looking, either. Now, if I didn't know you, and were to see that picture, I'd be more likely to think it was the picture of a well-to-do business man than a minister. (TESH *laughs deprecatingly*). Wouldn't you, Gene?

TESH. No, I should hardly say a business man.

MARY. Well, you'd never say a minister, would you?

TESH. No, I don't think I should.

MARY. Now, you see that, Loring!

TESH (*looking at the picture, with his head a bit to one side*). I'm afraid I'd be more inclined to think it might be the picture of an actor. (*There is a slight pause. MARY turns away smoothly, touching her hair, and moves over towards the right; and her husband, looking over his glasses at TESH, begins to melt, very visibly. Then he sways towards TESH, breaking into a very orthodox little chuckle.*)

RIGLEY (*taking the photograph*). That's very funny.

TESH. I daresay Mr. Rigley will be very much scandalized, but—

RIGLEY. No,—you're not the first that said that.

TESH (*glancing at MARY, who has come down to the right of the center table and is standing on a line with him*). No?

RIGLEY. My photographs invariably give that impression.

TESH. Is that so?

RIGLEY. Invariably.

TESH. Then, there must be some truth in it, Mr. Rigley.

RIGLEY (*vastly pleased*). Well, "what everybody says", you know! (*He bursts into delighted laughter.*)

TESH (*laughing with him*). Indeed, that's very true! (*As* MR. RIGLEY's *laughter continues,* TESH *glances at* MARY, *and she looks away.*)

RIGLEY. You know, Mr. Tesh, it's a most extraordinary thing—that nine out of ten persons who see this photograph, are of the impression that it is the photograph of a dramatic artist.

TESH. Yes?

RIGLEY. And, personally, I have never been able to understand why that should be so.

TESH. Well, frankly, Mr. Rigley, I can't see how anybody who would be at all familiar with the dramatic earmarks—could come to any other conclusion.

RIGLEY. Is that so?

TESH. Take this line here, for example.

RIGLEY (*looking closely*). You mean—

TESH. From the tip of your nose to the top of your upper lip.

RIGLEY. Yes, yes, I see what you mean!

TESH. That line is essentially dramatic.

RIGLEY. Is that so?

TESH. Essentially. Then, of course, the eye is an unfailing indication.

RIGLEY (*looking closely at the picture*). I don't know that I have ever noticed the eye particularly. Excuse me just a moment, till I get my other glasses!

TESH. That's quite all right.

RIGLEY (*hurrying to the mantelpiece, removing his nose glasses and putting them into a breast-pocket case as he goes*). It's rather difficult to see anything very closely with these. (TESH *glances at* MARY *significantly.*)

TESH. Mr. Rigley, have you ever seen a photograph of Edwin Booth?

RIGLEY (*picking up a pair of enormous, rimmed spectacles from the mantelpiece, and settling them on his nose*). Edwin Booth, the actor, you mean?

TESH. Yes.

RIGLEY (*coming forward*). Yes, I believe I have, Mr. Tesh.

TESH. Didn't anything strike you particularly?

RIGLEY. About Mr. Booth's picture, you mean?

TESH. Yes.

RIGLEY. Well, really, it's been so long ago, I would scarcely remember.

TESH. Well, the next time you have an opportunity of seeing a photograph of Mr. Booth, I'd like you to compare it, right in around the eyes, with your picture here—right in here (*he points to a certain spot on the picture, which* RIGLEY *is still holding*)—see if you don't get what I mean. (*He passes in front of* RIGLEY *and continues over towards the left; while* MARY *moves from her position at the right up towards the mantelpiece.* MR. RIGLEY, *however, remains perfectly still, looking intently at his photograph.*)

MRS. ZOOKER (*in the hallway out at the right*). Here we come right in, without ringing! (*Appearing at the hall door, and speaking back over her shoulder to* LENA, *who is evidently out at the street door*). Close that door, dear! (*To* MARY). I thought I'd like to have Lena meet Mr. Tesh! (*To* MR. RIGLEY, *who has turned from his contemplation of the photograph and is looking at her rather grandly*). Excuse me, Doctor. (RIGLEY *inclines his head, a bit condescendingly, and passes over in front of the table to the right, where he resumes his study of the picture*). Hurry, Lena! (*Addressing* MRS. RIGLEY, *as she comes into the room and takes up her position just to the left of the door*). I didn't think she'd be home from the lecture yet, but she sez it was over before five.

(LENA *has straggled in during this last speech, and comes
forward a few steps, when her eye lights upon* TESH;
*she stops dead, and looks at him steadily and apprais-
ingly; and he looks at her in puzzled curiosity.* MRS.
ZOOKER *stands looking from one to the other very affably.
Presently, she takes* LENA *by the arm and addresses herself to* TESH). This is the girl I was speakin' to you about
—our Lena. (TESH *advances a step or two, and* MARY
*passes above him, and goes down to the left of the
settee.*)

TESH (*bowing very graciously*). How do you do, Lena?

LENA (*casually*). Hello. (LENA, *as her mother has already
observed, will be fifteen the twenty-first of this coming
May. And she looks it; except for—perhaps just a bit
too much bust—if one may so say. But then* LENA *is
"perhaps just a bit too much" all over. And no wonder;
for she's forever eating. Something. Always chewing. One
of those little fatties that doesn't care where she is or
how she looks, so long as there's refreshments. And it's
very possible that "how she looks" is of less concern to
her than "where she is"; for she's been wearing the
same coat for the last five years. And it's a very dirty
coat too—by this time—naturally. A gray-green—long ago
outgrown, and without a button. But* LENA *doesn't mind
that. She never gets cold. She just gets red—the color of
her hat. A little pot hat of rose-colored felt, much too
narrow for the width of* LENA's *face, and trimmed
with a buckle of pea-green patent leather, and a brief,
frightened-looking little quill in the same shade. The hat
is secured by a broad, extremely tight-looking strap of
black elastic under the chin. Incidentally,* LENA *is just
about at an age when she can wear her mother's shoes,
and, at present, she appears to be taking advantage
of the possibility. Not with the most complete success,
however, as the shoes, an old brown pair, with tan-cloth
tops, have, owing to the weakness of* LENA's *ankles,
turned in and out respectively; an effect which is*

scarcely improved by the absence of the tongue of the right shoe and the consequent glimpse of the white stocking between the laces. When the coat is removed, there is revealed a washed-out middy blouse with a bow of broad red ribbon fastened with a ten-cent brooch—instead of the customary tie-effect—and a wide, black, patent leather belt around her waist. There is also a knee-length skirt of crimson satine, trimmed with two folds of itself near the bottom. Her hair is swept back from her face, rather than combed, and the short ends on top are tied with a little bow of red ribbon at the back of her head. The removal of her hat discloses perhaps the only surviving specimen of the old-fashioned circular back comb. And the heavy tan mittens have a past, too.)

MRS. ZOOKER (*snatching* LENA's *hat off, and rushing over to put it on the buffet at the right*). Mr. Tesh is an actor, dear; and I thought if you'd just run over one or two of them little pieces that you done New Year's Eve at the Guild, it might give him an idea of your talent. (*Running back and dragging* LENA's *coat off*). You remember that piece you done New Year's Eve, don't you?

LENA (*disinterestedly*). I done two pieces New Year's Eve.

MRS. ZOOKER. Yes, I know; but I mean the first one you done,—when they clapped you so; about ringin' the bells?

LENA. Oh, that was "Ring Out Wild Bells", by Alfred G. Tennyson.

MRS. ZOOKER. Yes, that's the one I mean. (*Speaking to* TESH, *as she crosses to place the coat on the armchair in front of the fireplace*). I don't think Mr. Tesh has ever heard that, have you, Mr. Tesh?

TESH. I don't believe I have, Mrs. Zooker.

MRS. ZOOKER (*settling the collar of* LENA's *blouse*). It's an awful dramatic thing, but I guess that's right in your line, ain't it?

TESH (*smiling*). Quite so.

MRS. ZOOKER (*guiding* LENA *to the center of the room*). Now, stand right there, dear, and do that for Mr. Tesh.

LENA. I don't think I remember it any more!

MRS. ZOOKER. Well, say what you remember, dear.

LENA (*to* TESH). I ain't spoke it since New Year's.

MRS. ZOOKER. Well, it'll come to you as you go along; (*turning to* TESH) and I'm sure Mr. Tesh won't mind, even if you do break down.

TESH. That's quite all right.

MARY. Sit here, Gene. (*He sits down on the settee, and* MARY *remains standing at the left.*)

MRS. ZOOKER (*backing away from* LENA *to the right*). Now, stand right up straight, dear; and don't forget your gestures.

RIGLEY (*for* TESH's *benefit*). Try and get the full, round tone, Lena. (*He glances at* TESH, *and then looks straight ahead.*

LENA. Yes, sir. (TESH *turns and looks at* MARY, *then waits for* LENA *to begin. She is busy, however, with the work of taking off her mittens, and, presently,* TESH *turns to see the cause of the delay. There is an end of lace—probably, from her petticoat or pants—hanging below the hem of her skirt; and* TESH *becomes conscious of it. Immediately* LENA *comprehends the object of his attention and tries to remedy the condition by pulling down her skirt. Then* TESH *turns away, and, looking straight ahead, awaits the ordeal.* LENA *extends her mittens towards her mother*). Hold these. (MRS. ZOOKER *advances, takes them, and resumes her place.* TESH *has turned to see the nature of this last postponement, and again resumes his attitude of resignation.*)

MRS. ZOOKER (*as* LENA *continues to prepare*). Go on, dear.

LENA (*holding the sides of her skirt with both hands, and breaking into a faint, flat voice*).

"Ring out, wild bells, to the wild sky,
The flying cloud, the frosty light;
The year is dying in the night;
Ring out, wild bells, and let him die."

MRS. ZOOKER. Louder, dear! (TESH *turns and looks at* MRS. ZOOKER; *so does* LENA). Louder.

LENA (*turning to resume, and speaking a little louder*).

"Ring out the old, ring in the new—
Ring, happy bells, across the snow;
The year is going, let him go;"

(*Here* LENA *makes a kind of lunging gesture towards* TESH, *which causes him to start slightly, and move quietly to the other end of the settee*).

"Ring out the false, ring in the true."

(*The telephone bell rings twice.*)

MRS. ZOOKER (*as* LENA *turns to her*). Go right on, dear. (*To* MARY, *and starting towards the telephone at the left of the hall door*). I'll answer it! (*Picking up the telephone*). Go right on, Lena!

LENA. I forget where I was now!

MRS. ZOOKER.

"Ring out the grief that saps the mind,"

LENA (*turning to* TESH, *smiling*). Oh, sure!

"Ring out the grief that saps the mind,
For those that here we see no more;"

MRS. ZOOKER (*into the telephone*). Mr. Who? (TESH *turns to* MARY, *but she is watching* MRS. ZOOKER.)

LENA.

"Ring out the feud of rich and poor,"

MRS. ZOOKER (*into the telephone*). Magoon? (RIGLEY *turns slowly and looks at* MRS. ZOOKER.)

LENA.

"Ring in redress to all mankind."

LENA and MRS. ZOOKER (*speaking at same time*).

(LENA). "Ring out a slowly dying cause,"

(MRS. ZOOKER, *into the telephone*). Why, there's nobody here by that name that I know of! (TESH *is in a still panic.*)

LENA.

"And ancient forms of paltry strife;"

LENA and MRS. ZOOKER (*speaking at same time*).

(LENA). "Ring in the nobler modes of life,"

(MRS. ZOOKER). Well just a minute, and I'll see!

LENA.

"With sweeter manners, purer laws."

LENA and MRS. ZOOKER (*speaking at same time*).

(LENA). "Ring out the care, the want, the sin,"

(MRS. ZOOKER, *turning to* MR. RIGLEY). There's a woman here lookin' for a man called Magoon!

LENA and RIGLEY (*speaking at same time*).

(LENA). "The faithless coldness of the times;"

(RIGLEY). She must have the wrong number.

MRS. ZOOKER. She must have.

LENA.

"Ring out, ring out, my mournful rhymes,"

LENA and MRS. ZOOKER (*speaking at same time*).

(LENA). "But ring the fuller minstrel in."

(MRS. ZOOKER, *into the telephone*). Why, Mr. Rigley sez you must have the wrong number.

LENA.

"Ring out false pride in place of blood,"

MRS. ZOOKER (*into the telephone*). This is Hillcrest, two four.

LENA.

"The civic slander and the spite;"

MRS. ZOOKER (*into the telephone*). You're welcome. (*She sets down the telephone.*)

LENA.

"Ring in the love of truth and right,"

MRS. ZOOKER (*tiptoeing back to her place at* LENA's *right, and speaking to* TESH *and* MARY *as she goes*). Excuse me.

LENA.

"Ring in the common love of good."

(*Here she pauses, and, placing her hand to her mouth, turns and looks at her mother.*)

MRS. ZOOKER. Can't you remember the rest of it, dear?

LENA. No, I think that's all I remember just now; (*turning to* TESH) it's been so long since I done it.

RIGLEY (*extending his arm magnificently, and breaking into declamation, as he struts across in front of the table towards* TESH).

"Ring out old shapes of foul disease,"

RIGLEY *and* LENA (*speaking at same time*).

(RIGLEY). "Ring out the narrowing lust of gold;"

(LENA, *turning suddenly to her mother*). Oh, yes, I know what it is now!

MRS. ZOOKER. Shut up, dear!

RIGLEY (*becoming more dramatic as he proceeds*). "Ring out (*He makes a gesture here that comes rather close to* TESH's *head*) the thousand wars of old; Ring in (*he repeats the same sweeping gesture here, knocking Abraham Lincoln's picture off the center table*) the thousand years of peace." (*As the picture is knocked off the table,* MRS. ZOOKER *utters a short screech, and rushes over to the right to pick it up.* RIGLEY *turns to* TESH). How is that?

TESH (*applauding, in which* LENA *joins*). Bravo, Mr. Rigley! Bravo! (MRS. ZOOKER *has picked up the photograph of Mr. Lincoln, and is giving it to* MARY, *who has crossed back of the settee to a point above the center table. As* MRS. ZOOKER *hands* MARY *the picture, she makes a whispered comment to the effect of its not being broken, to which* MARY *nods, as she rearranges it on the table.*)

RIGLEY. There's another verse or two, but they've escaped my mind. (*He goes up to the mantelpiece, shaking himself a bit, and laughing delightedly and self-consciously, and comes right down again.*)

TESH. I consider you a very great artist. (MR. RIGLEY *lifts his hand deprecatingly, and, still laughing delightedly, turns, and goes up to the mirror over the mantelpiece and comes down again.*)

MRS. ZOOKER (*having come down at the right of the table, and crossing in front of it towards* TESH). See here, Mr. Rigley! (RIGLEY *turns to her, from the center of the room*). Mr. Tesh said a while ago that I ought to be on the stage!

RIGLEY. He was flattering you, Mrs. Zooker.

MRS. ZOOKER. Well, maybe he was; but I think he ought to tell you the same thing. (LENA *is still standing in the spot where she delivered her recitation; but, at this point, her eye rests upon* TESH's *cane on the back of the armchair, and she moves towards it with the ostensible purpose of examining it more closely, but* MARY, *who is standing down at the right, observes her; and, anticipating her motive, steps to her side just as she is about to pick the cane up, and whispers that it might be safer to let it alone.* LENA *doesn't accept the suggestion with any too good grace, however; for, when* MARY *turns away, to resume her place,* LENA *turns on her heel with a sneer, for canes in general, and wanders back towards the settee.*)

RIGLEY (*overflowing with deprecation, as he passes in front of* TESH *to the left*). Oh, nonsense, Mrs. Zooker, nonsense!

MRS. ZOOKER. Don't you agree with me, Mr. Tesh?

TESH. Perfectly—perfectly—Mrs. Zooker! I'm afraid if the pulpit hadn't gotten Mr. Rigley—the theater would!

MRS. ZOOKER (*putting her arms around* LENA, *who has*

wandered in at her left). But, what do you think of *my* little girl, Mr. Tesh? (TESH *turns and looks at* LENA.)

TESH (*speaking very carefully*). Why, Mrs. Zooker—I think if your daughter lives—she has a future.

MRS. ZOOKER. Do you hear that, dear? (LENA *sneers and smiles, and buries her face in her mother's shoulder*). She does some comical pieces, too, but I guess she's forgotten them by this time, haven't you, dear? (LENA *shakes her head affirmatively, still keeping her face in her mother's shoulder*). Don't you remember that Irish piece you used to do, about the cook? (LENA *shakes her head negatively*). She used to do one of them pieces where she had to take off the Irish brogue,—and she'd have you dyin' in it.

TESH. I'd imagine she'd be delightful.

MRS. ZOOKER. You're sure you don't remember that piece, dear?

MARY (*coming a step or two forward from the right*). Well, I'm afraid Mr. Tesh won't have much time,—if you want to be back in town by six.

TESH (*rising*). Yes, I must go immediately. (*To* RIGLEY, *on his left*). I'm very sorry, Mr. Rigley. (RIGLEY *bows*.)

LENA (*standing right in his way, as he starts across to the back of the center table*). Is that your automobile out there?

TESH. Yes.

LENA. Do you travel around in that?

MRS. ZOOKER (*brushing* LENA *out of* TESH's *way*). No, dear, he travels round on the trains. (TESH *proceeds across to the center table and picks up his scarf and overcoat from the back of the armchair*). Where do you show to-morrow night, Mr. Tesh?

TESH. In—a—Akron, Ohio.

LENA. Where was you last night?

TESH. Erie. (*Handing his overcoat to* MARY). Please?

MRS. ZOOKER. P, A?

TESH. Yes.

MRS. ZOOKER. Oh, I'm sorry I didn't know! (*Addressing* LENA). He might have went out to see your Aunt Ida! (LENA *nods; and* TESH *puts on his scarf and then gets into the coat that* MARY *is holding for him*). I have a sister living right outside of Erie—at Overbrooke.

TESH. Is that so?

MRS. ZOOKER. Yes; you might have went out to see her.

TESH. Yes, it's too bad I didn't know about it.

LENA. Where do you go after you go where you go to-morrow night?

TESH (*laughing*). I think I shall have to send you my route, Lena.

MRS. ZOOKER (*coming forward at the left of the table, followed by* LENA). Oh, Mr. Tesh!—do you know a young man by the name of Harry Culverson? (TESH *comes down around the right of the table*). He's a distant relative of my husband's.

TESH. Why, I don't believe I do, Mrs. Zooker. Is he an actor?

MRS. ZOOKER. Oh, yes, he's right in your line; that's the reason I thought you might have run across him.

TESH. What company is he with?

MRS. ZOOKER. Why, the last letter we had from him, he had charge of the elephants, with the Barnum and Bailey Circus.

TESH. No, I'm afraid I don't know him, Mrs. Zooker, I'm sorry.

LENA. Do you ever get ashamed when you first come out?

MRS. ZOOKER. She means nervous.

TESH. Oh, sometimes, yes.

MRS. ZOOKER. Lena does, too.

TESH. Is that so? (MRS. ZOOKER *nods.*)

LENA. Is it true that Pearl White is the most beautiful woman in the world?

MRS. ZOOKER (*rather violently, and turning* LENA *towards the back, by the shoulder*). Shut your mouth, Lena!

MARY (*taking a step or two to the buffet, where she leans*). Don't forget your things, Gene.

TESH. No, I'm going immediately. (LENA *crosses above the table and comes forward at* TESH's *right*.)

MRS. ZOOKER. I suppose you run across some awful funny people travelin' round the country the way you do, don't you, Mr. Tesh?

TESH. Yes, very funny indeed, Mrs. Zooker,—very funny.

LENA. How do you get your laundry done, when you're always on the go?

MRS. ZOOKER (*sharply*). Don't ast so many questions, Lena! (LENA *gives her mother a withering look, then swishes a few steps to the right and slightly forward; then she stops, and makes a face of contempt for her mother.* TESH *stands watching her; so does* MRS. ZOOKER). Oh, there's a question I wanted to ast you, Mr. Tesh, before I forget it! Did you ever show in a place called Hutchinson, Kansas?

TESH. Hutchinson, Kansas? I believe I've passed through there several times.

MRS. ZOOKER. It's right outside of Dodge City.

TESH. Yes, I know where it is.

MRS. ZOOKER. Well, the reason I ast you, is 'cause we had a neighbor went out there to live some years ago,—

TESH. Oh, is that so?

MRS. ZOOKER. And she sent Lena the loveliest postal card of Niagara Falls. Lena saves them. (TESH *turns and looks at* LENA). She has quite a collection. So, if ever you run across a very fancy one, she'd be delighted to have you send it to her,—wouldn't you, dear?

LENA. Sure.

TESH. Well, when I get back to New York,—I'll send her one of the—Rocky Mountains. (*He starts to go, turning away from* MRS. ZOOKER *to the right.*)

LENA (*rather condescendingly, as* TESH *smiles at her in passing*). Thank you.

MARY. Have you everything, Gene?

TESH (*picking up his gloves from the table*). I think so. (MRS. ZOOKER *moves up to the center of the room, and* LENA *follows her, crossing in front of the center table.*)

MRS. ZOOKER. Well, Mr. Tesh, what do you think I ought to do about this girl? Do you think she belongs on the stage?—She's always acting!

LENA (*turning away, considerably embarrassed*). Oh, I am not! (TESH *laughs, and looks at* MARY, *who reflects his amusement.*)

MRS. ZOOKER. Now, you are too, dear!

TESH. There are very few of us who are *not* always acting, Mrs. Zooker; it's only when one learns how *not* to act,— that one really belongs on the stage.

MRS. ZOOKER. Well, what do you think I ought to do with her?

TESH. What are you doing with her now?

MRS. ZOOKER. Why, she's a waitress down in Schuster's Bakery—on Fridays and Saturdays; but she's terrible dissatisfied; sez she'd much rather be in the Moving Pictures.

TESH. Well, that isn't a bad idea; many waitresses have done very well in the pictures. However—personally, I think your daughter is a bit young to think of leaving the Bakery.

MRS. ZOOKER. Well, I think that myself.

TESH (*casually picking up his cane from the back of the armchair*). Besides, in a bakery, an actress can always be reasonably sure of getting something to eat.

MRS. ZOOKER. Yes, that's true enough.

TESH. However,—if her genius continues to develop,—I think it would not be a bad idea to take her to see a play occasionally.

MRS. ZOOKER (*a trifle disconcerted*). Well, of course, we don't go to the theater very much—on account of the church being opposed, you know.

TESH. Is your church opposed to the theater?

MRS. ZOOKER. Yes.

TESH. And why?

MRS. ZOOKER. Well, I guess Mr. Rigley can answer that question better than me.

RIGLEY. Well, I think Mr. Tesh understands that church people do not usually associate the two institutions.

TESH. But, I think they *should* be associated, Mr. Rigley.

RIGLEY. Well—

TESH. Personally, I've always regarded them as simply different branches of the same profession. (RIGLEY *makes a sound of amusement, but* TESH *cuts it off by a quick gesture*). Of course—I speak of the two institutions in their best sense.

RIGLEY. I'm afraid one doesn't see much of the best sense of the theater nowadays, Mr. Tesh.

TESH. One doesn't see anything at all, Mr. Rigley, if one doesn't look.

RIGLEY. That's true enough; but, then, one *hears* so many dreadful things of the people of the theater.

TESH. Perhaps, you mean one *reads* so many dreadful things.

RIGLEY. Well, probably, probably.

TESH. Frankly—I've read a great many very *shocking* things about church people (MRS. ZOOKER *looks at* RIGLEY), but I go to church occasionally; and I know some *very* good people who go to the theater regularly.

RIGLEY. No doubt indeed.

LENA. I know some girl's got a ticket to see you to-night.

TESH. I'll leave a ticket for *you*, Lena, if you want to see me.

LENA (*suddenly seizing her mother's arm*). Can I, Mom?

MRS. ZOOKER (*trying to silence her*). Sh-sh-sh-

LENA. Can I? (MRS. ZOOKER *glances at* TESH *with a shade of apology for* LENA's *eagerness*.)

MRS. ZOOKER. Well, you couldn't very well go alone, dear.

TESH. I shall leave a ticket for you, Mrs. Zooker; you can go with her.

MRS. ZOOKER (*laughing a little*). Well, I guess Mr. Rigley'd have to be consulted about that.

TESH. I shall leave a ticket for Mr. Rigley, also. (*They all laugh.*)

RIGLEY. Thank you very much.

TESH. Bring him along with you—and, if he sees anything in my play that in any way endangers your salvation—why—then he need never allow you to go to the theater again.

RIGLEY. What is the name of your play, Mr. Tesh?

TESH. The Open Mind.

RIGLEY. The Open Mind?

TESH. The Open Mind.

RIGLEY. And what is the idea of it?

TESH. It's about a man who had an idea that he was very good; and that everybody else was very bad; until one night he went to see a play; and in one part of this play, the theater was so dark that the audience couldn't see one another. And, presently, he heard various people around him—weeping—over—the injustice that was being done to the hero, and later applauding, when the villain was killed; and it gave him an idea—That if people sitting in the dark—where nobody can see them—will weep—over injustice, and applaud the downfall of iniquity—why—these things must be very vital to them;—

perhaps more so than they were to him, because he didn't weep; and he didn't applaud, either.

RIGLEY. What *did* he do?

TESH. He opened his mind, Mr. Rigley—wide open; because he saw that he had been mistaken all his life.

RIGLEY. And it took the theater to correct his mistake?

TESH. Precisely. The theater gave him the only opportunity that one has—of seeing people in the dark.

RIGLEY (*in a lighter vein*). What did he *do* then,—become an actor?

TESH. No, no,—he became a minister. (*They all laugh. MARY passes up to the hall door and takes TESH's hat off the hall-tree; then remains standing at the door*). So, you come along with Mrs. Zooker to-night, Mr. Rigley; you may get a very good idea for a sermon. (*He turns away to the right, and goes to the hall door. MRS. ZOOKER shoots across back of him and takes up her position just to the right of the door.*)

RIGLEY. Indeed, that's very true, I might.

TESH (*turning at the door*). And, Mrs. Zooker—(*He looks for her at the left of the door, and has a second's difficulty locating her*). I'll leave those tickets at the box-office for you. (*MRS. ZOOKER smiles and nods*). That'll be, one for you—and (*He turns to LENA on the left of the door, and she indicates herself with an abrupt gesture*). Lena—

RIGLEY. And Mrs. Rigley and myself.

TESH. Just the four of you?

RIGLEY. Just the four of us, yes.

TESH (*withdraws his eyes slowly from him, then turns and extends his hand to MRS. ZOOKER*). Good-by, Mrs. Zooker.

MRS. ZOOKER (*shaking hands*). Good-by, Mr. Tesh.

TESH. I'm very pleased to have met you.

MRS. ZOOKER. Thank you.

TESH. Although I'm sorry I couldn't have heard your daughter in one of her Irish numbers.

MRS. ZOOKER. Yes, it's too bad.

TESH. Well, some other time, I hope.

MRS. ZOOKER. I hope so too.

TESH (*turning to* LENA). And, Lena—(*She thrusts her hand and arm towards him before he can extend his hand. He takes her hand and looks away off*). Lena—I think I shall see you some day—on Broadway. (*She gives a sneering smile and slouches over to her mother,* TESH *watching her with amusement.*)

MRS. ZOOKER. Do you hear that, dear?

TESH (*turning to* RIGLEY, *who has come up at the left, and extending his hand*). Mr. Rigley, I've had a very charming visit (RIGLEY *bows*), and I shall look for you to-night at the theater.

RIGLEY (*shaking hands*). At the theater, yes; I'll call for those tickets at eight o'clock.

TESH. That'll be splendid. (*Turning to the door*). Good afternoon, Mrs. Zooker.

MRS. ZOOKER. Good afternoon, Mr. Tesh.

TESH (*nodding to* LENA). Lena. (*The curtain starts down very slowly.*)

LENA. Good afternoon.

TESH (*glancing over his shoulder to* MR. RIGLEY, *at the left of the door*). Mr. Rigley, good afternoon.

RIGLEY (*bowing*). Good afternoon, Mr. Tesh. (TESH *disappears into the hallway.*)

TESH. I suppose my chauffeur is frozen to death. I'm going to send you my route from Chicago, Mary, and I'd like you to let me know occasionally what's happening to you— (MRS. ZOOKER *starts to follow* TESH *out into the hallway, but* LENA *pushes her aside and rushes after him, much to the dismay of* MR. RIGLEY. MRS. ZOOKER *trails on out into the hallway after the rest of them, but*

MR. RIGLEY *remains standing just inside the hall door, to the left, looking intently at his resemblance to Edwin Booth in the photograph.*)

THE CURTAIN IS DOWN

THE TRIDGET OF GREVA

Translated from the Squinch

by Ring Lardner

CHARACTERS

LOUIS BARHOOTER, *the Tridget*
DESIRE CORBY, *a Corn Vitter*
BASIL LAFFLER, *a Wham Salesman*

THE TRIDGET OF GREVA

At the rise of the curtain, BARHOOTER, CORBY, *and* LAFFLER *are seated in three small flat-bottomed boats. They are fishing.*

LAFFLER. Well, boys, any luck? (*He looks from one to the other. Neither pays any attention.*)

CORBY (*after a pause, to* BARHOOTER). How's your wife, Louis?

BARHOOTER. She's in pretty bad shape.

CORBY (*who has paid no attention to the reply*). That's fine.

BARHOOTER. By the way, what was *your* mother's name before she was married?

CORBY. I didn't know her then.

LAFFLER. Do they allow people to fish at the Aquarium? (BARHOOTER *and* CORBY *ignore him.*)

BARHOOTER. You must know her first name.

CORBY. I don't. I always called her Mother.

BARHOOTER. But your father must have called her something.

CORBY. That's a hot one! (LAFFLER's *and* BARHOOTER's *fishlines become entangled.* BARHOOTER *gets out of his boat, untangles the lines, and resumes his place in the boat.*)

BARHOOTER (*to* CORBY). I wanted to ask you something about your sister, too.

CORBY. What about her?

BARHOOTER. Just anything. For instance, what's the matter with her?

CORBY. Who?

BARHOOTER. Your sister.

CORBY. I'm not married. (*After a pause*, BARHOOTER *and* CORBY *both laugh.*)

BARHOOTER (*to* LAFFLER). Do you know what we were laughing at?

LAFFLER. I have no idea.

BARHOOTER. I wish I knew who to ask. (*Moistens his finger and holds it up*). The wind's from off stage. (*He draws in his line, discovers the bait is gone*). That fellow got my bait. (*He throws his line out again without rebaiting it.*)

CORBY (*to* BARHOOTER). I understand you're an uncle.

BARHOOTER. Yes my sister's expecting a baby.

CORBY. On what train?

BARHOOTER. Yes, and do you want to know what happened?

CORBY. No.

BARHOOTER. Well, I'll tell you, two days before the baby was born, Bertha, that's my *sister*—she and her husband, that's her husband—were out driving up a steep hill and Harry tried to change into second speed.

CORBY. Who's Harry?

BARHOOTER. The fellow who was driving. He was Bertha's husband at the time. He made a mistake and shifted into reverse and the car went clear to the bottom of the hill.

CORBY. In reverse?

BARHOOTER. Yes. And the baby is very backward.

CORBY. It seems to me there is something wrong with all your sister's children. Look at Julia! (LAFFLER *looks in all directions, as if trying to locate* JULIA.)

LAFFLER. Where?

BARHOOTER (*to* CORBY). Can you imitate birds?

CORBY. I don't know. I never tried.

BARHOOTER. I wish you'd ask somebody. Somebody you can rely on. (*To* LAFFLER). Can *you* imitate birds?

LAFFLER. No. Why?

BARHOOTER. I'm always afraid I'll be near somebody that can imitate birds.

CORBY (*to* BARHOOTER). That reminds me, Louis—— Do you shave yourself?

BARHOOTER. Who would I shave?

CORBY. Well, when you shave, what do you do with your old whiskers?

BARHOOTER. I don't do anything with them.

CORBY. Will you save them for me?

BARHOOTER. What do you do with them?

CORBY. I play with them.

BARHOOTER (*with no apparent interest*). You're a scream, Corby. Where were you born?

CORBY. In bed. Where were you born?

BARHOOTER. Me? I was born out of wedlock.

CORBY. That's a mighty pretty country around there.

LAFFLER. Mr. Corby——

CORBY. Well?

LAFFLER. I often wonder how you spell your name.

CORBY. A great many people have asked me that. The answer is, I don't even try. I just let it go.

LAFFLER. I think that's kind of risky.

BARHOOTER (*to* LAFFLER). If I were you I'd wait till someone asked me what I thought. You're just making a fool of yourself.

CORBY. I'm getting hungry. I wish we could catch some fish.

BARHOOTER. I'm hungry, too, but not for fish.

LAFFLER. I can't eat fish either. I've got no teeth. (*Opens his mouth and shows his teeth*). About all I can eat is broth.

BARHOOTER. Well, let's go to a brothel.

LAFFLER. Let's—

THE APOLLO OF BELLAC
From the French of Jean Giraudoux

Adapted by Maurice Valency

CHARACTERS

AGNES

THERESE

THE CLERK

THE MAN

THE VICE-PRESIDENT

MR. CRACHETON

MR. LEPEDURA

MR. RASEMUTTE

MR. SCHULTZ

THE PRESIDENT

CHEVREDENT

THE CHAIRMAN OF THE BOARD

The Man from Bellac is not Apollo. The Man from Bellac is a little shabby fellow who doesn't know where his next meal is coming from. He is a vagabond and a poet, therefore an inventor. He dreams things up, but he does nothing and he has nothing. He was cast very sensibly on the Ford Omnibus television program, when Claude Dauphin played the role—a fine character-actor, not a matinee idol. The Man from Bellac must evoke Apollo, but visually he must remain the shabby little figure throughout the play. The moment he is cast as a big beautiful man with curly ringlets, the play is spoiled.

THE APOLLO OF BELLAC

SCENE: *The reception room of The International Bureau of
Inventions, S.A.*

*This is a large, well-appointed room on the second floor
of a magnificent office building in Paris. The French windows are open and afford us a view of tree-tops. There is
an elaborate crystal chandelier hanging from the ceiling.
The morning sun plays upon it. On a pedestal large enough
to conceal a man a bust of Archimedes is set. Four doors
open off the room. Three of them are marked Private.
These lead into the office of the* PRESIDENT, *Right, and the*
FIRST VICE-PRESIDENT *rear Right, and the Directors' Con-
ference Room rear Left. The effect is French and very ele-
gant, perhaps a trifle oppressive in its opulence.*

Behind a period desk sits the RECEPTION CLERK. *The
desk has an ivory telephone and a row of signal lights. It
has also a period blotter on which the clerk is writing something in an appointment book. The* CLERK *is well on in
years and his face makes one think of a caricature by
Daumier.*

TIME: *Autumn in Paris. The present or shortly before.*

AT RISE: *The CLERK is writing with a meticulous air. The outer door opens. AGNES comes in timidly from outer door, and stands in front of the desk. The CLERK does not look up.*

AGNES. Er—

CLERK. Yes?

AGNES. Is this the International Bureau of Inventions, Incorporated?

CLERK. Yes.

AGNES. Could I please see the Chairman of the Board?

CLERK (*looks up*). The Chairman of the Board? No one sees the Chairman of the Board.

AGNES. Oh. (*The outer door opens again. THERESE sweeps into the room. She is blond, shapely, thirty-five, dressed in expensive mink. CLERK rises respectfully.*)

CLERK. Good morning, Madame.

THERESE. Is the President in?

CLERK. Yes, Madame. Of course. (*THERESE walks haughtily to President's door. CLERK opens it for her and closes it behind her. He goes back to his desk where AGNES is waiting.*)

AGNES. Could I see the President?

CLERK. No one sees the President.

AGNES. But I have—

CLERK. What type of invention? Major? Intermediate? Minor?

AGNES. I beg pardon?

CLERK. Assistant Secretary to the Third Vice-President. Come back Tuesday. Name?

AGNES. My name?

CLERK. You have a name, I presume? (THE MAN FROM BELLAC *appears suddenly from outer door. He is nondescript, mercurial, shabby.*)

MAN. Yes. The young lady has a name. But what permits

you to conclude that the young lady's invention is as
minor as all that?

CLERK. Who are you?

MAN. What chiefly distinguishes the inventor is modesty.
You should know that by now. Pride is the invention of
non-inventors. (A STREET SINGER, *accompanied by violin and accordion, begins "La Seine" outside the windows.* CLERK *crosses to close them.*)

AGNES (*to the* MAN). Thanks very much, but—

MAN. To the characteristic modesty of the inventor, the
young lady adds the charming modesty of her sex— (*He
smiles at* AGNES). But— (CLERK *closes one of the windows*). how can you be sure, you, that she has not
brought us at last the invention which is destined to
transform the modern world?

CLERK (*closes the other window*). For world-transforma-
tions it's the Second Vice President. Mondays ten to
twelve.

MAN. Today is Tuesday.

CLERK. Now how can I help that?

MAN. So! While all humanity awaits with anguish the discovery which will at last utilize the moon's gravitation
for the removal of corns, and when we have every reason to believe that in all likelihood Mademoiselle—Mademoiselle?

AGNES. Agnes.

MAN. Mademoiselle Agnes has this discovery in her handbag— You tell her to come back Monday.

CLERK (*nervously*). There is going to be a Directors' meeting in just a few minutes. The Chairman of the Board
is coming. I must beg you to be quiet.

MAN. I will not be quiet. I am quiet Mondays.

CLERK. Now, please. I don't want any trouble.

MAN. And the Universal Vegetable? Five continents are
languishing in the hope of the Universal Vegetable which

will once and for all put an end to the ridiculous specialization of the turnip, the leek and the string-bean, which will be at one and the same time bread, meat, wine and coffee, and yield with equal facility cotton, potassium, ivory and wool. The Universal Vegetable which Paracelsus could not, and Burbank dared not, imagine! Yes, my friend. And while in this handbag, which with understandable concern she clutches to her charming bosom, the seeds of the Universal Vegetable await only the signal of your President to burst upon an expectant world, you say—come back Monday.

AGNES. Really, sir—

CLERK. If you wish an appointment for Monday, Mademoiselle—

MAN. She does not wish an appointment for Monday.

CLERK (*shrugs*). Then she can go jump in the lake.

MAN. What did you say?

CLERK. I said: She can go jump in the lake. Is that clear?

MAN. That's clear. Perfectly clear. As clear as it was to Columbus when— (*The BUZZER sounds on the* CLERK's *desk. A LIGHT flashes on.*)

CLERK. Excuse me. (*He crosses to the* VICE PRESIDENT's *door, knocks and enters.* MAN *smiles.* AGNES *smiles back wanly.*)

AGNES. But I'm not the inventor of the Universal Vegetable.

MAN. I know. I am.

AGNES. I'm just looking for a job.

MAN. Typist?

AGNES. Not really.

MAN. Stenographer?

AGNES. Not at all.

MAN. Copy-reader, translator, bookkeeper, editor, file-clerk—stop me when I come to it.

AGNES. You could go on like that for years before I could stop you.

MAN. Well then—your specialty? Charm? Coquetry, devotion, seduction, flirtation, passion, romance?

AGNES. That's getting warmer.

MAN. Splendid. The best career for a female is to be a woman.

AGNES. Yes, but—men frighten me.

MAN. Men frighten you?

AGNES. They make me feel weak all over.

MAN. That clerk frightens you?

AGNES. Clerks, presidents, janitors, soldiers. All a man has to do is to look at me, and I feel like a shoplifter caught in the act.

MAN. Caught in what act?

AGNES. I don't know.

MAN. Perhaps it's their clothes that frighten you. Their vests? Their trousers?

AGNES (shakes her head). I feel the same panic on the beach when they don't wear their trousers.

MAN. Perhaps you don't like men.

AGNES. Oh, no, I like them. I like their dog-like eyes, their hairiness, their big feet. And they have special organs which inspire tenderness in a woman—. Their Adam's apple, for instance, when they eat dinner or make speeches. But the moment they speak to me, I begin to tremble—

MAN (he looks appraisingly at her a moment). You would like to stop trembling?

AGNES. Oh yes. But— (She shrugs hopelessly.)

MAN. Would you like me to teach you the secret?

AGNES. Secret?

MAN. Of not trembling before men. Of getting whatever

you want out of them. Of making the directors jump, the presidents kneel and offer you diamonds?

AGNES. Are there such secrets?

MAN. One only. It is infallible.

AGNES. Will you really tell it to me?

MAN. Without this secret a girl has a bad time of it on this earth. With it, she becomes Empress of the World.

AGNES. Oh tell it to me quickly.

MAN (*peering about the room*). No one is listening?

AGNES (*whispers*). No one.

MAN. Tell them they're handsome.

AGNES. You mean, flatter them? Tell them they're handsome, intelligent, kind?

MAN. No. As for the intelligence and the kindness, they can shift for themselves. Tell them they're handsome.

AGNES. All?

MAN. All. The foolish, the wise, the modest, the vain, the young, the old. Say it to the professor of philosophy and he will give you a diploma. Say it to the butcher and he will give you a steak. Say it to the president here, and he will give you a job.

AGNES. But to say a thing like that, one has to know a person well—

MAN. Not at all. Say it right off. Say it before he has a chance even to open his mouth.

AGNES. But one doesn't say a thing like that before people.

MAN. Before people. Before all the world. The more witnesses, the better.

AGNES. But if they're not handsome—and for the most part they're not, you know—how can I tell them that they are?

MAN. Surely you're not narrow-minded, Agnes? (*She shrugs, not quite sure*). The ugly, the pimply, the crippled, the fat. Do you wish to get on in this world? Tell them they're handsome.

AGNES. Will they believe it?

MAN. They will believe it because they've always known it. Every man, even the ugliest, feels in his heart a secret alliance with beauty. When you tell him he's handsome, he will simply hear outwardly the voice he has been listening to inwardly all his life. And those who believe it the least will be the most grateful. No matter how ugly they may have thought themselves, the moment they find a woman who thinks them handsome, they grapple her to their hearts with hooks of steel. For them, she is the magic glass of truth, the princess of an enchanted world. When you see a woman who can go nowhere without a staff of admirers, it is not so much because they think she is beautiful, it is because she has told them they are handsome.

AGNES. There are women then who already know this secret?

MAN. Yes. But they know it without really knowing it. And usually they evade the issue, they go beside the point. They tell the hunchback he is generous, the walleyed that he's strong. There's no profit in that. I've seen a woman throw away a cool million in diamonds and emeralds because she told a clubfooted lover that he walked swiftly, when all he wanted to hear was—you know what. And now—to work. The President is in every day to those who come to tell him he's handsome.

AGNES. I'd better come back another day. I have to have training. I have a cousin who's not at all bad-looking— I'll practice on him tomorrow, and then the next day I'll—

MAN. You can practice right now. On the receptionist.

AGNES. That monster?

MAN. The monster is perfect for your purpose. After that, the Vice President. I know him. He's even better. Then the President. (*The* VICE PRESIDENT's *door opens. The* CLERK *comes in.*)

CLERK (*into the doorway*). Very good, sir.

VOICE. And another thing—

CLERK (*turns*). Yes sir?

VOICE. When the Chairman of the Board— (CLERK *goes back in and closes the door.*)

AGNES. No, I can't!

MAN (*indicating the bust of Archimedes at rear*). Begin with this bust then.

AGNES. Whose is it?

MAN. What does it matter? It's the bust of a man. It's all ears. Speak!

AGNES (*shuddering*). It has a beard.

MAN. Begin with what you like. With this chair. With this clock.

AGNES. They're not listening.

MAN. This fly, then. See? He's on your glove. He's listening.

AGNES. Is he a male?

MAN. Yes. Speak. Tell him.

AGNES (*with an effort*). How handsome he is!

MAN. No, no, no. Say it to him.

AGNES. How handsome you are!

MAN. You see? He's twirling his moustache. Go on. More. More. What is a fly especially vain of?

AGNES. His wings? His eyes?

MAN. That's it. Tell him.

AGNES. How beautiful your wings are, beautiful fly! They sparkle in the sun like jewels. And your eyes—so large, so sad, so sensitive!

MAN. Splendid. Shoo him away now. Here comes the clerk.

AGNES. He won't go. He's clinging to me.

MAN. Naturally.

AGNES (*to the fly*). You're bowlegged. (*She smiles*). He's gone.

MAN. You see? And now— (*The* VICE PRESIDENT'S *door opens slowly*). Here he comes.

AGNES (*in panic*). What must I say?

MAN. "How handsome you are." (CLERK *comes in and walks to his desk.* MAN *disappears behind the bust of Archimedes.*)

AGNES (*after an agony of indecision*). How handsome you are!

CLERK (*stops dead*). What?

AGNES. I said, how handsome you are!

CLERK. Do you get this way often?

AGNES. It's the first time in my life that I've ever—

CLERK (*finishing the sentence for her*). Called a chimpanzee handsome? Thanks for the compliment. But— why?

AGNES. You're right. Handsome is not the word. I should have said beautiful. Because, mind you, I never judge a face by the shape of the nose or the arch of the brow. To me, what counts is the ensemble.

CLERK. So what you're telling me is: your features are ugly, but they go beautifully together. Is that it?

AGNES. It serves me right. Very well— It's the first time I've ever told a man he was handsome. And it's going to be the last.

CLERK. Now don't get excited, please. I know girls. At your age a girl doesn't calculate; she says whatever comes into her head. I know you meant it. Only—why did you say it so badly? (MAN *sticks his head out and makes a face at* AGNES *behind the* CLERK'S *back.*)

AGNES (*to the* MAN). Did I say it badly? (*To the* CLERK, *who thinks it is said to him*). I thought you were handsome. I may have been wrong.

CLERK. Women are blind as bats. Even if there were something good about me, they'd never see it. What's so good about me? My face? God, no. My figure? Not at all.

Only my shadow. But of course you didn't notice that.

AGNES. Is that what you think? And when you leaned over to close the window, I suppose your shadow didn't lean over with you? And when you walked into the Vice President's office, did you put your shadow away in a drawer? (*She strokes his shadow with her hand*). How could I help noticing a shadow like that?

CLERK. You notice it now because I direct your attention to it.

AGNES. Have it your way. I thought I was looking at you, but what I saw was your shadow.

CLERK. Then you shouldn't say, what a handsome man. You should say, what a handsome shadow. (*He opens the window, the room is filled with MUSIC. It is still "La Seine."*)

AGNES. From now on, I shall say no more about it.

CLERK (*returning to desk*). Don't be angry, my dear. It's only because I'm a man of years and I have a right to warn you. I have a daughter of your age. I know what girls are. One day they see a fine shadow, and at once their heads are turned, the silly geese, and they think the man himself is handsome. Oh, I don't deny it, it's a rare thing, a fine shadow. And believe me it lasts you don't keep your hair, you don't keep your skin, but your shadow lasts all your life. Even longer, they say. But that's not the point. These little fools invariably insist on confusing the shadow with the man, and if the idiot lets himself be talked into it, in a moment it's all over and they've ruined their lives for nothing, the nitwits. No, my dear. Heed an old man's warning. You can't live your life among shadows. (MAN *sticks out his head and lifts an admonishing finger.*)

AGNES. How handsome you are!

CLERK. You know why? It's because when I'm angry I show my teeth. And the fact is, they are rather good. My dentist says they're perfect. It's no credit to me— It's because I eat hard foods. And when you— (*The BUZZER sounds again*). Ah—the Vice President needs me again. Wait just a minute, my dear. I'll make sure that he sees you at once. I'll say it's my niece.

AGNES (*as he bends over to close a drawer*). How beautiful it is, your shadow, when it leans over. One would say it belonged to Rodin's Thinker!

CLERK (*delighted*). Come, now, that will do. If you were my daughter, I'd give you a good slap on the—. Sit down a minute. I'll get him for you. (*Crosses to the* VICE PRESIDENT'S *door and goes out.* MAN *comes out from behind the bust. The MUSIC stops.*)

MAN. Well, it's a start.

AGNES. I think I'm better with flies.

MAN. Because in your mind the idea of beauty is inseparable from the idea of the caress. Women have no sense of the abstract—a woman admiring the sky is a woman caressing the sky. In a woman's mind beauty is something she needs to touch. And you didn't want to touch the clerk, not even his shadow.

AGNES. No.

MAN. With my method, it's not your hands that must speak, nor your cheek, nor your lips—. It's your brain.

AGNES. I had a narrow squeak. I almost lost him.

MAN. Yes, he had you there with his shadow. You're not ready to tackle a Vice President. No. Not yet.

AGNES. But there's no time. What shall I do?

MAN. Practice. Practice on me.

AGNES. You expect me to tell you you're handsome?

MAN. Is it so difficult?

AGNES. Not at all. Only—

MAN. Think. Think before you speak.

AGNES. Oh, you're not bad at all, you know, when you tease one like this.

MAN. Very feeble. Why when I tease one like this? The rest of the time, I'm not handsome?

AGNES. Oh yes. Always. Always.

MAN. Better. Now it's no longer your hands that are speaking.

AGNES. With you, all the same, they murmur a little something.

MAN. Good.

AGNES. The mass of your body is beautiful. The outline is beautiful. The face matters little.

MAN. What nonsense is this? My face matters little?

AGNES (*recovering quickly*). No more than the face of Rodin's Thinker.

MAN. In his case, doubtless the feet have more importance. Look here, Agnes, these little allusions to famous statues are ingenious. But is Rodin's Thinker the only one you know?

AGNES. Except for the Venus of Milo. But she wouldn't be much use to me with men.

MAN. That remains to be seen. In any case, we'd better extend your repertory. Forget The Thinker. Michelangelo's David is very good. Or his Moses. But best of all—the Apollo of Bellac—

AGNES. The Apollo of Bellac?

MAN. It doesn't exist. It will do perfectly.

AGNES. What does it look like?

MAN. A little like me, I think. I too come from Bellac. It's a little town in Limousin. I was born there.

AGNES. But they say the men of Limousin are so ugly. How does it happen that you are so handsome?

MAN. My father was a very handsome man, and he— Oh-oh. Good for you. (*He applauds.*)

AGNES (*pursuing her advantage*). Oh never! Not with you! You taught me the secret. With you I could be no other than honest.

MAN. At last. You understand. (*The* VICE PRESIDENT's *door opens.*) Here we are. (*Goes behind the bust.*)

CLERK (*comes in, smiling tenderly*). The Vice President will be out in a moment, my dear. No need to put yourself out. A shadow like his, you may see every day—in the zoo. (*He takes some papers from his desk and goes into where the Directors will meet.*)

AGNES (*whispers*). Help! Help! (MAN *thrusts his head out*). I feel faint!

MAN. Practice. Practice.

AGNES (*desperately*). On whom? On what?

MAN. On anything. The telephone.

AGNES (*she speaks to the telephone*). How handsome you are, my little telephone! (*She strokes it gently.*)

MAN. No! Not with the hands.

AGNES. But it's so much easier that way.

MAN. I know. Try the chandelier. That's one thing you can't touch.

AGNES. How handsome you are, my little, my great chandelier! (*The MUSIC begins again. Another tune*). Only when you're all lit up? Oh, don't say that. Other chandeliers, yes. Street lamps, store-fixtures, yes. Not you. See —you are full of sunshine. You are the chandelier of the sun. A desk lamp needs to be lit. A planet needs to be lit. But you have radiance of your own. You are as beautiful as a galaxy of stars, even more beautiful, for a galaxy is only an imitation chandelier, a cluster of uncertain lights swinging precariously in the eternal darkness. But you are a creature of crystal with limbs of ivory and gold, a living miracle! (*The chandelier LIGHTS up by itself.*)

MAN. Bravo!

VICE PRESIDENT (*the door opens. The* VICE PRESIDENT *comes in. His manner is important. His face is that of a gargoyle*). My dear young lady, I have exactly two minutes to give you. (*He crosses to close the window.*)

AGNES (*whispering in awe*). Oh!

VICE PRESIDENT *(stops and turns)*. Why do you stare at me like that? You've seen me before?

AGNES *(in a tone of wonder)*. No! On the contrary.

VICE PRESIDENT. And what does that mean, no, on the contrary?

AGNES. I was expecting to see the usual Vice President, stoop-shouldered, paunchy, bald— And all at once, I see you! (VICE PRESIDENT *freezes in his tracks.* MAN *thrusts out his head. He raises a warning finger. Hastily)*. How handsome you are!

VICE PRESIDENT. What? *(He turns.)*

AGNES. Nothing. I beg your pardon.

VICE PRESIDENT. I heard you distinctly. You said I was handsome. Don't deny it. *(He steps closer to her.* MUSIC *swells up)*. You know, it gave me rather a shock to hear you say it. However, it can't be true. If I were really— what you said—wouldn't some woman have told me before this?

AGNES. Oh, the fools! The fools!

VICE PRESIDENT. Whom are you calling fools, Mademoiselle? My sister, my mother, my niece?

AGNES *(giving up all at once. In a formal tone)*. Mr. Vice President, the truth is I am looking for a position. And I happened to hear through a friend of one of your directors, Mr. Lepédura— (MAN *thrusts out his head.)*

VICE PRESIDENT. Never mind Monsieur Lepédura. We are discussing me. As you probably know, I am one of the world's authorities in the field of dreams. It is I who work with those who are able to invent only while they sleep, and I have been able to extract from their dreams such extraordinary devices as the book that reads itself and the adjustable Martini, wonders of modern science which without my help would have remained mere figments of the imagination. If you appeared to me in a dream and told me I was handsome, I should have understood at once. But we are in a waking state, or are we?

One moment. (*He pinches himself*). Ow! I am awake.
Permit me. (*Pinches her.*)

AGNES. Ow!

VICE PRESIDENT. We're not dreaming, Mademoiselle. And
now, my dear— (*He takes her hand*). Why did you say
I was handsome? To flatter me?—I can see you are in-
capable of such baseness. To make fun of me? No—your
eye is gentle, your lips attract— Why did you say it,
Mademoiselle?

AGNES. I say you are handsome because you are handsome.
If your mother finds you ugly that's not my concern.

VICE PRESIDENT. I cannot permit you to form so low an
opinion of my mother's taste. Even when I was a boy,
my mother used to say I had the hands of an artist.

AGNES. If your niece prefers Charles Boyer—

VICE PRESIDENT. My niece? Only yesterday at dinner she
was saying that my eyebrows could have been drawn by
El Greco.

AGNES. If your sister—

VICE PRESIDENT. My sister has never quite admitted that I
am handsome, no, but she has always said that there
was something distinctive about my face. A friend of
hers, a history teacher, told her it's because in certain
lights, I resemble Lodovico Sforza. (*He makes a dep-
recating gesture.*)

AGNES. Lodovico Sforza? Never. The Apollo of Bellac, yes.

VICE PRESIDENT. The Apollo of Bellac?

AGNES. Wouldn't you say? Quite objectively?

VICE PRESIDENT. Well—if you really think so—perhaps just
a little. Although Lodovico Sforza, you know—I've seen
engravings—

AGNES. When I say the Apollo of Bellac, I mean, naturally,
the Apollo of Bellac in a beautifully tailored suit. You
see, I am frank. I say what I think. Yes, Mr. Vice President. You have the fault of all really handsome men—
you dress carelessly.

VICE PRESIDENT (*smiling*). What insolence! And this from a girl who tells every man she meets that he's handsome!

AGNES. I have said that to two men only in all my life. You are the second. (CLERK *comes in.*)

VICE PRESIDENT. What is it? Don't you see I'm busy?

CLERK. The Directors are on the way up, sir. It's time for the meeting.

VICE PRESIDENT. I'll be right in. (CLERK *goes into the Directors' room*). I'm sorry, Mademoiselle. I must go to this meeting. But we must certainly continue this wonderful conversation. Won't you come back and lunch with me? You know, my secretary is impossible. I'm having her transferred to the sales department. Now you're a first-rate typist, I'm told—

AGNES. I don't type. I play the piano.

VICE PRESIDENT. Ah, that's wonderful. And you take dictation?

AGNES. In longhand, yes.

VICE PRESIDENT. That's much the best way. That gives one time to think. Would you like to be my secretary?

AGNES. On one condition.

VICE PRESIDENT. A condition?

AGNES. On condition that you never wear this awful jacket again. When I think of these wonderful shoulders in that ill-fitting suit—!

VICE PRESIDENT. I have a beautiful blue silk suit. But it's for summer— It's a little light for the season.

AGNES. As you please.

VICE PRESIDENT. I'll wear it tomorrow.

AGNES. Good-bye.

VICE PRESIDENT. Don't forget. Lunch. (*He goes out, smiling, by way of the door to the Directors' room. The street MUSIC stops.* MAN *peers out from behind the bust.*)

AGNES. I kept my hands behind my back the whole time. I

pretended I had no hands. Now I can hardly move my fingers.

MAN. Here come the rest of the apes. Go to work.

AGNES. On the first?

MAN. On all. One after the other.

AGNES. But—(CLERK *throws open the doors of the Directors' room. The street MUSIC starts again. We have a glimpse of the Directors' table with chairs pulled back ready to receive the Directors. The* VICE PRESIDENT *is seen inside. He is posturing in front of a bookcase in the glass door of which he sees himself reflected, and he is trying vainly to give a smartly tailored appearance to his coat.* CLERK *glances at him in astonishment, then he stands by the outer door to announce the Directors as they appear. They come in through the outer door and cross the length of the reception room, one by one in time to the music, which is a waltz.*)

CLERK. Mr. Cracheton. (MR. CRACHETON *comes in, a lugubrious type, stiff and melancholy.*)

AGNES. How handsome he is!

CRACHETON (*he snaps his head about as if shot. His expression changes. He smiles. In a low voice*). Charming girl! (*He goes into the Directors' room, looking all the while over his shoulder.*)

CLERK. Mr. Lepédura.

LEPEDURA (*appears. He has a face full of suspicion and worry. As he passes* AGNES, *he tips his derby perfunctorily, recognizing her*). Good morning.

AGNES. How handsome you are!

LEPEDURA (*stops dead*). Who says so?

AGNES. Your wife's friend, the Baroness Chagrobis. She thinks you're wonderful.

LEPEDURA (*a changed man, gallant and charming*). She thinks I'm wonderful? Well, well, give her my love when you see her. And tell her I mean to call her up shortly myself. She has a pretty thin time of it with the Baron, you know. We have to be nice to her. Is she still at the same address?

AGNES. Oh yes. I'll tell her you're as handsome as ever.

LEPEDURA. Now don't exaggerate, my dear. We don't want to disappoint her. (*He gives her a radiant smile, and goes in, fully six inches taller and many pounds lighter. To the* CLERK). Delightful girl!

CLERK. Mr. Rasemutte and Mr. Schultz. (*They enter together, Mutt and Jeff.*)

AGNES. How handsome he is! (BOTH *stop as if at a signal.*)

RASEMUTTE. To which of us, Mademoiselle—

SCHULTZ. —Do you refer?

AGNES. Look at each other. You will see. (*They look at each other anxiously, and* BOTH *smile radiantly.*)

RASEMUTTE. Charming creature!

SCHULTZ. Lovely girl! (SCHULTZ *offers* RASEMUTTE *his arm. They walk into the Directors' room arm in arm like characters in "Alt Wien."* CLERK *blows* AGNES *a kiss, follows them in and closes the doors behind them.* MAN *pokes his head out from behind Archimedes. He shakes his head ruefully.*)

AGNES. I'm not doing it well? You're sad?

MAN. You're doing it much too well. I'm frightened.

AGNES. You?

MAN. Like Frankenstein. (*The door of the Directors' room is flung open.*)

CLERK. The President! (*As the* PRESIDENT *enters the room, we catch a glimpse of the* DIRECTORS. *Each has a mirror in his hand. While one combs his hair into waves, another settles his tie. Another preens his whiskers. The* VICE PRESIDENT *has taken off his jacket.*)

PRESIDENT. So you're the cause of it all, Miss— Miss—?

AGNES. Agnes.

PRESIDENT. Miss Agnes, for fifteen years this organization has been steeped in melancholy, jealousy and suspicion. And now suddenly this morning, everything is changed. My reception clerk, ordinarily a species of hyena— (*The* CLERK *smiles affably*) has become so affable he even bows to his own shadow on the wall— (CLERK *contemplates his silhouette in the sunshine with a nod of approval. It nods back*). The First Vice President, whose reputation for stuffiness and formality has never been seriously challenged, insists on sitting at the Directors' Meeting in his shirt-sleeves, God knows why. In the Directors' Room, around the table, mirrors flash like sunbeams in a forest, and my Directors gaze into them with rapture. Mr. Lepédura contemplates with joy the Adam's apple of Mr. Lepédura. Mr. Rasemutte stares with pride at the nose of Mr. Rasemutte. They are all in love with themselves and with each other. How in the world did you bring about this miracle, Miss Agnes? What was it you said to them?

AGNES. How handsome you are!

PRESIDENT. I beg your pardon?

AGNES. I said to them, to each of them, "How handsome you are!"

PRESIDENT. Ah! You conveyed it to them subtly by means of a smile, a wink, a promise—

AGNES. I said it in a loud clear voice. Like this: How handsome you are! (*In the Directors' Room, all heads turn suddenly.* CLERK *closes the doors.*)

PRESIDENT. I see. Like a child winding up a mechanical doll. Well, well! No wonder my mannikins are quivering with the joy of life. (*There is a round of applause from the Directors' Room*). Listen to that. It's Mr. Cracheton proposing the purchase of a new three-way mirror for the men's room. Miss Agnes, I thank you. You have made a wonderful discovery.

AGNES (*modestly*). Oh, it was nothing.

PRESIDENT. And the President? How does it happen that you don't tell the President?

AGNES. How handsome he is?

PRESIDENT. He's not worth the trouble, is that it? (*She looks at him with a smile full of meaning*). You've had enough of masculine vanity for one morning?

AGNES. Oh, Mr. President—you know the reason as well as I.

PRESIDENT. No. I assure you.

AGNES. But—I don't need to tell *you*. You *are* handsome.

PRESIDENT (*seriously*). Would you mind repeating that?

AGNES. You are handsome.

PRESIDENT. Think carefully, Miss Agnes. This is a serious matter. Are you quite sure that to you I seem handsome?

AGNES. You don't seem handsome. You are handsome.

PRESIDENT. You would be ready to repeat that before witnesses? Think. Much depends upon your answer. I have grave decisions to make today, and the outcome depends entirely upon you. Have you thought? Are you still of the same opinion?

AGNES. Completely.

PRESIDENT. Thank heaven. (*He goes to his private door, opens it and calls*) Chevredent! (CHEVREDENT *comes in. She is a thin, sour woman with an insolent air. Her nose is pinched. Her chin is high. Her hair is drawn up tightly. When she opens her mouth she appears to be about to bite.*)

CHEVREDENT. Yes? (*She looks at* AGNES *and sniffs audibly.*)

PRESIDENT. Chevredent, how long have you been my private secretary?

CHEVREDENT. Three years and two months. Why?

PRESIDENT. In all that time there has never been a morning when the prospect of finding you in my office has not made me shudder.

CHEVREDENT. Thanks very much. Same to you.

PRESIDENT. I wouldn't have put up with you for ten minutes if it had ever occurred to me that I was handsome.

CHEVREDENT. Ha-ha.

PRESIDENT. But because I thought I was ugly, I took your meanness for generosity. Because I thought I was ugly, I assumed that your evil temper concealed a good heart. I thought it was kind of you even to look at me. For I am ugly, am I not? (CHEVREDENT *sneers maliciously*). Thank you. And now listen to me. This young lady seems to be far better equipped to see than you. Her eyelids are not red like yours, her pupils are clear, her glance is limpid. Miss Agnes, look at me. Am I ugly?

AGNES. You are beautiful. (CHEVREDENT *shrugs.*)

PRESIDENT. This young lady's disinterested appraisal of my manly charms has no effect on your opinion?

CHEVREDENT. I never heard such rubbish in my life!

PRESIDENT. Quite so. Well, here is the problem that confronts us. I have the choice of spending my working time with any ugly old shrew who thinks I'm hideous or a delightful young girl who thinks I'm handsome. What do you advise?

CHEVREDENT. You intend to replace me with this little fool?

PRESIDENT. At once.

CHEVREDENT. We'll soon see about that, Mr. President. You may have forgotten, but your wife is inside in your office reading your mail. She should know about this.

PRESIDENT. She should. Tell her.

CHEVREDENT. With pleasure. (*She rushes into the* PRESIDENT's *office, slamming the door after her.*)

AGNES. I'm terribly sorry, Mr. President.

PRESIDENT. My dear, you come like an angel from heaven at the critical moment of my life. Today is my fifteenth wedding anniversary. My wife, with whose fury Chevredent threatens us, is going to celebrate the occasion by lunching with my Directors. I am going to present her with a gift. A diamond. (*He takes out a case and opens it*). Like it?

AGNES. How handsome it is!

PRESIDENT. Extraordinary! You praised the diamond in exactly the same tone you used for me. Is it yellow, by any chance? Is it flawed?

AGNES. It is beautiful. Like you.

PRESIDENT (*his door opens*). We are about to become less so, both of us. (*He puts the case in his pocket*). Here is my wife.

THERESE (THERESE, *the blond lady comes in with icy majesty. She looks* AGNES *up and down*). So.

PRESIDENT. Therese, my dear, permit me to present—

THERESE. Quite unnecessary. That will be all, Mademoiselle. You may go.

PRESIDENT. Agnes is staying, my dear. She is replacing Chevredent.

THERESE. Agnes! So she is already Agnes!

PRESIDENT. Why not?

THERESE. And why is Agnes replacing Chevredent?

PRESIDENT. Because she thinks I'm handsome.

THERESE. Are you mad?

PRESIDENT. No. Handsome.

THERESE (*to* AGNES). You think he's handsome?

AGNES. Oh yes.

THERESE. He makes you think of Galahad? Of Lancelot?

AGNES. Oh no. His type is classic. The Apollo of Bellac.

THERESE. The Apollo of Bellac?

PRESIDENT. Have you ever stopped to wonder, Therese, why the good Lord made women? Obviously they were not torn from our ribs in order to make life a torment for us. Women exist in order to tell men they are handsome. And those who say it the most are those who are

most beautiful. Agnes tells me I'm handsome. It's because she's beautiful. You tell me I'm ugly. Why?

MAN (*appears. He applauds*). Bravo! Bravo!

THERESE. Who is this maniac?

MAN. When one hears a voice which goes to the very heart
of humanity, it is impossible to keep silent.

PRESIDENT. My friend—

MAN. From the time of Adam and Eve, of Samson and
Delilah, of Antony and Cleopatra, the problem of man
and woman has made an impenetrable barrier between
man and woman. If, as it seems, we are able to solve
this problem once and for all, it will be a work of im-
measurable benefit to the human race.

THERESE. And you think we're getting somewhere with it
today, is that it?

MAN. Oh, yes.

THERESE. You don't think the final solution could be de-
ferred until tomorrow?

MAN. Till tomorrow? When the President has just posed the
problem so beautifully?

AGNES. So beautifully!

THERESE. The beautiful man poses a beautiful problem, eh,
Mademoiselle?

AGNES. I didn't say it. But I can say it. I say what I think.

THERESE. Little cheat!

PRESIDENT. I forbid you to insult Agnes!

THERESE. It's she who insults me!

PRESIDENT. When I'm called handsome, it's an insult to you
—is that it?

THERESE. I'm no liar.

PRESIDENT. No. You show us the bottom of your heart.

MAN. Agnes is telling the President the truth, Madame. Just
as Cleopatra told the truth, just as Isolt told the truth.
The truth about men is, they are beautiful, every last

one of them; and your husband is right, Madame, the woman who tells it to them never lies.

THERESE. So I am the liar!

MAN (*gently*). It's only because you don't see clearly. All you have to do to see the beauty of men is to watch as they breathe and move their limbs. Each has his special grace. His beauty of body. The heavy ones—how powerfully they hold the ground! The light ones—how well they hang from the sky! His beauty of position. A hunchback on the ridge of Notre Dame makes a masterpiece of Gothic sculpture. All you have to do is to get him up there. And, finally, his beauty of function. The steamfitter has the beauty of a steamfitter. The president has the beauty of a president. There is ugliness only when these beauties become confused—when the steamfitter has the beauty of a president, the president the beauty of a steamfitter.

AGNES. But there is no such confusion here.

THERESE. No. He has the beauty of a garbageman.

PRESIDENT. Thanks very much.

THERESE. My dear, I have known you too long to deceive you. You have many good qualities. But you're ugly.

PRESIDENT. Quiet!

THERESE. Yes. Yes. Ugly! This girl, whatever her motives, is just able to force her lips to whisper her lies. But with every part of me—my heart, my lungs, my arms, my eyes —I scream the truth at you. My legs! You're ugly! Do you hear?

PRESIDENT. I've heard nothing else for years.

THERESE. Because it's true.

MAN. There. And at last she's confessed.

THERESE. Confessed what? What have I confessed?

MAN. Your crime, Madame. You have injured this man. How could you expect him to be handsome in an environment that screamed at him constantly that he was ugly?

PRESIDENT. Ah! Now I understand!

THERESE. What do you understand? What's the matter with you all? What have I done?

PRESIDENT. Now I understand why I am always embarrassed not only in your presence, but in the presence of everything that belongs to you.

THERESE. Do you know what he is talking about?

PRESIDENT. The sight of your skirt on the back of a chair shortens my spine by three inches. Can you expect me to stand up like a man when you come in? Your stockings on the bureau tell me that I'm knock-kneed and thick-ankled. Is it any wonder if I stumble? Your nail file on my desk hisses at me that my fingers are thick and my gestures clumsy. What do you expect of me after that? And your onyx clock with the Dying Gaul on the mantelpiece—no wonder I always shiver when I go near the fire. Imagine—for fifteen years that Dying Gaul has been sneering at me in my own house, and I never realized why I was uncomfortable. Well, at last I understand. And this very evening—

THERESE. Don't you dare!

PRESIDENT. This very evening your Dying Gaul shall die. You will find him in the garbage with the rest of the conspiracy. Your Dresden china shepherd, your Arab sheik, your directoire chairs with their scratchy bottoms—

THERESE. Those chairs belonged to my grandmother!

PRESIDENT. From now on they belong to the garbage. What are your chairs covered with, Agnes?

AGNES. Yellow satin.

PRESIDENT. I knew it. And the statues on your table?

AGNES. There is only a bowl of fresh flowers on my table. Today it is white carnations.

PRESIDENT. Of course. And over your fireplace?

AGNES. A mirror.

PRESIDENT. Naturally.

THERESE. I warn you, if you so much as touch my chairs, I'll leave you forever.

PRESIDENT. As you please, my dear.

THERESE. I see. So this is my anniversary gift after fifteen years of devotion. Very well. Only tell me, what have you to complain of? In all these years has it ever happened that your roast was too rare? Did I ever give you your coffee too cold, too hot, too light, too sweet? Thanks to me, you are known as a man whose handkerchief is always fresh, whose socks are always new. Have you ever known what it was to have a hole in your toe? Has anyone ever seen a spot on your vest? And yet how you splash in your gravy, my friend! How you go through your socks!

PRESIDENT. Tell me one thing. Do you say I am ugly because you think I am ugly or merely to spite me?

THERESE. Because you are ugly.

PRESIDENT. Thank you, Therese. Go on.

THERESE. Then this woman appears. And at the first glance we can guess the fate of the unhappy creature who marries her. We see it all—the slippers with the inner sole curled up in a scroll. The nightly battle over the newspaper. The pajamas without buttons and always too small. The headaches without aspirin, the soup without salt, the shower without towels—

PRESIDENT. Agnes, one question. Do you tell me I'm handsome because you think I'm handsome or only to make fun of me?

AGNES. Because you're handsome.

PRESIDENT. Thank you, Agnes.

THERESE. You mean because he's rich.

AGNES. If he were the richest man in the world, I'd still say he was handsome.

THERESE. Very well. Marry her if she thinks you're so handsome. Well? What are you waiting for?

PRESIDENT. Nothing.

THERESE. Take him, you, with my compliments. After fifteen years I've had enough. If you like to hear snoring at night—

AGNES. You snore? How wonderful!

THERESE. If you like bony knees—

AGNES. I like legs that have character.

THERESE. Look at that face! Now tell me he has the brow of a Roman Senator.

AGNES. No, Madame.

THERESE. No?

AGNES. The brow of a king.

THERESE. I give up. Goodbye.

PRESIDENT. Goodbye, my love. (THERESE *rushes out through outer door*). And now, Agnes, in token of a happy future, accept this diamond. For me, one life has ended, and another begins. (CLERK *comes in and signs to him*). Forgive me just one moment, Agnes. I must address the Directors. The Chairman of the Board is evidently not coming. I'll be right back. (*He crosses to the door. To the* CLERK). Send down to the florist. I want all the white carnations he has. Agnes, you have made me the happiest of men.

AGNES. The handsomest. (*The* PRESIDENT *goes out by his door, the* CLERK *by outer door.*)

MAN. Well, there you are, my dear. You have everything— a job, a husband and a diamond. I can leave?

AGNES. Oh no! (*The street MUSIC starts afresh.*)

MAN. But what more do you want?

AGNES. Look at me. I have changed—haven't I?

MAN. Perhaps just a little. That can't be helped.

AGNES. It's your fault. I have told so many lies! I must tell the truth at last or I shall burst!

MAN. What truth do you want to tell?

AGNES. I want to tell someone who is really beautiful that he is beautiful. I want to tell the most beautiful man in the world that he is the most beautiful man in the world.

MAN. And to caress him, perhaps, just a little?

AGNES. Just a little.

MAN. There is the Apollo of Bellac.

AGNES. He doesn't exist.

MAN. What does it matter whether or not he exists? His beauty is the supreme beauty. Tell him.

AGNES. I can't. Unless I touch a thing I don't see it. You know that. I have no imagination.

MAN. Close your eyes.

AGNES (*closes them*). Yes?

MAN. Suppose, Agnes, it were the God of Beauty himself who visited you this morning. Don't be astonished. Perhaps it's true. Where else could this terrible power have come from? Or this extraordinary emotion you feel? Or this sense of oppression? And suppose that now the god reveals himself?

AGNES. It is you?

MAN. Don't open your eyes. Suppose I stand before you now in all my truth and all my splendor.

AGNES. I see you.

MAN. Call me thou.

AGNES. I see thee.

MAN. How do I seem?

AGNES. You seem—

MAN. I am taller than mortal men. My head is small and fringed with golden ringlets. From the line of my shoulders, the geometricians derived the idea of the square. From my eyebrows the bowmen drew the concept of the arc. I am nude and this nudity inspired in the musicians the idea of harmony.

AGNES. Your heels are winged, are they not?

MAN. They are not. You are thinking of the Hermes of St. Yrieix.

AGNES. I don't see your eyes.

MAN. As for the eyes, it's as well you don't see them. The eyes of beauty are implacable. My eyeballs are silver. My pupils are graphite. From the eyes of beauty poets derived the idea of death. But the feet of beauty are enchanting. They are not feet that touch the ground. They are never soiled and never captive. The toes are slender, and from them artists derived the idea of symmetry. Do you see me now?

AGNES. You dazzle my eyes.

MAN. But your heart sees me.

AGNES. I'm not so sure. Do not count on me too much, God of Beauty. My life is small. My days are long, and when I come back to my room each evening, there are five flights to climb in the greasy twilight amid smells of cooking. These five flights mark the beginning and the end of every event of my life, and oh, if you knew, Apollo, how lonely I am! Sometimes I find a cat waiting in a doorway. I kneel and stroke it for a moment, we purr together and it fills the rest of my day with joy. Sometimes I see a milk bottle that has fallen on its side. I set it right and the gesture comforts me. If I smell gas in the hallway I run and speak to the janitor. It is so good to speak to someone about something. Between the second story and the third, the steps sag. At this turning one abandons hope. At this turning one loses one's balance, and catches at the bannister, gasping with the anguish of those more fortunate ones who clutch at the rail on the heaving deck of a ship. That is my life, Apollo, a thing of shadows and tortured flesh. That is my conscience, Apollo, a staircase full of stale odors. If I hesitate to see you as you are, O beautiful god, it is because I need so much and I have so little and I must defend myself.

MAN. But I have rescued you, Agnes. You possess the secret.

AGNES. I know. From now on, my staircase will be new and full of light, the treads carpeted in velvet and adorned with initials. But to climb it with you would be unthinkable. Go away, God of Beauty. Leave me for always.

MAN. You wish that?

AGNES. If you were merely a handsome man, Apollo, thick and human in your flesh, with what joy I would take you in my arms! How I would love you! But you are too brilliant and too great for my staircase. I would do better to look at my diamond. Go, Apollo. Go away. Before I open my eyes, I implore you, vanish.

MAN. When I vanish, you will see before you an ordinary creature like yourself, covered with skin, covered with clothes.

AGNES. That is my destiny, and I prefer it. Let me kiss your lips, Apollo. And then—

MAN (*he kisses her*). Open your eyes, my dear. Apollo is gone. And I am going.

AGNES. How handsome you are!

MAN. Dear Agnes!

AGNES. Don't go. I will make you rich. I will order the President to buy your invention.

MAN. Which one?

AGNES. The Universal Vegetable. There must be a fortune in it.

MAN. I haven't quite got the hang of it yet. The roots don't hold the earth. I'll be back the moment I've perfected it.

AGNES. You promise?

MAN. We shall plant it together. And now—

AGNES. You are really leaving me? You think I shall marry the President?

MAN. No.

AGNES. Why not?

MAN. He's already married. And his wife has learned a lesson. You will see.

AGNES. Then whom shall I marry, if not the President?

CLERK. (*Enters. He crosses to the Directors' Room and throws open the door. Announces*). The Chairman of the Board! (*The* CHAIRMAN *enters from outer door.*)

MAN (*whispers*). He is a bachelor.

AGNES. How handsome he is!

MAN. Yes. (*He vanishes.*)

CHAIRMAN. Mademoiselle—

PRESIDENT (*the* PRESIDENT *comes in quickly in great excitement*). Agnes! Agnes! A miracle! My wife has just telephoned. I don't know what has come over her. She has thrown out the Dying Gaul and the china shepherd.

AGNES. Give her this diamond.

PRESIDENT. Thank you, Agnes. Thank you.

CHAIRMAN (*taking her hand*). And who is this charming girl who gives away diamonds?

AGNES. Her name is Agnes.

CHAIRMAN. Dear Agnes!

PRESIDENT. But what's happened to our friend? He isn't here?

AGNES. He is gone.

PRESIDENT. Call him back. He must have lunch with us. Do you know his name?

AGNES. His first name only. Apollo.

PRESIDENT (*runs to the outer door*). Apollo! Apollo! (*The* DIRECTORS *come in, all adorned with white carnations*). Gentlemen, gentlemen, let's call him! We can't let him go like that. Apollo! (*They each go to a door or a window save* AGNES *and the* CHAIRMAN *who remain standing hand in hand.*)

PRESIDENT and DIRECTORS. Apollo! Apollo!

CHAIRMAN. But whom are they shouting at? Is Apollo here?

AGNES. No. He just passed by.

CURTAIN

TRIFLES

by Susan Glaspell

TRIFLES

SCENE: *The kitchen in the now abandoned farmhouse of* JOHN WRIGHT, *a gloomy kitchen, and left without having been put in order—the walls covered with a faded wall paper.* D. R. *is a door leading to the parlor. On the* R. *wall above this door is a built-in kitchen cupboard with shelves in the upper portion and drawers below. In the rear wall at* R., *up two steps is a door opening onto stairs leading to the second floor. In the rear wall at* L. *is a door to the shed and from there to the outside. Between these two doors is an old-fashioned black iron stove. Running along the* L. *wall from the shed door is an old iron sink and sink shelf, in which is set a hand pump. Downstage of the sink is an uncurtained window. Near the window is an old wooden rocker. Center stage is an unpainted wooden kitchen table with straight chairs on either side. There is a small chair* D. R. *Unwashed pans under the sink, a loaf of bread outside the breadbox, a dish towel on the table— other signs of incompleted work. At the rear the shed door opens and the* SHERIFF *comes in followed by the* COUNTY ATTORNEY *and* HALE. *The* SHERIFF *and* HALE *are men in middle life, the* COUNTY ATTORNEY *is a young man; all are much bundled up and go at once to the stove. They are followed by the two women—the* SHERIFF'S *wife,* MRS. PETERS, *first; she is a slight wiry woman, a thin nervous face.* MRS. HALE *is larger and would ordinarily be called more comfortable looking, but she is disturbed now and looks fearfully about as she enters. The women have come in slowly, and stand close together near the door.*

COUNTY ATTORNEY (*at stove rubbing his hands*). This feels good. Come up to the fire, ladies.

MRS. PETERS (*after taking a step forward*). I'm not—cold.

SHERIFF (*unbuttoning his overcoat and stepping away from the stove to right of table as if to mark the beginning of official business*). Now, Mr. Hale, before we move things about, you explain to Mr. Henderson just what you saw when you came here yesterday morning.

COUNTY ATTORNEY (*crossing down to left of the table*). By the way, has anything been moved? Are things just as you left them yesterday?

SHERIFF (*looking about*). It's just the same. When it dropped below zero last night I thought I'd better send Frank out this morning to make a fire for us—(*sits right of center table*) no use getting pneumonia with a big case on, but I told him not to touch anything except the stove—and you know Frank.

COUNTY ATTORNEY. Somebody should have been left here yesterday.

SHERIFF. Oh—yesterday. When I had to send Frank to Morris Center for that man who went crazy—I want you to know I had my hands full yesterday. I knew you could get back from Omaha by today and as long as I went over everything here myself——

COUNTY ATTORNEY. Well, Mr. Hale, tell just what happened when you came here yesterday morning.

HALE (*crossing down to above table*). Harry and I had started to town with a load of potatoes. We came along the road from my place and as I got here I said, "I'm going to see if I can't get John Wright to go in with me on a party telephone." I spoke to Wright about it once before and he put me off, saying folks talked too much anyway, and all he asked was peace and quiet—I guess you know about how much he talked himself; but I thought maybe if I went to the house and talked about it before his wife, though I said to Harry that I didn't know as what his wife wanted made much difference to John——

COUNTY ATTORNEY. Let's talk about that later, Mr. Hale. I do want to talk about that, but tell now just what happened when you got to the house.

HALE. I didn't hear or see anything; I knocked at the door, and still it was all quiet inside. I knew they must be up, it was past eight o'clock. So I knocked again, and I thought I heard somebody say, "Come in." I wasn't sure, I'm not sure yet, but I opened the door—this door (*indicating the door by which the two women are still standing*) and there in that rocker—(*pointing to it*) sat Mrs. Wright. (*They all look at the rocker* D. L.)

COUNTY ATTORNEY. What—was she doing?

HALE. She was rockin' back and forth. She had her apron in her hand and was kind of—pleating it.

COUNTY ATTORNEY. And how did she—look?

HALE. Well, she looked queer.

COUNTY ATTORNEY. How do you mean—queer?

HALE. Well, as if she didn't know what she was going to do next. And kind of done up.

COUNTY ATTORNEY (*takes out notebook and pencil and sits left of center table*). How did she seem to feel about your coming?

HALE. Why, I don't think she minded—one way or other. She didn't pay much attention. I said, "How do, Mrs. Wright, it's cold, ain't it?" And she said, "Is it?"—and went on kind of pleating at her apron. Well, I was surprised; she didn't ask me to come up to the stove, or to set down, but just sat there, not even looking at me, so I said, "I want to see John." And then she—laughed. I guess you would call it a laugh. I thought of Harry and the team outside, so I said a little sharp: "Can't I see John?" "No," she says, kind o' dull like. "Ain't he home?" says I. "Yes," says she, "he's home." "Then why can't I see him?" I asked her, out of patience. "'Cause he's dead," says she. "*Dead?*" says I. She just nodded her head, not getting a bit excited, but rockin' back and forth. "Why—where is he?" says I, not knowing what to say. She just pointed upstairs—like that. (*Himself pointing to the room above*). I started for the stairs, with the

idea of going up there. I walked from there to here—
then I says, "Why, what did he die of?" "He died of a
rope round his neck," says she, and just went on pleatin'
at her apron. Well, I went out and called Harry. I
thought I might—need help. We went upstairs and there
he was lyin'——

COUNTY ATTORNEY. I think I'd rather have you go into that
upstairs, where you can point it all out. Just go on now
with the rest of the story.

HALE. Well, my first thought was to get that rope off. It
looked . . . (*stops, his face twitches*) . . . but Harry, he
went up to him, and he said, "No, he's dead all right,
and we'd better not touch anything." So we went back
downstairs. She was still sitting that same way. "Has
anybody been notified?" I asked. "No," says she, uncon-
cerned. "Who did this, Mrs. Wright?" said Harry. He
said it business-like—and she stopped pleatin' of her
apron. "I don't know," she says. "You don't *know?*" says
Harry. "No," says she. "Weren't you sleepin' in the bed
with him?" says Harry. "Yes," says she, "but I was on
the inside." "Somebody slipped a rope round his neck
and strangled him and you didn't wake up?" says Harry.
"I didn't wake up," she said after him. We must 'a'
looked as if we didn't see how that could be, for after a
minute she said, "I sleep sound." Harry was going to ask
her more questions but I said maybe we ought to let her
tell her story first to the coroner, or the sheriff, so Harry
went fast as he could to Rivers' place, where there's a
telephone.

COUNTY ATTORNEY. And what did Mrs. Wright do when
she knew that you had gone for the coroner?

HALE. She moved from the rocker to that chair over there
(*pointing to a small chair in the* D. R. *corner*) and just
sat there with her hands held together and looking down.
I got a feeling that I ought to make some conversation,
so I said I had come in to see if John wanted to put in a
telephone, and at that she started to laugh, and then

she stopped and looked at me—scared. (*The* COUNTY AT-
TORNEY, *who has had his notebook out, makes a note*).
I dunno, maybe it wasn't scared. I wouldn't like to say it
was. Soon Harry got back, and then Dr. Lloyd came,
and you, Mr. Peters, and so I guess that's all I know that
you don't.

COUNTY ATTORNEY (*rising and looking around*). I guess
we'll go upstairs first—and then out to the barn and
around there. (*To the* SHERIFF). You're convinced that
there was nothing important here—nothing that would
point to any motive?

SHERIFF. Nothing here but kitchen things. (*The* COUNTY
ATTORNEY, *after again looking around the kitchen, opens
the door of a cupboard closet in* R. *wall. He brings a
small chair from* R.—*gets up on it and looks on a shelf.
Pulls his hand away, sticky.*)

COUNTY ATTORNEY. Here's a nice mess. (*The women draw
nearer* U. C.)

MRS. PETERS (*to the other woman*). Oh, her fruit; it did
freeze. (*To the* LAWYER). She worried about that when
it turned so cold. She said the fire'd go out and her jars
would break.

SHERIFF (*rises*). Well, can you beat the women! Held for
murder and worryin' about her preserves.

COUNTY ATTORNEY (*getting down from chair*). I guess before we're through she may have something more serious
than preserves to worry about. (*Crosses down* R. C.)

HALE. Well, women are used to worrying over trifles. (*The
two women move a little closer together.*)

COUNTY ATTORNEY (*with the gallantry of a young politi-
cian*). And yet, for all their worries, what would we do
without the ladies? (*The women do not unbend. He
goes below the center table to the sink, takes a dipperful
of water from the pail and pouring it into a basin, washes
his hands. While he is doing this the* SHERIFF *and* HALE
cross to cupboard, which they inspect. The COUNTY AT-

TORNEY *starts to wipe his hands on the roller towel, turns it for a cleaner place*). Dirty towels! (*Kicks his foot against the pans under the sink*). Not much of a housekeeper, would you say, ladies?

MRS. HALE (*stiffly*). There's a great deal of work to be done on a farm.

COUNTY ATTORNEY. To be sure. And yet (*with a little bow to her*) I know there are some Dickson County farmhouses which do not have such roller towels. (*He gives it a pull to expose its full length again.*)

MRS. HALE. Those towels get dirty awful quick. Men's hands aren't always as clean as they might be.

COUNTY ATTORNEY. Ah, loyal to your sex, I see. But you and Mrs. Wright were neighbors. I suppose you were friends, too.

MRS. HALE (*shaking her head*). I've not seen much of her of late years. I've not been in this house—it's more than a year.

COUNTY ATTORNEY (*crossing to women U. C.*). And why was that? You didn't like her?

MRS. HALE. I liked her all well enough. Farmers' wives have their hands full, Mr. Henderson. And then——

COUNTY ATTORNEY. Yes——?

MRS. HALE (*looking about*). It never seemed a very cheerful place.

COUNTY ATTORNEY. No—it's not cheerful. I shouldn't say she had the homemaking instinct.

MRS. HALE. Well, I don't know as Wright had, either.

COUNTY ATTORNEY. You mean that they didn't get on very well?

MRS. HALE. No, I don't mean anything. But I don't think a place'd be any cheerfuller for John Wright's being in it.

COUNTY ATTORNEY. I'd like to talk more of that a little later. I want to get the lay of things upstairs now. (*He goes past the women to* U. R. *where steps lead to a stair door.*)

SHERIFF. I suppose anything Mrs. Peters does'll be all right. She was to take in some clothes for her, you know, and a few little things. We left in such a hurry yesterday.

COUNTY ATTORNEY. Yes, but I would like to see what you take, Mrs. Peters, and keep an eye out for anything that might be of use to us.

MRS. PETERS. Yes, Mr. Henderson. (*The men leave by* U. R. *door to stairs. The women listen to the men's steps on the stairs, then look about the kitchen.*)

MRS. HALE (*crossing* L. *to sink*). I'd hate to have men coming into my kitchen, snooping around and criticizing. (*She arranges the pans under sink which the* LAWYER *had shoved out of place.*)

MRS. PETERS. Of course it's no more than their duty. (*Crosses to cupboard* U. R.)

MRS. HALE. Duty's all right, but I guess that deputy sheriff that came out to make the fire might have got a little of this on. (*Gives the roller towel a pull*). Wish I'd thought of that sooner. Seems mean to talk about her for not having things slicked up when she had to come away in such a hurry. (*Crosses* R. *to* MRS. PETERS *at cupboard.*)

MRS. PETERS (*who has been looking through cupboard, lifts one end of a towel that covers a pan*). She had bread set. (*Stands still.*)

MRS. HALE (*eyes fixed on a loaf of bread beside the breadbox, which is on a low shelf of the cupboard*). She was going to put this in there. (*Picks up loaf, then abruptly drops it. In a manner of returning to familiar things*). It's a shame about her fruit. I wonder if it's all gone. (*Gets up on the chair and looks*). I think there's some here that's all right, Mrs. Peters. Yes—here; (*holding it toward the window*) this is cherries, too. (*Looking again*). I declare I believe that's the only one. (*Gets *down, jar in her hand. Goes to the sink and wipes it off on the outside).* She'll feel awful bad after all her hard work in the hot weather. I remember the afternoon I put up my cherries last summer. (*She puts the jar on the big kitchen table, center of the room. With a sigh, is about to sit down in the rocking chair. Before she is seated realizes what chair it is; with a slow look at it, steps back. The chair which she has touched rocks back and forth.* MRS. PETERS *moves to center table and they both watch the chair rock for a moment or two.*)

MRS. PETERS (*shaking off the mood which the empty rocking chair has evoked. Now in a businesslike manner she speaks*). Well, I must get those things from the front room closet. (*She goes to the door at the* R., *but, after looking into the other room, steps back*). You coming with me, Mrs. Hale? You could help me carry them. (*They go in the other room; reappear,* MRS. PETERS *carrying a dress, petticoat and skirt,* MRS. HALE *following with a pair of shoes*). My, it's cold in there. (*She puts the clothes on the big table, and hurries to the stove.*)

MRS. HALE (*right of center table examining the skirt*). Wright was close. I think maybe that's why she kept so much to herself. She didn't even belong to the Ladies' Aid. I suppose she felt she couldn't do her part, and then you don't enjoy things when you feel shabby. I heard she used to wear pretty clothes and be lively, when she was Minnie Foster, one of the town girls singing in the choir. But that—oh, that was thirty years ago. This all you was to take in?

MRS. PETERS. She said she wanted an apron. Funny thing to want, for there isn't much to get you dirty in jail, goodness knows. But I suppose just to make her feel more natural. (*Crosses to cupboard*). She said they was in the top drawer in this cupboard. Yes, here. And then her little shawl that always hung behind the door.

(*Opens stair door and looks*). Yes, here it is. (*Quickly shuts door leading upstairs.*)

MRS. HALE (*abruptly moving toward her*). Mrs. Peters?

MRS. PETERS. Yes, Mrs. Hale? (*At* U. R. *door.*)

MRS. HALE. Do you think she did it?

MRS. PETERS (*in a frightened voice*). Oh, I don't know.

MRS. HALE. Well, I don't think she did. Asking for an apron and her little shawl. Worrying about her fruit.

MRS. PETERS (*starts to speak, glances up, where footsteps are heard in the room above. In a low voice*). Mr. Peters says it looks bad for her. Mr. Henderson is awful sarcastic in a speech and he'll make fun of her sayin' she didn't wake up.

MRS. HALE. Well, I guess John Wright didn't wake when they was slipping that rope under his neck.

MRS. PETERS (*crossing slowly to table and placing shawl and apron on table with other clothing*). No, it's strange. It must have been done awful crafty and still. They say it was such a—funny way to kill a man, rigging it all up like that.

MRS. HALE (*crossing to left of* MRS. PETERS *at table*). That's just what Mr. Hale said. There was a gun in the house. He says that's what he can't understand.

MRS. PETERS. Mr. Henderson said coming out that what was needed for the case was a motive; something to show anger, or—sudden feeling.

MRS. HALE (*who is standing by the table*). Well, I don't see any signs of anger around here. (*She puts her hand on the dish towel which lies on the table, stands looking down at table, one-half of which is clean, the other half messy*). It's wiped to here. (*Makes a move as if to finish work, then turns and looks at loaf of bread outside the breadbox. Drops towel. In that voice of coming back to familiar things*). Wonder how they are finding things upstairs. (*Crossing below table to* D. R.). I hope she had it a little more red-up up there. You know, it seems kind of *sneaking*. Locking her up in town and then coming out here and trying to get her own house to turn against her!

MRS. PETERS. But, Mrs. Hale, the law is the law.

MRS. HALE. I s'pose 'tis. (*Unbuttoning her coat*). Better loosen up your things, Mrs. Peters. You won't feel them when you go out. (MRS. PETERS *takes off her fur tippet, goes to hang it on chair back left of table, stands looking at the work basket on floor near* D. L. *window.*)

MRS. PETERS. She was piecing a quilt. (*She brings the large sewing basket to the center table and they look at the bright pieces,* MRS. HALE *above the table and* MRS. PETERS *left of it.*)

MRS. HALE. It's a log cabin pattern. Pretty, isn't it? I wonder if she was goin' to quilt it or just knot it? (*Footsteps have been heard coming down the stairs. The* SHERIFF *enters followed by* HALE *and the* COUNTY ATTORNEY.)

SHERIFF. They wonder if she was going to quilt it or just knot it! (*The men laugh, the women look abashed.*)

COUNTY ATTORNEY (*rubbing his hands over the stove*). Frank's fire didn't do much up there, did it? Well, let's go out to the barn and get that cleared up. (*The men go outside by* U. L. *door.*)

MRS. HALE (*resentfully*). I don't know as there's anything so strange, our takin' up our time with little things while we're waiting for them to get the evidence. (*She sits in chair right of table smoothing out a block with decision*). I don't see as it's anything to laugh about.

MRS. PETERS (*apologetically*). Of course they've got awful important things on their minds. (*Pulls up a chair and joins* MRS. HALE *at the left of the table.*)

MRS. HALE (*examining another block*). Mrs. Peters, look at this one. Here, this is the one she was working on, and look at the sewing! All the rest of it has been so nice and even. And look at this! It's all over the place! Why, it looks as if she didn't know what she was about! (*After

*she has said this they look at each other, then start to
glance back at the door. After an instant* MRS. HALE
has pulled at a knot and ripped the sewing.)

MRS. PETERS. Oh, what are you doing, Mrs. Hale?

MRS. HALE (*mildly*). Just pulling out a stitch or two that's
not sewed very good. (*Threading a needle*). Bad sewing
always made me fidgety.

MRS. PETERS (*with a glance at door, nervously*). I don't
think we ought to touch things.

MRS. HALE. I'll just finish up this end. (*Suddenly stopping
and leaning forward*). Mrs. Peters?

MRS. PETERS. Yes, Mrs. Hale?

MRS. HALE. What do you suppose she was so nervous about?

MRS. PETERS. Oh—I don't know. I don't know as she was
nervous. I sometimes sew awful queer when I'm just
tired. (MRS. HALE *starts to say something, looks at* MRS.
PETERS, *then goes on sewing*). Well, I must get these
things wrapped up. They may be through sooner than
we think. (*Putting apron and other things together*). I
wonder where I can find a piece of paper, and string.
(*Rises.*)

MRS. HALE. In that cupboard, maybe.

MRS. PETERS (*crosses* R. *looking in cupboard*). Why,
here's a bird-cage. (*Holds it up*). Did she have a bird,
Mrs. Hale?

MRS. HALE. Why, I don't know whether she did or not—
I've not been here for so long. There was a man around
last year selling canaries cheap, but I don't know as
she took one; maybe she did. She used to sing real pretty
herself.

MRS. PETERS (*glancing around*). Seems funny to think of a
bird here. But she must have had one, or why would
she have a cage? I wonder what happened to it?

MRS. HALE. I s'pose maybe the cat got it.

MRS. PETERS. No, she didn't have a cat. She's got that feeling some people have about cats—being afraid of them. My cat got in her room and she was real upset and asked me to take it out.

MRS. HALE. My sister Bessie was like that. Queer, ain't it?

MRS. PETERS (*examining the cage*). Why, look at this door. It's broke. One hinge is pulled apart. (*Takes a step down to* MRS. HALE'S *right.*)

MRS. HALE (*looking too*). Looks as if someone must have been rough with it.

MRS. PETERS. Why, yes. (*She brings the cage forward and puts it on the table.*)

MRS. HALE (*glancing toward* U. L. *door*). I wish if they're going to find any evidence they'd be about it. I don't like this place.

MRS. PETERS. But I'm awful glad you came with me, Mrs. Hale. It would be lonesome for me sitting here alone.

MRS. HALE. It would, wouldn't it? (*Dropping her sewing*). But I tell you what I do wish, Mrs. Peters. I wish I had come over sometimes when *she* was here. I—(*looking around the room*)—wish I had.

MRS. PETERS. But of course you were awful busy, Mrs. Hale—your house and your children.

MRS. HALE (*rises and crosses* L.). I could've come. I stayed away because it weren't cheerful—and that's why I ought to have come. I—(*looking out* L. *window*)—I've never liked this place. Maybe because it's down in a hollow and you don't see the road. I dunno what it is, but it's a lonesome place and always was. I wish I had come over to see Minnie Foster sometimes. I can see now—— (*Shakes her head.*)

MRS. PETERS (*left of table and above it*). Well, you mustn't reproach yourself, Mrs. Hale. Somehow we just don't see how it is with other folks until—something turns up.

MRS. HALE. Not having children makes less work—but it makes a quiet house, and Wright out to work all day, and no company when he did come in. (*Turning from window*). Did you know John Wright, Mrs. Peters?

MRS. PETERS. Not to know him; I've seen him in town. They say he was a good man.

MRS. HALE. Yes—good; he didn't drink, and kept his word as well as most, I guess, and paid his debts. But he was a hard man, Mrs. Peters. Just to pass the time of day with him—— (*Shivers*). Like a raw wind that gets to the bone. (*Pauses, her eye falling on the cage*). I should think she would 'a' wanted a bird. But what do you suppose went with it?

MRS. PETERS. I don't know, unless it got sick and died. (*She reaches over and swings the broken door, swings it again, both women watch it.*)

MRS. HALE. You weren't raised round here, were you? (MRS. PETERS *shakes her head*). You didn't know—her?

MRS. PETERS. Not till they brought her yesterday.

MRS. HALE. She—come to think of it, she was kind of like a bird herself—real sweet and pretty, but kind of timid and—fluttery. How—she—did—change. (*Silence; then as if struck by a happy thought and relieved to get back to everyday things. Crosses* R. *above* MRS. PETERS *to cupboard, replaces small chair used to stand on to its original place* D. R.). Tell you what, Mrs. Peters, why don't you take the quilt in with you? It might take up her mind.

MRS. PETERS. Why, I think that's a real nice idea, Mrs. Hale. There couldn't possibly be any objection to it, could there? Now, just what would I take? I wonder if her patches are in here—and her things. (*They look in the sewing basket.*)

MRS. HALE (*crosses to right of table*). Here's some red. I expect this has got sewing things in it. (*Brings out a fancy box*). What a pretty box. Looks like something somebody would give you. Maybe her scissors are in here. (*Opens box. Suddenly puts her hand to her nose*). Why—— (MRS. PETERS *bends nearer, then turns her face away*). There's something wrapped up in this piece of silk.

MRS. PETERS. Why, this isn't her scissors.

MRS. HALE (*lifting the silk*). Oh, Mrs. Peters—it's—— (MRS. PETERS *bends closer.*)

MRS. PETERS. It's the bird.

MRS. HALE. But, Mrs. Peters—look at it! Its neck! Look at its neck! It's all—other side *to.*

MRS. PETERS. Somebody—wrung—its—neck. (*Their eyes meet. A look of growing comprehension, of horror. Steps are heard outside.* MRS. HALE *slips box under quilt pieces, and sinks into her chair. Enter* SHERIFF *and* COUNTY ATTORNEY. MRS. PETERS *steps* D. L. *and stands looking out of window.*)

COUNTY ATTORNEY (*as one turning from serious things to little pleasantries*). Well, ladies, have you decided whether she was going to quilt it or knot it? (*Crosses to* C. *above table.*)

MRS. PETERS. We think she was going to—knot it. (SHERIFF *crosses to right of stove, lifts stove lid and glances at fire, then stands warming hands at stove.*)

COUNTY ATTORNEY. Well, that's interesting, I'm sure. (*Seeing the bird-cage*). Has the bird flown?

MRS. HALE (*putting more quilt pieces over the box*). We think the—cat got it.

COUNTY ATTORNEY (*preoccupied*). Is there a cat? (MRS. HALE *glances in a quick covert way at* MRS. PETERS.)

MRS. PETERS (*turning from window takes a step in*). Well, not *now.* They're superstitious, you know. They leave.

COUNTY ATTORNEY (*to* SHERIFF PETERS, *continuing an interrupted conversation*). No sign at all of anyone having come from the outside. Their own rope. Now let's go up again and go over it piece by piece. (*They start upstairs*). It would have to have been someone who knew just the—— (MRS. PETERS *sits down left of table. The two women sit there not looking at one another, but as if*

*peering into something and at the same time holding
back. When they talk now it is in the manner of feeling
their way over strange ground, as if afraid of what they
are saying, but as if they cannot help saying it.)*

MRS. HALE (*hesitatively and in hushed voice*). She liked the
bird. She was going to bury it in that pretty box.

MRS. PETERS (*in a whisper*). When I was a girl—my kitten
—there was a boy took a hatchet, and before my eyes—
and before I could get there—— (*Covers her face an instant*). If they hadn't held me back I would have—
(*catches herself, looks upstairs where steps are heard,
falters weakly*)—hurt him.

MRS. HALE (*with a slow look around her*). I wonder how it
would seem never to have had any children around.
(*Pause*). No, Wright wouldn't like the bird—a thing that
sang. She used to sing. He killed that, too.

MRS. PETERS (*moving uneasily*). We don't know who killed
the bird.

MRS. HALE. I knew John Wright.

MRS. PETERS. It was an awful thing was done in this house
that night, Mrs. Hale. Killing a man while he slept,
slipping a rope around his neck that choked the life out
of him.

MRS. HALE. His neck. Choked the life out of him. (*Her
hand goes out and rests on the bird-cage.*)

MRS. PETERS (*with rising voice*). We don't know who
killed him. We don't *know*.

MRS. HALE (*her own feeling not interrupted*). If there'd
been years and years of nothing, then a bird to sing to
you, it would be awful—still, after the bird was still.

MRS. PETERS (*something within her speaking*). I know what
stillness is. When we homesteaded in Dakota, and my
first baby died—after he was two years old, and me with
no other then——

MRS. HALE (*moving*). How soon do you suppose they'll be
through looking for the evidence?

MRS. PETERS. I know what stillness is. (*Pulling herself back*). The law has got to punish crime, Mrs. Hale.

MRS. HALE (*not as if answering that*). I wish you'd seen Minnie Foster when she wore a white dress with blue ribbons and stood up there in the choir and sang. (*A look around the room*). Oh, I *wish* I'd come over here once in a while! That was a crime! That was a crime! Who's going to punish that?

MRS. PETERS (*looking upstairs*). We mustn't—take on.

MRS. HALE. I might have known she needed help! I know how things can be—for women. I tell you, it's queer, Mrs. Peters. We live close together and we live far apart. We all go through the same things—it's all just a different kind of the same thing. (*Brushes her eyes, noticing the jar of fruit, reaches out for it*). If I was you I wouldn't tell her her fruit was gone. Tell her it *ain't*. Tell her it's all right. Take this in to prove it to her. She—she may never know whether it was broke or not.

MRS. PETERS (*takes the jar, looks about for something to wrap it in; takes petticoat from the clothes brought from the other room, very nervously begins winding this around the jar. In a false voice*). My, it's a good thing the men couldn't hear us. Wouldn't they just laugh! Getting all stirred up over a little thing like a—dead canary. As if that could have anything to do with—with—wouldn't they *laugh*! (*The men are heard coming downstairs.*)

MRS. HALE (*under her breath*). Maybe they would—maybe they wouldn't.

COUNTY ATTORNEY. No, Peters, it's all perfectly clear except a reason for doing it. But you know juries when it comes to women. If there was some definite thing. (*Crosses slowly to above table*. SHERIFF *crosses* D. R. MRS. HALE *and* MRS. PETERS *remain seated at either side of table*). Something to show—something to make a story about—a thing that would connect up with this strange way of doing it—— (*The women's eyes meet for an instant. Enter* HALE *from outer door.*)

HALE (*remaining* U. L. *by door*). Well, I've got the team around. Pretty cold out there.

COUNTY ATTORNEY. I'm going to stay awhile by myself. (*To the* SHERIFF). You can send Frank out for me, can't you? I want to go over everything. I'm not satisfied that we can't do better.

SHERIFF. Do you want to see what Mrs. Peters is going to take in? (*The* LAWYER *picks up the apron, laughs.*)

COUNTY ATTORNEY. Oh, I guess they're not very dangerous things the ladies have picked out. (*Moves a few things about, disturbing the quilt pieces which cover the box. Steps back*). No, Mrs. Peters doesn't need supervising. For that matter a sheriff's wife is married to the law. Ever think of it that way, Mrs. Peters?

MRS. PETERS. Not—just that way.

SHERIFF (*chuckling*). Married to the law. (*Moves to* D. R. *door to the other room*). I just want you to come in here a minute, George. We ought to take a look at these windows.

COUNTY ATTORNEY (*scoffingly*). Oh, windows!

SHERIFF. We'll be right out, Mr. Hale. (HALE *goes outside. The* SHERIFF *follows the* COUNTY ATTORNEY *into the other room. Then* MRS. HALE *rises, hands tight together, looking intensely at* MRS. PETERS, *whose eyes make a slow turn, finally meeting* MRS. HALE'S. *A moment* MRS. HALE *holds her, then her own eyes point the way to where the box is concealed. Suddenly* MRS. PETERS *throws back quilt pieces and tries to put the box in the bag she is carrying. It is too big. She opens box, starts to take bird out, cannot touch it, goes to pieces, stands there helpless. Sound of a knob turning in the other room.* MRS. HALE *snatches the box and puts it in the pocket of her big coat. Enter* COUNTY ATTORNEY *and* SHERIFF, *who remains* D. R.)

COUNTY ATTORNEY (*crosses to* U. L. *door facetiously*). Well, Henry, at least we found out that she was not going to quilt it. She was going to—what is it you call it, ladies?

MRS. HALE (*standing* C. *below table facing front, her hand against her pocket*). We call it—knot it, Mr. Henderson.

CURTAIN

THE UGLY DUCKLING

by A. A. Milne

CHARACTERS

THE KING
THE QUEEN
THE PRINCESS CAMILLA
THE CHANCELLOR
DULCIBELLA
PRINCE SIMON
CARLO

THE UGLY DUCKLING

The SCENE *is the Throne Room of the Palace; a room of
many doors, or, if preferred, curtain-openings: simply furnished with three thrones for Their Majesties and Her
Royal Highness the* PRINCESS CAMILLA—*in other words,
with three handsome chairs. At each side is a long seat:
reserved, as it might be, for His Majesty's Council (if any),
but useful, as to-day, for other purposes. The* KING *is
asleep on his throne with a handkerchief over his face. He
is a king of any country from any story-book, in whatever
costume you please. But he should be wearing his crown.*

A VOICE (*announcing*). His Excellency the Chancellor!
(*The* CHANCELLOR, *an elderly man in horn-rimmed spectacles, enters, bowing. The* KING *wakes up with a start
and removes the handkerchief from his face.*)

KING (*with simple dignity*). I was thinking.

CHANCELLOR (*bowing*). Never, Your Majesty, was greater
need for thought than now.

KING. That's what I was thinking. (*He struggles into a more
dignified position*). Well, what is it? More trouble?

CHANCELLOR. What we might call the old trouble, Your
Majesty.

KING. It's what I was saying last night to the Queen. "Uneasy lies the head that wears a crown," was how I put it.

CHANCELLOR. A profound and original thought, which may
well go down to posterity.

KING. You mean it may go down well with posterity. I hope
so. Remind me to tell you some time of another little
thing I said to Her Majesty: something about a fierce
light beating on a throne. Posterity would like that, too.
Well, what is it?

CHANCELLOR. It is in the matter of Her Royal Highness'
wedding.

KING. Oh . . . yes.

CHANCELLOR. As Your Majesty is aware, the young Prince Simon arrives to-day to seek Her Royal Highness' hand in marriage. He has been travelling in distant lands and, as I understand, has not—er—has not—

KING. You mean he hasn't heard anything.

CHANCELLOR. It is a little difficult to put this tactfully, Your Majesty.

KING. Do your best, and I will tell you afterwards how you got on.

CHANCELLOR. Let me put it this way. The Prince Simon will naturally assume that Her Royal Highness has the customary—so customary as to be, in my own poor opinion, slightly monotonous—has what one might call the inevitable—so inevitable as to be, in my opinion again, almost mechanical—will assume, that she has the, as I think of it, faultily faultless, icily regular, splendidly—

KING. What you are trying to say in the fewest words possible is that my daughter is not beautiful.

CHANCELLOR. Her beauty is certainly elusive, Your Majesty.

KING. It is. It has eluded you, it has eluded me, it has eluded everybody who has seen her. It even eluded the Court Painter. His last words were, "Well, I did my best." His successor is now painting the view across the water-meadows from the West Turret. He says that his doctor has advised him to keep to landscape.

CHANCELLOR. It is unfortunate, Your Majesty, but there it is. One just cannot understand how it can have occurred.

KING. You don't think she takes after *me*, at all? You don't detect a likeness?

CHANCELLOR. Most certainly not, Your Majesty.

KING. Good. . . . Your predecessor did.

CHANCELLOR. I have often wondered what happened to my predecessor.

KING. Well, now you know. (*There is a short silence.*)

CHANCELLOR. Looking at the bright side, although Her Royal Highness is not, strictly speaking, beautiful——

KING. Not, truthfully speaking, beautiful——

CHANCELLOR. Yet she has great beauty of character.

KING. My dear Chancellor, we are not considering Her Royal Highness' character, but her chances of getting married. You observe that there is a distinction.

CHANCELLOR. Yes, Your Majesty.

KING. Look at it from the suitor's point of view. If a girl is beautiful, it is easy to assume that she has, tucked away inside her, an equally beautiful character. But it is impossible to assume that an unattractive girl, however elevated in character, has, tucked away inside her, an equally beautiful face. That is, so to speak, not where you want it—tucked away.

CHANCELLOR. Quite so, Your Majesty.

KING. This doesn't, of course, alter the fact that the Princess Camilla is quite the nicest person in the Kingdom.

CHANCELLOR (*enthusiastically*). She is indeed, Your Majesty. (*Hurriedly*). With the exception, I need hardly say, of Your Majesty—and Her Majesty.

KING. Your exceptions are tolerated for their loyalty and condemned for their extreme fatuity.

CHANCELLOR. Thank you, Your Majesty.

KING. As an adjective for your King, the word "nice" is ill-chosen. As an adjective for Her Majesty, it is—ill-chosen. (*At which moment* HER MAJESTY *comes in. The* KING *rises. The* CHANCELLOR *puts himself at right angles*.)

QUEEN (*briskly*). Ah. Talking about Camilla? (*She sits down*.)

KING (*returning to his throne*). As always, my dear, you are right.

QUEEN (*to* CHANCELLOR). This fellow, Simon—— What's he like?

CHANCELLOR. Nobody has seen him, Your Majesty.

QUEEN. How old is he?

CHANCELLOR. Five-and-twenty, I understand.

QUEEN. In twenty-five years he must have been seen by somebody.

KING (*to the* CHANCELLOR). Just a fleeting glimpse.

CHANCELLOR. I meant, Your Majesty, that no detailed report of him has reached this country, save that he has the usual personal advantages and qualities expected of a Prince, and has been travelling in distant and dangerous lands.

QUEEN. Ah! Nothing gone wrong with his eyes? Sunstroke or anything?

CHANCELLOR. Not that I am aware of, Your Majesty. At the same time, as I was venturing to say to His Majesty, Her Royal Highness' character and disposition are so outstandingly——

QUEEN. Stuff and nonsense. You remember what happened when we had the Tournament of Love last year.

CHANCELLOR. I was not myself present, Your Majesty. I had not then the honour of—I was abroad, and never heard the full story.

QUEEN. No; it was the other fool. They all rode up to Camilla to pay their homage—it was the first time they had seen her. The heralds blew their trumpets, and announced that she would marry whichever Prince was left master of the field when all but one had been unhorsed. The trumpets were blown again, they charged enthusiastically into the fight, and—— (*The* KING *looks nonchalantly at the ceiling and whistles a few bars.*)—don't do that.

KING. I'm sorry, my dear.

QUEEN (*to* CHANCELLOR). And what happened? They all simultaneously fell off their horses and assumed a posture of defeat.

KING. One of them was not quite so quick as the others. I was very quick. I proclaimed him the victor.

QUEEN. At the Feast of Betrothal held that night—

KING. We were all very quick.

QUEEN. The Chancellor announced that by the laws of the country the successful suitor had to pass a further test. He had to give the correct answer to a riddle.

CHANCELLOR. Such undoubtedly is the fact, Your Majesty.

KING. There are times for announcing facts, and times for looking at things in a broadminded way. Please remember that, Chancellor.

CHANCELLOR. Yes, Your Majesty.

QUEEN. I invented the riddle myself. Quite an easy one. What is it which has four legs and barks like a dog? The answer is, "A dog."

KING (to CHANCELLOR). You see that?

CHANCELLOR. Yes, Your Majesty.

KING. It isn't difficult.

QUEEN. He, however, seemed to find it so. He said an eagle. Then he said a serpent; a very high mountain with slippery sides; two peacocks; a moonlight night; the day after to-morrow—

KING. Nobody could accuse him of not trying.

QUEEN. *I* did.

KING. I *should* have said that nobody could fail to recognize in his attitude an appearance of doggedness.

QUEEN. Finally he said "Death." I nudged the King—

KING. Accepting the word "nudge" for the moment, I rubbed my ankle with one hand, clapped him on the shoulder with the other, and congratulated him on the correct answer. He disappeared under the table, and, personally, I never saw him again.

QUEEN. His body was found in the moat next morning.

CHANCELLOR. But what was he doing in the moat, Your Majesty?

KING. Bobbing about. Try not to ask needless questions.

CHANCELLOR. It all seems so strange.

QUEEN. What does?

CHANCELLOR. That Her Royal Highness, alone of all the Princesses one has ever heard of, should lack that invariable attribute of Royalty, supreme beauty.

QUEEN (*to the* KING). That was your Great-Aunt Malkin. She came to the christening. You know what she said.

KING. It was cryptic. Great-Aunt Malkin's besetting weakness. She came to *my* christening—she was one hundred and one then, and that was fifty-one years ago. (*To the* CHANCELLOR). How old would that make her?

CHANCELLOR. One hundred and fifty-two, Your Majesty.

KING (*after thought*). About that, yes. She promised me that when I grew up I should have all the happiness which my wife deserved. It struck me at the time—well, when I say "at the time," I was only a week old—but it did strike me as soon as anything could strike me—I mean of that nature—well, work it out for yourself, Chancellor. It opens up a most interesting field of speculation. Though naturally I have not liked to go into it at all deeply with Her Majesty.

QUEEN. I never heard anything less cryptic. She was wishing you extreme happiness.

KING. I don't think she was *wishing* me anything. However.

CHANCELLOR (*to the* QUEEN). But what, Your Majesty, did she wish Her Royal Highness?

QUEEN. Her other godmother—on my side—had promised her the dazzling beauty for which all the women in my family are famous—— (*She pauses, and the* KING *snaps his fingers surreptitiously in the direction of the* CHANCELLOR.)

CHANCELLOR (*hurriedly*). Indeed, yes, Your Majesty. (*The* KING *relaxes.*)

QUEEN. And Great-Aunt Malkin said—(*to the* KING)—what were the words?

KING.

> I give you with this kiss
> A wedding-day surprise.
> Where ignorance is bliss
> 'Tis folly to be wise.

I thought the last two lines rather neat. But what it *meant*——

QUEEN. We can all see what it meant. She was given beauty—and where is it? Great-Aunt Malkin took it away from her. The wedding-day surprise is that there will never be a wedding day.

KING. Young men being what they are, my dear, it would be much more surprising if there *were* a wedding day. So how—— (*The* PRINCESS *comes in. She is young, happy, healthy, but not beautiful. Or let us say that by some trick of make-up or arrangement of hair she seems plain to us: unlike the* PRINCESS *of the story-books.*)

PRINCESS (*to the* KING). Hallo, darling! (*Seeing the others*). Oh, I say! Affairs of state? Sorry.

KING (*holding out his hand*). Don't go, Camilla. (*She takes his hand.*)

CHANCELLOR. Shall I withdraw, Your Majesty?

QUEEN. You are aware, Camilla, that Prince Simon arrives to-day?

PRINCESS. He has arrived. They're just letting down the drawbridge.

KING (*jumping up*). Arrived! I must——

PRINCESS. Darling, you know what the drawbridge is like. It takes at *least* half an hour to let it down.

KING (*sitting down*). It wants oil. (*To the* CHANCELLOR). Have *you* been grudging it oil?

PRINCESS. It wants a new drawbridge, darling.

CHANCELLOR. Have I Your Majesty's permission——

KING. Yes, yes. (*The* CHANCELLOR *bows and goes out.*)

QUEEN. You've told him, of course? It's the only chance.

KING. Er—no. I was just going to, when——

QUEEN. Then I'd better. (*She goes to the door*). You can explain to the girl; I'll have her sent to you. You've told Camilla?

KING. Er—no. I was just going to, when——

QUEEN. Then you'd better tell her now.

KING. My dear, are you sure——

QUEEN. It's the only chance left. (*Dramatically to heaven*). My daughter! (*She goes out. There is a little silence when she is gone.*)

KING. Camilla, I want to talk seriously to you about marriage.

PRINCESS. Yes, father.

KING. It is time that you learnt some of the facts of life.

PRINCESS. Yes, father.

KING. Now the great fact about marriage is that once you're married you live happy ever after. All our history books affirm this.

PRINCESS. And your own experience too, darling.

KING (*with dignity*). Let us confine ourselves to history for the moment.

PRINCESS. Yes, father.

KING. Of course, there *may* be an exception here and there, which, as it were, proves the rule; just as—oh, well, never mind.

PRINCESS (*smiling*). Go on, darling. You were going to say that an exception here and there proves the rule that all princesses are beautiful.

KING. Well—leave that for the moment. The point is that it doesn't matter *how* you marry, or *who* you marry, as long as you *get* married. Because you'll be happy ever after in any case. Do you follow me so far?

PRINCESS. Yes, father.

KING. Well, your mother and I have a little plan——

PRINCESS. Was that it, going out of the door just now?

KING. Er—yes. It concerns your waiting-maid.

PRINCESS. Darling, I have several.

KING. Only one that leaps to the eye, so to speak. The one with the—well, with everything.

PRINCESS. Dulcibella?

KING. That's the one. It is our little plan that at the first meeting she should pass herself off as the Princess—a harmless ruse, of which you will find frequent record in the history books—and allure Prince Simon to his— that is to say, bring him up to the—— In other words, the wedding will take place immediately afterwards, and as quietly as possible—well, naturally in view of the fact that your Aunt Malkin is one hundred and fifty-two; and since you will be wearing the family bridal veil—which is no doubt how the custom arose—the surprise after the ceremony will be his. Are you following me at all? Your attention seems to be wandering.

PRINCESS. I was wondering why you needed to tell me.

KING. Just a precautionary measure, in case you happened to meet the Prince or his attendant before the ceremony; in which case, of course, you would pass yourself off as the maid——

PRINCESS. A harmless ruse, of which, also, you will find frequent record in the history books.

KING. Exactly. But the occasion need not arise.

A VOICE (*announcing*). The woman Dulcibella!

KING. Ah! (*To the* PRINCESS). Now, Camilla, if you will just retire to your own apartments, I will come to you there when we are ready for the actual ceremony. (*He leads her out as he is talking; and as he returns calls out*). Come in, my dear! (DULCIBELLA *comes in. She is beautiful, but dumb*). Now don't be frightened, there is nothing to be frightened about. Has Her Majesty told you what you have to do?

DULCIBELLA. Y-yes, Your Majesty.

KING. Well now, let's see how well you can do it. You are sitting here, we will say. (*He leads her to a seat*). Now imagine that I am Prince Simon. (*He curls his moustache and puts his stomach in. She giggles*). You are the beautiful Princess Camilla whom he has never seen. (*She giggles again*). This is a serious moment in your life, and you will find that a giggle will not be helpful. (*He goes to the door*). I am announced: "His Royal Highness Prince Simon!" That's me being announced. Remember what I said about giggling. You should have a far-away look upon the face. (*She does her best*). Farther away than that. (*She tries again*). No, that's too far. You are sitting there, thinking beautiful thoughts—in maiden meditation, fancy-free, as I remember saying to Her Majesty once . . . speaking of somebody else . . . fancy-free, but with the mouth definitely shut—that's better. I advance and fall upon one knee. (*He does so*). You extend your hand graciously—*graciously; you're not trying to push him in the face—that's better, and I raise it to my lips—so—and I kiss it—(*he kisses it warmly*)—no, perhaps not so ardently as that, more like this (*he kisses it again*), and I say, "Your Royal Highness, this is the most—er—— Your Royal Highness, I shall ever be—no— Your Royal Highness, it is the proudest——" Well, the point is that *he* will say it, and it will be something complimentary, and then he will take your hand in both of his, and press it to his heart. (*He does so*). And then—what do *you* say?

DULCIBELLA. Cool

KING. No, *not* Coo.

DULCIBELLA. Never had anyone do *that* to me before.

KING. That also strikes the wrong note. What you want to say is, "Oh, Prince Simon!" . . . Say it.

DULCIBELLA (*loudly*). Oh, Prince Simon!

KING. No, no. You don't need to shout until he has said "What?" two or three times. Always consider the possibility that he *isn't* deaf. Softly, and giving the words a dying fall, letting them play around his head like a flight of doves.

DULCIBELLA (*still a little overloud*). O-o-o-o-h, Prinsimon!

KING. Keep the idea in your mind of a flight of *doves* rather than a flight of panic-stricken elephants, and you will be all right. Now I'm going to get up, and you must, as it were, *waft* me into a seat by your side. (*She starts wafting*). *Not* rescuing a drowning man, that's another idea altogether, useful at times, but at the moment inappropriate. Wafting. Prince Simon will put the necessary muscles into play—all you require to do is to indicate by a gracious movement of the hand the seat you require him to take. Now! (*He gets up, a little stiffly, and sits next to her*). That was better. Well, here we are. Now, I think you give me a look: something, let us say, half-way between the breathless adoration of a nun and the voluptuous abandonment of a woman of the world; with an undertone of regal dignity, touched, as it were, with good comradeship. Now try that. (*She gives him a vacant look of bewilderment*). Frankly, that didn't quite get it. There was just a little something missing. An absence, as it were, of all the qualities I asked for, and in their place an odd resemblance to an unsatisfied fish. Let us try to get at it another way. Dulcibella, have you a young man of your own?

DULCIBELLA (*eagerly, seizing his hand*). Oo, yes, he's ever so smart, he's an archer, well not as you might say a real archer, he works in the armoury, but old Bottlenose, *you* know who I mean, the Captain of the Guard, says the very next man they ever has to shoot, my Eg shall take his place, knowing Father and how it is with Eg and me, and me being maid to Her Royal Highness and can't marry me till he's a real soldier, but ever so loving, and funny like, the things he says, I said to him once, "Eg," I said——

KING (*getting up*). I rather fancy, Dulcibella, that if you think of Eg all the time, *say* as little as possible, and, when thinking of Eg, see that the mouth is not more than partially open, you will do very well. I will show you where you are to sit and wait for His Royal Highness. (*He leads her out. On the way he is saying*). Now remember—*waft—waft*—not *hoick*. (PRINCE SIMON *wanders in from the back unannounced. He is a very ordinary-looking young man in rather dusty clothes. He gives a deep sigh of relief as he sinks into the* KING's *throne.* . . . CAMILLA, *a new and strangely beautiful* CAMILLA, *comes in.*)

PRINCESS (*surprised*). Well!

PRINCE. Oh, hallo!

PRINCESS. Ought you?

PRINCE (*getting up*). Do sit down, won't you?

PRINCESS. Who are you, and how did you get here?

PRINCE. Well, that's rather a long story. Couldn't we sit down? You could sit here if you liked, but it isn't very comfortable.

PRINCESS. That is the King's Throne.

PRINCE. Oh, is that what it is?

PRINCESS. Thrones are not meant to be comfortable.

PRINCE. Well, I don't know if they're meant to be, but they certainly aren't.

PRINCESS. Why were you sitting on the King's Throne, and who are you?

PRINCE. My name is Carlo.

PRINCESS. Mine is Dulcibella.

PRINCE. Good. And now couldn't we sit down?

PRINCESS (*sitting down on the long seat to the left of the throne and, as it were, wafting him to a place next to her*). You may sit here, if you like. Why are you so tired? (*He sits down.*)

PRINCE. I've been taking very strenuous exercise.

PRINCESS. Is that part of the long story?

PRINCE. It is.

PRINCESS (*settling herself*). I love stories.

PRINCE. This isn't a story really. You see, I'm attendant on Prince Simon, who is visiting here.

PRINCESS. Oh? I'm attendant on Her Royal Highness.

PRINCE. Then you know what he's here for.

PRINCESS. Yes.

PRINCE. She's very beautiful, I hear.

PRINCESS. Did you hear that? Where have you been lately?

PRINCE. Travelling in distant lands—with Prince Simon.

PRINCESS. Ah! All the same, I don't understand. Is Prince Simon in the Palace now? The drawbridge *can't* be down yet!

PRINCE. I don't suppose it is. *And* what a noise it makes coming down!

PRINCESS. Isn't it terrible?

PRINCE. I couldn't stand it any more. I just had to get away. That's why I'm here.

PRINCESS. But how?

PRINCE. Well, there's only one way, isn't there? That beech tree, and then a swing and a grab for the battlements, and don't ask me to remember it all—— (*He shudders.*)

PRINCESS. You mean you came across the moat by that beech tree?

PRINCE. Yes. I got so tired of hanging about.

PRINCESS. But it's terribly dangerous!

PRINCE. That's why I'm so exhausted. Nervous shock. (*He lies back and breathes loudly.*)

PRINCESS. Of course, it's different for *me*.

PRINCE (*sitting up*). Say that again. I must have got it wrong.

PRINCESS. It's different for me, because I'm used to it. Besides, I'm so much lighter.

PRINCE. You don't mean that *you*——

PRINCESS. Oh yes, often.

PRINCE. And I thought I was a brave man! At least, I didn't until five minutes ago, and now I don't again.

PRINCESS. Oh, but you are! And I think it's wonderful to do it straight off the first time.

PRINCE. Well, *you* did.

PRINCESS. Oh no, not the first time. When I was a child.

PRINCE. You mean that you crashed?

PRINCESS. Well, you only fall into the moat.

PRINCE. Only! Can you *swim?*

PRINCESS. Of course.

PRINCE. So you swam to the castle walls, and yelled for help, and they fished you out and walloped you. And next day you tried again. Well, if *that* isn't pluck——

PRINCESS. Of course I didn't. I swam back, and did it at once; I mean I tried again at once. It wasn't until the third time that I actually did it. You see, I was afraid I might lose my nerve.

PRINCE. Afraid she might lose her nerve!

PRINCESS. There's a way of getting over from this side, too; a tree grows out from the wall and you jump into another tree—I don't think it's quite so easy.

PRINCE. Not quite so easy. Good. You must show me.

PRINCESS. Oh, I will.

PRINCE. Perhaps it might be as well if you taught me how to swim first. I've often heard about swimming, but never——

PRINCESS. You can't swim?

PRINCE. No. Don't look so surprised. There are a lot of other things which I can't do. I'll tell you about them as soon as you have a couple of years to spare.

PRINCESS. You can't swim and yet you crossed by the beech tree! And you're *ever* so much heavier than I am! Now who's brave?

PRINCE (*getting up*). You keep talking about how light

you are. I must see if there's anything in it. Stand up! (*She stands obediently and he picks her up*). You're right, Dulcibella. I could hold you here for ever. (*Looking at her*). You're very lovely. Do you know how lovely you are?

PRINCESS. Yes. (*She laughs suddenly and happily.*)

PRINCE. Why do you laugh?

PRINCESS. Aren't you tired of holding me?

PRINCE. Frankly, yes. I exaggerated when I said I could hold you for ever. When you've been hanging by the arms for ten minutes over a very deep moat, wondering if it's too late to learn how to swim—(*he puts her down*)—what I meant was that I should *like* to hold you for ever. Why did you laugh?

PRINCESS. Oh, well, it was a little private joke of mine.

PRINCE. If it comes to that, I've got a private joke too. Let's exchange them.

PRINCESS. Mine's very private. One other woman in the whole world knows, and that's all.

PRINCE. Mine's just as private. One other man knows, and that's all.

PRINCESS. What fun. I love secrets. . . . Well, here's mine. When I was born, one of my godmothers promised that I should be very beautiful.

PRINCE. How right she was.

PRINCESS. But the other one said this:

> I give you with this kiss
> A wedding-day surprise.
> Where ignorance is bliss
> 'Tis folly to be wise.

And nobody knew what it meant. And I grew up very plain. And then, when I was about ten, I met my godmother in the forest one day. It was my tenth birthday. Nobody knows this—except you.

PRINCE. Except us.

PRINCESS. Except us. And she told me what her gift meant. It meant that I *was* beautiful—but everybody else was to go on being ignorant, and thinking me plain, until my wedding-day. Because, she said, she didn't want me to grow up spoilt and wilful and vain, as I should have done if everybody had always been saying how beautiful I was; and the best thing in the world, she said, was to be quite sure of yourself, but not to expect admiration from other people. So ever since then my mirror has told me I'm beautiful, and everybody else thinks me ugly, and I get a lot of fun out of it.

PRINCE. Well, seeing that Dulcibella is the result, I can only say that your godmother was very, very wise.

PRINCESS. And now tell me *your* secret.

PRINCE. It isn't such a pretty one. You see, Prince Simon was going to woo Princess Camilla, and he'd heard that she was beautiful and haughty and imperious—all *you* would have been if your godmother hadn't been so wise. And being a very ordinary-looking fellow himself, he was afraid she wouldn't think much of him, so he suggested to one of his attendants, a man called Carlo, of extremely attractive appearance, that *he* should pretend to be the Prince, and win the Princess' hand; and then at the last moment they would change places——

PRINCESS. How would they do that?

PRINCE. The Prince was going to have been married in full armour—with his visor down.

PRINCESS (*laughing happily*). Oh, what fun!

PRINCE. Neat, isn't it?

PRINCESS (*laughing*). Oh, very . . . very . . . very.

PRINCE. Neat, but not so terribly *funny*. Why do you keep laughing?

PRINCESS. Well, that's another secret.

PRINCE. If it comes to that, *I've* got another one up my sleeve. Shall we exchange again?

PRINCESS. All right. You go first this time.

PRINCE. Very well. . . . I am not Carlo. (*Standing up and speaking dramatically*). I am Simon!—*ow!* (*He sits down and rubs his leg violently.*)

PRINCESS (*alarmed*). What is it?

PRINCE. Cramp. (*In a mild voice, still rubbing*). I was saying that I was Prince Simon.

PRINCESS. Shall I rub it for you? (*She rubs.*)

PRINCE (*still hopefully*). I am Simon.

PRINCESS. Is that better?

PRINCE (*despairingly*). I am Simon.

PRINCESS. I know.

PRINCE. How did you know?

PRINCESS. Well, you told me.

PRINCE. But oughtn't you to swoon or something?

PRINCESS. Why? History records many similar ruses.

PRINCE (*amazed*). Is that so? I've never read history. I thought I was being profoundly original.

PRINCESS. Oh, no! Now I'll tell you *my* secret. For reasons very much like your own the Princess Camilla, who is held to be extremely plain, feared to meet Prince Simon. Is the drawbridge down yet?

PRINCE. Do your people give a faint, surprised cheer every time it gets down?

PRINCESS. Naturally.

PRINCE. Then it came down about three minutes ago.

PRINCESS. Ah! Then at this very moment your man Carlo is declaring his passionate love for my maid, Dulcibella. That, I think, is funny. (*So does the* PRINCE. *He laughs heartily*). Dulcibella, by the way, is in love with a man she calls Eg, so I hope Carlo isn't getting carried away.

PRINCE. Carlo is married to a girl he calls "the little woman," so Eg has nothing to fear.

PRINCESS. By the way, I don't know if you heard, but I said, or as good as said, that I am the Princess Camilla.

PRINCE. I wasn't surprised. History, of which I read a great deal, records many similar ruses.

PRINCESS (*laughing*). Simon!

PRINCE (*laughing*). Camilla! (*He stands up*). May I try holding you again? (*She nods. He takes her in his arms and kisses her*). Sweetheart!

PRINCESS. You see, when you lifted me up before, you said, "You're very lovely," and my godmother said that the first person to whom I would seem lovely was the man I should marry; so I knew then that you were Simon and I should marry you.

PRINCE. I knew directly I saw you that I should marry you, even if you were Dulcibella. By the way, which of you *am* I marrying?

PRINCESS. When she lifts her veil, it will be Camilla. (*Voices are heard outside*). Until then it will be Dulcibella.

PRINCE (*in a whisper*). Then good-bye, Camilla, until you lift your veil.

PRINCESS. Good-bye, Simon, until you raise your visor. (*The* KING *and* QUEEN *come in arm-in-arm, followed by* CARLO *and* DULCIBELLA, *also arm-in-arm. The* CHANCELLOR *precedes them, walking backwards, at a loyal angle.*)

PRINCE (*supporting the* CHANCELLOR *as an accident seems inevitable*). Careful! (*The* CHANCELLOR *turns indignantly round.*)

KING. Who and what is this? More accurately who and what are all these?

CARLO. My attendant, Carlo, Your Majesty. He will, with Your Majesty's permission, prepare me for the ceremony. (*The* PRINCE *bows.*)

KING. Of course, of course!

QUEEN (*to* DULCIBELLA). Your maid, Dulcibella, is it not, my love? (DULCIBELLA *nods violently*). I thought so.

(*To* CARLO). *She* will prepare Her Royal Highness. (*The* PRINCESS *curtsies.*)

KING. Ah, yes. Yes. *Most* important.

PRINCESS (*curtsying*). I beg pardon, Your Majesty, if I've done wrong, but I found the gentleman wandering—

KING (*crossing to her*). Quite right, my dear, quite right. (*He pinches her cheek, and takes advantage of this kingly gesture to say in a loud whisper*). We've pulled it off! (*They sit down; the* KING *and* QUEEN *on their thrones,* DULCIBELLA *on the* PRINCESS' *throne.* CARLO *stands behind* DULCIBELLA, *the* CHANCELLOR *on the* R. *of the* QUEEN, *and the* PRINCE *and* PRINCESS *behind the long seat on the left.*)

CHANCELLOR (*consulting documents*). H'r'm! Have I Your Majesty's authority to put the final test to His Royal Highness?

QUEEN (*whispering to* KING). Is this safe?

KING (*whispering*). Perfectly, my dear. I told him the answer a minute ago. (*Over his shoulder to* CARLO). Don't forget. *Dog.* (*Aloud*). Proceed, Your Excellency. It is my desire that the affairs of my country should ever be conducted in a strictly constitutional manner.

CHANCELLOR (*oratorically*). By the constitution of the country, a suitor to Her Royal Highness' hand cannot be deemed successful until he has given the correct answer to a riddle. (*Conversationally*). The last suitor answered incorrectly, and thus failed to win his bride.

KING. By a coincidence he fell into the moat.

CHANCELLOR (*to* CARLO). I have now to ask Your Royal Highness if you are prepared for the ordeal?

CARLO (*cheerfully*). Absolutely.

CHANCELLOR. I may mention, as a matter, possibly, of some slight historical interest to our visitor, that by the constitution of the country the same riddle is not allowed to be asked on two successive occasions.

KING (*startled*). What's that?

CHANCELLOR. This one, it is interesting to recall, was propounded exactly a century ago, and we must take it as a fortunate omen that it was well and truly solved.

KING (*to* QUEEN). I may want my sword directly.

CHANCELLOR. The riddle is this. What is it which has four legs and mews like a cat?

CARLO (*promptly*). A dog.

KING (*still more promptly*). Bravo, bravo! (*He claps loudly and nudges the* QUEEN, *who claps too.*)

CHANCELLOR (*peering at his documents*). According to the records of the occasion to which I referred, the correct answer would seem to be——

PRINCESS (*to* PRINCE). Say something, quick!

CHANCELLOR. —not dog, but——

PRINCE. Your Majesty, have I permission to speak? Naturally His Royal Highness could not think of justifying himself on such an occasion, but I think that with Your Majesty's gracious permission, I could——

KING. Certainly, certainly.

PRINCE. In our country, we have an animal to which we have given the name "dog," or, in the local dialect of the more mountainous districts, "doggie." It sits by the fireside and purrs.

CARLO. That's right. It purrs like anything.

PRINCE. When it needs milk, which is its staple food, it mews.

CARLO (*enthusiastically*). Mews like nobody's business.

PRINCE. It also has four legs.

CARLO. One at each corner.

PRINCE. In some countries, I understand, this animal is called a "cat." In one distant country to which His Royal Highness and I penetrated it was called by the very curious name of "hippopotamus."

CARLO. That's right. (*To the* PRINCE). Do you remember

that ginger-coloured hippopotamus which used to climb on to my shoulder and lick my ear?

PRINCE. I shall never forget it, sir. (*To the* KING). So you see, Your Majesty——

KING. Thank you. I think that makes it perfectly clear. (*Firmly to the* CHANCELLOR). You are about to agree?

CHANCELLOR. Undoubtedly, Your Majesty. May I be the first to congratulate His Royal Highness on solving the riddle so accurately?

KING. You may be the first to see that all is in order for an immediate wedding.

CHANCELLOR. Thank you, Your Majesty. (*He bows and withdraws. The* KING *rises, as do the* QUEEN *and* DULCIBELLA.)

KING (*to* CARLO). Doubtless, Prince Simon, you will wish to retire and prepare yourself for the ceremony.

CARLO. Thank you, sir.

PRINCE. Have I Your Majesty's permission to attend His Royal Highness? It is the custom of his country for Princes of the royal blood to be married in full armour, a matter which requires a certain adjustment——

KING. Of course, of course. (CARLO *bows to the* KING *and* QUEEN *and goes out. As the* PRINCE *is about to follow, the* KING *stops him*). Young man, you have a quality of quickness which I admire. It is my pleasure to reward it in any way which commends itself to you.

PRINCE. Your Majesty is ever gracious. May I ask for my reward *after* the ceremony? (*He catches the eye of the* PRINCESS, *and they give each other a secret smile.*)

KING. Certainly. (*The* PRINCE *bows and goes out. To* DULCIBELLA). Now, young woman, make yourself scarce. You've done your work excellently, and we will see that you and your—what was his name?

DULCIBELLA. Eg, Your Majesty.

KING. —that you and your Eg are not forgotten.

DULCIBELLA. Cool! (*She curtsies and goes out.*)

PRINCESS (*calling*). Wait for me, Dulcibella!

KING (*to* QUEEN). Well, my dear, we may congratulate ourselves. As I remember saying to somebody once, "You have not lost a daughter, you have gained a son." How does he strike you?

QUEEN. Stupid.

KING. They made a very handsome pair, I thought, he and Dulcibella.

QUEEN. Both stupid.

KING. I said nothing about stupidity. What I *said* was that they were both extremely handsome. That is the important thing. (*Struck by a sudden idea*). Or isn't it?

QUEEN. What do you think of Prince Simon, Camilla?

PRINCESS. I adore him. We shall be so happy together.

KING. Well, of course you will. I told you so. Happy ever after.

QUEEN. Run along now and get ready.

PRINCESS. Yes, mother. (*She throws a kiss to them and goes out.*)

KING (*anxiously*). My dear, have we been wrong about Camilla all this time? It seemed to me that she wasn't looking *quite* so plain as usual just now. Did *you* notice anything?

QUEEN (*carelessly*). Just the excitement of the marriage.

KING (*relieved*). Ah, yes, that would account for it.

CURTAIN

THE JEST OF HAHALABA

by Lord Dunsany

CHARACTERS

SIR ARTHUR STRANGWAYS
SNAGGS, *his butler*
AN ALCHEMIST
HAHALABA, *the Spirit of Laughter*

The 1928 version appeared in *Seven Modern Comedies* by Lord
Dunsany.

Reprinted by permission of Putnam & Company, Ltd., publishers, of London and New York.

THE JEST OF HAHALABA

SCENE: *The Smoking Room,* SIR ARTHUR STRANGWAYS' *house in London.* TIME: *The last moments of 1928. Bells are ringing in the New Year.* SIR ARTHUR *is in an armchair. Enter* SNAGGS, *his butler.*

SIR ARTHUR. A happy New Year to you, Snaggs.

SNAGGS. A happy New Year to you, Sir Arthur, and many of them.

SIR ARTHUR. Ah, thank you, Snaggs.

SNAGGS. There's a man to see you, Sir Arthur, who . . .

SIR ARTHUR. Oh yes, yes.

SNAGGS. . . . who says he wants to see you, Sir Arthur.

SIR ARTHUR. Yes, show him up, please.

SNAGGS. He's, if I may say so, Sir Arthur, a very strange person.

SIR ARTHUR. Yes, I know. Show him up.

SNAGGS. Very strange indeed.

SIR ARTHUR. Yes, I was expecting him.

SNAGGS. And it's very late, Sir Arthur.

SIR ARTHUR. Yes, never mind.

SNAGGS. As you wish, Sir Arthur.

SIR ARTHUR. Yes, show him up, please.

SNAGGS. As you wish. (*Exit, leaving* SIR ARTHUR *sitting thoughtful. Re-enter with the* ALCHEMIST *in a dull maroon cloak, elderly, bearded, and dressed like nobody later than Teniers.*)

SNAGGS. The man to see you, Sir Arthur. (SNAGGS *lingers.*)

SIR ARTHUR. Thank you, Snaggs. Thank you.

SNAGGS (*reluctantly dismissed*). Thank you, Sir Arthur.

SIR ARTHUR. You have the stuff? (ALCHEMIST *shows an old snuffbox and taps it, nodding his head*). And the words?

ALCHEMIST *(in a sort of whisper)*. Yes. (SIR ARTHUR *takes the snuffbox.*)

SIR ARTHUR *(extending hand)*. Give me the words.

ALCHEMIST. They may not be written. *(Re-enter* SNAGGS.*)*

SNAGGS. I will wait up, Sir Arthur, in case you should ring. If you should ring I would come at once.

SIR ARTHUR. Thank you, Snaggs. Thank you. *(Exit* SNAGGS. SIR ARTHUR *goes to door and locks it)*. You will tell me the words?

ALCHEMIST. There's laws in England against the likes of me.

SIR ARTHUR. Laws?

ALCHEMIST. Any time since the days of Edward the Confessor.

SIR ARTHUR. But you will tell me the words.

ALCHEMIST. Aye. But we must proceed softly.

SIR ARTHUR. All is quiet. We may start now.

ALCHEMIST. You have another door.

SIR ARTHUR. Oh, no one ever comes that way.

ALCHEMIST. It is better locked.

SIR ARTHUR. Perhaps it is. *(He locks it)*. Now.

ALCHEMIST. The powder then is placed upon the floor in a ring, wide enough to contain two feet, and two and a half times as wide should you dare to call up Eblis.

SIR ARTHUR. No, no. I shall not call up Eblis.

ALCHEMIST. That is something, Master. That is something. That is one thing to be thankful for in all this bad business. I couldn't have borne it, Master. His mouth alone: I couldn't have borne to look at it.

SIR ARTHUR. No, no. I do not wish to see Eblis.

ALCHEMIST. I couldn't have borne to see him.

SIR ARTHUR. You shan't see him. Tell me the words.

ALCHEMIST. Well, Master, you put the powder in a ring, wide enough to hold common feet, scarce larger than ours. And then, Master, if you must, you light it. If you must, Master, if you must. And it smoulders and the smoke goes away to the left and the right, and goes round the ring. And just as the two smokes meet, just then you say (*he whispers*). And you name the spirit that you would call up. And he must come. And he must grant one wish, the first demand that you make of him. And I wish I had never told you, and I wish I had never come.

SIR ARTHUR. Never mind that now. Let's get on with the business.

ALCHEMIST. Well, Master; then, there be many spirits. There's the spirit of Death, the spirit of Drought, the spirit of Fever.

SIR ARTHUR (*now preparing the ring*). No, no. I'll have some jolly spirit.

ALCHEMIST. Oh, Master, call up the spirit of Death, the spirit of Fever, even the spirit of Terror, but not the spirit of Laughter.

SIR ARTHUR. The spirit of Laughter? Why not? I like the sound of him. We'll have the spirit of Laughter.

ALCHEMIST. Oh, Master, not that spirit.

SIR ARTHUR. Why not?

ALCHEMIST. Why, Master, because all these spirits, they are all at enmity with man, and are over full of ingenuity: it always was so. And they sit for ages planning how to prevail against man. For ages, Master. You would hardly believe it. And when they have formed a plan they won't rest until they have tried it; you would not credit their malice. And most of all are they like this, most of all when they have been compelled to grant a wish. They are like it then most of all.

SIR ARTHUR. Then we won't have the spirit of Death.

ALCHEMIST. Oh, Master, the spirit of Laughter is the worst of all but one. His contrivances are beyond the wit of all the lesser spirits. You are not making the circle too wide, Master?

SIR ARTHUR. No, no. We'll only have the spirit of Laughter.

ALCHEMIST. Be warned, Master, and have none of him.

SIR ARTHUR. Come, tell me his name.

ALCHEMIST. Be warned, Master.

SIR ARTHUR. I've paid you well for this.

ALCHEMIST. Yes, Master, but be warned.

SIR ARTHUR. His name, then.

ALCHEMIST. His name, (oh, Master, call never upon this spirit,) his name is Hāhālābā.

SIR ARTHUR. So that's his name. The spell again. (SIR ARTHUR *now holds a matchbox.* ALCHEMIST *whispers in his ear.* SIR ARTHUR *ignites the powder and mutters the spell, ending with the name* HAHALABA. HAHALABA *steps through a curtain and stands in the ring, an athletic spirit, with small cloak slung over dark nude breast.*)

HAHALABA. What is your will of me?

ALCHEMIST. Oh, Master, nothing that he can turn to his advantage.

SIR ARTHUR. It shall be nothing. I have thought of all.

ALCHEMIST. Only a trifle, Master. Something too small for his contrivances, or . . .

SIR ARTHUR. It is only a trifle.

HAHALABA. What is your will of me?

SIR ARTHUR. Only a trifle. I wish to see a file of the *Times.*

HAHALABA. For what year?

SIR ARTHUR. For the year 1929.

ALCHEMIST. 1929!

HAHALABA (*pulling cloth from table and revealing a file of one year of the* Times). It is there.

SIR ARTHUR. Ha!

HAHALABA. Within an hour of midnight it will vanish.

SIR ARTHUR. Oh. We have not long then.

HAHALABA. It has far to go, and must be there by dawn.

SIR ARTHUR. Where?

HAHALABA. In the deeps of time. (*Exit.*)

SIR ARTHUR. Where has he gone?

ALCHEMIST. He has gone back.

SIR ARTHUR. To work, then.

ALCHEMIST (*as* SIR ARTHUR *gets half sheets and pencil and turns to the heap*). Oh, Master, I'm glad you asked for a little thing. It's a mercy, Master, a mercy.

SIR ARTHUR. A *little* thing, indeed!

ALCHEMIST. Aye, Master. For had you asked a great thing of such as him, he would have triumphed surely.

SIR ARTHUR. A little thing!

ALCHEMIST. Aye, Master, I know the ways of them.

SIR ARTHUR. A little thing, be damned. I shall make millions on this. Millions.

ALCHEMIST. Oh, Master, beware Hahalaba. Beware the spirit of Laughter.

SIR ARTHUR. I tell you I shall make millions. This alone for instance, this alone: December 31st, 1929: I see he's got December on the top the way the newspaper people keep it, they put the fresh paper on top of the one of the day before all the year round, and keep the lot like *this:* this number alone is worth all the money I've got, or you either. Patangas 104. You go down to the City and buy Patangas. But you don't understand.

ALCHEMIST. Master, I go to no city guided by Hahalaba.

SIR ARTHUR. He's got nothing to do with it. He's gone. But I read* in the *Times* that Patangas are 104. (*Jots down a word on half sheet, saying aloud "Patangas"*). I shall soon know if this file is genuine by waiting a few days and checking these. (*He lays his hand on the edges at bottom of heap.*)

---

* Present tense.

ALCHEMIST. Oh, it is genuine. He may not lie. But he is frivolous and cunning. I know Hahalaba.

SIR ARTHUR. If this is genuine (reads a line or two), as it evidently is, I shall make millions. There we are again, there we are again. Pocahontas 37. Who'd have thought it? I haven't paid you enough, old fellow. I haven't paid you enough.

ALCHEMIST. Master, I ask no more. I ask no more that comes from Hahalaba.

SIR ARTHUR. Nonsense. It comes out of the *Times*. And I'm the only man that's got a copy. November 20th this is, 1929. And the only one in the world. If you'd care for half a million you can have it. It will be nothing to me.

ALCHEMIST. No, Master. No.

SIR ARTHUR. Or a million for that matter.

ALCHEMIST. No, Master, I have no uses for it.

SIR ARTHUR. As you like. (*Lower down the file*). And here again. Tangerines at 80. Hullo. Here's old Perrot dead. He should have kept himself fit: he was no older than me. If he'd have played golf. Well, well. October 27th. —Fancy that. (*Takes another paper*). Hullo, hullo. (*Makes brief note*). I'll play hell with the Stock Exchange.

ALCHEMIST. Master.

SIR ARTHUR. Ha, ha! Lord! Bolivian United. Well, I never. (*Makes note.*)

ALCHEMIST. Master.

SIR ARTHUR. *And* Ecuador Guaranteed. Millions!

ALCHEMIST. Master.

SIR ARTHUR. Well.

ALCHEMIST. I have given you your desire, and you have paid me well. Our account is settled. May I go hence?

SIR ARTHUR. Go hence? Yes, if you like.

ALCHEMIST. Thank you, Master; for of all spirits of evil I fear most the spirit of Laughter.

SIR ARTHUR. Yes, you told me that. No one's keeping you. But wait a moment. Wait a moment. There's one thing I'll give you that you'll understand how to use. Wait a moment.

ALCHEMIST. Master, I go not to that city.

SIR ARTHUR. No, it's not the City. Wait a moment. Ah, here we have it. The Derby. Aurelian won. You back Aurelian for the Derby. (*Writes on a half sheet and gives it to* ALCHEMIST). There. Aurelian for the Derby.

ALCHEMIST. Master, I make no wager, lest in my hour of gain Hahalaba mock me. (*He puts paper down on a table*). And Master——

SIR ARTHUR. Well, never mind now. There's only a few more minutes, and I can't waste them talking. They're worth a million a minute.

ALCHEMIST. As you will, Master.

SIR ARTHUR. Well, good-bye then, and thank you very much. (ALCHEMIST *tries the door, it is locked*). Ah, the door. Give me a moment and I'll let you out. (*He takes key from pocket, but continues reading papers and making notes*). Another of them. Tromkins now. Why can't they keep themselves fit? Mexican Airways Limited! Well, well. (*Another note. Hastily turns over papers, making brief notes, till he nears the bottom of the heap*). Yes, yes. Well, that'll be enough. There's millions in it. I'll let you out now. (*Walks to the door with key in one hand, the last paper in the other.*)

ALCHEMIST. Thank you, Master, thank you.

SIR ARTHUR. And your friend Hahalaba will find it hard to laugh over this deal, for I'm the richest man in England now.

ALCHEMIST. Not yet, Master.

SIR ARTHUR. Well, I soon will be. (*Unlocks door.*)

ALCHEMIST. And Master. Read no more of these hidden

things. It is surely enough. Tempt Hahalaba no further.

SIR ARTHUR. I won't. I've read all I want. I've enough knowledge to put against the brains of all the financiers in London.

ALCHEMIST. Then read no further, Master. Put it down.

SIR ARTHUR. That? Do you know what that is? That is to-day's paper. January 1st, 1929, the last of the heap. I shall read to-day's paper before I go to bed. We're in 1929 now. Well, good-bye, and a happy New Year.

ALCHEMIST. Farewell, Master. (*Exit.* SIR ARTHUR *returns to his chair and settles down to the British habit of reading the day's* Times.)

SIR ARTHUR. Nothing of interest. Dull, I suppose, after the other. Hullo! What's this? What? What? But it can't be! But this is to-day's paper! But I'm alive! Good God. (*With breath coming short he goes to decanter of brandy, pours out, mixes, and drinks. He stands a little steadier, hand to heart now and then*). Bit of a shock that. Read that kind of thing. Silly Jugginses. Who can have been fool enough to invent a yarn like that? It's to-day's paper and I'm quite well. (*But the improvement was only momentary and he rings for* SNAGGS, *then he goes panting to the sofa and lies down*). Bit of a . . . shock, that. (*Enter* SNAGGS. *Goes to* SIR ARTHUR *on sofa. All the copies of the* Times *have vanished.*)

SNAGGS. Hullo. What's this has happened? (*Goes to table and sees* SIR ARTHUR'S *notes on half sheets*). Patangas? Mexican Airways? Nothing to account for it there. (*Almost absently he crumples them and throws them in the fire; then turns to the business in hand*). Now what should I do? (*A glance towards the sofa. Then he goes to the telephone*). Ah, would you please give me the *Times*. I don't know the number. Yes, the *Times* Office, please. Is that the *Times?* Oh, could I speak to the Editor? . . . Oh, well, perhaps he'd do. But it's important. . . . Tell him something sudden. . . . Oh, yes.

I'm butler to Sir Arthur Strangways. Mr. Snaggs is *my* name. . . . Well, I thought you'd like to know Sir Arthur has just died. . . . Sudden like. . . . Yes. (*Leaving the 'phone, he passes the other table on which* ALCHEMIST *had put down his slip. He picks it up and reads*). Aurelian for the Derby. *He's* no good.

CURTAIN

IN THE SHADOW
OF THE GLEN

by John M. Synge

CHARACTERS

DAN BURKE, *farmer and herd*
NORA BURKE, *his wife*
MICHEAL DARA, *a young herd*
A TRAMP

IN THE SHADOW OF THE GLEN

SCENE: *The last cottage at the head of a long glen in County Wicklow.*

(*Cottage kitchen; turf fire on the right; a bed near it against the wall with a body lying on it covered with a sheet. A door is at the other end of the room, with a low table near it, and stools, or wooden chairs. There are a couple of glasses on the table, and a bottle of whisky, as if for a wake, with two cups, a teapot, and a home-made cake. There is another small door near the bed.*
NORA BURKE *is moving about the room, settling a few things, and lighting candles on the table, looking now and then at the bed with an uneasy look. Some one knocks softly at the door. She takes up a stocking with money from the table and puts it in her pocket. Then she opens the door.*)

TRAMP (*outside*). Good evening to you, lady of the house.

NORA. Good evening, kindly stranger, it's a wild night, God help you, to be out in the rain falling.

TRAMP. It is, surely, and I walking to Brittas from the Aughrim fair.

NORA. Is it walking on your feet, stranger?

TRAMP. On my two feet, lady of the house, and when I saw the light below I thought maybe if you'd a sup of new milk and a quiet decent corner where a man could sleep. (*He looks in past her and sees the dead man*). The Lord have mercy on us all!

NORA. It doesn't matter anyway, stranger, come in out of the rain.

TRAMP (*coming in slowly and going towards the bed*). Is it departed he is?

NORA. It is, stranger. He's after dying on me, God forgive

him, and there I am now with a hundred sheep beyond on the hills, and no turf drawn for the winter.

TRAMP (*looking closely at the dead man*). It's a queer look is on him for a man that's dead.

NORA (*half-humorously*). He was always queer, stranger, and I suppose them that's queer and they living men will be queer bodies after.

TRAMP. Isn't it a great wonder you're letting him lie there, and he is not tidied, or laid out itself?

NORA (*coming to the bed*). I was afeard, stranger, for he put a black curse on me this morning if I'd touch his body the time he'ld die sudden, or let any one touch it except his sister only, and it's ten miles away she lives in the big glen over the hill.

TRAMP (*looking at her and nodding slowly*). It's a queer story he wouldn't let his own wife touch him, and he dying quiet in his bed.

NORA. He was an old man, and an odd man, stranger, and it's always up on the hills he was thinking thoughts in the dark mist. (*She pulls back a bit of the sheet*). Lay your hand on him now, and tell me if it's cold he is surely.

TRAMP. Is it getting the curse on me you'ld be, woman of the house? I wouldn't lay my hand on him for the Lough Nahanagan and it filled with gold.

NORA (*looking uneasily at the body*). Maybe cold would be no sign of death with the like of him, for he was always cold, every day since I knew him,—and every night, stranger,—(*she covers up his face and comes away from the bed*); but I'm thinking it's dead he is surely, for he's complaining a while back of a pain in his heart, and this morning, the time he was going off to Brittas for three days or four, he was taken with a sharp turn. Then he went into his bed and he was saying it was destroyed he was, the time the shadow was going up through the glen, and when the sun set on the bog beyond he made a great lep, and let a great cry out of him, and stiffened himself out the like of a dead sheep.

TRAMP (*crosses himself*). God rest his soul.

NORA (*pouring him out a glass of whisky*). Maybe that would do you better than the milk of the sweetest cow in County Wicklow.

TRAMP. The Almighty God reward you, and may it be to your good health. (*He drinks.*)

NORA (*giving him a pipe and tobacco*). I've no pipes saving his own, stranger, but they're sweet pipes to smoke.

TRAMP. Thank you kindly, lady of the house.

NORA. Sit down now, stranger, and be taking your rest.

TRAMP (*filling a pipe and looking about the room*). I've walked a great way through the world, lady of the house, and seen great wonders, but I never seen a wake till this day with fine spirits, and good tobacco, and the best of pipes, and no one to taste them but a woman only.

NORA. Didn't you hear me say it was only after dying on me he was when the sun went down, and how would I go out into the glen and tell the neighbours, and I a lone woman with no house near me?

TRAMP (*drinking*). There's no offence, lady of the house?

NORA. No offence in life, stranger. How would the like of you, passing in the dark night, know the lonesome way I was with no house near me at all?

TRAMP (*sitting down*). I knew rightly. (*He lights his pipe so that there is a sharp light beneath his haggard face*). And I was thinking, and I coming in through the door, that it's many a lone woman would be afeard of the like of me in the dark night, in a place wouldn't be as lonesome as this place, where there aren't two living souls would see the little light you have shining from the glass.

NORA (*slowly*). I'm thinking many would be afeard, but I never knew what way I'd be afeard of beggar or bishop or any man of you at all. (*She looks towards the window and lowers her voice*). It's other things than the like of you, stranger, would make a person afeard.

TRAMP (*looking round with a half-shudder*). It is surely, God help us all!

NORA (*looking at him for a moment with curiosity*). You're saying that, stranger, as if you were easy afeard.

TRAMP (*speaking mournfully*). Is it myself, lady of the house, that does be walking round in the long nights, and crossing the hills when the fog is on them, the time a little stick would seem as big as your arm, and a rabbit as big as a bay horse, and a stack of turf as big as a towering church in the city of Dublin? If myself was easily afeard, I'm telling you, it's long ago I'ld have been locked into the Richmond Asylum, or maybe have run up into the back hills with nothing on me but an old shirt, and been eaten with crows the like of Patch Darcy the Lord have mercy on him—in the year that's gone.

NORA (*with interest*). You knew Darcy?

TRAMP. Wasn't I the last one heard his living voice in the whole world?

NORA. There were great stories of what was heard at that time, but would any one believe the things they do be saying in the glen?

TRAMP. It was no lie, lady of the house. . . . I was passing below on a dark night the like of this night, and the sheep were lying under the ditch and every one of them coughing, and choking, like an old man, with the great rain and the fog. Then I heard a thing talking—queer talk, you wouldn't believe at all, and you out of your dreams,—and "Merciful God," says I, "if I begin hearing the like of that voice out of the thick

mist, I'm destroyed surely." Then I run, and I run, and
I run, till I was below in Rathvanna. I got drunk that
night, I got drunk in the morning, and drunk the day
after,—I was coming from the races beyond—and the
third day they found Darcy. . . . Then I knew it was
himself I was after hearing, and I wasn't afeard any
more.

NORA (*speaking sorrowfully and slowly*). God spare
Darcy, he'ld always look in here and he passing up or
passing down, and it's very lonesome I was after him a
long while (*she looks over at the bed and lowers her
voice, speaking very clearly*), and then I got happy
again—if it's ever happy we are, stranger,—for I got
used to being lonesome. (*A short pause; then she stands
up.*)

NORA. Was there any one on the last bit of the road,
stranger, and you coming from Aughrim?

TRAMP. There was a young man with a drift of mountain ewes, and he running after them this way and that.

NORA (*with a half-smile*). Far down, stranger?

TRAMP. A piece only. (*She fills the kettle and puts it on
the fire.*)

NORA. Maybe, if you're not easy afeard, you'ld stay here
a short while alone with himself.

TRAMP. I would surely. A man that's dead can do no hurt.

NORA (*speaking with a sort of constraint*). I'm going a
little back to the west, stranger, for himself would go
there one night and another and whistle at that place,
and then the young man you're after seeing—a kind of
a farmer has come up from the sea to live in a cottage
beyond—would walk round to see if there was a thing
we'ld have to be done, and I'm wanting him this night,
the way he can go down into the glen when the sun
goes up and tell the people that himself is dead.

TRAMP (*looking at the body in the sheet*). It's myself

will go for him, lady of the house, and let you not be destroying yourself with the great rain.

NORA. You wouldn't find your way, stranger, for there's a small path only, and it running up between two sluigs where an ass and cart would be drowned. (*She puts a shawl over her head*). Let you be making yourself easy, and saying a prayer for his soul, and it's not long I'll be coming again.

TRAMP (*moving uneasily*). Maybe if you'd a piece of a grey thread and a sharp needle—there's great safety in a needle, lady of the house—I'ld be putting a little stitch here and there in my old coat, the time I'll be praying for his soul, and it going up naked to the saints of God.

NORA (*takes a needle and thread from the front of her dress and gives it to him*). There's the needle, stranger, and I'm thinking you won't be lonesome, and you used to the back hills, for isn't a dead man itself more company than to be sitting alone, and hearing the winds crying, and you not knowing on what thing your mind would stay?

TRAMP (*slowly*). It's true, surely, and the Lord have mercy on us all! (NORA *goes out. The* TRAMP *begins stitching one of the tags in his coat, saying the "De Profundis" under his breath. In an instant the sheet is drawn slowly down, and* DAN BURKE *looks out. The* TRAMP *moves uneasily, then looks up, and springs to his feet with a movement of terror.*)

DAN (*with a hoarse voice*). Don't be afeard, stranger; a man that's dead can do no hurt.

TRAMP (*trembling*). I meant no harm, your honour; and won't you leave me easy to be saying a little prayer for your soul? (*A long whistle is heard outside.*)

DAN (*sitting up in his bed and speaking fiercely*). Ah, the devil mend her. . . . Do you hear that, stranger? Did ever you hear another woman could whistle the like of that with two fingers in her mouth? (*He looks at*

the table hurriedly). I'm destroyed with the drouth,
and let you bring me a drop quickly before herself
will come back.

TRAMP (*doubtfully*). Is it not dead you are?

DAN. How would I be dead, and I as dry as a baked
bone, stranger?

TRAMP (*pouring out the whisky*). What will herself say
if she smells the stuff on you, for I'm thinking it's not for
nothing you're letting on to be dead?

DAN. It is not, stranger, but she won't be coming near me
at all, and it's not long now I'll be letting on, for
I've a cramp in my back, and my hip's asleep on me,
and there's been the devil's own fly itching my nose.
It's near dead I was wanting to sneeze, and you blathering about the rain, and Darcy (*bitterly*)—the devil
choke him—and the towering church. (*Crying out impatiently*). Give me that whisky. Would you have herself come back before I taste a drop at all? (TRAMP
gives him the glass.)

DAN (*after drinking*). Go over now to that cupboard,
and bring me a black stick you'll see in the west corner
by the wall.

TRAMP (*taking a stick from the cupboard*). Is it that?

DAN. It is, stranger; it's a long time I'm keeping that stick
for I've a bad wife in the house.

TRAMP (*with a queer look*). Is it herself, master of the
house, and she a grand woman to talk?

DAN. It's herself, surely, it's a bad wife she is—a bad wife
for an old man, and I'm getting old, God help me,
though I've an arm to me still. (*He takes the stick in
his hand*). Let you wait now a short while, and it's a
great sight you'll see in this room in two hours or three.
(*He stops to listen*). Is that somebody above?

TRAMP (*listening*). There's a voice speaking on the path.

DAN. Put that stick here in the bed and smooth the sheet
the way it was lying. (*He covers himself up hastily*).

Be falling to sleep now and don't let on you know anything, or I'll be having your life. I wouldn't have told you at all but it's destroyed with the drouth I was.

TRAMP (*covering his head*). Have no fear, master of the house. What is it I know of the like of you that I'ld be saying a word or putting out my hand to stay you at all? (*He goes back to the fire, sits down on a stool with his back to the bed and goes on stitching his coat.*)

DAN (*under the sheet, querulously*). Stranger.

TRAMP (*quickly*). Whisht, whisht. Be quiet I'm telling you, they're coming now at the door. (NORA *comes in with* MICHEAL DARA, *a tall, innocent young man behind her.*)

NORA. I wasn't long at all, stranger, for I met himself on the path.

TRAMP. You were middling long, lady of the house.

NORA. There was no sign from himself?

TRAMP. No sign at all, lady of the house.

NORA (*to* MICHEAL). Go over now and pull down the sheet, and look on himself, Micheal Dara, and you'll see it's the truth I'm telling you.

MICHEAL. I will not, Nora, I do be afeard of the dead. (*He sits down on a stool next the table facing the* TRAMP. NORA *puts the kettle on a lower hook of the pot-hooks, and piles turf under it.*)

NORA (*turning to* TRAMP). Will you drink a sup of tea with myself and the young man, stranger, or (*speaking more persuasively*) will you go into the little room and stretch yourself a short while on the bed, I'm thinking it's destroyed you are walking the length of that way in the great rain.

TRAMP. Is it to go away and leave you, and you having a wake, lady of the house? I will not surely. (*He takes a drink from his glass which he has beside him*). And it's none of your tea I'm asking either. (*He goes on stitching.* NORA *makes the tea.*)

MICHEAL (*after looking at the* TRAMP *rather scornfully for a moment*). That's a poor coat you have, God help you, and I'm thinking it's a poor tailor you are with it.

TRAMP. If it's a poor tailor I am, I'm thinking it's a poor herd does be running back and forward after a little handful of ewes the way I seen yourself running this day, young fellow, and you coming from the fair. (NORA *comes back to the table.*)

NORA (*to* MICHEAL *in a low voice*). Let you not mind him at all, Micheal Dara, he has a drop taken and it's soon he'll be falling asleep.

MICHEAL. It's no lie he's telling, I was destroyed surely. They were that wilful they were running off into one man's bit of oats, and another man's bit of hay, and tumbling into the red bogs till it's more like a pack of old goats than sheep they were. Mountain ewes is a queer breed, Nora Burke, and I'm not used to them at all.

NORA (*settling the tea things*). There's no one can drive a mountain ewe but the men do be reared in the Glen Malure, I've heard them say, and above by Rathvanna, and the Glen Imaal, men the like of Patch Darcy, God spare his soul, who would walk through five hundred sheep and miss one of them, and he not reckoning them at all.

MICHEAL (*uneasily*). Is it the man went queer in his head the year that's gone?

NORA. It is surely.

TRAMP (*plaintively*). That was a great man, young fellow, a great man I'm telling you. There was never a lamb from his own ewes he wouldn't know before it was marked, and he'ld run from this to the city of Dublin and never catch for his breath.

NORA (*turning round quickly*). He was a great man surely, stranger, and isn't it a grand thing when you hear a living man saying a good word of a dead man, and he mad dying?

TRAMP. It's the truth I'm saying, God spare his soul. (*He puts the needle under the collar of his coat, and settles himself to sleep in the chimney-corner.* NORA *sits down at the table; their backs are turned to the bed.*)

MICHEAL (*looking at her with a queer look*). I heard tell this day, Nora Burke, that it was on the path below Patch Darcy would be passing up and passing down, and I heard them say he'ld never pass it night or morning without speaking with yourself.

NORA (*in a low voice*). It was no lie you heard, Micheal Dara.

MICHEAL. I'm thinking it's a power of men you're after knowing if it's in a lonesome place you live itself.

NORA (*giving him his tea*). It's in a lonesome place you do have to be talking with some one, and looking for some one, in the evening of the day, and if it's a power of men I'm after knowing they were fine men, for I was a hard child to please, and a hard girl to please (*she looks at him a little sternly*), and it's a hard woman I am to please this day, Micheal Dara, and it's no lie I'm telling you.

MICHEAL (*looking over to see that the* TRAMP *is asleep, and then pointing to the dead man*). Was it a hard woman to please you were when you took himself for your man?

NORA. What way would I live and I an old woman if I didn't marry a man with a bit of a farm, and cows on it, and sheep on the back hills?

MICHEAL (*considering*). That's true, Nora, and maybe it's no fool you were, for there's good grazing on it, if it is a lonesome place, and I'm thinking it's a good sum he's left behind.

NORA (*taking the stocking with money from her pocket, and putting it on the table*). I do be thinking in the long nights it was a big fool I was that time, Micheal Dara, for what good is a bit of a farm with cows on it, and sheep on the back hills, when you do be sitting looking out from a door the like of that door, and seeing nothing but the mists rolling down the bog, and the mists again, and they rolling up the bog, and hearing nothing but the wind crying out in the bits of broken trees were left from the great storm, and the streams roaring with the rain.

MICHEAL (*looking at her uneasily*). What is it ails you, this night, Nora Burke? I've heard tell it's the like of that talk you do hear from men, and they after being a great while on the back hills.

NORA (*putting out the money on the table*). It's a bad night, and a wild night, Micheal Dara, and isn't it a great while I am at the foot of the back hills, sitting up here boiling food for himself, and food for the brood sow, and baking a cake when the night falls? (*She puts up the money, listlessly, in little piles on the table*). Isn't it a long while I am sitting here in the winter and the summer, and the fine spring, with the young growing behind me and the old passing, saying to myself one time, to look on Mary Brien who wasn't that height (*holding out her hand*), and I a fine girl growing up, and there she is now with two children, and another coming on her in three months or four. (*She pauses.*)

MICHEAL (*moving over three of the piles*). That's three pounds we have now, Nora Burke.

NORA (*continuing in the same voice*). And saying to myself another time, to look on Peggy Cavanagh, who had the lightest hand at milking a cow that wouldn't be easy, or turning a cake, and there she is now walking round on the roads, or sitting in a dirty old house, with no teeth in her mouth, and no sense and no more hair than you'ld see on a bit of a hill and they after burning the furze from it.

MICHEAL. That's five pounds and ten notes, a good sum, surely! . . . It's not that way you'll be talking when you marry a young man, Nora Burke, and they were saying in the fair my lambs were the best lambs, and I got a grand price, for I'm no fool now at making a bargain when my lambs are good.

NORA. What was it you got?

MICHEAL. Twenty pound for the lot, Nora Burke. . . . We'ld do right to wait now till himself will be quiet awhile in the Seven Churches, and then you'll marry me in the chapel of Rathvanna, and I'll bring the sheep up on the bit of a hill you have on the back mountain, and we won't have anything we'ld be afeard to let our minds on when the mist is down.

NORA (*pouring him out some whisky*). Why would I marry you, Mike Dara? You'll be getting old and I'll be getting old, and in a little while I'm telling you, you'll be sitting up in your bed—the way himself was sitting—with a shake in your face, and your teeth falling, and the white hair sticking out round you like an old bush where sheep do be leaping a gap. (DAN BURKE *sits up noiselessly from under the sheet, with his hand to his face. His white hair is sticking out round his head.*)

NORA (*goes on slowly without hearing him*). It's a pitiful thing to be getting old, but it's a queer thing surely. It's a queer thing to see an old man sitting up there in his bed with no teeth in him, and a rough word in his mouth, and his chin the way it would take the bark from the edge of an oak board you'ld have building a door. . . . God forgive me, Micheal Dara, we'll all be getting old, but it's a queer thing surely.

MICHEAL. It's too lonesome you are from living a long time with an old man, Nora, and you're talking again like a herd that would be coming down from the thick mist (*he puts his arm round her*), but it's a fine life you'll have now with a young man, a fine life surely. . . . (DAN *sneezes violently.* MICHEAL *tries to get to the door, but before he can do so,* DAN *jumps out of the bed in queer white clothes, with his stick in his hand, and goes over and puts his back against it.*

MICHEAL. Son of God deliver us. (*Crosses himself, and goes backward across the room.*)

DAN (*holding up his hand at him*). Now you'll not marry her the time I'm rotting below in the Seven Churches, and you'll see the thing I'll give you will follow you on the back mountains when the wind is high.

MICHEAL (*to* NORA). Get me out of it, Nora, for the love of God. He always did what you bid him, and I'm thinking he would do it now.

DAN (*turning towards her*). It's little you care if it's dead or living I am, but there'll be an end now of your fine times, and all the talk you have of young men and old men, and of the mist coming up or going down. (*He opens the door*). You'll walk out now from that door, Nora Burke, and it's not to-morrow, or the next day, or any day of your life, that you'll put in your foot through it again.

TRAMP (*standing up*). It's a hard thing you're saying for an old man, master of the house, and what would the like of her do if you put her out on the roads?

DAN. Let her walk round the like of Peggy Cavanagh below, and be begging money at the cross-road, or selling songs to the men. (*To* NORA). Walk out now, Nora Burke, and it's soon you'll be getting old with that life, I'm telling you; it's soon your teeth'll be falling and your head'll be the like of a bush where sheep do be leaping a gap. (*He pauses: she looks round at* MICHEAL.)

MICHEAL (*timidly*). There's a fine Union below in Rathdrum.

DAN. The like of her would never go there. . . . It's lonesome roads she'll be going and hiding herself away till the end will come, and they find her stretched like a dead sheep with the frost on her, or the big spiders, maybe, and they putting their webs on her, in the butt of a ditch.

NORA (*angrily*). What way will yourself be that day, Daniel Burke? What way will you be that day and you lying down a long while in your grave? For it's bad you are living, and it's bad you'll be when you're dead. (*She looks at him a moment fiercely, then half turns away and speaks plaintively again*). Yet, if it is itself, Daniel Burke, who can help it at all, and let you be getting up into your bed, and not be taking your death with the wind blowing on you, and the rain with it, and you half in your skin.

DAN. It's proud and happy you'ld be if I was getting my death the day I was shut of yourself. (*Pointing to the door*). Let you walk out through that door, I'm telling you, and let you not be passing this way if it's hungry you are, or wanting a bed.

TRAMP (*pointing to* MICHEAL). Maybe himself would take her.

NORA. What would he do with me now?

TRAMP. Give you the half of a dry bed, and good food in your mouth.

DAN. Is it a fool you think him, stranger, or is it a fool you were born yourself? Let her walk out of that door, and let you go along with her, stranger—if it's raining itself—for it's too much talk you have surely.

TRAMP (*going over to* NORA). We'll be going now, lady of the house—the rain is falling, but the air is kind and maybe it'll be a grand morning by the grace of God.

NORA. What good is a grand morning when I'm destroyed surely, and I going out to get my death walking the roads?

TRAMP. You'll not be getting your death with myself, lady of the house, and I knowing all the ways a man can put food in his mouth. . . . We'll be going now, I'm telling you, and the time you'll be feeling the cold, and the frost, and the great rain, and the sun again, and the south wind blowing in the glens, you'll not be sitting up on a wet ditch, the way you're after sitting in the place, making yourself old with looking on each day, and it passing you by. You'll be saying one time, "It's a grand evening, by the grace of God," and another time, "It's a wild night, God help us, but it'll pass surely." You'll be saying—

DAN (*goes over to them crying out impatiently*). Go out of that door, I'm telling you, and do your blathering below in the glen. (NORA *gathers a few things into her shawl.*)

TRAMP (*at the door*). Come along with me now, lady of the house, and it's not my blather you'll be hearing only, but you'll be hearing the herons crying out over the black lakes, and you'll be hearing the grouse and the owls with them, and the larks and the big thrushes when the days are warm, and it's not from the like of them you'll be hearing a talk of getting old like Peggy Cavanagh, and losing the hair off you, and the light of your eyes, but it's fine songs you'll be hearing when the sun goes up, and there'll be no old fellow wheezing, the like of a sick sheep, close to your ear.

NORA. I'm thinking it's myself will be wheezing that time with lying down under the Heavens when the night is cold; but you've a fine bit of talk, stranger, and it's with yourself I'll go. (*She goes towards the door, then turns to* DAN). You think it's a grand thing you're after doing with your letting on to be dead, but what is it at all? What way would a woman live in a lonesome place the like of this place, and she not making a talk with the men passing? And what way will yourself live from this day, with none to care for you? What is it you'll have now but a black life, Daniel Burke, and it's not long I'm telling you, till you'll be lying again under that sheet, and you dead surely. (*She goes out with the*

TRAMP. MICHEAL *is slinking after them, but* DAN *stops him.*)

DAN. Sit down now and take a little taste of the stuff, Micheal Dara. There's a great drouth on me, and the night is young.

MICHEAL (*coming back to the table*). And it's very dry I am, surely, with the fear of death you put on me, and I after driving mountain ewes since the turn of the day.

DAN (*throwing away his stick*). I was thinking to strike you, Micheal Dara, but you're a quiet man, God help you, and I don't mind you at all. (*He pours out two glasses of whisky, and gives one to* MICHEAL.)

DAN. Your good health, Micheal Dara.

MICHEAL. God reward you, Daniel Burke, and may you have a long life, and a quiet life, and good health with it. (*They drink.*)

CURTAIN

CATHLEEN NI HOULIHAN

by William Butler Yeats

CHARACTERS

PETER GILLANE
MICHAEL GILLANE, *his son, going to be married*
PATRICK GILLANE, *a lad of twelve, Michael's brother*
BRIDGET GILLANE, *Peter's wife*
DELIA CAHEL, *engaged to Michael*
THE POOR OLD WOMAN
NEIGHBOURS

CATHLEEN NI HOULIHAN

Interior of a cottage close to Killala, in 1798. BRIDGET *is standing at a table undoing a parcel.* PETER *is sitting at one side of the fire,* PATRICK *at the other.*

PETER. What is the sound I hear?

PATRICK. I don't hear anything. (*He listens*). I hear it now. It's like cheering. (*He goes to the window and looks out*). I wonder what they are cheering about. I don't see anybody.

PETER. It might be a hurling.

PATRICK. There's no hurling to-day. It must be down in the town the cheering is.

BRIDGET. I suppose the boys must be having some sport of their own. Come over here, Peter, and look at Michael's wedding clothes.

PETER (*shifts his chair to table*). Those are grand clothes, indeed.

BRIDGET. You hadn't clothes like that when you married me, and no coat to put on of a Sunday more than any other day.

PETER. That is true, indeed. We never thought a son of our own would be wearing a suit of that sort for his wedding, or have so good a place to bring a wife to.

PATRICK (*who is still at the window*). There's an old woman coming down the road. I don't know is it here she is coming.

BRIDGET. It will be a neighbour coming to hear about Michael's wedding. Can you see who it is?

PATRICK. I think it is a stranger, but she's not coming to the house. She's turned into the gap that goes down where Maurteen and his sons are shearing sheep. (*He turns towards* BRIDGET). Do you remember what Winny of the Cross-Roads was saying the other night about

the strange woman that goes through the country whatever time there's war or trouble coming?

BRIDGET. Don't be bothering us about Winny's talk, but
go and open the door for your brother. I hear him
coming up the path.

PETER. I hope he has brought Delia's fortune with him
safe, for fear the people might go back on the bargain
and I after making it. Trouble enough I had making
it. (PATRICK *opens the door and* MICHAEL *comes in.*)

BRIDGET. What kept you, Michael? We were looking out
for you this long time.

MICHAEL. I went round by the priest's house to bid him
be ready to marry us to-morrow.

BRIDGET. Did he say anything?

MICHAEL. He said it was a very nice match, and that
he was never better pleased to marry any two in his
parish than myself and Delia Cahel.

PETER. Have you got the fortune, Michael?

MICHAEL. Here it is. (MICHAEL *puts bag on table and goes
over and leans against chimney-jumb,* BRIDGET, *who has
been all this time examining the clothes, pulling the
seams and trying the lining of the pockets, etc., puts
the clothes on the dresser.*)

PETER (*getting up and taking the bag in his hand and
turning out the money*). Yes, I made the bargain well
for you, Michael. Old John Cahel would sooner have
kept a share of this a while longer. 'Let me keep the
half of it until the first boy is born,' says he. 'You will
not,' says I. 'Whether there is or is not a boy, the whole
hundred pounds must be in Michael's hands before he
brings your daughter to the house.' The wife spoke to
him then, and he gave in at the end.

BRIDGET. You seem well pleased to be handling the
money, Peter.

PETER. Indeed, I wish I had had the luck to get a hundred
pounds, or twenty pounds itself, with the wife I married.

BRIDGET. Well, if I didn't bring much I didn't get much. What had you the day I married you but a flock of hens and you feeding them, and a few lambs and you driving them to the market at Ballina? (*She is vexed and bangs a jug on the dresser*). If I brought no fortune I worked it out in my bones, laying down the baby, Michael that is standing there now, on a stook of straw, while I dug the potatoes, and never asking big dresses or anything but to be working.

PETER. That is true, indeed. (*He pats her arm.*)

BRIDGET. Leave me alone now till I ready the house for the woman that is to come into it.

PETER. You are the best woman in Ireland, but money is good, too. (*He begins handling the money again and sits down*). I never thought to see so much money within my four walls. We can do great things now we have it. We can take the ten acres of land we have the chance of since Jamsie Dempsey died, and stock it. We will go to the fair at Ballina to buy the stock. Did Delia ask any of the money for her own use, Michael?

MICHAEL. She did not, indeed. She did not seem to take much notice of it, or to look at it at all.

BRIDGET. That's no wonder. Why would she look at it when she had yourself to look at, a fine, strong young man? It is proud she must be to get you; a good steady boy that will make use of the money, and not be running through it or spending it on drink like another.

PETER. It's likely Michael himself was not thinking much of the fortune either, but of what sort the girl was to look at.

MICHAEL (*coming over towards the table*). Well, you would like a nice comely girl to be beside you, and to go walking with you. The fortune only lasts for a while, but the woman will be there always.

PATRICK (*turning round from the window*). They are cheering again down in the town. Maybe they are landing horses from Enniscrone. They do be cheering when the horses take the water well.

MICHAEL. There are no horses in it. Where would they be going and no fair at hand? Go down to the town, Patrick, and see what is going on.

PATRICK (*opens the door to go out, but stops for a moment on the threshold*). Will Delia remember, do you think, to bring the greyhound pup she promised me when she would be coming to the house?

MICHAEL. She will surely. (PATRICK *goes out, leaving the door open.*)

PETER. It will be Patrick's turn next to be looking for a fortune, but he won't find it so easy to get it and he with no place of his own.

BRIDGET. I do be thinking sometimes, now things are going so well with us, and the Cahels such a good back to us in the district, and Delia's own uncle a priest, we might be put in the way of making Patrick a priest some day, and he so good at his books.

PETER. Time enough, time enough. You have always your head full of plans, Bridget.

BRIDGET. We will be well able to give him learning, and not to send him tramping the country like a poor scholar that lives on charity.

MICHAEL. They're not done cheering yet. (*He goes over to the door and stands there for a moment, putting up his hand to shade his eyes.*)

BRIDGET. Do you see anything?

MICHAEL. I see an old woman coming up the path.

BRIDGET. Who is it, I wonder? It must be the strange woman Patrick saw a while ago.

MICHAEL. I don't think it's one of the neighbours anyway, but she has her cloak over her face.

BRIDGET. It might be some poor woman heard we were making ready for the wedding and came to look for her share.

PETER. I may as well put the money out of sight. There is no use leaving it out for every stranger to look at. (*He goes over to a large box in the corner, opens it and puts the bag in and fumbles at the lock.*)

MICHAEL. There she is, father! (*An* OLD WOMAN *passes the window slowly. She looks at* MICHAEL *as she passes*). I'd sooner a stranger not to come to the house the night before my wedding.

BRIDGET. Open the door, Michael; don't keep the poor woman waiting. (*The* OLD WOMAN *comes in.* MICHAEL *stands aside to make way for her.*)

OLD WOMAN. God save all here!

PETER. God save you kindly!

OLD WOMAN. You have good shelter here.

PETER. You are welcome to whatever shelter we have.

BRIDGET. Sit down there by the fire and welcome.

OLD WOMAN (*warming her hands*). There is a hard wind outside. (MICHAEL *watches her curiously from the door.* PETER *comes over to the table.*)

PETER. Have you travelled far to-day?

OLD WOMAN. I have travelled far, very far; there are few have travelled so far as myself, and there's many a one that doesn't make me welcome. There was one that had strong sons I thought were friends of mine, but they were shearing their sheep, and they wouldn't listen to me.

PETER. It's a pity indeed for any person to have no place of their own.

OLD WOMAN. That's true for you indeed, and it's long I'm on the roads since I first went wandering.

BRIDGET. It is a wonder you are not worn out with so much wandering.

OLD WOMAN. Sometimes my feet are tired and my hands are quiet, but there is no quiet in my heart. When the people see me quiet, they think old age has come on me and that all the stir has gone out of me. But when the trouble is on me I must be talking to my friends.

BRIDGET. What was it put you wandering?

OLD WOMAN. Too many strangers in the house.

BRIDGET. Indeed you look as if you'd had your share of trouble.

OLD WOMAN. I have had trouble indeed.

BRIDGET. What was it put the trouble on you?

OLD WOMAN. My land that was taken from me.

PETER. Was it much land they took from you?

OLD WOMAN. My four beautiful green fields.

PETER (aside to BRIDGET). Do you think could she be the widow Casey that was put out of her holding at Kilglass a while ago?

BRIDGET. She is not. I saw the widow Casey one time at the market in Ballina, a stout fresh woman.

PETER (to OLD WOMAN). Did you hear a noise of cheering, and you coming up the hill?

OLD WOMAN. I thought I heard the noise I used to hear when my friends came to visit me. (She begins singing half to herself).

> I will go cry with the woman,
> For yellow-haired Donough is dead,
> With a hempen rope for a neck-cloth,
> And a white cloth on his head, —

MICHAEL (coming from the door). What is it that you are singing, ma'am?

OLD WOMAN. Singing I am about a man I knew one time, yellow-haired Donough that was hanged in Galway. (She goes on singing, much louder).

> I am come to cry with you, woman,
> My hair is unwound and unbound;
> I remember him ploughing his field,
> Turning up the red side of the ground,

> And building his barn on the hill
> With the good mortared stone;
> O! we'd have pulled down the gallows
> Had it happened in Enniscrone!

MICHAEL. What was it brought him to his death?

OLD WOMAN. He died for love of me: many a man has died for love of me.

PETER (*aside to* BRIDGET). Her trouble has put her wits astray.

MICHAEL. Is it long since that song was made? Is it long since he got his death?

OLD WOMAN. Not long, not long. But there were others that died for love of me a long time ago.

MICHAEL. Were they neighbours of your own, ma'am?

OLD WOMAN. Come here beside me and I'll tell you about them. (MICHAEL *sits down beside her on the hearth*). There was a red man of the O'Donnells from the north, and a man of the O'Sullivans from the south, and there was one Brian that lost his life at Clontarf by the sea, and there were a great many in the west, some that died hundreds of years ago, and there are some that will die to-morrow.

MICHAEL. Is it in the west that men will die to-morrow?

OLD WOMAN. Come nearer, nearer to me.

BRIDGET. Is she right, do you think? Or is she a woman from beyond the world?

PETER. She doesn't know well what she's talking about, with the want and the trouble she has gone through.

BRIDGET. The poor thing, we should treat her well.

PETER. Give her a drink of milk and a bit of the oaten cake.

BRIDGET. Maybe we should give her something along with that, to bring her on her way. A few pence or a shilling itself, and we with so much money in the house.

PETER. Indeed I'd not begrudge it to her if we had it to

spare, but if we go running through what we have, we'll soon have to break the hundred pounds, and that would be a pity.

BRIDGET. Shame on you, Peter. Give her the shilling and your blessing with it, or our own luck will go from us. (PETER *goes to the box and takes out a shilling.*)

BRIDGET (*to the* OLD WOMAN). Will you have a drink of milk, ma'am?

OLD WOMAN. It is not food or drink that I want.

PETER (*offering the shilling*). Here is something for you.

OLD WOMAN. This is not what I want. It is not silver I want.

PETER. What is it you would be asking for?

OLD WOMAN. If anyone would give me help he must give me himself, he must give me all. (PETER *goes over to the table staring at the shilling in his hand in a bewildered way, and stands whispering to* BRIDGET.)

MICHAEL. Have you no one to care for you in your age, ma'am?

OLD WOMAN. I have not. With all the lovers that brought me their love I never set out the bed for any.

MICHAEL. Are you lonely going the roads, ma'am?

OLD WOMAN. I have my thoughts and I have my hopes.

MICHAEL. What hopes have you to hold to?

OLD WOMAN. The hope of getting my beautiful fields back again; the hope of putting the strangers out of my house.

MICHAEL. What way will you do that, ma'am?

OLD WOMAN. I have good friends that will help me. They are gathering to help me now. I am not afraid. If they are put down to-day they will get the upper hand to-morrow. (*She gets up*). I must be going to meet my friends. They are coming to help me and I must be there to welcome them. I must call the neighbours together to welcome them.

MICHAEL. I will go with you.

BRIDGET. It is not her friends you have to go and welcome, Michael; it is the girl coming into the house you have to welcome. You have plenty to do; it is food and drink you have to bring to the house. The woman that is coming home is not coming with empty hands; you would not have an empty house before her. (*To the* OLD WOMAN). Maybe you don't know, ma'am, that my son is going to be married to-morrow.

OLD WOMAN. It is not a man going to his marriage that I look to for help.

PETER (*to* BRIDGET). Who is she, do you think, at all?

BRIDGET. You did not tell us your name yet, ma'am.

OLD WOMAN. Some call me the Poor Old Woman, and there are some that call me Cathleen, the daughter of Houlihan.

PETER. I think I knew some one of that name, once. Who was it, I wonder? It must have been some one I knew when I was a boy. No, no; I remember, I heard it in a song.

OLD WOMAN (*who is standing in the doorway*). They are wondering that there were songs made for me; there have been many songs made for me. I heard one on the wind this morning. (*Sings*).

> Do not make a great keening
> When the graves have been dug to-morrow.
> Do not call the white-scarfed riders
> To the burying that shall be to-morrow.
> Do not spread food to call strangers
> To the wakes that shall be to-morrow;
> Do not give money for prayers
> For the dead that shall die to-morrow. . . .

They will have no need of prayers, they will have no need of prayers.

MICHAEL. I do not know what that song means, but tell me something I can do for you.

PETER. Come over to me, Michael.

MICHAEL. Hush, father, listen to her.

OLD WOMAN. It is a hard service they take that help me. Many that are red-cheeked now will be pale-cheeked; many that have been free to walk the hills and the bogs and the rushes will be sent to walk hard streets in far countries; many a good plan will be broken; many that have gathered money will not stay to spend it; many a child will be born and there will be no father at its christening to give it a name. They that have red cheeks will have pale cheeks for my sake, and for all that, they will think they are well paid. (*She goes out; her voice is heard outside singing*).

> They shall be remembered for ever,
> They shall be alive for ever,
> They shall be speaking for ever,
> The people shall hear them for ever.

BRIDGET (*to* PETER). Look at him, Peter; he has the look of a man that has got the touch. (*Raising her voice*). Look here, Michael, at the wedding clothes. Such grand clothes as these are! You have a right to fit them on now; it would be a pity to-morrow if they did not fit. The boys would be laughing at you. Take them, Michael, and go into the room and fit them on. (*She puts them on his arm.*)

MICHAEL. What wedding are you talking of? What clothes will I be wearing to-morrow?

BRIDGET. These are the clothes you are going to wear when you marry Delia Cahel to-morrow.

MICHAEL. I had forgotten that. (*He looks at the clothes and turns towards the inner room, but stops at the sound of cheering outside.*)

PETER. There is the shouting come to our own door.

What is it has happened? (*Neighbours come crowding in,* PATRICK *and* DELIA *with them.*)

PATRICK. There are ships in the Bay; the French are landing at Killala! (PETER *takes his pipe from his mouth and his hat off, and stands up. The clothes slip from* MICHAEL's *arm.*)

DELIA. Michael (*He takes no notice*). Michael! (*He turns towards her*). Why do you look at me like a stranger? (*She drops his arm.* BRIDGET *goes over towards her.*)

PATRICK. The boys are all hurrying down the hillside to join the French.

DELIA. Michael won't be going to join the French.

BRIDGET (*to* PETER). Tell him not to go, Peter.

PETER. It's no use. He doesn't hear a word we're saying.

BRIDGET. Try and coax him over to the fire.

DELIA. Michael, Michael! You won't leave me! You won't join the French, and we going to be married! (*She puts her arms about him, he turns towards her as if about to yield.* OLD WOMAN's *voice outside*).

>   They shall be speaking for ever,
>   The people shall hear them for ever.

(MICHAEL *breaks away from* DELIA, *stands for a second at the door, then rushes out, following the* OLD WOMAN's *voice.* BRIDGET *takes* DELIA, *who is crying silently, into her arms.*)

PETER (*to* PATRICK, *laying a hand on his arm*). Did you see an old woman going down the path?

PATRICK. I did not, but I saw a young girl, and she had the walk of a queen.

CURTAIN

A MARRIAGE PROPOSAL

by Anton Chekhov

English Version by

Hilmar Baukhage and

Barrett H. Clark

CHARACTERS

STEPAN STEPANOVITCH TSCHUBUKOV, *a country farmer*
NATALIA STEPANOVNA, *his daughter (aged 25)*
IVAN VASSILIYITCH LOMOV, *Tschubukov's neighbor*

SCENE: *Reception-room in* TSCHUBUKOV'S *country home, Russia.*

TIME: *The present.*

A MARRIAGE PROPOSAL

SCENE: *The reception room in* TSCHUBUKOV's *home.*
TSCHUBUKOV *discovered as the curtain rises. Enter* LOMOV,
wearing a dress-suit.

TSCHUB (*going toward him and greeting him*). Who is
this I see? My dear fellow! Ivan Vassiliyitch! I'm so
glad to see you! (*Shakes hands*). But this is a surprise!
How are you?

LOMOV. Thank you! And how are you?

TSCHUB. Oh, so-so, my friend. Please sit down. It isn't
right to forget one's neighbor. But tell me, why all this
ceremony? Dress clothes, white gloves and all? Are you
on your way to some engagement, my good fellow?

LOMOV. No, I have no engagement except with you,
Stepan Stepanovitch.

TSCHUB. But why in evening clothes, my friend? This isn't
New Year's!

LOMOV. You see, it's simply this, that—(*Composing himself.*) I have come to you, Stepan Stepanovitch, to

trouble you with a request. It is not the first time I
have had the honor of turning to you for assistance,
and you have always, that is—I beg your pardon, I am a
bit excited! I'll take a drink of water first, dear Stepan
Stepanovitch. (*He drinks.*)

TSCHUB (*aside*). He's come to borrow money! I won't give
him any! (*To* LOMOV). What is it, then, dear Lomov?

LOMOV. You see—dear—Stepanovitch, pardon me, Stepan
—Stepan—dearvitch—I mean—I am terribly nervous,
as you will be so good as to see—! What I mean to say—
you are the only one who can help me, though I don't
deserve it, and—and I have no right whatever to make
this request of you.

TSCHUB. Oh, don't beat about the bush, my dear fellow.
Tell me!

LOMOV. Immediately—in a moment. Here it is, then: I
have come to ask for the hand of your daughter, Natalia
Stepanovna.

TSCHUB (*joyfully*). Angel! Ivan Vassiliyitch! Say that once
again! I didn't quite hear it!

LOMOV. I have the honor to beg——

TSCHUB (*interrupting*). My dear, dear man! I am so happy
that everything is so—everything! (*Embraces and kisses
him*). I have wanted this to happen for so long. It has
been my dearest wish! (*He represses a tear*). And I
have always loved you, my dear fellow, as my own
son! May God give you His blessings and His grace
and—I always wanted it to happen. But why am I
standing here like a blockhead? I am completely dumbfounded with pleasure, completely dumbfounded. My
whole being—I'll call Natalia——

LOMOV. Dear Stepan Stepanovitch, what do you think?
May I hope for Natalia Stepanovna's acceptance?

TSCHUB. Really! A fine boy like you—and you think she
won't accept on the minute? Lovesick as a cat and all
that—! (*He goes out, right.*)

LOMOV. I'm cold. My whole body is trembling as though I was going to take my examination! But the chief thing is to settle matters! If a person meditates too much, or hesitates, or talks about it, waits for an ideal or for true love, he never gets it. Brrr! It's cold! Natalia is an excellent housekeeper, not at all bad-looking, well educated—what more could I ask? I'm so excited my ears are roaring! (*He drinks water*). And not to marry, that won't do! In the first place, I'm thirty-five—a critical age, you might say. In the second place, I must live a well-regulated life. I have a weak heart, continual palpitation, and I am very sensitive and always getting excited. My lips begin to tremble and the pulse in my right temple throbs terribly. But the worst of all is sleep! I hardly lie down and begin to doze before something in my left side begins to pull and tug, and something begins to hammer in my left shoulder—and in my head, too! I jump up like a madman, walk about a little, lie down again, but the moment I fall asleep I have a terrible cramp in the side. And so it is all night long! (*Enter* NATALIA STEPANOVNA.)

NATALIA. Ah! It's you. Papa said to go in: there was a dealer in there who'd come to buy something. Good afternoon, Ivan Vassiliyitch.

LOMOV. Good day, my dear Natalia Stepanovna.

NATALIA. You must pardon me for wearing my apron and this old dress: we are working to-day. Why haven't you come to see us oftener? You've not been here for so long! Sit down. (*They sit down*). Won't you have something to eat?

LOMOV. Thank you, I have just had lunch.

NATALIA. Smoke, do, there are the matches. To-day it is beautiful and only yesterday it rained so hard that the workmen couldn't do a stroke of work. How many bricks have you cut? Think of it! I was so anxious that I had the whole field mowed, and now I'm sorry I did it, because I'm afraid the hay will rot. It would have been better if I had waited. But what on earth is this? You are in evening clothes! The latest cut! Are you on your way to a ball? And you seem to be looking better, too—really. Why are you dressed up so gorgeously?

LOMOV (*excited*). You see, my dear Natalia Stepanovna —it's simply this: I have decided to ask you to listen to me—of course it will be a surprise, and indeed you'll be angry, but I—(*Aside*). How fearfully cold it is!

NATALIA. What is it? (*A pause*). Well?

LOMOV. I'll try to be brief. My dear Natalia Stepanovna, as you know, for many years, since my childhood, I have had the honor to know your family. My poor aunt and her husband, from whom, as you know, I inherited the estate, always had the greatest respect for your father and your poor mother. The Lomovs and the Tschubukovs have been for decades on the friendliest, indeed the closest, terms with each other, and furthermore my property, as you know, adjoins your own. If you will be so good as to remember, my meadows touch your birch woods.

NATALIA. Pardon the interruption. You said "my meadows" —but are they yours?

LOMOV. Yes, they belong to me.

NATALIA. What nonsense! The meadows belong to us—not to you!

LOMOV. No, to me! Now, my dear Natalia Stepanovna!

NATALIA. Well, that is certainly news to me. How do they belong to you?

LOMOV. How? I am speaking of the meadows lying between your birch woods and my brick-earth.

NATALIA. Yes, exactly. They belong to us.

LOMOV. No, you are mistaken, my dear Natalia Stepanovna, they belong to me.

NATALIA. Try to remember exactly, Ivan Vassiliyitch. Is it so long ago that you inherited them?

LOMOV. Long ago! As far back as I can remember they
  have always belonged to us.

NATALIA. But that isn't true! You'll pardon my saying so.

LOMOV. It is all a matter of record, my dear Natalia
  Stepanovna. It is true that at one time the title to the
  meadows was disputed, but now everyone knows they
  belong to me. There is no room for discussion. Be so
  good as to listen: my aunt's grandmother put these
  meadows, free from all costs, into the hands of your
  father's grandfather's peasants for a certain time while
  they were making bricks for my grandmother. These
  people used the meadows free of cost for about forty
  years, living there as they would on their own property.
  Later, however, when——

NATALIA. There's not a word of truth in that! My grandfather, and my great-grandfather, too, knew that their
  estate reached back to the swamp, so that the meadows
  belong to us. What further discussion can there be? I
  can't understand it. It is really most annoying.

LOMOV. I'll show you the papers, Natalia Stepanovna.

NATALIA. No, either you are joking, or trying to lead
  me into a discussion. That's not at all nice! We have
  owned this property for nearly three hundred years, and
  now all at once we hear that it doesn't belong to us.
  Ivan Vassiliyitch, you will pardon me, but I really can't
  believe my ears. So far as I am concerned, the meadows
  are worth very little. In all they don't contain more
  than five acres and they are worth only a few hundred
  roubles, say three hundred, but the injustice of the
  thing is what affects me. Say what you will, I can't
  bear injustice.

LOMOV. Only listen until I have finished, please! The
  peasants of your respected father's grandfather, as I
  have already had the honor to tell you, baked bricks
  for my grandmother. My aunt's grandmother wished to
  do them a favor——

NATALIA. Grandfather! Grandmother! Aunt! I know nothing about them. All I know is that the meadows belong to us, and that ends the matter.

LOMOV. No, they belong to me!

NATALIA. And if you keep on explaining it for two days, and put on five suits of evening clothes, the meadows are still ours, ours, ours! I don't want to take your property, but I refuse to give up what belongs to us!

LOMOV. Natalia Stepanovna, I don't need the meadows, I am only concerned with the principle. If you are agreeable, I beg of you, accept them as a gift from me!

NATALIA. But I can give them to you, because they belong to me! That is very peculiar, Ivan Vassiliyitch! Until now we have considered you as a good neighbor and a good friend; only last year we lent you our threshing machine so that we couldn't thresh until November, and now you treat us like thieves! You offer to give me my own land. Excuse me, but neighbors don't treat each other that way. In my opinion, it's a very low trick—to speak frankly—

LOMOV. According to you I'm a usurper, then, am I? My dear lady, I have never appropriated other people's property, and I shall permit no one to accuse me of such a thing! (*He goes quickly to the bottle and drinks water*). The meadows are mine!

NATALIA. That's not the truth! They are mine!

LOMOV. Mine!

NATALIA. Eh? I'll prove it to you! This afternoon I'll send my reapers into the meadows.

LOMOV. W—h—a—t?

NATALIA. My reapers will be there to-day!

LOMOV. And I'll chase them off!

NATALIA. If you dare!

LOMOV. The meadows are mine, you understand? Mine!

NATALIA. Really, you needn't scream so! If you want to scream and snort and rage you may do it at home, but here please keep yourself within the limits of common decency.

LOMOV. My dear lady, if it weren't that I were suffering from palpitation of the heart and hammering of the arteries in my temples, I would deal with you very differently! (*In a loud voice*). The meadows belong to me!

NATALIA. Us!

LOMOV. Me! (*Enter* TSCHUBUKOV, *right.*)

TSCHUB. What's going on here? What is he yelling about?

NATALIA. Papa, please tell this gentleman to whom the meadows belong, to us or to him?

TSCHUB (*to* LOMOV). My dear fellow, the meadows are ours.

LOMOV. But, merciful heavens, Stepan Stepanovitch, how do you make that out? You at least might be reasonable. My aunt's grandmother gave the use of the meadows free of cost to your grandfather's peasants; the peasants lived on the land for forty years and used it as their own, but later when——

TSCHUB. Permit me, my dear friend. You forget that your grandmother's peasants never paid, because there had been a lawsuit over the meadows, and everyone knows that the meadows belong to us. You haven't looked at the map.

LOMOV. I'll prove to you that they belong to me!

TSCHUB. Don't try to prove it, my dear fellow.

LOMOV. I will!

TSCHUB. My good fellow, what are you shrieking about? You can't prove anything by yelling, you know. I don't ask for anything that belongs to you, nor do I intend to give up anything of my own. Why should I? If it has gone so far, my dear man, that you really intend to claim the meadows, I'd rather give them to the peasants than you, and I certainly shall!

LOMOV. I can't believe it! By what right can you give away property that doesn't belong to you?

TSCHUB. Really, you must allow me to decide what I am to do with my own land! I'm not accustomed, young man, to have people address me in that tone of voice. I, young man, am twice your age, and I beg you to address me respectfully.

LOMOV. No! No! You think I'm a fool! You're making fun of me! You call my property yours and then expect me to stand quietly by and talk to you like a human being. That isn't the way a good neighbor behaves, Stepan Stepanovitch! You are no neighbor, you're no better than a landgrabber. That's what you are!

TSCHUB. Wh—at? What did he say?

NATALIA. Papa, send the reapers into the meadows this minute!

TSCHUB. (to LOMOV). What was that you said, sir?

NATALIA. The meadows belong to us and I won't give them up! I won't give them up! I won't give them up!

LOMOV. We'll see about that! I'll prove in court that they belong to me.

TSCHUB. In court! You may sue in court, sir, if you like! Oh, I know you, you are only waiting to find an excuse to go to law! You're an intriguer, that's what you are! Your whole family were always looking for quarrels. The whole lot!

LOMOV. Kindly refrain from insulting my family. The entire race of Lomov has always been honorable! And never has one been brought to trial for embezzlement, as your dear uncle was!

TSCHUB. And the whole Lomov family were insane!

NATALIA. Every one of them!

TSCHUB. Your grandmother was a dipsomaniac, and the younger aunt, Nastasia Michailovna, ran off with an architect.

LOMOV. And your mother limped. (*He puts his hand over his heart*). Oh, my side pains! My temples are bursting! Lord in Heaven! Water!

TSCHUB. And your dear father was a gambler—and a glutton!

NATALIA. And your aunt was a gossip like few others!

LOMOV. And you are an intriguer. Oh, my heart! And it's an open secret that you cheated at the elections— my eyes are blurred! Where is my hat?

NATALIA. Oh, how low! Liar! Disgusting thing!

LOMOV. Where's the hat—? My heart! Where shall I go? Where is the door—? Oh—it seems—as though I were dying! I can't—my legs won't hold me—(*Goes to the door.*)

TSCHUB (*following him*). May you never darken my door again!

NATALIA. Bring your suit to court! We'll see! (LOMOV *staggers out, center.*)

TSCHUB (*angrily*). The devil!

NATALIA. Such a good-for-nothing! And then they talk about being good neighbors!

TSCHUB. Loafer! Scarecrow! Monster!

NATALIA. A swindler like that takes over a piece of property that doesn't belong to him and then dares to argue about it!

TSCHUB. And to think that this fool dares to make a proposal of marriage!

NATALIA. What? A proposal of marriage?

TSCHUB. Why, yes! He came here to make you a proposal of marriage.

NATALIA. Why didn't you tell me that before?

TSCHUB. That's why he had on his evening clothes! The poor fool!

NATALIA. Proposal for me? Oh! (*Falls into an armchair and groans*). Bring him back! Bring him back!

TSCHUB. Bring whom back?

NATALIA. Faster, faster, I'm sinking! Bring him back! (*She becomes hysterical.*)

TSCHUB. What is it? What's wrong with you? (*His hands to his head*). I'm cursed with bad luck! I'll shoot myself! I'll hang myself!

NATALIA. I'm dying! Bring him back!

TSCHUB. Bah! In a minute! Don't bawl! (*He rushes out, center.*)

NATALIA (*groaning*). What have they done to me? Bring him back! Bring him back!

TSCHUB (*comes running in*). He's coming at once! The devil take him! Ugh! Talk to him yourself, I can't.

NATALIA (*groaning*). Bring him back!

TSCHUB. He's coming, I tell you! "Oh, Lord! What a task it is to be the father of a grown daughter!" I'll cut my throat! I really will cut my throat! We've argued with the fellow, insulted him, and now we've thrown him out! —and you did it all, you!

NATALIA. No, you! You haven't any manners, you are brutal! If it weren't for you, he wouldn't have gone!

TSCHUB. Oh, yes, I'm to blame! If I shoot or hang myself, remember you'll be to blame. You forced me to it! You! (LOMOV *appears in the doorway*). There, talk to him yourself! (*He goes out.*)

LOMOV. Terrible palpitation!— My leg is lamed! My side hurts me——

NATALIA. Pardon us, we were angry, Ivan Vassiliyitch. I remember now—the meadows really belong to you.

LOMOV. My heart is beating terribly! My meadows—my eyelids tremble—(*They sit down*). We were wrong. It was only the principle of the thing—the property isn't worth much to me, but the principle is worth a great deal.

NATALIA. Exactly, the principle! Let us talk about something else.

LOMOV. Because I have proofs that my aunt's grandmother had, with the peasants of your good father——

NATALIA. Enough, enough. (*Aside*). I don't know how to begin. (*To* LOMOV). Are you going hunting soon?

LOMOV. Yes, heath-cock shooting, respected Natalia Stepanovna. I expect to begin after the harvest. Oh, did you hear? My dog, Ugadi, you know him—limps!

NATALIA. What a shame! How did that happen?

LOMOV. I don't know. Perhaps it's a dislocation, or maybe he was bitten by some other dog. (*He sighs*). The best dog I ever had—to say nothing of his price! I paid Mironov a hundred and twenty-five roubles for him.

NATALIA. That was too much to pay, Ivan Vassiliyitch.

LOMOV. In my opinion it was very cheap. A wonderful dog!

NATALIA. Papa paid eighty-five roubles for his Otkatai, and Otkatai is much better than your Ugadi.

LOMOV. Really? Otkatai is better than Ugadi? What an idea! (*He laughs*). Otkatai better than Ugadi!

NATALIA. Of course he is better. It is true Otkatai is still young; he isn't full-grown yet, but in the pack or on the leash with two or three, there is no better than he, even——

LOMOV. I really beg your pardon, Natalia Stepanovna, but you quite overlooked the fact that he has a short lower jaw, and a dog with a short lower jaw can't snap.

NATALIA. Short lower jaw? That's the first time I ever heard that!

LOMOV. I assure you, his lower jaw is shorter than the upper.

NATALIA. Have you measured it?

LOMOV. I have measured it. He is good at running, though.

NATALIA. In the first place, our Otkatai is pure-bred, a

full-blooded son of Sapragavas and Stameskis, and as for your mongrel, nobody could ever figure out his pedigree; he's old and ugly, and as skinny as an old hag.

LOMOV. Old, certainly! I wouldn't take five of your Otkatais for him! Ugadi is a dog and Otkatai is—it is laughable to argue about it! Dogs like your Otkatai can be found by the dozens at any dog dealer's, a whole pound-full!

NATALIA. Ivan Vassiliyitch, you are very contrary to-day. First our meadows belong to you and then Ugadi is better than Otkatai. I don't like it when a person doesn't say what he really thinks. You know perfectly well that Otkatai is a hundred times better than your silly Ugadi. What makes you keep on saying he isn't?

LOMOV. I can see, Natalia Stepanovna, that you consider me either a blindman or a fool. But at least you may as well admit that Otkatai has a short lower jaw!

NATALIA. It isn't so!

LOMOV. Yes, a short lower jaw!

NATALIA (loudly). It's not so!

LOMOV. What makes you scream, my dear lady?

NATALIA. What makes you talk such nonsense? It's disgusting! It is high time that Ugadi was shot, and yet you compare him with Otkatai!

LOMOV. Pardon me, but I can't carry on this argument any longer. I have palpitation of the heart!

NATALIA. I have always noticed that the hunters who do the most talking know the least about hunting.

LOMOV. My dear lady, I beg of you to be still. My heart is bursting! (He shouts). Be still!

NATALIA. I won't be still until you admit that Otkatai is better! (Enter TSCHUBUKOV.)

TSCHUB. Well, has it begun again?

NATALIA. Papa, say frankly, on your honor, which dog is better: Otkatai or Ugadi?

LOMOV. Stepan Stepanovitch, I beg of you, just answer this: has your dog a short lower jaw or not? Yes or no?

TSCHUB. And what if he has? Is it of such importance? There is no better dog in the whole country.

LOMOV. My Ugadi is better. Tell the truth, now!

TSCHUB. Don't get so excited, my dear fellow! Permit me. Your Ugadi certainly has his good points. He is from a good breed, has a good stride, strong haunches, and so forth. But the dog, if you really want to know it, has two faults; he is old and he has a short lower jaw.

LOMOV. Pardon me, I have palpitation of the heart!—Let us keep to facts—just remember in Maruskins's meadows, my Ugadi kept ear to ear with the Count Rasvachai and your dog.

TSCHUB. He was behind, because the Count struck him with his whip.

LOMOV. Quite right. All the other dogs were on the fox's scent, but Otkatai found it necessary to bite a sheep.

TSCHUB. That isn't so!—I am sensitive about that and beg you to stop this argument. He struck him because everybody looks on a strange dog of good blood with envy. Even you, sir, aren't free from the sin. No sooner do you find a dog better than Ugadi than you begin to —this, that—his, mine—and so forth! I remember distinctly.

LOMOV. I remember something, too!

TSCHUB (*mimicking him*). I remember something, too! What do you remember?

LOMOV. Palpitation! My leg is lame—I can't——

NATALIA. Palpitation! What kind of hunter are you? You ought to stay in the kitchen by the stove and wrestle with the potato peelings, and not go fox-hunting! Palpitation!

TSCHUB. And what kind of hunter are you? A man with your diseases ought to stay at home and not jolt around in the saddle. If you were a hunter—! But you only ride round in order to find out about other people's dogs, and make trouble for everyone. I am sensitive! Let's drop the subject. Besides, you're no hunter.

LOMOV. You only ride around to flatter the Count!—My heart! You intriguer! Swindler!

TSCHUB. And what of it? (*Shouting*). Be still!

LOMOV. Intriguer!

TSCHUB. Baby! Puppy! Walking drug-store!

LOMOV. Old rat! Jesuit! Oh, I know you!

TSCHUB. Be still! Or I'll shoot you—with my worst gun, like a partridge! Fool! Loafer!

LOMOV. Everyone knows that—oh, my heart!—that your poor late wife beat you. My leg—my temples—Heavens —I'm dying—I——

TSCHUB. And your housekeeper wears the trousers in your house!

LOMOV. Here—here—there—there—my heart has burst! My shoulder is torn apart. Where is my shoulder? I'm dying! (*He falls into a chair*). The doctor! (*Faints.*)

TSCHUB. Baby! Half-baked clam! Fool!

NATALIA. Nice sort of hunter you are! You can't even sit on a horse. (*To* TSCHUB). Papa, what's the matter with him? (*She screams*). Ivan Vassiliyitch! He is dead!

LOMOV. I'm ill! I can't breathe! Air!

NATALIA. He is dead! (*She shakes* LOMOV *in the chair*). Ivan Vassiliyitch! What have we done! He is dead! (*She sinks into a chair*). The doctor—doctor! (*She goes into hysterics.*)

TSCHUB. Ahh! What is it? What's the matter with you?

NATALIA (*groaning*). He's dead!—Dead!

TSCHUB. Who is dead? Who? (*Looking at* LOMOV). Yes, he is dead! Good God! Water! The doctor! (*Holding the glass to* LOMOV's *lips*). Drink! No, he won't drink! He's dead! What a terrible situation! Why didn't I shoot myself? Why have I never cut my throat? What am I waiting for now? Only give me a knife! Give me a pistol! (LOMOV *moves*). He's coming to! Drink some water—there!

LOMOV. Sparks! Mists! Where am I?

TSCHUB. Get married! Quick, and then go to the devil! She's willing! (*He joins the hands of* LOMOV *and* NATALIA). She's agreed! Only leave me in peace!

LOMOV. Wh—what? (*Getting up*). Whom?

TSCHUB. She's willing! Well? Kiss each other and—the devil take you both!

NATALIA (*groans*). He lives! Yes, yes, I'm willing!

TSCHUB. Kiss each other!

LOMOV. Eh? Whom? (NATALIA *and* LOMOV *kiss*). Very nice—! Pardon me, but what is this for? Oh, yes, I understand! My heart—sparks—I am happy, Natalia Stepanovna. (*He kisses her hand*). My leg is lame!

NATALIA. I'm happy, too!

TSCHUB. Ahh! A load off my shoulders! Ahh!

NATALIA. And now at least you'll admit that Ugadi is worse than Otkatai!

LOMOV. Better!

NATALIA. Worse!

TSCHUB. Now the domestic joys have begun.—Champagne!

LOMOV. Better!

NATALIA. Worse, worse, worse!

TSCHUB (*trying to drown them out*). Champagne, champagne!

CURTAIN

SPREADING THE NEWS

by Lady Gregory

CHARACTERS

BARTLEY FALLON
MRS. FALLON
JACK SMITH
SHAWN EARLY
TIM CASEY
JAMES RYAN
MRS. TARPEY
MRS. TULLY
A POLICEMAN (JO MULDOON)
A REMOVABLE MAGISTRATE

SPREADING THE NEWS

SCENE—*The outskirts of a Fair.*

When the CURTAIN *rises,* MRS. TARPEY *is sitting at an apple stall. The* MAGISTRATE *and the* POLICEMAN *enter.*

MAGISTRATE. So that is the Fair Green. Cattle and sheep and mud. No system. What a repulsive sight!

POLICEMAN. That is so, indeed.

MAGISTRATE. I suppose there is a good deal of disorder in this place?

POLICEMAN. There is.

MAGISTRATE. Common assault?

POLICEMAN. It's common enough.

MAGISTRATE. Agrarian crime, no doubt?

POLICEMAN. That is so.

MAGISTRATE. Boycotting? Maiming of cattle? Firing into houses?

POLICEMAN. There was one time, and there might be again.

MAGISTRATE. That is bad. Does it go any further than that?

POLICEMAN. Far enough, indeed.

MAGISTRATE. Homicide, then! This district has been shamefully neglected! I will change all that. When I was in the Andaman Islands, my system never failed. Yes, yes, I will change all that. What has that woman on her stall?

POLICEMAN. Apples mostly—and sweets.

MAGISTRATE. Just see if there are any unlicensed goods underneath—spirits or the like. We had evasions of the salt tax in the Andaman Islands.

POLICEMAN (*sniffing cautiously and upsetting a heap of apples*). I see no spirits here—or salt.

MAGISTRATE (*to* MRS. TARPEY). Do you know this town well, my good woman?

MRS. TARPEY (*holding out some apples*). A penny the half-dozen, Your Honour.

POLICEMAN (*shouting*). The gentleman is asking do you know the town! He's the new magistrate!

MRS. TARPEY (*rising and ducking*). Do I know the town? I do, to be sure.

MAGISTRATE (*shouting*). What is its chief business?

MRS. TARPEY. Business, is it? What business would the people here have but to be minding one another's business?

MAGISTRATE. I mean what trade have they?

MRS. TARPEY. Not a trade. No trade at all but to be talking.

MAGISTRATE. I shall learn nothing here. (JAMES RYAN *comes in, pipe in mouth. Seeing the* MAGISTRATE *he retreats quickly, taking the pipe from his mouth.*)

MAGISTRATE. The smoke from that man's pipe had a greenish look; he may be growing unlicensed tobacco at home. I wish I had brought my telescope to this district. Come to the post-office, I will telegraph for it. I found it very useful in the Andaman Islands. (*The* MAGISTRATE *and the* POLICEMAN *go out* L.)

MRS. TARPEY. Bad luck to Jo Muldoon, knocking my apples this way and that way. (*She arranges them*). Showing off he was to the new magistrate. (BARTLEY FALLON *and* MRS. FALLON *enter.*)

BARTLEY. Indeed it's a poor country and a scarce country to be living in. But I'm thinking if I went to America it's long ago the day I'd be dead!

MRS. FALLON. So you might, indeed. (*She rests her basket on a barrel and begins putting parcels in it, taking them from under her cloak.*)

BARTLEY. And it's a great expense for a poor man to be buried in America.

MRS. FALLON. Never fear, Bartley Fallon, but I'll give you a good burying the day you'll die.

BARTLEY. Maybe it's yourself will be buried in the grave-yard of Cloonmara before me, Mary Fallon, and I myself that will be dying unbeknownst some night, and no-one a-near me. And the cat itself may be gone stray-ing through the country, and the mice squealing over the quilt.

MRS. FALLON. Leave off talking of dying. It might be twenty years you'll be living yet.

BARTLEY (*with a deep sigh*). I'm thinking if I'll be living at the end of twenty years it's a very old man I'll be then!

MRS. TARPEY (*turns and sees them*). Good morrow, Bart-ley Fallon; good morrow, Mrs. Fallon. Well, Bartley, you'll find no cause for complaining today; they are all saying it was a good fair.

BARTLEY (*raising his voice*). It was not a good fair, Mrs. Tarpey. It was a scattered sort of a fair. If we didn't expect more, we got less. That's the way with me al-ways; whatever I have to sell goes down and whatever I have to buy goes up. If there's ever any misfortune coming to this world, it's on myself it pitches, like a flock of crows on seed potatoes.

MRS. FALLON. Leave off talking of misfortunes, and listen to Jack Smith that is coming the way, and he singing.

JACK SMITH (*off; singing*).

I thought, my first love,
There'd be but one house between you and me,
And I thought I would find
Yourself coaxing my child on your knee.
Over the tide
I would leap with the leap of a swan,
Till I came to the side
Of the wife of the Red-haired man!

(JACK SMITH *enters. He is a red-haired man, and is carrying a hayfork.*)

MRS. TARPEY. That should be a good song if I had my hearing.

MRS. FALLON (*shouting*). It's *The Red-haired Man's Wife.*

MRS. TARPEY. I know it well. That's the song that has a skin on it! (*She turns her back on them and goes on arranging her apples.*)

MRS. FALLON. Where's herself, Jack Smith?

JACK SMITH. She was delayed with her washing; bleaching the clothes on the hedge she is, and she daren't leave them with all the tinkers that do be passing to the fair. It isn't to the fair I came myself, but up to the Five Acre Meadow I'm going, where I have a contract for the hay. We'll get a share of it into tramps today. (*He lays down the hayfork and lights his pipe.*)

BARTLEY. You will not get it into tramps today. The rain will be down on it by evening, and on myself too. It's seldom I ever started on a journey but the rain would come down on me before I'd find any place of shelter.

JACK SMITH. If it didn't itself, Bartley, it is my belief you would carry a leaky pail on your head in place of a hat, the way you'd not be without some cause of complaining.

A VOICE (*off*). Go on, now, go out o' that. Go on I say.

JACK SMITH. Look at that young mare of Pat Ryan's that is backing into Shaughnessy's bullocks with the dint of the crowd! Don't be daunted, Pat, I'll give you a hand with her. (JACK SMITH *goes out* R. *leaving his hayfork.*)

MRS. FALLON. It's time for ourselves to be going home. I have all I bought put in the basket. Look at there, Jack Smith's hayfork he left after him! He'll be wanting it. (*She calls*). Jack Smith! He's gone through the crowd—hurry after him, Bartley, he'll be wanting it.

BARTLEY. I'll do that. This is no safe place to be leaving it. (*He takes up the fork awkwardly and upsets the basket*). Look at that now! If there is any basket in the fair upset, it must be our own basket! (BARTLEY *goes out* R.)

MRS. FALLON. Get out of that! It is your own fault, it is. Talk of misfortunes and misfortunes will come. Glory be! Look at my new egg-cups rolling in every part—and my two pound of sugar with the paper broke . . .

MRS. TARPEY (*turning from the stall*). God help us, Mrs. Fallon, what happened your basket?

MRS. FALLON. It's himself that knocked it down, bad manners to him. (*Picking things up*). My grand sugar that's destroyed, and he'll not drink his tea without it. I had best go back to the shop for more, much good may it do him! (TIM CASEY *enters*.)

TIM CASEY. Where is Bartley Fallon, Mrs. Fallon? I want a word with him before he'll leave the fair. I was afraid he might have gone home by this, for he's a temperate man.

MRS. FALLON. I wish he did go home! It'd be best for me if he went home straight from the fair green, or if he never came with me at all! Where is he, is it? He's gone up the road—(*she jerks her elbow*) following Jack Smith with a hayfork. (MRS. FALLON *goes out* L.)

TIM CASEY. Following Jack Smith with a hayfork! Did ever anyone hear the like of that. (*He shouts*). Did you hear that news, Mrs. Tarpey?

MRS. TARPEY. I heard no news at all.

TIM CASEY. Some dispute I suppose it was that rose between Jack Smith and Bartley Fallon, and it seems Jack made off, and Bartley is following him with a hayfork!

MRS. TARPEY. Is he now? Well, that was quick work! It's not ten minutes since the two of them were here, Bartley going home and Jack going to the Five Acre Meadow; and I had my apples to settle up, that Jo Muldoon of the police had scattered, and when I looked round again Jack Smith was gone, and Bartley Fallon was gone, and Mrs. Fallon's basket upset, and all in it strewed upon the ground—the tea here—the two pound of sugar there—the egg-cups there. Look, now, what a great hardship the deafness puts upon me, that I didn't hear the commincement of the fight! Wait till I tell James Ryan that I see below; he is a neighbour of Bartley's, it would be a pity if he wouldn't hear the news! (MRS. TARPEY *goes out.* SHAWN EARLY *and* MRS. TULLY *enter.*)

TIM CASEY. Listen, Shawn Early! Listen, Mrs. Tully, to the news! Jack Smith and Bartley Fallon had a falling out, and Jack knocked Mrs. Fallon's basket into the road, and Bartley made an attack on him with a hayfork, and away with Jack, and Bartley after him. Look at the sugar here yet on the road!

SHAWN EARLY. Do you tell me so? Well, that's a queer thing, and Bartley Fallon so quiet a man!

MRS. TULLY. I wouldn't wonder at all. I would never think well of a man that would have that sort of a mouldering look. It's likely he has overtaken Jack by this. (JAMES RYAN *and* MRS. TARPEY *enter.*)

JAMES RYAN. That is great news Mrs. Tarpey was telling me! I suppose that's what brought the police and the magistrate up this way. I was wondering to see them in it a while ago.

SHAWN EARLY. The police after them? Bartley Fallon must have injured Jack so. They wouldn't meddle in a fight that was only for show!

MRS. TULLY. Why wouldn't he injure him? There was many a man killed with no more of a weapon than a hayfork.

JAMES RYAN. Wait till I run north as far as Kelly's bar to spread the news! (JAMES RYAN *exits.*)

TIM CASEY. I'll go tell Jack Smith's first cousin that is standing there south of the church after selling his lambs. (TIM CASEY *exits.*)

MRS. TULLY. I'll go telling a few of the neighbours I see beyond to the west. (MRS. TULLY *exits.*)

SHAWN EARLY. I'll give word of it beyond at the east of the green. (*He is about to go.*)

MRS. TARPEY (*seizing hold of him*). Stop a minute, Shawn Early, and tell me did you see red Jack Smith's wife, Kitty Keary, in any place?

SHAWN EARLY (*breaking away*). Laying out a drying clothes on the hedge as I passed.

MRS. TARPEY. What did you say she was doing?

SHAWN EARLY (*breaking away*). Laying out a sheet on the hedge. (SHAWN EARLY *exits.*)

MRS. TARPEY. Laying out a sheet for the dead! The Lord have mercy on us! Jack Smith dead, and his wife laying out a sheet for his burying! (*She calls out*). Why didn't you tell me that before, Shawn Early? Isn't the deafness the great hardship? Half the world might be dead without me knowing of it or getting word of it at all! (*She sits down and rocks herself*). Oh, my poor Jack Smith! To be going to his work so nice and so hearty, and to be left stretched on the ground in the full light of the day! (TIM CASEY *enters.*)

TIM CASEY. What is it, Mrs. Tarpey? What happened since?

MRS. TARPEY. Oh, my poor Jack Smith!

TIM CASEY. Did Bartley overtake him?

MRS. TARPEY. Oh, the poor man!

TIM CASEY. Is it killed he is?

MRS. TARPEY. Stretched in the Five Acre Meadow!

TIM CASEY. The Lord have mercy on us! Is that a fact?

MRS. TARPEY. And the wife laying out a sheet for a ha'porth!

TIM CASEY. Who was telling you?

MRS. TARPEY. And the wife laying out a sheet for his corpse. (*She sits and wipes her eyes*). I suppose they'll

wake him the same as another (MRS. TULLY, SHAWN
EARLY, *and* JAMES RYAN *enter.*)

MRS. TULLY. There is great talk about this work in every
quarter of the fair.

MRS. TARPEY. Ochone! Cold and dead. And myself maybe
the last he was speaking to!

JAMES RYAN. The Lord save us! Is it dead he is?

TIM CASEY. Dead surely, and the wife getting provision
for the wake.

SHAWN EARLY. Well, now, hadn't Bartley Fallon great
venom in him?

MRS. TULLY. You may be sure he had some cause. Why
would he have made an end of him if he had not?
(*To* MRS. TARPEY, *raising her voice*). What was it rose
the dispute at all, Mrs. Tarpey?

MRS. TARPEY. Not a one of me knows. The last I saw of
them, Jack Smith was standing there, and Bartley Fallon was standing there, quiet and easy and he listening
to *The Red-haired Man's Wife.*

MRS. TULLY. Do you hear that Tim Casey? Do you hear
that, Shawn Early and James Ryan? Bartley Fallon
was here this morning listening to Red Jack Smith's wife
Kitty Keary that was! Listening to her and whispering
with her! It was she started the fight so!

SHAWN EARLY. She must have followed him from her own
house. It is likely some person roused him.

TIM CASEY. I never knew, before, Bartley Fallon was great
with Jack Smith's wife.

MRS. TULLY. How would you know it? Sure it's not in the
streets they would be calling it. If Mrs. Fallon didn't
know of it, and if I that have the next house to them
didn't know of it, and if Jack Smith himself didn't know
of it, it is not likely you would know of it, Tim Casey.

SHAWN EARLY. Let Bartley Fallon take charge of her from
this out so, and let him provide for her. It is little pity
she will get from any person in this parish.

TIM CASEY. How can he take charge of her? Sure he has a wife of his own. Sure you don't think he'd turn souper and marry her in a Protestant church?

JAMES RYAN. It would be easy for him to marry her if he brought her to America.

SHAWN EARLY. With or without Kitty Keary, believe me it is for America he's making at this minute. I saw the new magistrate and Jo Muldoon of the police going into the post-office as I came up—there was hurry on them —you may be sure it was to telegraph they went, the way he'll be stopped in the docks at Queenstown!

MRS. TULLY. It's likely Kitty Keary is gone with him, and not minding a sheet or a wake at all. The poor man, to be deserted by his own wife, and the breath hardly gone out yet from his body that is lying bloody in the field! (MRS. FALLON *enters.*)

MRS. FALLON. What is it the whole of the town is talking about? And what is it you yourselves are talking about? Is it about my man Bartley Fallon you are talking? Is it lies about him you are telling, saying that he went killing Jack Smith? My grief that ever he came into this place at all!

JAMES RYAN. Be easy now, Mrs. Fallon. Sure there is no-one at all in the whole fair but is sorry for you!

MRS. FALLON. Sorry for me is it? Why would anyone be sorry for me? Let you be sorry for yourselves, and that there may be shame on you for ever and at the day of judgement, for the words you are saying and the lies you are telling to take away the character of my poor man, and take the good name off of him, and to drive him to destruction! That is what you are doing!

SHAWN EARLY. Take comfort now, Mrs. Fallon. The police are not so smart as they think. Sure he might give them the slip yet, the same as Lynchehaun.

MRS. TULLY. If they do get him, and if they do put a rope

around his neck, there is no-one can say he does not deserve it!

MRS. FALLON. Is that what you are saying, Bridget Tully, and is that what you think? I tell you it's too much talk you have, making yourself out to be such a great one, and to be running down every respectable person! A rope, is it? It isn't much of a rope was needed to tie up your own furniture the day you came into Martin Tully's house, and you never bringing as much as a blanket, or a penny, or a suit of clothes with you and I myself bringing seventy pounds and two feather beds. And now you are stiffer than a woman would have a hundred pounds! It is too much talk the whole of you have. A rope is it? I tell you the whole of this town is full of liars and schemers that would hang you up for half a glass of whiskey. (*Turning to go*). People they are you wouldn't believe as much as daylight from without you'd get up to have a look at it yourself. Killing Jack Smith indeed! Where are you at all, Bartley, till I bring you out of this? My nice quiet little man! My decent comrade! He that is as kind and as harmless as an innocent beast of the field! He'll be doing no harm at all if he'll shed the blood of some of you after this day's work! That much would be no harm at all. (*She calls out*). Bartley! Bartley Fallon! Where are you? (*Going*). Did anyone see Bartley Fallon? (MRS. FALLON *exits* L. *All turn to look after her.*)

JAMES RYAN. It is hard for her to believe any such a thing. God help her! (BARTLEY FALLON *enters* R., *carrying the hayfork.*)

BARTLEY. It is what I often said to myself, if there is ever any misfortune coming to this world it is on myself it is sure to come! (*All turn round and face him*). To be going about with this fork and to find no-one to take it, and no place to leave it down, and I wanting to be gone out of this. Is that you, Shawn Early? (*He holds out the fork*). It's well I met you. You have no call to be leaving the fair for a while the way I have, and how can I go till I'm rid of this fork? Will you take it and keep it until such time as Jack Smith . . .

SHAWN EARLY (*backing*). I will not take it, Bartley Fallon, I'm very thankful to you!

BARTLEY (*turning to the apple stall*). Look at it now, Mrs Tarpey, it was here I got it; let me thrust it in under the stall. It will lie there safe enough, and no-one will take notice of it until such time as Jack Smith . . .

MRS. TARPEY. Take your fork out of that! Is it to put trouble on me and to destroy me you want? Putting it there for the police to be rooting it out maybe. (*She thrusts him back.*)

BARTLEY. That is a very unneighbourly thing for you to do, Mrs. Tarpey. Hadn't I enough care on me with that fork before this, running up and down with it like the swinging of a clock, and afeard to lay it down in any place! I wish I never touched it or meddled with it at all!

JAMES RYAN. It is a pity, indeed, you ever did.

BARTLEY. Will you yourself take it, James Ryan? You were always a neighbourly man.

JAMES RYAN (*backing*). There is many a thing I would do for you, Bartley Fallon, but I won't do that!

SHAWN EARLY. I tell you there is no man will give you any help or any encouragement for this day's work. If it was something agrarian now . . .

BARTLEY. If no-one at all will take it, maybe it's best to give it up to the police.

TIM CASEY. There'd be a welcome for it with them surely! (*Laughter.*)

MRS. TULLY. And it is to the police Kitty Keary herself will be brought.

MRS. TARPEY (*rocking to and fro*). I wonder now who will take the expense of the wake for poor Jack Smith?

BARTLEY. The wake for Jack Smith!

TIM CASEY. Why wouldn't he get a wake as well as another? Would you begrudge him that much?

BARTLEY. Red Jack Smith dead! Who was telling you?

SHAWN EARLY. The whole town knows of it by this.

BARTLEY. Do they say what way did he die?

JAMES RYAN. You don't know that yourself, I suppose, Bartley Fallon? You don't know he was followed and that he was laid dead with the stab of a hayfork?

BARTLEY. The stab of a hayfork!

SHAWN EARLY. You don't know, I suppose, that the body was found in the Five Acre Meadow?

BARTLEY. The Five Acre Meadow!

TIM CASEY. It is likely you don't know that the police are after the man that did it?

BARTLEY. The man that did it!

MRS. TULLY. You don't know, maybe, that he was made away with for the sake of Kitty Keary, his wife?

BARTLEY. Kitty Keary, his wife! (*He sits down bewildered.*)

MRS. TULLY. And what have you to say now, Bartley Fallon?

BARTLEY (*crossing himself*). I to bring that fork here, and to find that news before me! It is much if I can ever stir from this place at all, or reach as far as the road!

TIM CASEY. Look, boys, at the new magistrate, and Jo Muldoon along with him! It's best for us to quit this.

SHAWN EARLY. That is so. It is best not to be mixed in this business at all.

JAMES RYAN. Bad as he is, I wouldn't like to be an informer against any man. (ALL *hurry away except* MRS. TARPEY, *who remains behind her stall. The* MAGISTRATE *and the* POLICEMAN *enter.*)

MAGISTRATE. I knew the district was in a bad state, but I did not expect to be confronted with a murder at the first fair I came to.

POLICEMAN. I am sure you did not, indeed.

MAGISTRATE. It was well I had not gone home. I caught a few words here and there that roused my suspicions.

POLICEMAN. So they would, too.

MAGISTRATE. You heard the same story from everyone you asked?

POLICEMAN. The same story—or if it was not altogether the same, anyway it was no less than the first story.

MAGISTRATE. What is that man doing? He is sitting alone with a hayfork. He has a guilty look. The murder was done with a hayfork!

POLICEMAN (*in a whisper*). That's the very man they say did the act; Bartley Fallon himself!

MAGISTRATE. He must have found escape difficult—he is trying to brazen it out. A convict in the Adaman Islands tried the same game, but he could not escape my system! Stand aside. Don't go far—have the handcuffs ready. (*He walks up to* BARTLEY, *folds his arms, and stands before him*). Here, my man, do you know anything of John Smith . . .

BARTLEY. Of John Smith! Who is he, now?

POLICEMAN. Jack Smith, sir—Red Jack Smith!

MAGISTRATE (*coming a step nearer and tapping him on the shoulder*). Where is Jack Smith?

BARTLEY (*with a deep sigh, and shaking his head slowly*). Where is he, indeed?

MAGISTRATE. What have you to tell?

BARTLEY. It is where he was this morning, standing in this spot, singing his share of songs—no, but lighting his pipe —scratching a match on the sole of his shoe . . .

MAGISTRATE. I ask you, for the third time, where is he?

BARTLEY. I wouldn't like to say that. It is a great mystery, and it is hard to say of any man, did he earn hatred or love.

MAGISTRATE. Tell me all you know.

BARTLEY. All that I know. Well, there are the three estates; there is Limbo and there is Purgatory, and there is . . .

MAGISTRATE. Nonsense! This is trifling! Get to the point.

BARTLEY. Maybe you don't hold with the clergy so? That is the teaching of the clergy. Maybe you hold with the old people. It is what they do be saying, that the shadow goes wandering, and the soul is tired, and the body is taking a rest. The shadow! (*He starts up*). I was nearly sure I saw Jack Smith not ten minutes ago at the corner of the forge, and I lost him again. Was it his ghost I saw, do you think?

MAGISTRATE (*to the* POLICEMAN). Conscience-struck! He will confess all now!

BARTLEY. His ghost to come before me! It is likely it was on account of the fork! I to have it and he to have no way to defend himself the time he met with his death!

MAGISTRATE (*to the* POLICEMAN). I must note down his words. (*He takes out a notebook. To* BARTLEY). I warn you that your words are being noted.

BARTLEY. If I had ha'run faster in the beginning, this terror would not be on me at the latter end! Maybe he will cast it up against me at the day of judgement—I wouldn't wonder at all at that.

MAGISTRATE (*writing*). At the day of judgement . . .

BARTLEY. It was soon for his ghost to appear to me—is it coming after me always by day it will be, and stripping the clothes off in the night-time? I wouldn't wonder at all at that, being as I am an unfortunate man!

MAGISTRATE (*sternly*). Tell me this truly. What was the motive of this crime?

BARTLEY. The motive, is it?

MAGISTRATE. Yes; the motive; the cause.

BARTLEY. I'd sooner not say that.

MAGISTRATE. You had better tell me truly. Was it money?

BARTLEY. Not at all! What did poor Jack Smith ever have

in his pockets unless it might be his hands that would be in them?

MAGISTRATE. Any dispute about land?

BARTLEY (*indignantly*). Not at all! He never was a grabber or grabbed from anyone!

MAGISTRATE. You will find it better for you if you tell me at once.

BARTLEY. I tell you I wouldn't for the whole world wish to say what it was—it is a thing I would not like to be talking about.

MAGISTRATE. There is no use in hiding it. It will be discovered in the end.

BARTLEY. Well, I suppose it will, seeing that mostly everybody knows it before. Whisper here now. I will tell no lie; where would be the use? (*He puts his hand to his mouth and the* MAGISTRATE *stoops down*). Don't be putting the blame on the parish, for such a thing was never done in the parish before—it was done for the sake of Kitty Keary, Jack Smith's wife.

MAGISTRATE (*to the* POLICEMAN). Put on the handcuffs. We have been saved some trouble. I knew he would confess if taken in the right way. (*The* POLICEMAN *puts on the handcuffs.*)

BARTLEY. Handcuffs now! Glory be! I always said, if there was ever any misfortune coming to this place it was on myself it would fall. I to be in handcuffs! There's no wonder at all in that. (MRS. FALLON *enters followed by the rest. She is looking back at them as she speaks.*)

MRS. FALLON. Telling lies the whole of the people of this town are; telling lies, telling lies as fast as a dog will trot! Speaking against my poor respectable man! Saying he made an end of Jack Smith! My decent comrade! There is no better man and no kinder man in the whole of the five parishes! It's little annoyance he ever gave to anyone! (*She turns and sees him*). What in the earthly world do I see before me? Bartley Fallon in charge of the police! Handcuffs on him! Oh, Bartley, what did you do at all at all?

BARTLEY. Oh, Mary, there has a great misfortune come upon me! It is what I always said, that if there is ever any misfortune . . .

MRS. FALLON. What did he do at all, or is it bewitched I am?

MAGISTRATE. This man has been arrested on a charge of murder.

MRS. FALLON. Whose charge is that? Don't believe them! They are all liars in this place! Give me back my man!

MAGISTRATE. It is natural you should take his part, but you have no cause of complaint against your neighbours. He has been arrested for the murder of John Smith, on his own confession.

MRS. FALLON. The saints of heaven protect us! And what did he want killing Jack Smith?

MAGISTRATE. It is best you should know all. He did it on account of a love affair with the murdered man's wife.

MRS. FALLON (*sitting down*). With Jack Smith's wife! With Kitty Keary! Ochone, the traitor!

THE CROWD. A great shame, indeed. He is a traitor, indeed.

MRS. TULLY. To America he was bringing her, Mrs. Fallon.

BARTLEY. What are you saying, Mary? I tell you . . .

MRS. FALLON. Don't say a word! I won't listen to any word you'll say! (*She stops her ears*). Oh, isn't he the treacherous villain? Ochone go deo!

BARTLEY. Be quiet till I speak! Listen to what I say!

MRS. FALLON. Sitting beside me on the ass-car coming to the town, so quiet and so respectable, and treachery like that in his heart!

BARTLEY. Is it your wits you have lost or is it I myself that have lost my wits?

MRS. FALLON. And it's hard I earned you, slaving, slaving—and you grumbling, and sighing, and coughing, and

discontented, and the priest wore out anointing you,
with all the times you threatened to die!

BARTLEY. Let you be quiet till I tell you!

MRS. FALLON. You to bring such a disgrace into the parish.
A thing that was never heard of before!

BARTLEY. Will you shut your mouth and hear me
speaking?

MRS. FALLON. And if it was for any sort of a fine handsome woman, but for a little fistful of a woman like
Kitty Keary, that's not four feet high hardly, and not
three teeth in her head unless she got new ones!
May God reward you, Bartley Fallon, for the black
treachery in your heart and the wickedness in your
mind, and the red blood of poor Jack Smith that is
wet upon your hand!

JACK SMITH (*off; singing*).

> The sea shall be dry,
> The earth under mourning and ban!
> Then loud shall he cry
> For the wife of the red-haired man!

BARTLEY. It's Jack Smith's voice—I never knew a ghost
to sing before. It is after myself and the fork he is
coming! (JACK SMITH *enters*). Let one of you give him
the fork and I will be clear of him now and for eternity!

MRS. TARPEY. The Lord have mercy on us! Red Jack Smith!
The man that was going to be waked!

JAMES RYAN. Is it back from the grave you are come?

SHAWN EARLY. Is it alive you are, or is it dead you are?

TIM CASEY. Is it yourself at all that's in it?

MRS. TULLY. Is it letting on you were to be dead?

MRS. FALLON. Dead or alive, let you stop Kitty Keary,
your wife, from bringing my man away with her to
America!

JACK SMITH. It is what I think, the wits are gone astray

on the whole of you. What would my wife want bringing Bartley Fallon to America?

MRS. FALLON. To leave yourself, and to get quit of you she wants, Jack Smith, and to bring him away from myself. That's what the two of them had settled together.

JACK SMITH. I'll break the head of any man that says that! Who is it says it? (*To* TIM CASEY). Was it you said it? (*To* SHAWN EARLY). Was it you?

ALL (*together; backing and shaking their heads*). It wasn't I said it!

JACK SMITH. Tell me the name of any man that said it!

ALL (*together; pointing to* BARTLEY). It was *him* that said it!

JACK SMITH. Let me at him till I break his head! (BARTLEY *backs in terror. Neighbours hold* JACK SMITH *back. Trying to free himself*). Let me at him! Isn't he the pleasant sort of a scarecrow for any woman to be crossing the ocean with! It's back from the docks of New York he'd be turned, (*trying to rush at him again*) with a lie in his mouth and treachery in his heart, and another man's wife by his side, and he passing her off as his own! Let me at him, can't you. (*He makes another rush, but is held back.*)

MAGISTRATE (*pointing to* JACK SMITH). Policeman put the handcuffs on this man. I see it all now. A case of false impersonation, a conspiracy to defeat the ends of justice. There was a case in the Andaman Islands, a murderer of the Mopsa tribe, a religious enthusiast . . .

POLICEMAN. So he might be, too.

MAGISTRATE. We must take both these men to the scene of the murder. We must confront them with the body of the real Jack Smith.

JACK SMITH. I'll break the head of any man that will find my dead body!

MAGISTRATE. I'll call more help from the barracks. (*He blows the* POLICEMAN'S *whistle.*)

BARTLEY. It is what I am thinking, if myself and Jack Smith are put together in the one cell for the night, the handcuffs will be taken off him, and his hands will be free, and murder will be done that time surely!

MAGISTRATE. Come on! (*They turn to the* R.)

CURTAIN

A FLORENTINE TRAGEDY

by Oscar Wilde

This play is only a fragment and was never completed. The well-known poet, Mr. T. Sturge Moore, has written an opening scene for the purpose of presentation, but only Oscar Wilde's work is given here.

A private performance was given by the Literary Theatre Club in 1906. The first public presentation was given by the New English Players at The Cripplegate Institute, Golden Lane, E. C., in 1907.

A FLORENTINE TRAGEDY

(*Enter* THE HUSBAND)

SIMONE. My good wife, you come slowly, were it not better to run to meet your lord? Here, take my cloak. Take this pack first. 'Tis heavy. I have sold nothing: Save a furred robe unto the Cardinal's son, who hopes to wear it when his father dies, and hopes that will be soon. But who is this? Why you have here some friend. Some kinsman doubtless, newly returned from foreign lands and fallen upon a house without a host to greet him? I crave your pardon, kinsman. For a house lacking a host is but an empty thing and void of honour; a cup without its wine, a scabbard without steel to keep it straight, a flowerless garden widowed of the sun. Again I crave your pardon, my sweet cousin.

BIANCA. This is no kinsman and no cousin neither.

SIMONE. No kinsman, and no cousin! You amaze me. Who is it then who with such courtly grace deigns to accept our hospitalities?

GUIDO. My name is Guido Bardi.

SIMONE. What! The son of that great Lord of Florence whose dim towers like shadows silvered by the wandering moon I see from out my casement every night! Sir Guido Bardi, you are welcome here, twice welcome. For I trust my honest wife, most honest if uncomely to the eye, hath not with foolish chatterings wearied you, as is the wont of women.

GUIDO. Your gracious lady, whose beauty is a lamp that pales the stars and robs Diana's quiver of her beams has welcomed me with such sweet courtesies that if it be her pleasure, and your own, I will come often to your simple house. And when your business bids you walk abroad I will sit here and charm her loneliness

lest she might sorrow for you overmuch. What say you,
good Simone!

SIMONE. My noble Lord, you bring me such high honour
that my tongue like a slave's tongue is tied, and cannot
say the word it would. Yet not to give you thanks were
to be too unmannerly. So, I thank you, from my heart's
core. It is such things as these that knit a state together,
when a Prince so nobly born and of such fair address,
forgetting unjust Fortune's differences, comes to an honest burgher's honest home as a most honest friend. And
yet, my Lord, I fear I am too bold. Some other night we
trust that you will come here as a friend, to-night you
come to buy my merchandise. Is it not so? Silks, velvets,
what you will, I doubt not but I have some dainty
wares will woo your fancy. True, the hour is late, but
we poor merchants toil both night and day to make our
scanty gains. The tolls are high, and every city levies
its own toll, and prentices are unskilful, and wives even
lack sense and cunning, though Bianca here has brought
me a rich customer to-night. Is it not so, Bianca? But
I waste time. Where is my pack? Where is my pack, I
say? Open it, my good wife. Unloose the cords. Kneel
down upon the floor. You are better so. Nay not that
one, the other. Despatch, despatch! Buyers will grow
impatient oftentimes. We dare not keep them waiting.
Ay! 'tis that, give it to me; with care. It is most costly.
Touch it with care. And now, my noble Lord— Nay,
pardon, I have here a Lucca damask, the very web of
silver and the roses so cunningly wrought that they lack
perfume merely to cheat the wanton sense. Touch it,
my Lord. Is it not soft as water, strong as steel? And
then the roses! Are they not finely woven? I think
the hillsides that best love the rose, at Bellosguardo
or at Fiesole, throw no such blossoms on the lap of
spring, or if they do their blossoms droop and die. Such
is the fate of all the dainty things that dance in wind
and water. Nature herself makes war on her own
loveliness and slays her children like Medea. Nay but,

my Lord, look closer still. Why in this damask here it
is summer always, and no winter's tooth will ever blight
these blossoms. For every ell I paid a piece of gold.
Red gold, and good, the fruit of careful thrift.

GUIDO. Honest Simone, enough, I pray you. I am well
content, to-morrow I will send my servant to you, who
will pay twice your price.

SIMONE. My generous Prince! I kiss your hands. And now
I do remember another treasure hidden in my house
which you must see. It is a robe of state: woven by a
Venetian: the stuff, cut-velvet: the pattern, pomegran-
ates: each separate seed wrought of a pearl: the collar
all of pearls, as thick as moths in summer streets at
night, and whiter than the moons that madmen see
through prison bars at morning. A male ruby burns
like a lighted coal within the clasp. The Holy Father
has not such a stone, nor could the Indies show a
brother to it. The brooch itself is of most curious art,
Cellini never made a fairer thing to please the great
Lorenzo. You must wear it. There is none worthier in
our city here, and it will suit you well. Upon one side
a slim and horned satyr leaps in gold to catch some
nymphs of silver. Upon the other stands Silence with a
crystal in her hand, no bigger than the smallest ear of
corn, that wavers at the passing of a bird, and yet
so cunningly wrought that one would say it breathed,
or held its breath.

Worthy Bianca, would not this noble and most costly
robe suit young Lord Guido well?

Nay, but entreat him; he will refuse you nothing,
though the price be as a prince's ransom. And your
profit shall not be less than mine.

BIANCA. Am I your prentice? Why should I chaffer for
your velvet robe?

GUIDO. Nay, fair Bianca, I will buy the robe, and all things
that the honest merchant has I will buy also. Princes

must be ransomed, and fortunate are all high lords
who fall into the white hands of so fair a foe.

SIMONE. I stand rebuked. But you will buy my wares?
Will you not buy them? Fifty thousand crowns would
scarce repay me. But you, my Lord, shall have them
for forty thousand. Is that price too high? Name your
own price. I have a curious fancy to see you in this
wonder of the loom amidst the noble ladies of the
court, a flower among flowers.

They say, my Lord, these high-born dames do so af-
fect your Grace that where you go they throng like flies
around you, each seeking for your favour. I have heard
also of husbands that wear horns, and wear them
bravely, a fashion most fantastical.

GUIDO. Simone, your reckless tongue needs curbing; and
besides, you do forget this gracious lady here whose
delicate ears are surely not attuned to such coarse music.

SIMONE. True: I had forgotten, nor will offend again. Yet,
my sweet Lord, you'll buy the robe of state. Will you
not buy it?

But forty thousand crowns. 'Tis but a trifle, to one
who is Giovanni Bardi's heir.

GUIDO. Settle this thing to-morrow with my steward
Antonio Costa. He will come to you. And you will have
a hundred thousand crowns if that will serve your
purpose.

SIMONE. A hundred thousand! Said you a hundred thousand? Oh! be sure that will for all time, and in everything make me your debtor. Ay! from this time forth
my house, with everything my house contains is yours,
and only yours.

A hundred thousand! My brain is dazed. I will be
richer far than all the other merchants. I will buy
vineyards, and lands, and gardens. Every loom from
Milan down to Sicily shall be mine, and mine the
pearls that the Arabian seas store in their silent caverns.

Generous Prince, this night shall prove the herald

of my love, which is so great that whatsoe'er you ask it will not be denied you.

GUIDO. What if I asked for white Bianca here?

SIMONE. You jest, my Lord, she is not worthy of so great a Prince. She is but made to keep the house and spin. Is it not so, good wife? It is so. Look! Your distaff waits for you. Sit down and spin. Women should not be idle in their homes, for idle fingers make a thoughtless heart. Sit down, I say.

BIANCA. What shall I spin?

SIMONE. Oh! spin some robe which, dyed in purple, sorrow might wear for her own comforting: or some longfringed cloth in which a newborn and unwelcome babe might wail unheeded; or a dainty sheet which, delicately perfumed with sweet herbs, might serve to wrap a dead man. Spin what you will; I care not, I.

BIANCA. The brittle thread is broken, the dull wheel wearies of its ceaseless round, the duller distaff sickens of its load; I will not spin to-night.

SIMONE. It matters not. To-morrow you shall spin, and every day shall find you at your distaff. So Lucretia was found by Tarquin. So, perchance, Lucretia waited for Tarquin. Who knows? I have heard strange things about men's wives. And now, my Lord, what news abroad? I heard to-day at Pisa that certain of the English merchants there would sell their woollens at a lower rate than the just laws allow, and have entreated the Signory to hear them.

　　Is this well? Should merchant be to merchant as a wolf? And should the stranger living in our land seek by enforced privilege or craft to rob us of our profits?

GUIDO. What should I do with merchants or their profits? Shall I go and wrangle with the Signory on your count? And wear the gown in which you buy from fools, or sell to sillier bidders? Honest Simone, wool-selling or wool-gathering is for you. My wits have other quarries.

BIANCA. Noble Lord, I pray you pardon my good husband here, his soul stands ever in the market-place, and his heart beats but at the price of wool. Yet he is honest in his common way. (*To* SIMONE). And you, have you no shame? A gracious Prince comes to our house, and you must weary him with most misplaced assurance. Ask his pardon.

SIMONE. I ask it humbly. We will talk to-night of other things. I hear the Holy Father has sent a letter to the King of France bidding him cross that shield of snow, the Alps, and make a peace in Italy, which will be worse than war of brothers, and more bloody than civil rapine or intestine feuds.

GUIDO. Oh! we are weary of that King of France, who never comes, but ever talks of coming. What are these things to me? There are other things closer, and of more import, good Simone.

BIANCA (*to* SIMONE). I think you tire our most gracious guest. What is the King of France to us? As much as are your English merchants with their wool.

SIMONE. Is it so then? Is all this mighty world narrowed into the confines of this room with but three souls for poor inhabitants? Ay! there are times when the great universe, like cloth in some unskilful dyer's vat, shrivels into a handsbreadth, and perchance that time is now! Well! let that time be now. Let this mean room be as that mighty stage whereon kings die, and our ignoble lives become the stakes God plays for. I do not know why I speak thus. My ride has wearied me. And my horse stumbled thrice, which is an omen that bodes not good to any. Alas! my Lord, how poor a bargain is this life of man, and in how mean a market are we sold! When we are born our mothers weep, but when we die there is none weep for us. No, not one. (*Passes to back of stage.*)

BIANCA. How like a common chapman does he speak! I hate him, soul and body. Cowardice has set her pale

seal on his brow. His hands whiter than poplar leaves
in windy springs, shake with some palsy; and his stammering mouth blurts out a foolish froth of empty words
like water from a conduit.

GUIDO. Sweet Bianca, he is not worthy of your thought
or mine. The man is but a very honest knave full of
fine phrases for life's merchandise, selling most dear
what he must hold most cheap, a windy brawler in a
world of words. I never met so eloquent a fool.

BIANCA. Oh, would that Death might take him where he
stands!

SIMONE (*turning round*). Who spake of Death? Let no
one speak of Death. What should Death do in such a
merry house, with but a wife, a husband, and a friend
to give it greeting? Let Death go to houses where there
are vile, adulterous things, chaste wives who growing
weary of their noble lords draw back the curtains of
their marriage beds, and in polluted and dishonoured
sheets feed some unlawful lust. Ay! 'tis so strange, and
yet so. *You* do not know the world. *You* are too single
and too honourable. I know it well. And would it
were not so, but wisdom comes with winters. My hair
grows grey, and youth has left my body. Enough of
that. To-night is ripe for pleasure, and indeed, I would
be merry, as beseems a host who finds a gracious and
unlooked-for guest waiting to greet him. (*Takes up a
lute*). But what is this, my Lord? Why, you have
brought a lute to play to us. Oh! play, sweet Prince.
And, if I am bold, pardon, but play.

GUIDO. I will not play to-night. Some other night, Simone.
(*To* BIANCA). You and I together, with no listeners but
the stars, or the more jealous moon.

SIMONE. Nay, but my Lord! Nay, but I do beseech you.
For I have heard that by the simple fingering of a string,
or delicate breath breathed along hollowed reeds, or
blown into cold mouths of cunning bronze, those who
are curious in this art can draw poor souls from prison-

houses. I have heard also how such strange magic lurks within these shells and innocence puts vine-leaves in her hair, and wantons like a mænad. Let that pass. Your lute I know is chaste. And therefore play: ravish my ears with some sweet melody; my soul is in a prison-house, and needs music to cure its madness. Good Bianca, entreat our guest to play.

BIANCA. Be not afraid. Our well-loved guest will choose his place and moment: that moment is not now. You weary him with your uncouth insistence.

GUIDO. Honest Simone, some other night. To-night I am content with the low music of Bianca's voice, who, when she speaks, charms the too amorous air. And makes the reeling earth stand still, or fix his cycle round her beauty.

SIMONE. You flatter her. She has her virtues as most women have, but beauty is a gem she may not wear. It is better so, perchance. Well, my dear Lord, if you will not draw melodies from your lute to charm my moody and o'er-troubled soul you'll drink with me at least? (*Sees table*). Your place is laid. Fetch me a stool, Bianca. Close the shutters. Set the great bar across. I would not have the curious world with its small prying eyes to peer upon our pleasure. Now, my Lord, give us a toast from a full brimming cup. (*Starts back*). What is this stain upon the cloth? It looks as purple as a wound upon Christ's side. Wine merely is it? I have heard it said when wine is spilt blood is spilt also, but that's a foolish tale. My Lord, I trust my grape is to your liking? The wine of Naples is fiery like its mountains. Our Tuscan vineyards yield a more wholesome juice.

GUIDO. I like it well, honest Simone; and, with your good leave, will toast the fair Bianca when her lips have like red rose-leaves floated on this cup and left its vintage sweeter. Taste, Bianca. (BIANCA *drinks*). Oh, all the honey of Hyblean bees, matched with this draught were bitter! Good Simone, you do not share the feast.

SIMONE. It is strange, my Lord, I cannot eat or drink with you, to-night. Some humour, or some fever in my blood, at other seasons temperate, or some thought that like an adder creeps from point to point, that like a madman crawls from cell to cell, poisons my palate and makes appetite a loathing, not a longing. (*Goes aside.*)

GUIDO. Sweet Bianca, this common chapman wearies me with words. I must go hence. To-morrow I will come. Tell me the hour.

BIANCA. Come with the youngest dawn! Until I see you all my life is vain.

GUIDO. Ah! loose the falling midnight of your hair, and in those stars, your eyes, let me behold mine image, as in mirrors. Dear Bianca, though it be but a shadow, keep me there, nor gaze at anything that does not show some symbol of my semblance. I am jealous of what your vision feasts on.

BIANCA. Oh! be sure your image will be with me always. Dear, love can translate the very meanest thing into a sign of sweet remembrances. But come before the lark with its shrill song has waked a world of dreamers. I will stand upon the balcony.

GUIDO. And by a ladder wrought out of scarlet silk and sewn with pearls will come to meet me. White foot after foot, like snow upon a rose-tree.

BIANCA. As you will. You know that I am yours for love or Death.

GUIDO. Simone, I must go to mine house.

SIMONE. So soon? Why should you? The great Duomo's bell has not yet tolled its midnight, and the watchmen who with their hollow horns mock the pale moon lie drowsy in their towers. Stay awhile. I fear we may not

see you here again, and that fear saddens my too simple heart.

GUIDO. Be not afraid, Simone. I will stand most constant
in my friendship. But to-night I go to mine own
home, and that at once. To-morrow, sweet Bianca.

SIMONE. Well, well, so be it. I would have wished for fuller
converse with you, my new friend, my honourable
guest, but that it seems may not be. And besides I do
not doubt your father waits for you, wearying for voice
or footstep. You, I think, are his one child? He has no
other child. You are the gracious pillar of his house,
the flower of a garden full of weeds. Your father's
nephews do not love him well. So run folk's tongues
in Florence. I meant but that; men say they envy your
inheritance and look upon your vineyard with fierce
eyes as Ahab looked on Naboth's goodly field. But that
is but the chatter of a town where women talk too
much. Good night, my Lord. Fetch a pine torch,
Bianca. The old staircase is full of pitfalls, and the
churlish moon grows, like a miser, niggard of her
beams. And hides her face behind a muslin mask as
harlots do when they go forth to snare some wretched
soul in sin. Now, I will get your cloak and sword.
Nay, pardon, my good Lord, it is but meet that I should
wait on you who have so honoured my poor burgher's
house, drunk of my wine, and broken bread, and
made yourself a sweet familiar. Oftentimes my wife and
I will talk of this fair night and its great issues. Why,
what a sword is this! Ferrara's temper, pliant as a snake,
and deadlier, I doubt not. With such steel one need
fear nothing in the moil of life. I never touched so
delicate a blade. I have a sword too, somewhat rusted
now. We men of peace are taught humility. And to
bear many burdens on our backs, and not to murmur
at an unjust world. And to endure unjust indignities.
We are taught that, and like the patient Jew find profit
in our pain. Yet I remember how once upon the road

to Padua a robber sought to take my pack-horse from me, I slit his throat and left him. I can bear dishonour, public insult, many shames, shrill scorn, and open contumely, but he who filches from me something that is mine, Ay! though it be the meanest trencher-plate from which I feed mine appetite—oh! he perils his soul and body in the theft and dies for his small sin. From what strange clay we men are moulded!

GUIDO. Why do you speak like this?

SIMONE. I wonder, my Lord Guido, if my sword is better tempered than this steel of yours? Shall we make trial? Or is my state too low for you to cross your rapier against mine. In jest, or earnest?

GUIDO. Naught would please me better than to stand fronting you with naked blade in jest, or earnest. Give me mine own sword. Fetch yours. To-night will settle the great issue whether the Prince's or the merchant's steel is better tempered. Was not that your word? Fetch your own sword. Why do you tarry, sir?

SIMONE. My Lord, of all the gracious courtesies that you have showered on my barren house this is the highest. Bianca, fetch my sword. Thrust back that stool and table. We must have an open circle for our match at arms. And good Bianca here shall hold the torch lest what is but a jest grow serious.

BIANCA (*to* GUIDO). Oh! kill him, kill him!

SIMONE. Hold the torch, Bianca. (*They begin to fight.*)

SIMONE. Have at you! Ah! Ha! would you? (*He is wounded by* GUIDO). A scratch, no more. The torch was in mine eyes. Do not look sad, Bianca. It is nothing. Your husband bleeds, 'tis nothing. Take a cloth, bind it about mine arm. Nay, not so tight. More softly, my good wife. And be not sad, I pray you be not sad. No: take it off. What matter if I bleed? (*Tears bandage off*). Again! again! (SIMONE *disarms* GUIDO). My gentle Lord, you see that I was right. My sword is better tempered, finer steel, but let us match our daggers.

BIANCA (*to* GUIDO). Kill him! kill him!

SIMONE. Put out the torch, Bianca. (BIANCA *puts out torch*). Now, my good Lord, now to the death of one, or both of us, or all the three it may be. (*They fight*). There and there. Ah, devil! do I hold thee in my grip? (SIMONE *overpowers* GUIDO *and throws him down over table*.)

GUIDO. Fool! take your strangling fingers from my throat. I am my father's only son; the State has but one heir, and that false enemy France waits for the ending of my father's line to fall upon our city.

SIMONE. Hush! your father when he is childless will be happier. As for the State, I think our state of Florence needs no adulterous pilot at its helm. Your life would soil its lilies.

GUIDO. Take off your hands. Take off your damned hands. Loose me, I say!

SIMONE. Nay, you are caught in such a cunning vice that nothing will avail you, and your life narrowed into a single point of shame ends with that shame and ends most shamefully.

GUIDO. Oh! let me have a priest before I die!

SIMONE. What wouldst thou have a priest for? Tell thy sins to God, whom thou shalt see this very night and then no more for ever. Tell thy sins to Him who is most just, being pitiless, most pitiful being just. As for myself. . . .

GUIDO. Oh! help me, sweet Bianca! help me, Bianca, thou knowest I am innocent of harm.

SIMONE. What, is there life yet in those lying lips? Die like a dog with lolling tongue! Die! Die! And the dumb river shall receive your corse and wash it all unheeded to the sea.

GUIDO. Lord Christ receive my wretched soul to-night!

SIMONE. Amen to that. Now for the other. (*He dies.* SIMONE *rises and looks at* BIANCA. *She comes towards him as one dazed with wonder and with outstretched arms.)*

BIANCA. Why did you not tell me you were so strong?

SIMONE. Why did you not tell me you were beautiful?
(He kisses her on the mouth.)

CURTAIN

BIOGRAPHICAL NOTES

ARTHUR MILLER

(1915–   )

Arthur Miller says he never read a good book until he was seventeen. After he graduated from high school in New York, where he was born, he came across *The Brothers Karamazov* and it changed his life—all at once he knew he was born to be a writer. He was inspired by a novel then, this playwright, not by a play; and he has said: "My aim is what it has been from the beginning—to bring to the stage the thickness, awareness, and complexity of the novel." After receiving his degree from the University of Michigan, he returned to New York to write. He worked for radio, wrote a novel, *Focus,* and then had his first big success in 1947 with *All My Sons.* In 1949 he won the Pulitzer Prize for *Death of a Salesman,* one of the most powerful and moving plays of our time. Of it John Gassner wrote: ". . . it represents a culmination of American playwrights' efforts to create a significant American drama." *The Crucible* appeared in 1953 and in 1955, *A View From the Bridge* won both the Pulitzer Prize and the New York Drama Critics' Circle Award. In 1959 he was awarded the Gold Medal for Drama by the National Institute of Arts and Letters, and his cinema novel, *The Misfits,* was published in 1961.

TERENCE RATTIGAN

(1914–   )

Terence Rattigan, who was born in London, embarked on his career as a dramatist at the age of eleven with what he admits was "a somewhat unwieldy masterpiece." After attending Oxford he wrote five scripts in two years, one of which, *French without Tears,* encouraged him by its success. He served in World War II and then returned home to continue his playwrighting. He had the magic touch. With *While the Sun Shines,* and *O Mistress Mine* he fulfilled the promise he had shown, and went on to even greater success with such plays as *The Winslow Boy* and *The Browning Version.* Next came *Who is Sylvia?* and *The Deep Blue Sea,* which was produced in New York in 1950. Two of his plays—*Separate Tables* and *The Sleeping Prince*—ran simultaneously on Broadway during the 1956–57 season, and

Ross, based on the life of the famed Lawrence of Arabia, was produced here in 1961–62. Many of Rattigan's plays have been made into motion pictures; he has frequently been translated into other languages; and he often writes for television. He has one of the widest audiences of any living playwright.

TENNESSEE WILLIAMS
(1914–   )

Possessing one of the most powerful and distinctive voices in the theater today, Tennessee Williams has, in a little more than ten years, carved a permanent place for himself as a playwright. Born in Columbus, Mississippi, he moved north to St. Louis with his family when he was twelve. He got his education in between part-time jobs and serious bouts with poor health, and finally graduated from the University of Iowa. His first play, *Battle of Angels,* starring Miriam Hopkins, closed in Boston during its tryout. He subsisted on odd jobs, which included being an elevator operator and movie usher; finally he went to Hollywood and managed to save enough money to support himself while he wrote his first smash success, *The Glass Menagerie* (in which, incidentally, Laurette Taylor made her exciting comeback). The story after that is familiar to everyone interested in the theater. In 1947 *A Streetcar Named Desire* won both the Pulitzer Prize and the Drama Critics' Circle Award. Then came *Summer and Smoke, The Rose Tattoo, Camino Real,* and, in 1955, *Cat on a Hot Tin Roof,* which again gave Williams both the Drama Critics' Circle Award and the Pulitzer Prize. These were followed by *Orpheus Descending, The Garden District, Sweet Bird of Youth, Period of Adjustment,* and *Night of the Iguana,* which won the 1961 Drama Critics' Circle Award. Most of Williams' plays have been made into equally successful films.

LUCILLE FLETCHER
(1913–   )

Sorry, Wrong Number has had an almost unparalleled career. As a radio script, a film, a television play, a novel, and on records, it has chilled millions of people to the bone. It is probably the most repeated play in the history of radio. Lucille Fletcher was born in Brooklyn, New York. She insists that writing is only a hobby with her, that she spends far less time at it than in running her house. Most of her work has been for radio and motion pictures, although she has published three novels: *The Daughters of Jasper Clay, Blindfold,* and . . . *And Presumed Dead.*

WILLIAM INGE

(1913–   )

William Inge is that rarity among writers—a man who, during his formative years, had no desire to write at all. He was born in Independence, Kansas, and graduated from the University of Kansas; he taught in a high school for a time and then at Stephens College, and at Washington University in St. Louis. It was while he was a drama critic for the *St. Louis Star-Times* during the forties that he first became interested in writing for the theater, although he had always wanted to be an actor. Then he saw Tennessee Williams' *The Glass Menagerie* and his mind was made up. Margo Jones produced Inge's first play in Dallas. His first real success, however, was *Come Back, Little Sheba,* and the New York drama critics acclaimed him "the most promising new playwright of 1950." Three years later he received both the Pulitzer Prize and the New York Drama Critics' Circle Award for *Picnic.* Then came the smash hit *Bus Stop* and, in 1958, *The Dark at the Top of the Stairs,* which Brooks Atkinson called "Mr. Inge's finest play." *A Loss of Roses* appeared in 1959. Mr. Inge lives in New York.

NOEL COWARD

(1899–   )

Playwright, composer, director, actor, producer, Noel Coward is one of the most brilliant and versatile men in the theater. He was born at Teddington on the Thames and received an education of sorts in and about London. After performing such service as his frail health would allow in World War I, he turned to playwrighting. His first play was bought, but not produced. *The Vortex* in 1923 was his first hit, and then one brilliant success followed another: *Hay Fever, Bitter Sweet, Private Lives, Design for Living,* and a dozen others. During and after World War II, Coward turned to motion-picture making, and with such films as *In Which We Serve, This Happy Breed,* and *Brief Encounter,* and the delightful film version of his *Blithe Spirit,* he showed that he could be every bit as entertaining and effective in a new medium. Coward is also a successful short story author, and his novel, *Pomp and Circumstance,* was published in 1960.

In 1961, he again turned his attention to the stage with the musical, *Sail Away*.

STEPHEN VINCENT BENET

(1898–1943)

Stephen Vincent Benét, who never followed any profession except writing, was born in Bethlehem, Pennsylvania, and part of his youth was spent on various army posts to which his father, an officer, was assigned. He published his first book—six dramatic monologues in verse—when he was seventeen. He received his M.A. from Yale in 1920 and thereafter managed to earn his living from his pen, though there were lean years. As a boy he had been fascinated by the military books in his father's library and he was obsessed by the idea of writing a long narrative poem about America and the Civil War. This appeared in 1928 as *John Brown's Body* and won him the Pulitzer Prize for poetry. A little less than ten years later he again published a work which was to become a minor American classic; this was the story, *The Devil and Daniel Webster*. Since then it has been done as a play, first in the form of an opera, and as a movie. Aside from his constant output of poems and stories, he also was active as a reviewer and as a member of the American Academy of Arts and Letters. He died in New York City.

THORNTON WILDER

(1897–   )

Brooks Atkinson once remarked about Thornton Wilder that he "takes his own time as a writer." It is true that in the more than thirty years since his first novel appeared in 1925 he has not written a body of work that is impressive in size; but most people agree that it makes up in quality what it lacks in length. He has won three Pulitzer Prizes—one for his first successful novel, *The Bridge of San Luis Rey*, and two for the plays *Our Town*, that poignant picture of life and death that uses no scenery, and *The Skin of Our Teeth*, a lively, provocative allegory, which has been successfully revived since its first production in 1942. *The Matchmaker* arrived on Broadway in 1954, and a trio of one-act plays, *Infancy, Childhood*, and *Lust*, were produced off-Broadway in 1961 under the title, *Plays for Bleecker Street*. They are the first of a projected cycle of fourteen one-act plays covering The Seven Ages of Man and The Seven Deadly Sins. Wilder's novels include *Heaven's My Destination* and *The*

Ides of March, considered by many to be one of the finest pieces of modern fiction.

Wilder was born in Madison, Wisconsin, and when he was nine he was taken to China, where his father was an American consul general. He completed his education at Yale and Princeton, and in one way or another he has been associated with the academic world ever since. He says his profession is teaching rather than writing and this has perhaps made him feel free to write for pleasure rather than profit. In any case, all his work bears the stamp of a truly original mind.

DOROTHY PARKER

(1893–   )

Born in West End, New Jersey, and educated at Miss Dana's School in Morristown and the Blessed Sacrament Convent in New York City, Dorothy Parker began her literary career as a critic—a drama critic on *Vanity Fair* and a book critic on *The New Yorker*. Although she is best known for her short stories, which glisten with a sardonic, acidulous wit, and light verse, she has done considerable writing for the screen. In 1949, with Ross Evans, she wrote a play called *The Coast of Illyria*, based on the life of the English essayist, Charles Lamb, which Margo Jones produced in Dallas. In 1953, *Ladies of the Corridor*, which she wrote with Arnaud d'Usseau, had a successful run in New York. She now lives in California, and for several years has been a regular contributor to *Esquire* Magazine as book critic.

MARC CONNELLY

(1890–   )

Marc Connelly was born in McKeesport, Pennsylvania, and after graduating from Trinity Hall School he became a reporter and then a humorous columnist in Pittsburgh. He came to New York to see a show which was using some lyrics he had written—and stayed. His first play, *Dulcy*, written in collaboration with George S. Kaufman, was a great success. In 1929, however, he wrote and directed a play which has since taken its place as one of the most beloved dramas in the American theater, *The Green Pastures* (it was adapted from Roark Bradford's *Ol' Man Adam and His Children*). It received the Pulitzer Prize for that year. In addition to his plays, which have always shown him to be a superior writer of high comedy, he has written two musical comedies, again with Kaufman. For a time he was on the faculty of Yale University, and, though his permanent residence is New York, he continues to conduct seminars at universities around the country, helping teach young playwrights what he has learned after many rich years in the theater.

GEORGE S. KAUFMAN

(1889–1961)

For all his biting wit and brusque manner, George Kaufman had, as Moss Hart said, a heart as hard and tough as a marshmallow. For more than thirty years he refreshed the theater—and the films—with his talent and personality. Though he wrote only one play by himself (*The Butter and Egg Man*, 1925), his collaboration with other writers produced success after success in films and on the stage. Here are a few landmarks in his career. His first play, written with Marc Connelly, was *Dulcy*, produced in 1921, with Lynn Fontanne rising to stardom as a result; again with Connelly, he wrote *To The Ladies* and *Merton of the Movies*. Then he wrote, in collaboration, with Edna Ferber (*The Royal Family, Dinner at Eight, Stage Door*), Alexander Woollcott (*The Channel Road*), Moss Hart (*Once in a Lifetime, The Man Who Came to Dinner, You Can't Take It With You, George Washington Slept Here*), Morris Ryskind (*Of Thee I Sing, Let 'Em Eat Cake*), J. P. Marquand (*The Late George Apley*), and Howard Teichmann (*The Solid Gold Cadillac*), to list a few. *Of Thee I Sing* and *You Can't Take It With You* won Pulitzer Prizes. Kaufman was born in Philadelphia, and first made his name as a contributor to F.P.A.'s column. His film work included several scripts for the Marx Brothers, and in 1951 he directed the stage production of *Guys and Dolls*.

EUGENE O'NEILL

(1888–1953)

High on any list of the world's foremost dramatists, Eugene O'Neill has been the most influential and respected of modern American playwrights. The son of a famous romantic actor, O'Neill spent his youth in the atmosphere of the theater. After a year at Princeton and a brief career prospecting for gold in the Honduras, he went to sea (storing up impressions which were later used in many of his plays). Then came short sojourns as actor and reporter before his health broke down: he was tubercular. With time to think, he decided he wanted to write plays, and when he was recovered he enrolled in George Baker's famous "Forty-Seven Workshop." The Provincetown Theatre gave him his real chance, however: they put on his first play, *Bound East for Cardiff*, in 1916. In 1920 his first full-length play, *Beyond the Horizon*, was produced in New York; it received the Pulitzer Prize. From that time on there was never any doubt that he was the leading playwright of his time. He received two more Pulitzer Prizes and was given the Nobel Prize for literature in 1936. In the middle thirties he began a cycle of nine long plays with the general title *A Tale of the Possessors Self-Possessed*. Several of these plays he destroyed before his death; others he wished to be delayed for production until twenty-five years after he died. (Two of these, however, have been released by his wife and have been produced—*A Long Day's Journey into Night* and *A Touch of the Poet*. Another, *More Stately Mansions*, discovered after O'Neill's death, was edited and produced in Stockholm in 1962.) Other major plays: *The Hairy Ape, Anna Christie, Desire Under the Elms, Strange Interlude, Mourning Becomes Electra, The Iceman Cometh, A Moon for the Misbegotten*.

WILLIAM OLIPHANT DOWN

Born at Bridgewater, Somerset, and educated at Warminster School, Wiltshire, William Oliphant Down studied to be a Chartered Accountant but to his father's dismay gave up a business career in favor of writing. Volunteering during the first few months of the war in 1914, he served in the front lines and won the Military Cross. Not long afterward he was killed.

GEORGE EDWARD KELLY

(1887–)

George Kelly, who was born in Philadelphia, followed his brother's footsteps into the proscenium and played juvenile roles for about five years on the road. He then entered vaudeville, traveling with the Keith and Orpheum circuits, where he began writing his own sketches. In 1922 his first full-length play, *The Torch-bearers*, was produced, and with *The Show-Off* in 1924 he became one of the most talked-about playwrights of the season. The Pulitzer Prize was awarded to his *Craig's Wife* in 1925. His last two plays, both comedies about middle-aged women with delusions, were *The Deep Mrs. Sykes* in 1945 and *The Fatal Weakness* in 1946.

RING LARDNER

(1885–1933)

Ring Lardner began his career as a journalist when he took, on an Indiana newspaper, a job which his brother had been unable to accept. He was born in Niles, Michigan, and went to Chicago to study engineering, but found that wasn't really what he wanted to do. His newspaper career led him into the field of sports, and after considerable success as a reporter and editor, he began to write humorous stories about a baseball pitcher which were read by millions in *The Saturday Evening Post* and were later published in book form as *You Know Me, Al.* Lardner was more than a light humorist, however; his later stories— "Golden Honeymoon," "The Love Nest," and many others— showed a modern Swift at work under the entertaining nonsense. Moreover, hardly any other writer in his day could rival Lardner's ear for the American language and speech rhythms. He collaborated with George M. Cohan on *Elmer the Great*, and in 1930 wrote a satire called *June Moon* with George S. Kaufman. Both of these plays were successful on Broadway. He died at East Hampton, Long Island, after several years of poor health.

JEAN GIRAUDOUX

(1882–1944)

One of France's most distinguished modern playwrights, Jean Giraudoux did not discover the drama until he was forty-six, when, with Jouvet's help, he converted one of his own novels into a play, *Siegfried,* which was followed by the highly successful *Amphitryon 38.* His earlier life was by turns brilliant, aimless, adventurous. He studied the classics and once began to prepare to teach, but thought better of it. He wrote stories, but not with a career in mind; finally he decided to see the world. He wandered, sometimes on foot and often broke, through many countries, including Germany, Norway, the Balkans, the United States, and Mexico. He then entered the service of the French Government and began to take his writing more seriously —at least he did more of it. One collection of his short stories sold thirty copies in four years. Of course it was with his plays —with their wonderful mixture of wit, style, and paradox—that he made his fame and fortune. It was only after his death, however, that plays such as *The Madwoman of Chaillot, The Enchanted, Ondine,* and *Tiger at the Gates* were produced in this country.

SUSAN GLASPELL

(1882-1948)

Born in Iowa, Susan Glaspell spent her youth in the Middle West. She never wanted to do anything but write. Her interest turned from her successful stories and novels to playwrighting after she helped her husband found the Provincetown Players on Cape Cod in 1915. She began, of course, with one-act plays, of which *Trifles* was one of the earliest. She lived in Greece for a while, and after her husband died in 1924 she returned to America, though she liked to visit France and England. In 1931 she won the Pulitzer Prize Drama award with *Alison's House.* After that, she wrote no more plays, but she did publish two novels. She died in Provincetown.

ALAN ALEXANDER MILNE

(1882-1956)

After graduating from Trinity College, Cambridge, A. A. Milne returned to London, where he was born, to enter a journalistic career. His progress was hardly spectacular, but suddenly he was offered an editorial position on *Punch* and gradually became known as a humorist. During World War I, in which he served, his interest turned to the drama, and he wrote many plays which enjoyed huge success; among them are *Mr. Pim Passes By, The Dover Road,* and *The Perfect Alibi* (a mystery). He also wrote several novels, and published many collections of both essays and short stories, the last of which, *Year In, Year Out,* appeared in 1956. Of course the most important fact in Milne's life to most people is that he has a son named Christopher Robin. The *Pooh* books have become so phenomenally successful that they threaten to overwhelm all of the author's more serious work. This no doubt caused considerable anguish to the dramatist—but there are millions of people, old and young, who wouldn't have missed Winnie-the-Pooh and Christopher Robin for anything. Milne died at his Sussex home in January 1956.

LORD DUNSANY

(Edward John Moreton Drax Plunkett)

(1878–1957)

An Irishman born in, of all places, London, this prolific writer of stories, plays and poems is the 18th Baron of Dunsany. His work was a great deal more popular several generations ago than it is now, but in the over fifty books he has published there is a good deal of first-rate writing. Reversing the usual order, Lord Dunsany was a playwright before he turned to stories (he was "discovered" by the Abbey Theatre) and during World War II he composed hundreds of poems for English newspapers. Always a facile writer, he was often more interested in hunting and other outdoor activities than in literature. Soldier, scholar, sportsman, Lord Dunsany led a full life. His writings have been influenced most by his study of the Bible and Greek mythology.

JOHN MILLINGTON SYNGE

(1871–1909)

When Lady Gregory, W. B. Yeats and George Moore founded the Irish National Theatre Society (later the Abbey Theatre), John M. Synge had two fine one-act plays ready for them to produce: *In the Shadow of the Glen* (which was hissed by easily offended Dublin audiences) and the justly famous *Riders to the Sea*. Synge, who was born in a Dublin suburb and rarely traveled much further than walking distance from the capital, originally wanted to become a musician. Then he wanted to become a critic. It was only after a meeting with Yeats that he finally knew what he had to do. The high point of his career most certainly came with the writing of the full-length play, *The Playboy of the Western World*, one of the finest plays of his or any other generation.

WILLIAM BUTLER YEATS

(1865–1939)

W. B. Yeats, easily one of the greatest poets of all time, was born in Dublin. He is one of the few poets in history whose work became better as he grew older. When he died at seventy-three he was at the height of his powers. His life was a varied one. As a youth he was pretentious and something of a mystic; he fell in love with the beautiful Maud Gonne and immortalized her in verse—but could not win her. He later became passionately involved in the Irish Literary Movement along with Lady Gregory, and not only wrote many plays for the Abbey Theatre but helped produce them; in the twenties, partly through the influence of his wife, his latent fascination with mysticism awoke again, though otherwise he remained a man of eminent sensibility and reason. In 1932 he was awarded the Nobel Prize for Literature. In his old age he often expressed disillusionment with Ireland and life, but without bitterness, for he loved them both. He had, after all, given more poetic beauty to the world than anyone else of his century. His most famous plays include: *The Countess Kathleen, The Land of Heart's Desire, Cathleen ni Houlihan,* and many others.

ANTON CHEKHOV

(1860–1904)

Russian literature of the nineteenth century produced half a dozen of the greatest writers of all time. Only two of them however—Pushkin and Chekhov—became playwrights of note. Chekhov was born in Tananrog, near the Crimea. He attended a medical school in Moscow in 1884 and in 1892 played an important role in putting down a cholera epidemic. But the young Chekhov had another love besides medicine: writing. In 1885 he wrote his first one-act play, *On the Highroad,* after trying his hand at short stories in a comic vein. And it wasn't long before writing—both short stories and plays—became the most important thing in his life. His most successful plays were produced by the Moscow Art Theatre, and were soon translated into many languages. Productions of *The Cherry Orchard, The Three Sisters, The Seagull,* and *Uncle Vanya* are known the world over; Katherine Cornell's production of *The Three Sisters* was a landmark of the 1942–43 theatrical season in New York. Chekhov suffered from tuberculosis in his later years, and he finally died of it at Badenweiler, in the Black Forest.

LADY GREGORY

(Isabella Augusta Persse)

(1859–1932)

Lady Gregory, who was born in County Galway, Ireland, only accidentally became interested in writing and the arts when she began editing her husband's autobiography after he died in 1892. Thereafter she turned to Irish folklore and history. In 1898 she met William Butler Yeats and became one of the prime movers behind the establishment of the famous Abbey Theatre. She was often called "the Godmother of the Abbey Theatre," and she devoted her life to its success. To the theater she was everything —writer, stage and business manager, guiding spirit. Altogether she wrote thirty-one plays, of which *The Workhouse Ward*, *Spreading the News*, and *The Rising of the Moon* are the best known.

OSCAR WILDE

(1856–1900)

Oscar Wilde was born in Dublin and educated at Trinity College, Dublin, and Magdalen College, Oxford. While at Oxford his unusual behavior and mode of attire became the pattern for an aesthetic cult that enjoyed a violent, if short-lived, vogue, which was caricatured so tellingly in Gilbert and Sullivan's *Patience*. Wilde was a versatile genius. His poems, his fairy tales, his novel, *The Picture of Dorian Gray*, were in themselves enough to win him fame, and the wit and repartee in his plays *Lady Windermere's Fan*, *A Woman of No Importance*, and *The Importance of Being Earnest* still burn brightly enough to ensure frequent revivals to this very day. Wilde's private life was the scandal of London, and, in 1895, after a celebrated trial, he was committed to prison for two years. The experience wrecked his life, but also inspired *The Ballad of Reading Gaol* and *De Profundis*. *Salomé*, Wilde's only serious play, was written in 1893, and so profoundly did it shock English authorities that the ban on its performance in public was not lifted until 1931.